ZÜRICH

NORTHERN
SWITZERLAND

**NORTHERN
SWITZERLAND**
Pages 134–157

ZÜRICH
Pages 158–175

CENTRAL
SWITZERLAND
AND TICINO

EASTERN
SWITZERLAND AND
GRAUBÜNDEN

0 km   50

0 miles   50

**CENTRAL
SWITZERLAND
AND TICINO**
Pages 206–239

**EASTERN
SWITZERLAND
AND GRAUBÜNDEN**
Pages 176–205

EYEWITNESS TRAVEL
SWITZERLAND

EYEWITNESS TRAVEL

SWITZERLAND

ADRIANA CZUPRYN
MAŁGORZATA OMILANOWSKA
ULRICH SCHWENDIMANN

LONDON, NEW YORK,
MELBOURNE, MUNICH AND DELHI
www.dk.com

Produced by Hachette Livre Polska sp. z o.o., Warsaw, Poland

EDITORS Teresa Czerniewicz-Umer, Joanna Egert-Romanowska

DESIGNER Paweł Pasternak
CARTOGRAPHERS Magdalena Polak, Olaf Rodowald
PHOTOGRAPHERS Wojciech and Katarzyna Mędrzakowie,
Oldrich Karasek
ILLUSTRATORS Michał Burkiewicz, Paweł Marczak

CONTRIBUTORS
Małgorzata Omilanowska, Ulrich Schwendimann,
Adriana Czupryn, Marek Pernal, Marianna Dudek

FOR DORLING KINDERSLEY
EDITOR Lucilla Watson
CONSULTANTS Gerhard Brüschke, Matthew Teller
TRANSLATOR Magda Hannay
PRODUCTION CONTROLLER Louise Minihane

Printed and bound by South China Printing Co. Ltd., China.

First American edition, 2005

13 14 15 16 10 9 8 7 6 5 4 3 2 1

Published in the United States by DK Publishing,
375 Hudson Street, New York, NY 10014

Reprinted with revisions 2008, 2010, 2013

Copyright © 2005, 2013 Dorling Kindersley Limited, London
A Penguin Company

A CATALOG RECORD IS AVAILABLE FROM THE LIBRARY OF CONGRESS

ISSN 1542-1554
ISBN 978 0 7566 9514 9

Front cover main image: The Matterhorn, Swiss Alps

MIX
Paper from
responsible sources
FSC
www.fsc.org   FSC™ C018179

◁ The Matterhorn, Zermatt

CONTENTS

The massive towers of the
Grossmünster, Zürich

INTRODUCING
SWITZERLAND

Emblem of Zürich, Schweizerisches Landesmuseum, Zürich

Lake Lucerne, at the geographical and historical heart of Switzerland

Panel from the 1513 altarpiece in
the Église des Cordeliers, Fribourg

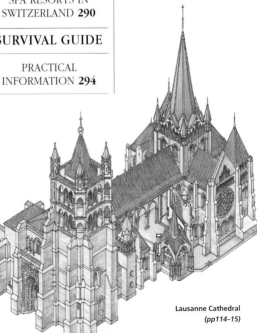

Lausanne Cathedral
(pp114–15)

HOW TO USE THIS GUIDE

This guide helps you to get the most from your visit to Switzerland. *Introducing Switzerland* maps the country and sets it in its historical and cultural context. Features cover topics from wildlife to geology. The eight sections comprising *Switzerland Region by Region*, three of which focus on Bern, Geneva and Zürich, describe the main

sights, with photographs, maps and illustrations. Restaurant and hotel listings, and information about winter sports and many other outdoor activities can be found in *Travellers' Needs*. The *Survival Guide* contains practical tips on everything from using the Swiss rail network to choosing the best times of year to visit Switzerland.

BERN

A separate section is devoted to Switzerland's capital city. Each of Bern's main sights is shown on the map of the city centre and described in numerical order.

Sights at a Glance lists key places of interest.

A locator map shows where you are in relation to other areas of the city.

1 City Map
For easy reference, sights are numbered and located on a map. The main streets, bus stations, railway stations and tourist offices are also shown.

A suggested route for a walk is marked by a broken red line.

2 Street-by-Street Map
This gives a bird's-eye view of the key areas described in each section.

3 Detailed Information
All the sights in each city are described individually. Addresses and opening hours are given for each sight, and if there is an admission charge, this will be indicated. The key to symbols is on the back flap.

1 Introduction
An overview of the history and character of a major city or region of Switzerland is given here.

SWITZERLAND REGION BY REGION
In this book, the country is described in eight chapters, three of which focus on Switzerland's major cities and five on its distinctive regions. The map on the inside front cover shows this regional division. The sights listed are shown and numbered on the *Regional Map* at the beginning of each chapter.

2 Regional Map
This shows the main road network and gives an illustrated overview of the whole region. All sights covered in the chapter are numbered and there are useful tips on getting around.

Each area of Switzerland is identified by colour-coded thumb tabs corresponding to the map on the inside front cover.

3 Detailed Information
All towns, villages and other places to visit are described individually and listed in order, following the numbering given on the Regional Map. *Each entry also contains practical information such as museum opening times.*

Story boxes explore some of the region's historical and cultural subjects in detail.

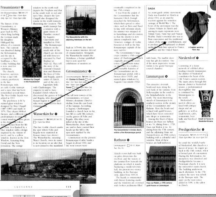

A Visitors' Checklist provides a summary of the practical information you need to plan your visit.

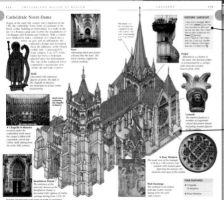

4 Switzerland's Top Sights
These are given two or more full pages. Historic buildings are often dissected so as to reveal their interiors. Stars indicate sights that visitors should not miss.

INTRODUCING SWITZERLAND

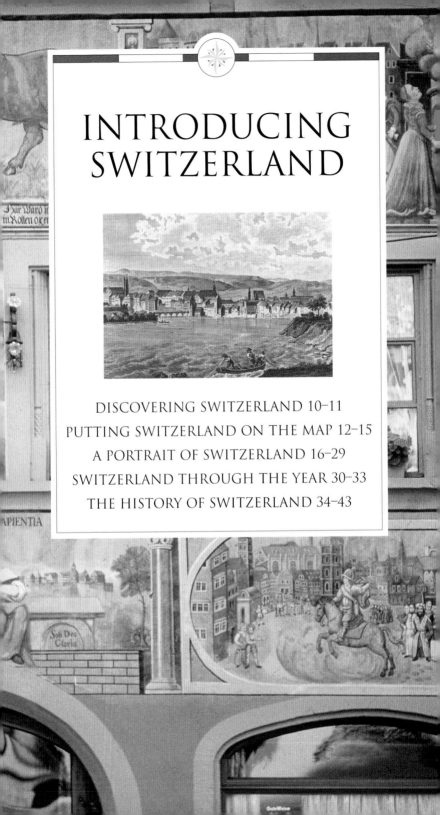

DISCOVERING SWITZERLAND

Each of Switzerland's eight regions has its own unique history. Landscapes, cuisine, architecture and even languages change as otherwise invisible borders are crossed. You can also explore the independent country of Liechtenstein, which is surrounded by Switzerland. From the gnomes of Zürich to the grotesquely costumed Vogel Gryff carnival dancers in Basel to the smiling citizens of Bern, the Swiss are a people who revel in their own stereotypes, celebrating their diversity while enjoying an unrivalled reputation for making a business out of welcoming strangers with one of the world's best tourist infrastructures.

Snowboarding in Verbier

Snowy scene with the peak of the Matterhorn in the distance

BERN

- **Well-preserved Old Town**
- **Art at the Kunstmuseum**
- **Bear Park**

Bern is Switzerland's most affable and affordable big city, and arguably the easiest capital city in Europe to negotiate. The local people are polite, and seldom in a hurry. Enjoy a stroll through the **Old Town** (see pp52–3), a UNESCO World Heritage Site with stone arcades and more than 100 fountains. The **Kunstmuseum** (see pp56–7) and the cluster of museums in the Kirchenfeld district merit special attention, as do the **Zytglogge** (see p55), **Münster** (see pp58–9), **Käfigturm** (see p55) and the **Bear Park** (see p60), home to the city's popular brown bears.

MITTELLAND, BERNESE OBERLAND AND VALAIS

- **World-class ski resorts**
- **Grand St Bernard Pass**
- **Awe-inspiring peaks**

A region of ice-covered peaks and verdant valleys, this area also includes Switzerland's biggest expanse of flat farm land – the Mittelland. Among the world-class ski resorts here are **Zermatt** (see p89), and **Verbier** (see p85). The Jungfrau train travels through the Eiger, terminating at 3,454 m (11,333 ft). The **Matterhorn** (see p90) is the world's most enigmatic mountain and the **Aletsch** (see p91) is the largest glacier in the Alps.

No trip to the Valais is complete without a visit to the eponymous dogs at the **St Bernard Pass** (see p84), or to see the fighting cows of the Herens breed. Relax with the region's Fendant wine or soak in the thermal spas at **Leukerbad** (see p89).

GENEVA

- **Decadent luxury shopping**
- **Characterful old town**
- **Europe's tallest fountain**

Bustling with bankers and diplomats, Switzerland's most cosmopolitan city is an expensive but exciting place to stay. It is a shoppers paradise, known for watches and antiques (see pp106–7). Top attractions include the **UN Headquarters** (see p101) but Geneva's pride and joy is the landmark **Jet d'Eau** fountain (see p97). Also rewarding is Geneva's Old Town, in particular the Gothic **Cathédrale St-Pierre** and its gorgoyles (see pp98–9).

WESTERN SWITZERLAND

- **Elegant Swiss Riviera**
- **Fairytale Château de Chillon**
- **Verdant lakeside vineyards**

The romantic poets Byron and Shelley, as well as modern

Bern's medieval Old Town, with the River Aare running through it

◁ Painted façade of the Roter Ochsen, a house on the Rathausplatz in Stein am Rhein

The Château de Chillon on the eastern shore of Lake Geneva

legends like Charlie Chaplin and Freddy Mercury, made the **Swiss Riviera** *(see pp112–19)* on the north shores of Lake Geneva their home. On the eastern shore of Lake Geneva is the the beautiful **Château de Chillon** *(see pp122–3)*. Lush vineyards grow on the hillsides of Lake Geneva and **Lake Neuchâtel** *(see pp130–1)* is a town renowned for its wines. The Roman town of **Avenches** *(see p124)* and the dairy country of **Gruyères** *(see p124)* are fascinating areas to tour, as are the rolling hills of the Jura mountains.

NORTHERN SWITZERLAND

- **Basel on the Rhine**
- **Outstanding art collections**
- **Fairytale medieval villages**

Most of the northern region is flat and industrialized, with the exceptions of the wine-growing villages of Regensberg and Eglisau. Sharing borders with Germany and France, **Basel** *(see 138–47)* is exceptionally diverse and open to artistic expression, as witnessed in its street festivals. Basel's **Kunstmuseum** *(see pp146–7)* alone is worth travelling far to see and **Winterthur** *(see pp156–7)* also has superb art collections. **Baden** – the "baths" spa resort *(see pp154–5)* – is built around a picture-postcard medieval Old Town.

ZURICH

- **Finance and fashion capital**
- **Contemporary art**
- **Bahnhofstrasse shopping**

A city of guarded banks, and a world centre of gold trading, Zürich surprises visitors with its amazingly ruch and vibrant contemporary art and cultural scene. The vast **National Museum** *(see pp162–3)* and **Kunsthaus** *(see pp170–1)* art gallery are both world class attractions. With cobblestoned streets, tree-lined promenades and lakeside quays, Zürich is one of the most seductive European cities for strolling. There are thousands of architectural treasures to be discovered in small alleys, shows to be seen in intimate cabarets *(see pp172–3)*, and luxury items to be bought on the expensive **Bahnhofstrasse** *(see p164)*.

Colourful carnival in the streets of Basel, a dynamic, artistic city

EASTERN SWITZERLAND AND GRAUBUNDEN

- **Swiss National Park**
- **Engadine's "Graffiti" houses**
- **Heidi's homeland**

This is the Switzerland of storybook and legend. The Rhine flows through broad flower- and fruit-filled valleys celebrated in the **Heidi** story *(see pp190–1)*. The **Swiss National Park** *(see pp202–3)* offers a pristine wilderness of wildlife and rare flowers. Ancient towns of trade and learning with magnificent medieval buildings are found across the region, while houses with unusual painted façades can be seen in the **Engadine valley** *(see p200)*. Winter sports entertain the jet set in **St Moritz** *(see p204)*, and **Klosters** *(see p191)*.

Ibex grazing in the Swiss National Park, a much-loved nature reserve

CENTRAL SWITZERLAND AND TICINO

- **Chapel Bridge, Luzern**
- **Scenic lakes**
- **Baroque Einsiedeln Kloster**

Birthplace of the legendary William Tell, this region runs from Switzerland's heart to the Italian-speaking Ticino. The lakes of **Lugano** *(see pp210–11)* and **Maggiore** *(see pp216–17)* are blessed with a warm climate while **Luzern** *(see pp232–3)*, is one of Europe's most scenic cities. The **Kloster Einsiedeln** is a Baroque masterpiece *(see pp226–7)*.

Putting Switzerland on the Map

Located in the Alpine region of central Europe,
Switzerland is a landlocked country covering some
41,300 sq km (15,950 sq miles) and inhabited by
7.9 million people, 22 per cent of whom are non-
Swiss. It borders Germany to the north, Austria and
Liechtenstein to the east, Italy to the south, and France
to the west and northwest. Switzerland consists of
three distinct geographical regions, which stretch
across the country southwest to northeast: the Jura
mountains, covering a small area in the northwest;
the Mittelland, a central plateau, and the Alps in
the south and east. The capital city is Bern.

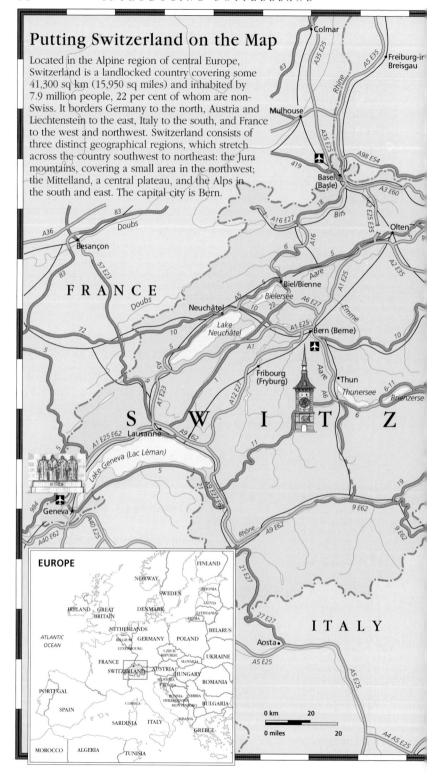

Aerial view of Bern's Old Town

Villingen-
-Schwenningen

Danube

GERMANY

Schaffhausen

Konstanz

*Bodensee
(Lake Constance)*

Winterthur

Thur

Bregenz

Dornbirn

Zürich

Reuss

Töss

Feldkirch

AUSTRIA

Luzern
(Lucerne)

Vaduz

Bludenz

Lech

Rhine

Chur

Inn

E   R   L   A   N   D

Ticino

Bellinzona

Adda

Lugano

*Lake
Como*

*Lake
Lugano*

*Lake
Maggiore*

Lecco

Varese

Como

Oglio

Bergamo

KEY

Busto
Arsizio

Monza

--- National border

✈ International airport

═ Motorway

═ Major road

— Railway line

Ticino

Milan

Novara

Adda

Switzerland's Cantons and Linguistic Regions

Switzerland is divided into 26 cantons, six of which (Appenzell-Ausserrhoden, Appenzell-Innerrhoden, Basel-Landschaft, Basel-Stadt, Nidwalden and Obwalden) are known as half-cantons but operate as full cantons. Each canton has its own constitution, legislation and financial autonomy. The country is divided into three main linguistic regions. While German predominates in northern, eastern and central Switzerland, French is spoken in the west, and Italian in the south. Valais, or Wallis, has distinct French- and German-speaking regions. Romansh is the language of a small minority of people in Graubünden, where German and Italian predominate.

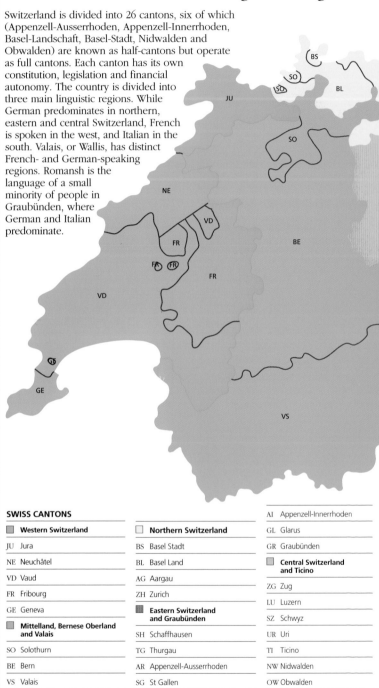

SWISS CANTONS

▨ Western Switzerland	▨ Northern Switzerland	AI Appenzell-Innerrhoden
JU Jura	BS Basel Stadt	GL Glarus
NE Neuchâtel	BL Basel Land	GR Graubünden
VD Vaud	AG Aargau	▨ Central Switzerland and Ticino
FR Fribourg	ZH Zurich	
GE Geneva	▨ Eastern Switzerland and Graubünden	ZG Zug
▨ Mittelland, Bernese Oberland and Valais		LU Luzern
	SH Schaffhausen	SZ Schwyz
SO Solothurn	TG Thurgau	UR Uri
BE Bern	AR Appenzell-Ausserrhoden	TI Ticino
VS Valais	SG St Gallen	NW Nidwalden
		OW Obwalden

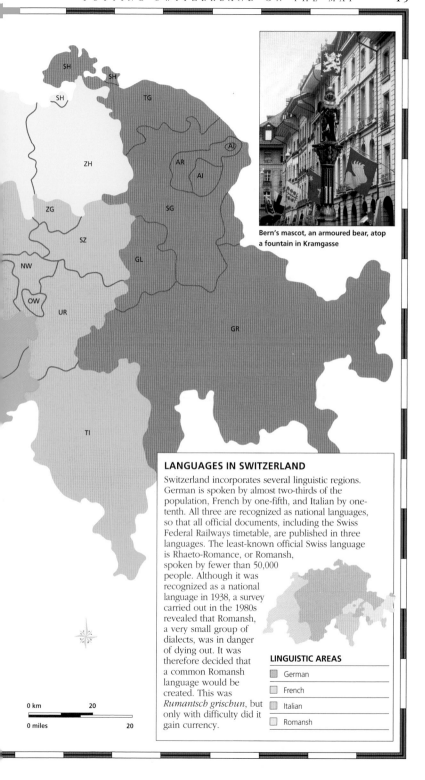

Bern's mascot, an armoured bear, atop a fountain in Kramgasse

LANGUAGES IN SWITZERLAND

Switzerland incorporates several linguistic regions. German is spoken by almost two-thirds of the population, French by one-fifth, and Italian by one-tenth. All three are recognized as national languages, so that all official documents, including the Swiss Federal Railways timetable, are published in three languages. The least-known official Swiss language is Rhaeto-Romance, or Romansh, spoken by fewer than 50,000 people. Although it was recognized as a national language in 1938, a survey carried out in the 1980s revealed that Romansh, a very small group of dialects, was in danger of dying out. It was therefore decided that a common Romansh language would be created. This was *Rumantsch grischun*, but only with difficulty did it gain currency.

LINGUISTIC AREAS

▢	German
▢	French
▢	Italian
▢	Romansh

0 km   20

0 miles   20

A PORTRAIT OF SWITZERLAND

A landlocked country in the cultural and geographical heart of Europe, Switzerland has a distinct character and dynamism. While the country is admired for the beauty of its Alpine environment, its people are respected for their industry and technical ingenuity, as well as their social responsibility and direct democratic system of government. It is also one of the world's richest countries.

Switzerland has virtually no natural borders. The Alpine mass of which it mostly consists extends eastwards into Austria, westwards into France, and southwards to form valleys that run down to Lombardy, where the border straddles several lakes. Although Switzerland's northern border follows the course of the Rhine, even here it crosses this natural feature, bulging out around Basel and taking in a mosaic of German and Swiss enclaves around Schaffhausen.

This mountainous country has engendered a robust spirit of independence and enterprise and a zealous work ethic in its population. Both Catholic and Protestant,

"Welcome to the Swiss Alps"

and with diverse cultural roots, the Swiss are remarkable for their strong sense of unified nationhood. Switzerland's national character has also been moulded by its neutrality. Having avoided many of the major conflicts that shaped the culture of other European nations, Switzerland stands at a slight remove from the wider world.

Switzerland today is a prosperous and highly industrialized nation with a cosmopolitan lifestyle. On the one hand, it is forward-looking and innovative. On the other, it is traditional and conservative, valuing stability above change, with a keenness to maintain cultural continuity and links with the past.

The Aletsch Glacier seen from the Eggishorn, whose peak reaches 2,927 m (9,603 ft)

◁ The Église St-Jean and Fontaine St-Jean in Fribourg

Biel/Bienne, the Bielersee and St Petersinsel, seen from Boezingenberg, in the Jura mountains

POPULATION, LANGUAGE AND RELIGION

The Jura mountains, in the north, and the Alpine region, to the south, are sparsely populated. The highest population density, and most of the country's industrial activity, is in the central Mittelland, concentrated in and around the capital Bern, and also in the lakeside cities of Geneva, Lausanne, Luzern and Zürich.

Switzerland's linguistic and religious divisions are also distinctive. The German-speaking population inhabits the northern slopes and valleys of the Alps and a large section of the Mittelland plateau. The northern shores of Lake Geneva, the gentle slopes of the Jura mountains and the western Alps are inhabited by French-speaking Swiss.

Traditional folk costume of the Fribourg region

Italian is spoken south of the main Alpine ridge, while the Romansh-speaking minority inhabits a few isolated high mountain valleys in the east. German is spoken by two-thirds of the population, French by one fifth, Italian by one tenth and Romansh by no more than about 1 per cent. Switzerland is almost equally divided between Protestant and Catholic, these religions crossing linguistic divides. The population also includes a small number of Jews and Muslims.

Divisions between French, Italian and German speakers, and between Protestants and Catholics, which have dogged the unity of the Confederation throughout its history, are still tangible today.

DEMOCRACY IN ACTION

Switzerland is a federal republic consisting of 26 cantons. With its own tax, legal, fiscal and educational systems, each canton is virtually an independent state, enjoying considerable autonomy within the Swiss Confederation.

The country is governed by a Federal Assembly, a bicameral parliament consisting of a directly elected Federal Council and a Council of States, whose delegates represent the individual cantons. Switzerland's main political parties are the Swiss

Regatta on Lej da Silvaplana in Graubünden

People's Party, the Social Democrats, the Free Democrats and the Christian Democrats. Certain major issues are decided directly by the people, by referendum. Voting, on matters ranging from the national speed limit to concerns of strictly local relevance, takes place at national, cantonal and communal level.

Alpine festival in Beatenberg, on the Thunersee

THE ECONOMY

The Swiss economy is based on banking and international trade, the service industries, manufacturing, agriculture and tourism. Standards of living are high, unemployment is low and per capita income is one of the highest in the world.

The country's major exports are precision machinery, clocks and watches, textiles, chemicals and pharmaceuticals. Chocolate and dairy products, including cheese, are also major exports.

Although only 5 per cent of the population is engaged in agriculture, this sector of the economy enjoys a privileged status, with some of the highest subsidies in the world. This is not only of benefit to farmers but, since it contributes to the preservation of Switzerland's picturesque landscape, it also supports the country's hugely important tourist industry. Livestock accounts for almost three-quarters of Swiss farming, and dairy farming and agriculture for one quarter. Half of the country's cheese production is exported, chiefly in the form of Emmental and Gruyère.

ARTS AND SCIENCES

A highly cultured country, Switzerland plays a leading role in the arts, hosting such important events as the Lucerne Music Festival, the Montreux Jazz Festival and the Rose d'Or television awards. Art Basel is the world's premier contemporary art fair, and the Kunsthaus in Zürich is a national art gallery with collections of international importance.

The best-known of all Swiss intellectuals is the philosopher Jean-Jacques Rousseau (1712–78), who was born in Geneva but who spent most of his life in France. Other important Swiss writers include the German-born dramatists Max Frisch (1911–91) and Friedrich Dürrenmatt (1921–90). Herman Hesse (1877–1962), who was born in Germany, became a Swiss citizen and wrote many of his greatest works in Switzerland. Many

Cattle returning from mountain pastures, in the Schwarzenburg region

Swiss artists and architects have also won international recognition. Among the most prominent is the architect Le Corbusier (1887–1965), who was born and grew up in La-Chaux-de-Fonds, but who is more closely associated with France, and the sculptor and painter Alberto Giacometti (1901–66), a native of Graubünden, who spent nearly all his adult life in Paris. Although he retained his German citizenship, the artist Paul Klee (1879–1940), who was born near Bern, is treated as Swiss. Other notable Swiss artists include the painter Ferdinand Hodler (1853–1918), the sculptor Jean Tinguely (1925–91) and the polymath Max Bill (1908–94).

Since the 1930s, Switzerland has produced several architects of international renown. Mario Botta (b. 1943) designed the Museum of Modern of Art in San Francisco, and Jacques Herzog and Pierre de Meuron are the architects who designed the world's largest steel structure, the 2008 Olympic Stadium in Beijing.

Switzerland also has a tradition of excellence in the sciences. It was in Bern that Albert Einstein developed his theory of relativity, and to date an impressive number of 25 Swiss citizens have won Nobel prizes. The Federal Institute of Technology in

Clearing, an installation by Gillian White, depicting the links between art and nature

Zürich and the prestigious European Centre for Nuclear Research near Geneva have put Switzerland at the forefront of scientific research.

TRADITIONAL ACTIVITIES

A sport-loving nation, the Swiss make the most of their Alpine country. Skiing, snowboarding, sledging and skating are popular winter sports. Kayaking, rafting, hiking and a host of other active summer sports have a large following among the Swiss.

Certain rural areas are home to distinctive types of sport. These include *Schwingen*, an Alpine form of wrestling, *Hornussen*, a ball game played with long, curved bats, and cow fights *(combats des reines)*, staged in the canton of Valais. Yodelling and alphorn-playing are also an integral part of the Alpine way of life. However, many

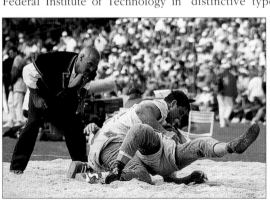

Contestants in a *Schwingen* match, a Swiss form of wrestling

young town folk, regardless of region, are deeply indifferent to these traditional activities, as they are to the *Waffenlauf*, a long-distance race run by competitors dressed in uniforms and carrying rucksacks and rifles on their backs.

Swiss Guards at a ceremony at the Vatican in Rome

ENVIRONMENTAL ISSUES

The Swiss have a punctilious approach to preserving their natural environment. Two examples of this are a remarkably developed and well coordinated public transport system, and a scrupulous approach to recycling waste.

Switzerland is the first country to have made compulsory the fitting of catalytic converters to cars, and national regulations concerning the emission of toxic gases and other substances are among the most stringent in the world. Such consideration towards the environment has had a measurable effect on the quality of life in Switzerland. Even in towns or cities the size of Luzern, Bern or Zürich, the rivers and lakes are so clean that it is perfectly safe to swim in them.

Most Alpine plants and many wild animals are protected by law, and certain animals, such as the ibex, wolf and bear, have been reintroduced. Forests, which cover about a third of the country, are also protected. Forestry is tightly regulated and logging of large areas, which heightens the risk of landslides and avalanches, is forbidden. Switzerland is a signatory to the 1999 Alpine Convention, drawn up together with eight other Alpine nations to protect the Alpine environment from the harmful effects of tourism and motorized transport.

SWITZERLAND ON THE WORLD STAGE

Although it is a neutral country, Switzerland maintains a citizen army to defend its borders. National service is compulsory. However, except in time of war, the Swiss army has no active units and no top general, although regular training takes place. The last mobilization occurred during World War II. Today, the only Swiss mercenaries are the Swiss Guards, who defend the Vatican and act as the papal bodyguard in Rome.

Switzerland has the European headquarters of the UN and the world headquarters of the International Red Cross based in Geneva, and sees its role in international affairs as a largely humanitarian one.

Kayaking on the Valser Rhine in Graubünden

The Swiss Alps

About two-thirds of Swiss territory consists of Alpine and sub-Alpine areas. At lower elevations up to 1,500 m (5,000 ft) agricultural land and deciduous trees predominate. These give way to coniferous forest, which above 2,200 m (7,200 ft) in turn gives way to scrub and alpine pastures. At altitudes above 3,000 m (9,800 ft) mosses and lichens cover a desolate rocky landscape, above which are snowfields, glaciers and permanently snow-covered peaks. While snow and rainfall increase with altitude, the Alpine climate is affected by two seasonal winds, the cold, dry easterly *bise* and the warm southerly *Föhn*, which brings clear, sunny skies then rainfall to the western Alps.

Meadow and pasture *cover almost half of Switzerland. Wild clover and campanula grow abundantly in the high meadows of the Bernese Oberland.*

Glacial lakes, *formed by the melting of glaciers, are a common sight in Alpine valleys. The Bachalpsee, near which rises the Wetterhorn, lies at the heart of a particularly scenic part of the Swiss Alps.*

Mosses and lichens cling to the surface of rugged crests and precipitous scree-filled gorges.

Scrub, including dwarf mountain pine, as well as rhododendron and alder, cover the transitional zone between the forests and the high mountain peaks. At this altitude the growing season, from June to August, is brief.

Lush vegetation thrives on sheltered slopes and along gulleys cut by mountain streams.

High alpine meadows provide lush summer grazing for cattle.

MOUNTAIN LANDSCAPE

The Alps are cut through by deep valleys, terraces, cols and gorges. To the south of the Alps lies the canton of Ticino, which enjoys a Mediterranean climate. To their north are the long limestone sub-Alpine ranges, whose sheer rockfaces merge into the flatter Mittelland, central Switzerland's relatively low-lying plateau.

Forests *in Switzerland are closely monitored and protected. Clearing hillsides, which increases the danger of avalanches, is forbidden.*

Alpine streams *flowing through dense pine forests are a part of the extraordinarily beautiful scenery in the Swiss National Park.*

Spruce predominates in forests at higher altitudes

Areas of grassland, *like this one around the Schwarzsee, a lake at the foot of the Matterhorn, provide summer grazing for sheep. Thick snow covers these pastures during winter.*

ALPINE PLANTS AND ANIMALS

In spring Switzerland's high Alpine meadows are covered with a carpet of flowers, including aster, edelweiss, campion, and several species of gentian. Most Alpine flowers are protected and it is forbidden to pick them. Alpine wildlife includes ibex and chamois, marmot, Alpine hare, golden eagle, bearded vulture, and the rarely seen European lynx. Several species of these animals, including those that have been reintroduced, are also protected.

Edelweiss, *the symbol of Switzerland, grows among rocks at altitudes up to 3,500 m (11,500 ft). It has star-shaped flowers and woolly leaves.*

Alpenrose, *a species of rhododendron, grows mostly at altitudes of 2,500 m (8,200 ft). Its flowers create large areas of dense colour.*

Gentian *grows mainly in rock crevices and in woodlands. Its roots are used in the pharmaceutical industry.*

The Alpine ibex *lives above the tree line for most of the year. A species of wild goat, it is extremely agile over mountainous terrain.*

The chamois, *a goat antelope, frequents regions between wooded mountainsides and the snow line. Agile and shy, it is seldom seen at close range.*

The marmot *lives in burrows in Alpine meadows. When disturbed, it emits a piercing, high-pitched whistle.*

Formation of the Alps

About 70 million years ago, the Adriatic Microplate began to drift northward, colliding with the rigid European Plate. While the oceanic floor that lay between them was forced downwards, the Adriatic Microplate was thrust upwards, creating the Alps. This up-heaval, which continued until 2 million years ago, caused the upper strata of rock to fold over on themselves. The older metamorphic rocks, thrust up from the substratum, thus form the highest part of the Alps, while the more recent sedimentary and igneous rocks make up the lower levels. The action of glaciers during successive ice ages then scoured and sculpted the Alps, giving them their present appearance.

The Matterhorn, *carved by the action of ice, is the most distinctive and best-known of Switzerland's peaks. Lofty and awe-inspiring, it rises to a height of 4,478 m (14,691 ft).*

The Aletsch Glacier, *in the Bernese Alps, covers about 86 sq km (33 sq miles) and is about 900 m (2,952 ft) deep. It is the largest glacier in the Alps.*

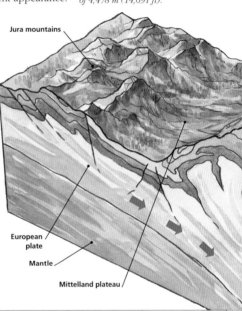

Jura mountains

European plate

Mantle

Mittelland plateau

ALPINE GLACIERS

Vestiges of the Ice Age, Alpine glaciers continue their erosive action. As they advance, they scour valley floors and sides, carrying away rocks which are ground and then deposited as lateral and terminal moraines. Glacial lakes fill basins scooped out by glaciers. Hanging valleys were created when glaciers deepened the main valley.

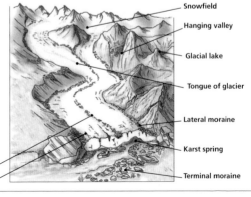

Snowfield

Hanging valley

Glacial lake

Tongue of glacier

Lateral moraine

Karst spring

Terminal moraine

Medial moraine

Crevasses

The Jura mountains, *consisting of fossil-rich marl and limestone, are relatively low. They feature caves, sinkholes and underground streams. Because of their exceptionally well-preserved strata, the mountains gave their name to a geological period, the Jurassic.*

THE SWISS ALPS

Apart from those in the eastern part of the canton of Graubünden, the Swiss Alps, like the French Alps, belong to the Western Alpine Group, which in turn consists of ten separate ranges. This part of the Alpine range has the highest and steepest peaks and most contorted geological formations. It is also where Switzerland's landscapes of snow and ice are at their most breathtaking. The Valais Alps contain many of Switzerland's most impressive peaks, including the Matterhorn and Dufourspitze, which at 4,634 m (15,203 ft) is the country's highest mountain. The southern Alps lie in the canton of Ticino. The eastern Alps contain the Swiss National Park.

KEY

	Western Alps
	Eastern Alps
	Southern Alps
	Swiss upland
	Jura mountains

Western Alps

Southern Alps

Direction of tectonic thrust

Adriatic Plate

Mantle

ALPINE LANDSCAPE

Shaped by the action of ice, the landscape of the Alps was created during a succession of ice ages that occurred 600,000 to 10,000 years ago. During periods of glaciation, the ice sheet was up to 2,000 m (6,500 ft) thick. Typical of the glacial landscape are sharp ridges, steep gullies, flat-bottomed valleys carved out by advancing glaciers, glacial lakes and hanging valleys with waterfalls creating streams.

The Swiss National Park *is situated in the Rhaetian Alps, which form part of the Eastern Alpine Group. Its pristine Alpine landscape, covering 170 sq km (66 sq miles) in Graubünden, ranges from evergreen forest to desolate rocky areas and permanent snow at high altitudes.*

Swiss Architecture

Tympanum of Basel's Romanesque Münster

Serene Romanesque abbeys, lofty Gothic cathedrals, lavishly decorated Baroque churches and town houses with painted façades all form part of Switzerland's architectural heritage. For most of its history, however, Swiss architecture reflected various European influences – German in the north and east, French in the west, and Italian in the south – without developing a distinctive style until the mid-20th century. Swiss vernacular architecture, however, has always been distinctive. It is epitomized by the Alpine chalet, of which there are several local variants.

Painted façade *of a fine 16th-century town house in Stein-am-Rhein, Schaffhausen.*

ROMANESQUE (10TH–12TH CENTURIES)

As elsewhere in western Europe, the flowering of the Romanesque style in Switzerland was due largely to the diffusion of religious orders, which spearheaded a renewal in religious architecture. Romanesque buildings are characterized by massive walls, rounded arches, groin vaulting, and a restrained use of decorative carving. Among the finest examples of the style in Switzerland are the Benedictine monastery at St Gallen, the Münster zu Allerheiligen in Schaffhausen, and its culmination, Basel's remarkable Münster.

The Grossmünster *in Zürich, begun in the 11th century, was stripped of its interior decor during the Reformation.*

The Romanesque crypt of Basel's 12th-century Münster

GOTHIC (13TH–15TH CENTURIES)

Characterized by pointed arches, ribbed vaulting and flying buttresses, the Gothic style emphasizes vertical perspectives, with stained-glass windows admitting light to lofty interiors and decoration on towers and portals. Fine examples of Swiss Gothic architecture include the Cathédrale St-Pierre in Geneva and Cathédrale de Nôtre-Dame in Lausanne, both of French inspiration, and the Münster in Bern, in the German Gothic style. Important Gothic secular buildings include the Château de Vufflens and Château de Chillon, and Bellinzona's three castles, Montebello, Sasso Corbaro and Castelgrande.

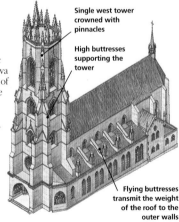

Single west tower crowned with pinnacles

High buttresses supporting the tower

Flying buttresses transmit the weight of the roof to the outer walls

The Cathédrale St-Nicolas *in Fribourg, built in the 14th and 15th centuries, exemplifies the High Gothic style.*

The Château de Chillon, *built by the Dukes of Savoy on an islet near Montreux, is one of the finest extant examples of Gothic fortified architecture in Switzerland.*

RENAISSANCE (15TH–16TH CENTURIES)

Coinciding with the Reformation, the Renaissance reached Switzerland in the late 15th to early 16th centuries. The style is most clearly seen in secular buildings, such as town halls, mansions with arcaded courtyards and fine town houses, like those in Bern. While the Gothic style tended to persist in the country's German-speaking regions, Renaissance influence was strongest in central and southern Switzerland.

The Rathaus in Luzern, completed in 1606, is built in the style of a Renaissance Florentine palazzo but its mansard roof reflects Swiss traditions.

The Collegio Pontificio di Papio in Ascona, built around 1584, has a fine Renaissance arcaded courtyard with a double tier of beautifully proportioned arches.

BAROQUE (17TH–18TH CENTURIES)

The end of the Thirty Years' War in 1648 was marked by a renewal in building activity in Switzerland. In the country's Catholic regions many new churches were built, and older ones remodelled, in the Baroque style. Characterized by extensive ornamentation, painted ceilings, scrollwork and gilding, the Baroque in Switzerland came under foreign influences and has north Italian and south German variants. The finest examples of Baroque architecture in Switzerland are the Klosterkirche in Einsiedeln, completed in 1745, and St Gallen Cathedral, completed in 1768.

The Klosterkirche at Einsiedeln has an ornate gilt and polychrome ceiling typical of the Baroque style.

St Gallen Cathedral, a fine example of Swiss Baroque architecture

THE SWISS CHALET

Characteristic of Switzerland and other adjacent Alpine areas, the chalet was originally a herdsman's house. Although there are many regional variations, the chalet is typically built of timber, generally to a square plan, and is covered with a low-pitched roof made of wood, slate or stone. The roof usually projects both at the eaves and at the gables, and the gable end is sometimes filled with a triangular area of sloping roof. Many chalets also have balconies, which may be fronted with decoratively carved railings.

Doors of wooden houses are of panel construction, and are usually covered with decorations and reinforced with ornamental metalwork.

Half-timbered chalet at the Freilichtmuseum Ballenberg

Rural house typical of the Bern region of the Mittelland during the Baroque period. The roof is designed to enable it to withstand heavy coverings of snow.

Tunnels and Railways

The building of Switzerland's renowned railways, tunnels and viaducts began in the mid-19th century, driven by the needs of a precociously industrialized economy and made possible by the technological advances of the age. As track was laid along seemingly inaccessible mountain routes, tunnels were driven beneath mountains and viaducts built to span deep valleys. By the end of the 19th century, narrow- and full-gauge rail networks, including rack-and-pinion track on the steepest inclines, covered the country. While part of the rail network caters for visitors, it is used mainly by modern express, intercity and high-speed trains.

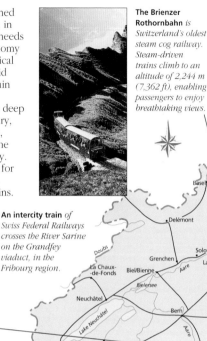

The Brienzer Rothornbahn *is Switzerland's oldest steam cog railway. Steam-driven trains climb to an altitude of 2,244 m (7,362 ft), enabling passengers to enjoy breathtaking views.*

An intercity train *of Swiss Federal Railways crosses the River Sarine on the Grandfey viaduct, in the Fribourg region.*

Map labels: Basel, Delémont, Doubs, Solothurn, Grenchen, Langenthal, La Chaux-de-Fonds, Biel/Bienne, Aare, Neuchâtel, Bielersee, Burgc, Lake Neuchâtel, Bern, Aare, Yverdon, Payerne, Fribourg, Thun, Spiez, Inter, Lausanne, Gruyères, Vevey, Gstaad, Montreux, Lake Geneva (Lac Léman), Geneva (Genève), Sion, Saa, Le Châtelard, Martigny, Zermatt, Orsières, Chamonix-Mont-Blanc, Grand St Bernard

The funicular train *from Mülenen takes visitors up the Niesen, whose peak rises to 2,362 m (7,749 ft). From the summit there is a magnificent view of the Thunersee, Spiez and the Jungfrau range.*

An intercity train *on a main line that opened in 1996. Skirting Lake Geneva, it passes near the beautiful Château de Chillon.*

The Glacier Express *crosses 291 bridges and viaducts and runs through 91 tunnels on its scenic route between Zermatt and St Moritz.*

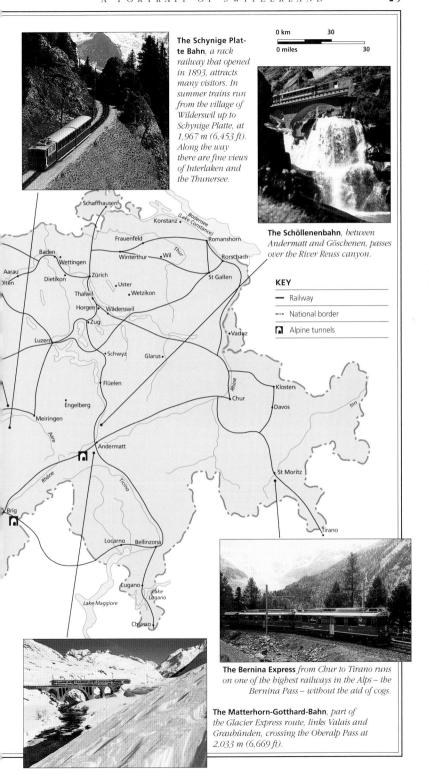

The Schynige Platte Bahn, *a rack railway that opened in 1893, attracts many visitors. In summer trains run from the village of Wilderswil up to Schynige Platte, at 1,967 m (6,453 ft). Along the way there are fine views of Interlaken and the Thunersee.*

0 km   30

0 miles   30

The Schöllenenbahn, *between Andermatt and Göschenen, passes over the River Reuss canyon.*

KEY

— Railway

--- National border

🔲 Alpine tunnels

Schaffhausen
Konstanz — Bodensee (Lake Constance)
Frauenfeld
Romanshorn
Baden
Wettingen
Winterthur • Wil
Thur
Rorschach
Aarau
Dietikon
Zürich
St Gallen
Olten
Thalwil • Uster • Wetzikon
Horgen • Wädenswil
• Zug
Luzern
• Schwyz
Glarus •
Vaduz
Flüelen
Engelberg
Klosters
Chur
Meiringen
Davos
Aare
Rhône
Inn
Andermatt
Ticino
St Moritz
Rhône
Brig
Tirano
Locarno Bellinzona
Lugano
Lake Lugano
Lake Maggiore
Chiasso

The Bernina Express *from Chur to Tirano runs on one of the highest railways in the Alps – the Bernina Pass – without the aid of cogs.*

The Matterhorn-Gotthard-Bahn, *part of the Glacier Express route, links Valais and Graubünden, crossing the Oberalp Pass at 2,033 m (6,669 ft).*

SWITZERLAND THROUGH THE YEAR

The Swiss enjoy a great variety of festivals. These range from colourful spectacles in which entire towns, cities and villages take part, to sophisticated art, music and film festivals, some of which are internationally famous. Among these are the Lucerne Festival of classical music and Bern's International Jazz Festival (March–May).

Alphorn, seen at folk festivals

While the country unites to celebrate its origins on National Day (1 August), a large proportion of popular festivals, such as Bern's onion fair in November, have a more local, though no less historic, significance. Many folk festivals, particularly those ushering in the arrival of spring, have pagan roots, and in mountain villages cows are honoured in ceremonies that mark the spring and autumn transhumance – the seasonal movement of livestock.

Between December and March, the country also hosts many winter sports events, including several world championships.

Chalandamarz, a children's spring festival in the Engadine on 1 March

SPRING

The early spring is a time of transition. As the winter sports season nears its end, cold dark days begin to brighten and the first of the spring festivals, at which winter is ritually despatched, take place. Open-air voting sessions resume, cows are ceremonially taken up to their summer pastures, and in the Valais the first cow fights of the year are held.

MARCH

International Jazzfestival *(March–May)*, Bern. Major three-month festival of blues, jazz and gospel music.
Chalandamarz *(1 March)*, villages all over the Engadine. Children's spring festival, with costumed parades.
Engadine Ski Marathon *(2nd Sunday in March)*.

Major cross-country skiing marathon run from Maloja to S-chanf with about 13,000 participants.
International Motor Show *(March)*, Geneva. Prestigious annual event.
Verbier Xtreme *(mid-March)*. Daredevil off piste skiing and boarding, Verbier.
Snow and Symphony *(late March–early April)*, St Moritz. World-famous orchestras and soloists present a series of 20 concerts of classical music and jazz.
Oesterfestspiele *(around Easter)*, Luzern. Festival of Easter music.

APRIL

Sechseläuten *(3rd Monday in April)*, Zürich. Spring festival with parade of medieval guilds and the ritual burning of Böögg (Old Man Winter).

Basel World, Basel. Watch and jewellery fair.
Lugano Festival *(mid-April–June)*, Lugano. Classical music concerts.
Fête de la Tulipe *(mid-April–mid-May)*, Morges. Colourful tulip festival.
Fête du Soleil *(late April–May)*, Lausanne. Carnival with bands and markets.
Combat des Reines *(mid-April–May)*, Valais. Traditional cow fighting takes place in four Swiss valleys – Heremence, Herens, Anniviers and Bagnes.
Landsgemeinde *(last Sunday in April)*, Appenzell Innerrhoden. Open-air cantonal voting session.

MAY

Landsgemeinde *(1st Sunday in May)*, Glarus. An open-air cantonal voting session conducted by a show of hands.
International Rowing Regattas *(late May)*, Luzern. World-class rowing races on the Rotsee.

Traditional cow fights, held in Valais in spring

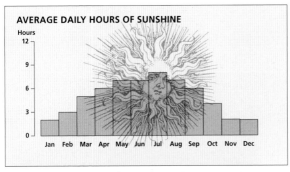

AVERAGE DAILY HOURS OF SUNSHINE

Sunshine Chart
July is the sunniest month, but May, June and August also feature sunny weather. The cloudiest months are in winter, from November to January.

Dancers in traditional costume at a summer folk festival in Appenzell

SUMMER

In mountain villages summer is celebrated with a host of folk festivals, with much eating, drinking and merriment. Elsewhere, the first of many open-air events, including music festivals and summer sporting events, takes place. At the height of summer, Swiss National Day (1 August) is celebrated in every town and village with bonfires and fireworks.

JUNE

Alpaufzug *(mid-June)*, across the Alps. Cows, adorned with flowers, are herded to high Alpine meadows, while celebrations are held in villages.
Art Basel *(mid-June)*, Basel. Major international contemporary art fair in leading galleries across the city.

Participant in the Fêtes des Vignerons, Vevey

Jazz Ascona *(late June)*, Ascona. The music of New Orleans, in the largest jazz event outside the USA.
William Tell *(late June–mid-September)*, Interlaken. Open-air performances of Schiller's play about the Swiss hero.

JULY

Open-Air Rock and Pop Music Festival *(early July)*, St Gallen.
Montreux Jazz Festival *(July)*, Montreux. Festival of jazz blues, rock, reggae and soul music. Free concerts on the promenade.
Avenches Opera Festival *(6–21 July)*. World-class opera productions at the 6,000-seat Roman amphitheatre.
Swiss Open *(mid-July)*, Gstaad. International men's tennis tournament.
Moon and Stars *(mid-July)*, Locarno. Rock and pop music in the city's Piazza Grande.

AUGUST

National Day *(1 August)*, throughout Switzerland. Celebrations, with fireworks, music, street illuminations and lantern processions, marking the birth of the Swiss Confederation in 1291.
Fêtes de Genève *(early August)*, Geneva. Music, street theatre, firework displays and sport.
International Film Festival *(early August)*, Locarno. Some 7,000 spectators enjoy outdoor viewings on Europe's biggest cinema screen.
Street Parade *(either of the first two weekends in August)*, Zürich. Huge open-air gathering of a million techno-music fans.
Inferno Triathlon *(mid-August)*, Jungfrau region. Bike and run 5,500 m (18,045 ft) uphill, then swim 3,100 m (2 miles) to cool off.
Luzern Festival *(mid-August–mid-September)*, Luzern. The famous festival of classical music, with international orchestras, conductors and soloists.

Celebrations on National Day in Oberhofen, on the Thunersee

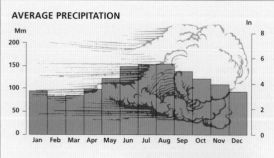

AVERAGE PRECIPITATION

Jan Feb Mar Apr May Jun Jul Aug Sep Oct Nov Dec

Precipitation
*The heaviest rainfall
in Switzerland occurs
during the summer
months. Winter brings
heavy snowfalls,
especially at high
altitudes. However, the
annual precipitation
in some regions, such
as Valais, is lower than
the national average.*

AUTUMN

When the trees on the
Alpine hillsides start to take
on autumnal colours and the
vines are heavy with ripe
grapes, it is time to give thanks
for the harvest. Colourful agricultural fairs are held across
the country; chestnut and wine
festivals take place everywhere
and the cows are returned to
their valley pastures, where
they will spend the winter.

SEPTEMBER

European Masters *(early
September)*, Crans Montana.
Switzerland's premier golfing
event, a highlight of the
PGA European tour.
La Bénichon *(mid-September–
October)*, Canton Fribourg.
Festival of thanksgiving.
Knabenschiessen *(2nd
weekend in September)*,
Zürich. Shooting contest for
boys and girls aged 12–16.
Wine Festival *(late
September)*, Neuchâtel.
The largest of its kind in
Switzerland. Others are held
throughout the country.
Fête de la Désalpe *(last
Saturday in September)*, across
the Alps. Celebrations as cows
decorated with flowers are
brought down from their
summer grazing in the high
Alpine meadows.

OCTOBER

Combats des Reines *(early
October)*, Martigny. Cow fighting in the Roman amphitheatre,
the ultimate winner being
proclaimed Reine des Reines
(Queen of the Queens).
Autumn Fair *(early October)*,

Festivities marking the return of
cows from their Alpine pastures

Basel. Switzerland's largest and
longest-established food fair
and funfair runs for two weeks.
La Bénichon *(3rd Sunday
in October)*, Châtel-St-Denis.
Harvest thanksgiving, with
procession in traditional dress.
Älplerchilbi *(October–early
November)*, Obwalden and

Nidwalden. Folk festival with
alphorns and yodelling.

NOVEMBER

Expovina *(first two weeks of
November)*, Zürich. Fair, with
wine-tastings, at which wines
imported from all over the
world are put on display
on ships moored along
Bürkliplatz.
Räben-Chilbi *(2nd Saturday
in November)*, Richterswil.
Young people carrying
lanterns made of turnips join
in a procession.
Bach Festival *(two weeks in
early November)*, Lausanne.
Gansabhauet *(mid-November)*,
Sursee. Ancient harvest festival
rite in which blindfolded contestants try to behead a dead
goose with a blunt sword.
Zibelemärit *(4th Monday in
November)*, Bern. Onion fair,
with confetti battle and other
festive activities marking the
beginning of winter.

September Wine Festival, Neuchâtel

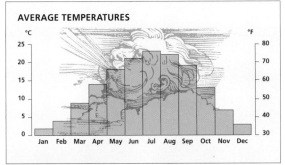

AVERAGE TEMPERATURES

Temperatures
Temperatures are highest in June, July and August, though they rarely exceed 30° C (86° F). The coldest month is December, when temperatures often drop below freezing.

Ice sculptures at the World Snow Festival in Grindelwald

WINTER

Advent, Christmas and the Feast of St Nicholas are the main focus of fairs and festivals in December. New Year is exuberantly celebrated throughout the country. In some parts of Switzerland it is marked twice, first in accordance with the current Gregorian calendar, and again according to the older Julian calendar. This is also the season of a variety of winter sports events, from ice hockey and curling to horse-racing on ice. Between New Year and mid-March, countless carnival balls, folk festivals with masquerades and fancy dress keep spirits up through the cold winter months. They culminate in Fasnacht, a three-day festival held in many parts of Switzerland, which precedes Lent.

Carnival participant, in devil's costume

DECEMBER

St Nicholas Day *(on or around 6 December)*, all over Switzerland. Parades and fairs celebrating Santa Claus' arrival.
Fête de l'Escalade *(1st Sat in December)*, Geneva. Festival commemorating the Duke of Savoy's failed attempt to capture Geneva in 1602.
Spengler Cup *(late December)*, Davos. World ice-hockey tournament.
New Year's Eve *(31 December)*, villages of Appenzell. Masked characters with cow-bells usher in the New Year.
New Year's Eve *(31 December)*, Verbier. The biggest, wildest outdoor rave in the Alps with hours of fireworks broadcast live on TV.

JANUARY

Vogel Gryff *(mid-to late January)*, Basel. Three-day folk festival involving a lion, a griffin and Wild Man of the Woods.
Coppa Romana *(mid-Jan)*,

Silvaplana. Europe's largest open-air curling contest.
World Snow Festival *(mid-January)*, Grindelwald. Fantastic ice-sculpture contest, held on a natural skating rink.
Hot-Air Balloon Week *(late Jan)*, Château d'Oex. Week-long spectacle as the skies fill with colourful hot-air balloons.
Cartier Polo World Cup on Snow *(late January)*, St Moritz. Polo played on the frozen lake at St Moritz.

FEBRUARY

Roitschäggättä *(week before Ash Wednesday)*, Lötschental. Nocturnal parades by men wearing grotesque masks.
White Turf *(1st half of February)*, St Moritz. International horse races held on the frozen lake.
Fasnacht *(February or early March)*, Basel. Major spring carnival lasting three days and three nights, with thousands of costumed figures playing drums and piccolos. Also celebrated around the same time in Luzern, Bern and other towns.

PUBLIC HOLIDAYS
New Year's Day (1 Jan)
Good Friday
(Karfreitag, Vendredi Saint)
Easter Monday
(Ostermontag,
Lundi de Paques)
Ascension Day
(Himmelfahrt, Ascension)
Whit Monday
(Pfingstmontag,
Lundi de Pentecôte)
National Day (1 Aug)
Christmas Holiday (25
& 26 Dec)

THE HISTORY OF SWITZERLAND

The history of Switzerland began in 1291, when three small cantons formed an alliance against their foreign overlords, the Habsburgs. As other cantons joined, the alliance expanded, but there followed centuries of instability, with bitter conflict between cantons and religious groups. It was not until 1848 that a central government was established and that modern Switzerland was born.

HELVETI AND RHAETIANS

From about 500 BC, the lands that now comprise Switzerland were settled by two peoples, the Rhaetians, possibly an Etruscan people who settled in a small area in the east, and the Helveti, a powerful Celtic tribe, who settled in the west. The Helveti established several small townships here, including La Tène, near Neuchâtel.

Bust of Marcus Aurelius from Avenches

FROM ROMAN TO FRANKISH RULE

By 58 BC both Helvetia and Rhaetia, as they were known, were incorporated in the Roman Empire, the Helveti becoming allies of the Romans against warlike tribes to the north. Under Roman rule Aventicum (Avenches), capital of the Helveti, became a Roman province. Other towns with villas were built, agriculture flourished and new roads were laid out. In AD 260, Helvetia and Rhaetia were once again attacked by Germanic tribes. While the eastern region was taken by the Alemani, driving the Rhaetians into the hinterland, the western region was seized by Burgundians. In 401 the Romans abandoned their Alpine province.

By the 6th century, the Swiss territories of the Alemani and Burgundians had been taken by the Franks. These lands were later incorporated into Charlemagne's Holy Roman Empire, and in 843 they were divided between his grandsons.

ALLIANCE OF THE CANTONS

In 1033, Burgundy was reunited within the Holy Roman Empire. However, as imperial power declined, feudal dynasties came to prominence. The most powerful was that of the Habsburgs. In 1291, the free peasants of the Forest Cantons of Schwyz, Uri and Unterwalden formed an alliance against Habsburg power, their delegates meeting in Rütli Meadow to swear their mutual allegiance. This was the nucleus of what later became the Swiss Confederation. In the 14th century they were joined by the cantons of Luzern, Zürich, Glarus, Zug and Bern. In their attempts to break the Confederation, the Habsburgs suffered crushing defeats in a succession of battles with the Confederates, who eventually won their independence in 1499.

TIMELINE

5th century BC The Helveti and Rhaetians begin to settle in the Alps	**AD 69** Uprising of the Helveti against the Romans	**6th century** Franks conquer Aleman and Burgundian territories	**1033** Burgundy incorporated in the Holy Roman Empire
	260 First incursions by the Alemani		**1291** The three Forest Cantons form an alliance
200 BC	**AD 1**	**500**	**1000**	**1500**
c. 500 BC The Helveti establish the settlement of La Tène	**401** The Romans abandon their Alpine province	**5th century** Settlement by the Alemani, Burgundians and Lombards	*Reliquary in the shape of a foot*	**1499** Switzerland gains independence

◁ **Representatives of the three Forest Cantons swearing the oath of allegiance on Rütli Meadow in 1291**

The Struggle for Independence

In 1291, on the death of Emperor Rudolf I, representatives of the cantons of Schwyz, Uri and Unterwalden decided to form an alliance against the power and tyranny of the Habsburgs. The oath of mutual allegiance that they swore at Rütli Meadow in August that year laid the foundations of the Swiss Confederation. The wars that the Confederates fought against the Habsburgs and the Burgundians in the 14th and 15th centuries demonstrated the superiority of agile peasant troops over heavily armed knights. The Swiss also became renowned for their valour as soldiers and were sought after as mercenaries throughout Europe.

Officer of the Swiss Guard
The reputation of the Swiss as courageous soldiers prompted Pope Julius II to form the Swiss Guard in 1506, to act as his bodyguards and to protect the Vatican.

Battle of Dornach (1499)
Confederate soldiers launched a surprise attack on troops commanded by Heinrich von Fürstenberg, who was killed in the battle.

Mercenary troops sent by Charles VII of France to aid the Habsburg cause march on Basel.

Battle of Morgarten (1315)
The army of Duke Leopold of Habsburg suffered a crushing defeat when it fought against peasant Confederate forces at the Battle of Morgarten.

Shield of Schwyz
Originally plain red, as here, the shield of Schwyz was later charged with a white cross. A red cross on a white ground became the Confederation's emblem.

Confederate soldiers at the foot of a tower rally behind a banner with the emblem of Basel.

Crossbow
The crossbow was the basic weapon in the Swiss army's arsenal.

Defensive walls around Basel

Confederate defenders in a fortified camp around the church.

St Jakob's Church

William Tell's Arrow
According to legend, William Tell was sentenced to death by the Austrian bailiff Hermann Gessler for refusing to acknowledge Habsburg power but won a reprieve by shooting an apple off his son's head with his crossbow. William Tell later killed Gessler.

BATTLE OF ST JAKOB

In 1444, at the request of the Habsburg king Friedrich III, Charles VII of France sent a 20,000-strong army of mercenaries to Switzerland. In their fortified camp at St Jakob, on the River Birs, near Basel, defenders of the Confederation put up a heroic defence but were slaughtered.

Battle of Laupen (1339)
After the siege of Bern, the armies of Bern and Luzern give thanks to God for their defeat of the Duke of Burgundy and his ally, the canton of Fribourg.

Defeat of the Swiss at the Battle of Marignano (1515)

Reformation in Switzerland were the humanist Ulrich Zwingli (1484–1531), who was active in Zürich, and Jean Calvin (1509–64), who led the movement in Geneva. While the urban cantons embraced the Reformation, the poorer and more conservative cantons of central Switzerland remained faithful to Catholicism. Despite this rift, the cantons remained loyal to the Confederation throughout the wars of religion that swept through Europe in the 17th century.

THE PEAK OF TERRITORIAL POWER

Emboldened by independence, yet surrounded by territories held by the Habsburgs and other powers, the Swiss Confederation attempted to secure and expand its territory to the north, east and south. In 1512, Confederate troops conquered Lombardy, occupying Locarno and Lugano. However, their stand against combined French and Venetian forces at Marignano in 1515 ended in defeat, after which Switzerland abandoned its policy of expansion and moved towards military neutrality. The Confederation itself, however, continued to grow, Fribourg and Solothurn joining in 1481, Basel and Schaffhausen in 1501 and Appenzell in 1513. The cantons now numbered 13.

Bed made in Bern in the 16th century

THE REFORMATION

The great religious and political movement to reform the Roman Catholic Church originated in Germany in the early 16th century and quickly spread throughout western Europe. At the vanguard of the

PROSPERITY AND INDUSTRY

The Swiss Confederation's independence from the Austrian Empire was formally recognized by the Peace of Westphalia, which ended the Thirty Years' War (1618–48). Switzerland did not take part in the conflict, and this contributed to a boost in the country's economy.

During the war Switzerland had in fact played a key role in trade throughout Europe, and the arrival of refugees, particularly Huguenots, revitalized Switzerland's textile

Burning of religious paintings, in response to Zwingli's preaching against the worship of images

TIMELINE

Louis XIV and representatives of the Swiss Confederation

William Tell victorious over the dragon of the French Revolution, a symbol of Swiss resistance

the short-lived and unpopular Helvetic Republic. The Swiss Confederation, as it was now known, was restored in 1803, although it remained under French control until the fall of Napoleon in 1815.

THE SWISS CONFEDERATION

Six further cantons – St Gallen, Graubünden, Aargau, Thurgau, Ticino and Vaud – joined the Confederation in 1803, and Valais, Neuchâtel and Geneva in 1815. Internal religious hostilities continued, however, and in 1845 seven Catholic cantons formed a military alliance known as the Sonderbund. Condemned as unconstitutional by the Protestant cantons, this led to civil war, and the defeat of the Catholic faction by Protestant forces.

A new constitution was drawn up in 1848, transforming what had until then been a loose confederation of cantons into a union ruled by a Federal Assembly in Bern, which was chosen as the Swiss capital. National unity was, however, tested again in 1857, when Prussia threatened to take the canton of Neuchâtel. The 100,000-strong Swiss army sent to the Rhine border repelled Prussian ambitions.

industry. Industrial expansion continued in the 18th century, when the weaving of silk, linen and cotton became mechanized, while clockmaking, introduced to Switzerland by French and Italian refugees in the 16th century, became one of the country's most important industries.

THE HELVETIC REPUBLIC

The principles of the French Revolution were supported by Switzerland's French-speaking regions, but this was a threat to the stability of the Confederation. In 1798, having conquered northern Italy, and wishing to control routes between Italy and France, Napoleon invaded Switzerland. Under Napoleon the 13 cantons of the Confederation were abolished and replaced with

The Swiss army bound for the Rhine to defend Neuchâtel in 1857

1723 Leonhard Euler, founder of modern mathematics and author of almost 900 publications, graduates at Basel

1815 Napoleon is defeated. Congress of Vienna reaffirms the eternal neutrality of the Swiss Confederation

1857 The Confederation repels Prussia's attempt to take the canton of Neuchâtel

Henri Dunant

| 1750 | 1800 | 1850 | 1900 |

1798 Invasion by the French. Establishment of the Helvetic Republic

French grenadier

1847 Civil war and defeat of the Sonderbund

1864 Henri Dunant founds the International Red Cross in Geneva

1848 The new constitution establishes central government

Economic Growth

As early as the 17th century, Switzerland already had active textile and clockmaking industries, the foundations of which were laid by Huguenot refugees from France. By the second half of the 18th century, aided by its neutrality in international politics, the growing affluence of the middle classes and long periods of domestic peace, Switzerland was becoming as industrially advanced as other countries in Europe. Swiss economic growth accelerated in the 19th century, when the textile industry was mechanized and exports increased. This was also a boom period for precision engineering and the chemicals industry. Swiss foods, including Philippe Suchard's chocolate, Henri Nestlé's powdered milk and Julius Maggi's stock cubes became international brands.

Excited crowds gather around the Egyptian-style statue personifying industry.

Allegory of Justice

A locomotive, symbol of modern technical achievement.

Women workers operating belt-driven machinery.

An entrepreneur presenting his products to interested merchants.

The Swiss Pavilion at the Great Exhibition of 1851
The 270 exhibits in the Swiss Pavilion included textiles and lace, clocks and watches, and pharmaceuticals. There was also a model of Strasbourg Cathedral made by Jules Leemann, a sculptor from Bern.

Invention of the Telegraph
The first electric telegraph was built by the physicist Georges-Louis in Geneva in 1774.

Development of the Railway Network
Zürich's imposing Hauptbahnhof, or central station, was built in 1867.

Clock- and Watchmaking
The Swiss clock is a symbol of accuracy and reliability.

Allegory of Industry

Poster for St Moritz
From the 19th century, the popularity of Swiss resorts and tourist regions began to grow rapidly.

Road Through the Alps
In the 19th century Switzerland's dramatic Alpine scenery began to attract numerous visitors.

A group of clients, including a German visitor wearing a coat with a fur collar, and an American donning a wide-brimmed hat.

APEX OF INDUSTRIAL DEVELOPMENT
This monumental fresco in the Musée d'Art et d'Histoire in Neuchâtel (*see p131*) portrays the achievements of Swiss industry in the 19th century. Through allegory the painting depicts the environment in which Swiss industry consolidated its position in the international market.

ST GOTTHARD PASS
The gateway over the Alps between central and southern Switzerland, the St Gotthard Pass lies at 2,108 m (6,919 ft) above sea level. On one of the main transport routes between Germany and Italy, it is also one of Europe's crucial arteries. With international funding of 102 billion Swiss francs, work on building a tunnel and a railway line beneath the pass began in 1871. It opened to traffic in 1882.

Driving a mail waggon *over the pass was arduous, sometimes dangerous and, because of heavy snow, possible only in summer.*

Italian workers *who were employed to drill the tunnel staged a strike in 1875. Intervention by the army eventually brought a return to work.*

Swiss Chocolate
Among Swiss chocolate manufacturers whose brands became known worldwide in the 19th century was Philippe Suchard (1797–1884).

First assembly of the League of Nations, Geneva, in 1920

WORLD WAR I

At the outbreak of World War I, maintaining its neutrality was one of Switzerland's principal concerns. Relations between French- and German-speaking Swiss deteriorated, as both linguistic groups supported opposing sides in the war. However, appeals for national unity averted the danger of open conflict.

By 1915, some 100,000 Swiss troops had been mobilized to guard the country's frontiers. As the war went on, Switzerland embarked on a wide-ranging aid programme for some 68,000 prisoners of war and refugees. Political asylum-seekers who had come to Switzerland included many heads of state and political figures, including the Bolshevik leader Lenin and the Russian revolutionaries Trotsky and Zinoviev.

The revolutionary socialist ideas that they brought fomented unrest among Swiss workers, which culminated in the General Strike of 1918. The strike was quickly broken by the army but, as a result of their action, the workers won proportional representation, improved welfare and a 48-hour working week.

THE INTER-WAR YEARS

In 1920 Switzerland voted to join the newly formed League of Nations and, in tribute to the country's neutrality, Geneva was chosen as the organization's headquarters.

While the 1920s had been a period of prosperity, Switzerland, like the rest of Europe, fell prey to the Depression of the early 1930s. Also at this time, Switzerland's pacific stance and democracy were threatened by Nazi and Fascist sympathisers among its population.

By the late 1930s, as war seemed imminent, Switzerland's economy accelerated, fuelled partly by the booming arms industry in which the country was involved and by the fact that Swiss banks now played an important role in international finance.

General Henri Guisan, Commander-in-Chief of the armed forces, at the outbreak of war in 1939

TIMELINE

1900	1910	1920	1930	1940	1950

1901 Henri Dunant, founder of the International Red Cross, receives the first Nobel Peace Prize to be awarded

1918 General Strike and introduction of the 48-hour week

1934 Carl G. Jung, founder of analytical psychology, becomes head of the Department of Psychology at Zürich University

1914–18 Switzerland maintains neutrality during World War I

1920 Switzerland joins the League of Nations

1922 The Simplon Tunnel opens

1939–45 Switzerland maintains neutrality during World War II

Drilling the Simplon Tunnel

Swiss artists and scientists were also coming to prominence. Among them were the artists Paul Klee (1879–1940) and Alberto Giacometti (1901–66), the architect Le Corbusier (1887–1965) and the psychologist Carl G. Jung (1875–1961).

WORLD WAR II

In 1940, with Nazi Germany to the north and east, France under German occupation to the west and Fascist Italy to the south, Switzerland was surrounded. Invasion seemed inevitable, collaboration with Germany was suspected and the advantages of submitting to Germany were even contemplated. General Henri Guisan, Commander-in-Chief of the Swiss army, responded by assembling his officers on Rütli Meadow, birthplace of the Confederation, in 1291. Here he reaffirmed Switzerland's neutrality and demanded that all officers renew their vows of allegiance to the Confederation.

Although Switzerland was not directly drawn into World War II, it played a part in the conflict. The country acted as a secret meeting place between leaders of the Allied and Axis powers and set up anonymous bank accounts for German Jews. Swiss banks also provided currency for the purchase of military equipment and exchanged gold pillaged by the Germans for currency needed by the Third Reich.

POSTWAR YEARS TO THE PRESENT

Unlike all other European countries, Switzerland remained untouched by the upheaval of war and detached from the postwar new world order. It

Demonstration in 1963 by women demanding the right to vote in national elections

was not until 1971 that women won the right to vote in federal elections and the country continues to reject membership of the European Union, although popular opinion is divided on this issue. Switzerland did, however, vote to join the United Nations in 2002. In line with increasing globalization, Switzerland has softened its isolationist stance, and its relations with the EU remain at the top of the political agenda.

In late 1996, the country was rocked by the "Nazi Gold" scandal, when it was alleged that Swiss banks were holding gold looted by the Nazis and the assets of Jews who had perished in the Holocaust. Under strong US pressure, Switzerland agreed, in August 1998, to pay $1.25 billion in compensation to families of Holocaust victims and to certain Jewish organizations – leaving a severe impression on the national psyche.

Diego by Alberto Giacometti

OUI
À L'EEE, CAR LES FEMMES, REGARDENT L'AVENIR EN FACE.
FEMMES SUISSES EN FAVEUR DE L'EEE

Poster for Swiss membership of the European Union

Carl G. Jung (1875–1961)

1971 Women obtain federal voting rights

1992 Switzerland rejects membership of the EU

2002 Switzerland votes to join the United Nations

2008 Switzerland becomes a member of the Schengen Agreement

1960	1970	1980	1990	2000	2010	2020

1960 Professor Auguste Piccard's son Jacques reaches a record depth of 10,911 m (35,800 ft) in the Pacific Ocean in a bathysphere designed by his father

1996 The "Nazi Gold" scandal emerges

Celebratory salute on the 700th anniversary of the Swiss Confederation in 1991

2011 Switzerland decides to phase out nuclear power

SWITZERLAND REGION BY REGION

Switzerland at a Glance

From the snow-bound Alps and verdant Jura mountains to the more densely populated plateau of the Mittelland that lies between them, Switzerland offers a wealth of different impressions. It has no coastline but the shimmering waters of its large, clean lakes amply make up for this. Picturesque mountain villages and atmospheric medieval towns of its remoter areas contrast with the cosmopolitan cities of Bern, Zürich, Lausanne, Luzern and Basel. For many, the Alps, which offer unrivalled skiing and other winter sports, as well as a pristine natural environment, are the country's greatest attraction. South of the Alps, the canton of Ticino is a different world, with a lively Italian culture and a warm Mediterranean-style climate.

Bern, *the capital of Switzerland, is a historic city with a medieval layout and many fine historic buildings. Its emblem is the bear.*

0 km   25

0 miles

Lausanne, *on the north side of Lake Geneva, is a vibrant cultural centre. The cathedral, in the medieval city centre, is one of Switzerland's most important Gothic buildings.*

WESTERN SWITZERLAND
Pages 108–133

BERN
Pages 48–65

MITTELLAND, BERNESE OBERLAND AND VALAIS
Pages 66–91

GENEVA
Pages 92–107

Geneva *enjoys a magnificent setting on the largest lake in the country. A city with a cosmopolitan culture, it is the headquarters of over 250 international organizations and NGOs.*

The Matterhorn *is the most distinctive and dramatic peak in the Swiss Alps. The resort of Zermatt lies in a valley at the foot of the mountain.*

◁ **Ponte dei Salti, a 17th-century bridge near Lavertezzo, in Ticino**

Schaffhausen, *the capital of Switzerland's northernmost canton, has an atmospheric medieval town centre. The Munot, a Renaissance fortress in the east of the city, towers over the Rhine.*

Zürich, *on the River Limmat, is Switzerland's largest city, and the centre of Swiss banking and trade in gold. The central landmark of the Old Town is the imposing twin-towered Grossmünster.*

NORTHERN SWITZERLAND
Pages 134–157

ZURICH
Pages 158–175

Val Bregaglia *is one of Graubünden's many scenic Alpine valleys. Surrounded by granite peaks and containing a variety of rock formations, it is regarded as a rock-climber's paradise.*

CENTRAL SWITZERLAND AND TICINO
Pages 206–239

EASTERN SWITZERLAND AND GRAUBÜNDEN
Pages 176–205

The Hofkirche *is one of Luzern's many fine buildings. This charming city, set on Lake Luzern and surrounded by mountains, is the cultural capital of central Switzerland.*

Bellinzona, *the capital of Ticino, owes its importance to its strategic position. It is the starting point of roads leading to the St Gotthard and San Bernardino passes.*

BERN

With a picturesque setting on the River Aare and fine buildings lining the cobbled streets of its medieval centre, Bern is one of the most beautiful of Switzerland's historic towns. Although it is the Swiss capital, it retains the atmosphere of a provincial town. Bern is also a university city, the seat of the Federal Assembly and the headquarters of several international organizations.

Bern lies on a narrow, elevated spit of land set in a sharp, steep-banked bend of the River Aare. It was founded by Berthold V, Duke of Zähringen, in 1191, and its coat of arms features a bear. According to legend, the duke decided to name the new settlement after the first animal that he killed in the next hunt: this was a bear (Bär), and the duke duly named the town Bärn. After the demise of the Zähringen dynasty, Bern became a free town. Growing in power and prosperity, it joined the Swiss Confederation in 1353.

After a fire destroyed its timber buildings in 1405, the town was rebuilt in stone. It is from this period that the appearance of Bern's beautiful Old Town largely dates.

In 1528 the Bernese declared themselves in favour of the Reformation, and supported the Protestant cause. By the 16th century, Bern, led by a prosperous nobility, was a powerful city-state that, in the 17th and 18th centuries, further expanded its territory through the annexation of surrounding lands. Invaded by Napoleonic forces in 1798, Bern lost some of its territories but remained important enough to be chosen as the federal capital in 1848.

In the 20th century and into the 21st, Bern has continued to expand. Today, with a mostly German-speaking population, it is Switzerland's political and educational hub, and the base of major industries. Its historic Old Town is a UNESCO World Heritage Site.

The Rathaus, Bern's town hall, dating from the 15th century and with later alterations

◁ The Bundeshaus, the Federal Assembly building, from the Monbijoubrücke across the River Aare

Bern at a Glance

With many of its streets restricted to pedestrians and public transport, Bern's compact Old Town (Altstadt) is both easy and pleasant to explore on foot. Set on a narrow rocky ridge, the Old Town stretches from the Nydeggbrücke, in the east, to the Käfigturm, a tower that was originally a city gate, in the west. The main artery through the Old Town is Marktgasse, lined with old houses that have been converted into shops. The museums in the Kirchenfeld district, on the opposite bank of the Aare, are easily reachable on foot via the Kirchenfeldbrücke.

SEE ALSO

• **Where to Stay** p244

• **Where to Eat** pp268–9

Statue of Samson subduing a lion, dating from 1545, on the Samsonbrünnen, a fountain in Kramgasse

KEY

▨	Street-by-Street map pp52–3
🚉	Railway station
🚌	Coach station
🅿	Parking
ℹ	Tourist information
✚	Hospital
🚓	Police station
✝	Church

Display in the Museum für Kommunikation

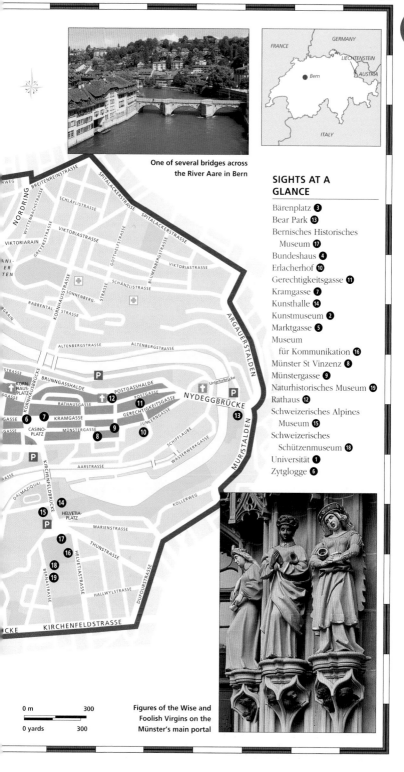

One of several bridges across
the River Aare in Bern

SIGHTS AT A GLANCE

Figures of the Wise and
Foolish Virgins on the
Münster's main portal

0 m   300

0 yards   300

Street-by-Street: The Old Town

With long cobbled streets lined with red-roofed houses and picturesque arcades, Bern's Old Town (Altstadt) is the best-preserved historic town centre in Switzerland. The layout of its streets, which are punctuated by colourfully painted fountains, has remained largely unchanged since the early 15th century. This was also the period when the Münster and the Rathaus, two of its great landmarks, were built. While the western district of the Old Town is filled with shops and busy street markets, the older eastern district has a more restful atmosphere.

Kornhaus
Now a cultural centre, this 18th-century granary was built over large vaulted wine cellars that currently house a restaurant.

Marktgasse
The main axis through the western part of the Old Town begins at the Käfigturm (Prison Tower). This tower was the city's western gate in the 13th and 14th centuries **5**

Französische Kirche is the oldest church in Bern.

Bärenplatz
This square overlies the spot where a moat once ran, along Bern's west side **3**

Heiliggeistkirche is Switzerland's finest Protestant church.

```
0 m        100
0 yards     100
```

STAR SIGHTS

★ Münster

★ Zytglogge

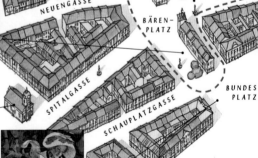

Bundesplatz
The Bundeshaus, with its paintings of historical events, overlooks this square.

Rathaus
The town hall is fronted by a double staircase and a Gothic loggia that leads through to the main entrance ⑫

Gerechtigkeitsgasse
This is the eastern section of the main axis through the Old Town. The house at No. 68 is the Weavers' Guild, the façade featuring a gilt griffin. Another striking landmark is a fountain with a statue of Justice ⑪

LOCATOR MAP
See pp50–51.

POSTGASSE

GERECHTIG- KEITSGASSE

KORNHAUSPLATZ

RATHAUSGASSE

KRAMGASSE

THEATER-PLATZ

MÜNSTERGASSE

AMTHAUSGASSE

★ Münster
The most striking feature of Bern's Gothic cathedral is the magnificent central portal, surrounded by painted figures ⑧

Münstergasse
On Tuesday and Saturday mornings the arcades along this street are filled with a bustling street market ⑨

Kramgasse
The main axis through the Old Town is continued by Kramgasse. This street begins at the Zytglogge, the clock tower marking the western limit of the oldest part of the Old Town ⑦

★ Zytglogge
From 1191 to 1250 the clock tower was the city's western gate, and it was later used as a prison. Its elaborate chimes begin at four minutes before the hour ⑥

KEY

– – – Suggested route

Universität ❶

Hochschulstrasse 4.

Although the University of Bern was founded in 1834, the city's academic traditions go back to the 16th century. In 1528 a theological school was established, and it occupied a former Franciscan monastery that stood on the site of the Casino on what is now Casinoplatz.

In 1805 the school became an academy, which in turn was elevated to the status of university, its premises still being the former monastery.

As the university grew, with increasing numbers of students and the addition of new faculties, larger premises were required. These were built in 1899–1903, on the embankment of Grosse Schanze (the Great Rampart) that formed part of Bern's 17th-century defence system. This is now the main university building and is a monumental structure in an eclectic mixture of the Neo-Renaissance and Neo-Baroque styles.

Kunstmuseum ❷

See pp56–7.

Bärenplatz ❸

This elongated esplanade has the appearance of a wide street rather than a square, particularly because it is seamlessly continued by another square, Waisenhaus-platz, on its north side. Only a fountain marks the division between the two.

Bärenplatz (Bear Square) is named after the bear pit once located here, while Waisenhausplatz (Orphanage Square) owes its name to the former orphanage, in a fine Baroque building that is now the police headquarters.

Both squares were laid out on the course of the moat that was dug on the western side of the town in 1256. On the east sides of both squares stand the Dutch Tower and the **Käfigturm** (Prison Tower).

The Bundeshaus from a bridge on the River Aare

The Käfigturm has a steeply pitched roof with a slender lantern tower topped by a spire. It was incorporated into a wall that was built to the west as Bern expanded, and was the town gate from 1250 until 1350. From 1643 to 1897 the tower was used as a prison and since 1999 it has served as a centre of political discourse, being the venue for political seminars, meetings with politicians and exhibitions.

On its southern side Bären-platz adjoins Bundesplatz, an esplanade dominated by the Bundeshaus. Bundesplatz is lined with cafés, and a fruit and flower market is held here on Tuesday and Saturday.

🚇 **Käfigturm**
Marktgasse 67. **Tel** 031 322 75 00.
⬜ 8am–6pm Mon–Fri,
10am–4pm Sat.

Bundeshaus ❹

Bundesplatz 3. **Tel** 031 322 85 22.
📷 11:30am & 3pm Mon–Sat (also 2pm early Jul–late Aug).
www.parlament.ch

The imposing seat of the Federal Assembly stands on a cliff overlooking the Aare valley. Although it faces north onto Bundesplatz, its most attractive aspect is from the south – from Monbijoubrücke, a bridge on the Aare.

The Bundeshaus (parliament building) was designed by W. H. Auer in a bold Neo-Renaissance style, and completed in 1902. The central part of the building contains a spacious domed hall. The hall is decorated with paintings illustrating important events in Swiss history, the dome has

FERDINAND HODLER (1853–1918)

One of the most outstanding Swiss painters of his time, Ferdinand Hodler was born in Bern but spent most of his

Self-portrait by Hodler

life in Geneva. He initially produced exquisitely realistic landscapes and portraits but later became a leading exponent of Symbolism. Often allegorical, his Symbolist paintings have a haunting beauty and typically feature groups of stylized, symmetrically arranged figures. Hodler was also well known for his monumental wall paintings. His late work, which has a more spontaneous style, anticipated the development of Expressionism.

stained-glass panels featuring the emblems of Switzerland's regions and cantons, and stained-glass windows with allegories of justice, education, public works and defence. The main assembly hall, in the south wing, is decorated with paintings depicting delegates of the cantons of Uri, Schwyz and Unterwalden swearing the oath of alliance on Rütli Meadow (see p35).

Visitors are able to listen to debates from the public gallery. You can tell when parliament is in session by the flag flying from the Bundeshaus.

The Bundeshaus is flanked by two other government buildings. That to the east was designed by Auer and built in 1892, and the building to the west was designed by F. Studer and built in 1857.

The Bundesterrasse, a wide promenade behind the Bundeshaus, offers a panoramic view of the Alps. A funicular near the western side of the Bundeshaus takes visitors down to the bottom of the Aare valley.

The Käfigturm, the former gate at the western end of Marktgasse

Marktgasse ❺

Laid out in the 13th century, as the town expanded west-wards, Marktgasse runs east to west from the Zytglogge, the original town gate, to the Käfigturm, the later gate.

Marktgasse is now the centre of Bern's shopping district,

and the arcades lining it are filled with shops, restaurants and cafés. Marktgasse also has two Renaissance fountains: the **Anna-Seiler-Brunnen**, which commemorates the woman who founded Bern's first hospital, in 1354, and the **Schützenbrunnen** (Marksman Fountain).

At its eastern end Marktgasse forms a right angle with Kornhausplatz, which follows the line of the earliest town walls. On this square is the macabre **Kindlifresserbrunnen** (Ogre Fountain), with an ogre eating an infant.

Off the northwestern side of Kornhausgasse stands the **Französische Kirche** (French Church). Built in the 12th century as part of a monastery, it is the oldest church in Bern. It was taken over by French Protestants, most of them Huguenot refugees, in the 17th century.

Zytglogge ❻

Marktgasse. **Tel** 031 328 12 12. 🗓 Apr–Oct: 2:30–3:20pm daily (also 26–31 Dec). 🖼

Also widely known as the Zeitglockenturm, the tower is Bern's central landmark. It was the town's west gate from 1191 to 1250, when it was superseded by the Käfigturm. Rebuilt after the fire of 1405, the Zytglogge was then used to imprison prostitutes.

Its astronomical clock was made by Caspar Brunner in 1527–30. The clock contains mechanical figures, including bears and a crowing cock, that begin their procession on the clock's east face at four minutes before the clock strikes the hour.

The guided tour allows visitors to observe the clock's mechanism at close quarters, see the rooms in the tower and admire the view.

Restaurant in an arcade on Kramgasse

Clockface on the Zytglogge

Kramgasse ❼

With Gerechtigkeitsgasse, its eastern extension, Kramgasse marks the main axis of Bern's early medieval town plan, which was laid out in the late 12th century. Both sides of Kramgasse are lined with fine historic buildings and guild houses fronted by long arcades.

Also on Kramgasse are three fountains: the **Zähringer-brunnen** (1542), with a bear in armour hold-ing the standard of Berthold von Zähringer, Bern's founder; the **Simsonbrunnen** (1545), with a figure of Samson subduing a lion; and the unadorned **Kreuzgassbrunnen** (1778). At Kramgasse 49 is the **Einsteinhaus**, where the great German physicist and mathematician Albert Einstein lived from 1903 to 1905 and where he began to develop the theory of relativity while working at the patent office. Einstein's apartment is now a museum, displaying his writing desk and other objects from his time in Bern.

🏛 **Einsteinhaus,**
Kramgasse 49. **Tel** 031 312 00 91.
🕐 Mar–Oct: 10am–6pm daily; Oct–mid Dec: 10am–5pm Tue–Fri, 10am–4pm Sat. 🖼 www.einstein-bern.ch

Kunstmuseum ②

Bern's Museum of Fine Arts houses a collection of over 3,000 paintings of international importance. Spanning the 14th to the 20th centuries, it includes Early Renaissance paintings, 16th- and 17th-century Old Master paintings, and 19th- and 20th-century French paintings, including works by Delacroix, Manet, Monet, Cézanne, Braque, Gris, Picasso, Klee and Kandinsky. Swiss artists, among them Ferdinand Hodler and Albert Anker, are well represented.

Ice on the River
This winter landscape of broken ice carried downstream by a wide river was painted in 1882 by the French Impressionist Claude Monet.

Main entrance

★ The Chosen One
Consisting of an alignment of stylized figures, this painting by Ferdinand Hodler, dating from 1893–4, is typical of the artist's mature style. He called this method of painting Parallelism.

GALLERY GUIDE
The collection of Old Master paintings is displayed in the basement. The 19th-century paintings are exhibited on the ground floor. The 20th-century collection occupies the first floor and the wing, a modern extension.

★ The Temptation of St Anthony by Demons
This painting by the 16th-century Bernese artist Niklaus Manuel Deutsch is one of a pair. Its pendant depicts the temptation of St Anthony by women.

Dans un Jardin Meridional
This rare 1914 garden fantasy by Pierre Bonnard (1867–1947) is a splendid example of his love for intense colour.

VISITORS' CHECKLIST

Hodlerstrasse 8–12.
Tel *031 328 09 44.*
⏰ 10am–9pm Tue, 10am–5pm
Wed–Sun. ♿ 📷 🎧
www.kunstmuseumbern.ch

First floor

★ Ad Parnassum
Paul Klee produced this painting at a time when he was fascinated with Pointillism, painting with small dots of pigment.

Blue Horse
This painting by Franz Marc reflects the artist's fondness for the colour blue and his love of horses, to which he ascribed great spirituality.

 Ground floor

Drunken Doze
The museum's large collection of paintings by Picasso includes works from his early Blue Period, including this portrait.

Basement

KEY

- ☐ Old Master Paintings
- ☐ 19th-century Paintings
- ☐ Modern Paintings
- ☐ Temporary Exhibitions

STAR PAINTINGS

- ★ Ad Parnassum
- ★ The Chosen One
- ★ The Temptation of St Anthony

Münster St Vinzenz ❽

A splendid example of the German-influenced late Gothic style, Bern's Münster is the most recent of Switzerland's great Gothic cathedrals. The architect was Matthäus Ensinger of Strasbourg, who designed it as a three-aisle basilica with fan vaulting, side chapels and a tower. Work on the cathedral began in 1421 and continued into the 16th century. It was not, however, until 1893, when the spire was added, that the building was finally completed. Exactly 100 m (328 ft) high, the Münster is the country's tallest church and largest ecclesiastical building. The tower is still inhabited by tower-keepers.

Nave
Flanked by square pillars, the lofty nave culminates in the stained-glass windows of the choir. On the keystones are busts of Christ, Mary and other biblical figures.

The rib vaulting, by Daniel Heintz, dates from the 1570s.

Pulpit
Like the Münster's other furnishings, the finely carved pulpit (1470) was badly damaged during the Reformation. The figures are later replacements.

Main entrance

★ **Tympanum**
A striking depiction of the Last Judgment fills the tympanum in the 15th-century central portal. While the damned occupy the left half of the tympanum, the saved are on the right.

★ Stained Glass
The choir is lit by stained-glass windows (1441–50). The central panel depicts Christ's Passion and Crucifixion.

Flying buttresses
transmit the weight of
the roof outwards and
downwards to the outer walls.

STAR FEATURES

★ Stained Glass

★ Tympanum

Münstergasse 9

Running parallel to
Kramgasse, Münstergasse
links Theaterplatz with
Münsterplatz, which is lined
with arcaded buildings.
On Tuesday and Sat-
urday mornings (and
Thursday from April
to October), this
square is filled with
a busy meat and
cheese market.
During Advent, it is
replaced by a large
Christmas market.

At the junction of
Münstergasse and
Theaterplatz stands
the **Stadt- und
Universitäts-
bibliothek**, the City
and University Library. This
18th-century building stages
exhibitions of books and
manuscripts on the history of
Bern and on literary subjects.

At the point where Münstergasse joins Münsterplatz stands
the **Mosesbrunnen** (1791),
a fountain with the figure of
Moses holding the Ten
Commandments. He points to
the second of them, which
forbids idolatry, a stricture
that was one of the main
tenets of the Reformation.

**Figure of Moses on
the Mosesbrunnen**

Colourful flags along Münstergasse

On the Münster's south side is
the Münsterplattform, a terrace
with trees and Baroque pavilions from which there are
beautiful views over the Aare.

**Stadt- und Universitäts-
bibliothek**
Münstergasse 61. *Tel 031 631 92
11.* 8am–7pm Mon–Fri, 8am–
noon Sat.

Erlacherhof 10

Junkerngasse 47. Closed to visitors.

East of Münsterplatz,
Münsterplatz is continued by
Junkerngasse, a street once
inhabited by Bern's
wealthiest citizens.

At no. 47 is the **Erlacherhof**,
a Baroque mansion built by
Hieronymus von Erlach,
mayor of Bern,
and completed
in 1752. It is
designed in the
French style, with
wings set at a right
angle to the main
building, enclosing a
grand courtyard.
To the rear is a
formal garden, also
in the French style.

The Erlacherhof is now
the official residence of the
mayor of Bern and the seat
of the city's government.

Gerechtigkeits-gasse 11

Some of the oldest and
most beautiful arcaded
buildings in Bern line this
street. Many of them were
built as guild houses, and
their façades are heavily
decorated with motifs
reflecting the relevant trade.

Gerechtigkeitsgasse, or
Street of Justice, also has a
fountain, the **Gerechtigkeits-
brunnen**, which features a
figure personifying Justice.

In the side alley at no. 31
is the Berner Puppen Theater
(see p63), a puppet theatre
that stages shows for children
and also produces puppet
plays for adult audiences.

At its eastern extremity,
Gerechtigkeitsgasse leads to
Nydegggasse. This is where a
castle stood, probably about
100 years before Berthold V
chose the location as a secure
spot on which to establish a
new town *(see p49)*. In the
late 15th century the castle was
replaced by a small church,
the **Nydeggkirche**, and in the
19th century a stone bridge,
the **Nydeggbrücke**, was built
over the deep gorge of the
Aare, connecting the Old Town
with Bern's eastern district.

The Rosengarten with a view of Bern Old Town

Rathaus ⑫

Rathausplatz 2. **Tel** 031 633 75 50.
8:30am–noon & 1:15–5pm Mon–Thu.

The seat of the canton and
city of Bern's legislative
assemblies since it was built
in 1406–16, the Rathaus is
an attractive building with
an elegant Gothic façade *(see
illustration on p49)*.

Since the 15th century the
Rathaus has undergone major
restoration, and the ground
floor was completely rebuilt
in 1939–42. However, it still
retains its authentic Gothic
character, making it typical of
Bernese architecture. The
building is fronted by a double
staircase with balustrades decorated with tracery. Beneath
the balustrades are a pair of
stone reliefs featuring human
figures. On the loggia at the
top of the staircase are a
clock and statues set on
canopied consoles.

Near the Rathaus stands the
Kirche St Peter- und St Paul,
a Catholic church in the
Neo-Gothic style, completed
in 1858.

**One of the pair of stone reliefs on
the façade of the Rathaus**

Bear Park ⑬

Bärengraben. 8am–5pm daily.

Brown bears, indelibly
associated with Bern since
the town was founded in
1191 *(see p49)*, were kept in
pits *(Bärengraben)* on the far
side of the Nydeggbrücke,
across the river from the Old
Town's eastern extremity,
from the early 16th century.

The bear pits have been
transformed into a forested
6,000-sq-m (64,590-sq-ft)
modern park, opened in 2009.
Sloping down from the old
bear pits to the river, it has
numerous caves and pools
that provide the bears with a
truly natural environment.

Next to the old bear pits, in
a former tram depot, is one of
the town's two helpful tourist
offices, where there is also a
restaurant serving local
cuisine and beer brewed on
the premises. The tourist
office also presents the **Bern
Show**, a visual history of Bern
told through a model of the
city, slides and spoken
commentary.

The steep path from the old
bear pits leads up to the
Rosengarten. Laid out on a
hillside, with a scenic view of
the Old Town across the Aare,
this rose garden contains over
200 varieties of roses.

Bern Show
Am Bärengraben. Grosse Muristalden.
Tel 031 328 12 12. Mar–May:
10am–4pm daily; Jun–Sep:
9am–6pm daily; Oct: 10am–4pm
daily; Nov–Feb: 11am–4pm Fri–Sun.
Show (in English) every 20 mins.
www.baerenpark-bern.ch

Kunsthalle ⑭

Helvetiaplatz 1. **Tel** 031 350 00 40.
11am–6pm Tue–Fri, 10am–6pm
Sat–Sun. **www**.kunsthalle-bern.ch

Kirchenfeldbrücke leads
from Casinoplatz, in the Old
Town, over the Aare to
Helvetiaplatz, on the south
bank of the river, where
many of Bern's museums
are located.

The Kunsthalle, a building
in the Modernist style, was
founded in 1918 and has
retained its prominence as a
showcase for modern art. It
has no permanent collection
but stages a continuous
programme of exhibitions.
Past events include one-man
shows of the work of such
artists as Paul Klee, Alberto
Giacometti and Henry Moore.
Details of upcoming shows
here are available from the
Kunsthalle itself and from
Bern's tourist offices.

**Landscape by Alexandre Calame,
Schweizerisches Alpines Museum**

Schweizerisches
Alpines Museum ⑮

Helvetiaplatz 4. **Tel** 031 350 04 40.
10am–5pm daily (to 8pm Thu).
www.alpinesmuseum.ch

Through videos, photographs,
dioramas, models, and paintings inspired by the Alps'
magnificent scenery, the
museum describes the Alps'
geology, topography, climate
and natural history, and documents all aspects of human
activity in the mountains.

The displays include a
graphic explanation of how
glaciers are formed, how they

are melting, and a model of the Bernese Oberland. Separate sections are devoted to various aspects of Alpine life, including transport, industry, tourism and winter sports. The daily life and culture of Alpine people are also described, as are modern concerns for environmental protection.

One exhibit in the section devoted to the history of mountaineering is *The Climb and the Fall*, two dioramas by Ferdinand Hodler illustrating the conquest of the Matterhorn *(see p54)*.

Museum für Kommunikation **16**

Helvetiastrasse 16. **Tel** *031 357 55 55.* ◯ *10am–5pm Tue–Sun.* www.

The history of the human endeavour to communicate over long distances is compellingly presented at the Museum of Communication. The displays span the gamut from bonfires to satellites, and multimedia presentations usher the visitor into the complex world of modern telephone exchanges and state-of-the-art mailsorting systems.

The museum also holds one of the world's largest collections of postage stamps. Numbering over half a million, they include such rarities as an 1840 Penny Black. A programme of temporary exhibitions complements the museum's permanent displays.

Mural, Bernisches Historisches Museum

Bernisches Historisches Museum **17**

Helvetiaplatz 5. **Tel** *031 350 77 11.* ◯ *10am–5pm Tue–Sun.* www.bhm.ch

Laid out on seven floors of a Neo-Gothic building reminiscent of a medieval fortified castle, the artifacts displayed at Bern's Museum of History are highly diverse.

Among the most interesting exhibits here are some of the original sandstone figures from the west front of the late Gothic Münster *(see pp58–9)* and a spine-chilling depiction of the Dance of Death, a copy of a 16th-century monastic wall painting.

The pride of the museum, however, is its collection of twelve Burgundian tapestries, the oldest of which date from the 15th century. Among the most notable is the Millefleurs-tapisserie (Thousand Flowers Tapestry), which once belonged to Charles the Bold, Duke of Burgundy.

Other sections are devoted to archaeology, with displays of Stone Age, Ancient Egyptian, Roman and Celtic artifacts. Exhibits of coins and medals and of items of armour can be seen, as well as a spectacular collection of Islamic artifacts. A scale model of Bern as it was in 1800 is also on show.

Schweizerisches Schützenmuseum **18**

Bernastrasse 5. **Tel** *031 351 01 27.* ◯ *2–5pm Tue–Sat, 10am–noon & 2–5pm Sun.* www.schuetzenmuseum.ch

The origins of the Swiss Rifle Museum go back to 1885, when the participants in a shooting festival decided to create a rifle section within the Bernisches Historisches Museum. The pieces now form a museum collection in their own right.

Consisting of a vast array of guns, the collection illustrates the history of firearms from the early 19th century. Also on display are cups, medals and other trophies awarded at shooting festivals.

Naturhistorisches Museum **19**

Bernastrasse 15. **Tel** *031 350 71 11.* ◯ *2–5pm Mon, 9am–5pm Tue, Thu & Fri, 9am–6pm Wed, 10am–5pm Sat–Sun.* www.nmbe.ch

With roots going back to the early 19th century, Bern's Museum of Natural History is one of the oldest museums in Switzerland.

It is best known for its numerous dioramas in which stuffed animals are shown in re-creations of their natural habitats. There are sections devoted to the reptiles, birds and mammals of Africa, Asia and the Arctic, but the most impressive displays are those focusing on the wildlife of the Alps. Also on view is the stuffed body of Barry, a St Bernard famous for his feats of mountain rescue in the 19th century *(see p84)*. The museum also has a large collection of Alpine minerals and fossils.

A manually operated telephone exchange, Museum für Kommunikation

ENTERTAINMENT IN BERN

Bern's vibrant cultural scene offers entertainment of every kind, from ballet to jazz and in styles ranging from the classic to the avant-garde. The city's many cultural centres host a varied programme of art and photography exhibitions as well as other cultural events. Classic plays presented at the Stadt-theater are complemented by fringe

Street musician in Bern

productions staged in many small independent theatres. While the prestigious Bern Symphony Orchestra makes the city a focus of the classical music repertoire, Bern also has a long-standing tradition of hosting major jazz and rock festivals. Like those of many other capital cities, the streets and squares of Bern are enlive-ned by street musicians. Bern is also well endowed with nightclubs.

INFORMATION/TICKETS

The best source of information on entertainment and cultural events in Bern is the city's tourist office **(Bern Tourismus)**. *Bern Aktuell,* a free guide available at the tourist office, gives listings of mainstream events in German, French and English. The Thursday edition of *Berner Zeitung,* the daily newspaper, includes *Agenda,* a supplement with listings in German.

THEATER VIS-A-VIS
Tel. 031 / 311 72 55
Gerechtigkeitsgasse 44

Signboard for a theatre on Gerechtigkeitsgasse

Tickets for major events can be purchased at the tourist office and from agencies, including **BZ-BillettZentrale, Ticket Corner, Konzertkasse Casino** and **Starticket**.

THEATRE AND CINEMA

The focal point of theatrical entertainment in Bern is the **Stadttheater**, where classic and contemporary

productions (in German or in French) are staged. Plays from the mainstream repertoire are also staged at the **Kornhaus** arts centre. Two other major theatrical venues in Bern are the **DAS Theater an der Effingerstrasse**, which specializes in modern drama, and the **Theater am Käfigturm**, which is often used by visiting drama companies.

Bern also has an unusually large number of fringe theatres, many of them tucked away in the cellars of houses along the streets of the Old Town. Information about fringe performances is available from the Stadttheater's box office.

Bern's 23 cinemas screen a regular programme of international films, many in their original language. Art-house films are shown at the Kunstmuseum *(see p57).*

The Stadttheater, on Kornhausplatz

Poster advertising a concert by the Bern Symphony Orchestra

FESTIVALS

From chamber music to jazz, Bern is alive to the sound of live music, with several music festivals taking place throughout the summer months. The city's largest and best-known annual musical event is the celebrated **Internationales Jazzfestival Bern**, which takes place from March to May, with concerts staged at many venues throughout the town.

Bern Dance Days skip through most of the month of June, from stage to roller-skating rink to café tabletops.

The **Gurtenfestival** is over the penultimate weekend in July. This large-scale rock-music event is staged in Gurtenpark, over the Aare to the south of the Old Town. Altstadtsommer is a series of summer concerts organized in the Old Town.

The Kultur Casino Bern, on Herrengasse

CULTURAL CENTRES

Bern's main cultural centre is the **Kornhaus**, a former granary. This large building is the venue for a wide range of events, including exhibitions of architecture, design and photography, and seminars, concerts and theatrical productions.

Another of the town's major cultural centres is the **Kulturhallen Dampfzentrale**, installed in a disused boiler house. The spacious auditorium here is used as a dance, film and jazz theatre, and the centre also has a restaurant, pub and bar.

The **Reitschule** (also known as the Reithalle) was established in the 1980s when protesters took over a former riding school. Fashionably alternative and politically controversial, the Reitschule is run as a cooperative and

stages film shows and concerts. There is also a nightclub and a café bar.

MUSIC AND CLUBS

Most concerts given by the renowned Bern Symphony Orchestra take place in the **Kultur Casino Bern**. The orchestra also plays at other venues, including the Kornhaus, and occasionally in churches.

Bern boasts several music clubs, some devoted to a variety of musical styles. They include the famous **Marians Jazzroom**, where traditional jazz is played. Other clubs specialize in rock, funk and other types of popular music. Peculiar to Bern are music clubs occupying disused factories, a fact that is often reflected in their names. Very popular are the concerts organized in Musig-Bistrot, **Gaskessel** and **Wasserwerk**, which concentrates on techno music and which have a bar, disco and live music on certain nights.

Gaskessel is also a popular nightclub. Others include **Shakira**, a South American bar and disco, and Babalu, on Gurtengasse, which specializes in techno and house music.

GAMBLING

Bern's main casino is the Grand Casino in the Allegro hotel at Kornhausstrasse 3. As well as gambling tables and slot machines, it has a restaurant and bars, open until 2am.

CHILDREN

Bern offers several indoor and outdoor entertainments for the young. The **Berner Puppen Theater** puts on puppet shows that will amuse children even if they do not speak German.

With its European animals, **Dählhölzli Tierpark Zoo** offers a close-up experience of many kinds of wildlife.

A Bern bear at Dählhölzli Tierpark Zoo

DIRECTORY

SHOPPING IN BERN

Bern's shopping district lies along Gerechtigkeitsgasse Kramgasse, Marktgasse and Spitalgasse, streets that form a continuous east–west axis through the centre of the Old Town. Shops also line Postgasse, which runs parallel to Gerechtigkeitsgasse on its northern side.

Beneath arcades with vaulted roofs that cover the pavement below are shops selling an almost endless variety of goods. On offer here is a range of souvenirs,

Chocolate bear from Bern

including bears in all imaginable guises, as well as Swiss-made shoes, high-quality clothes and leather goods, fine jewellery and watches, Swiss army knives and musical boxes, handwoven textiles and woodcarvings, and, of course, the famous Swiss chocolate. On the squares at the Old Town's western extremity are several open-air markets, with colourful flower and produce stalls, and two large department stores on Spitalgasse.

Display of handcrafted goods at Heimatwerk, on Kramgasse

MARKETS AND FAIRS

Twice a week several of the squares in Bern's Old Town are filled with lively open-air markets. On Tuesdays and Saturdays from April, and daily from May to October, a large fruit, vegetable and flower market is held on Bärenplatz and the adjoining Bundesplatz. There is also a lively meat and dairy produce market on Münstergasse on Tuesday and Saturday mornings. This also takes place on Thursdays from April to October. A general market takes place on Waisenhausplatz all day Tuesday and Saturday. A flea market is held on Mühleplatz, in the Matte district, on the third Saturday of the month from May to October.

Bern's annual fairs are major attractions. The magnificent Geranienmarkt, or Geranium

Fair, takes place on Bundesplatz, Bärenplatz and Waisenhausplatz in April or May. In late November a party atmosphere breaks out as Zibelemärit, the onion fair, gets under way (see p32). A **Christmas market**, with gifts and handicrafts, is held on Waisenhausplatz and Münsterplatz daily through December.

ART AND ANTIQUES

The best art galleries and antique shops in Bern are located on Kramgasse, Postgasse and Gerechtigkeitsgasse. Some art galleries also hold exhibitions of contemporary art. Antique dolls and toys, meanwhile, are the speciality of **Puppenklinik**, on Gerechtigkeitsgasse.

CRAFTS AND SOUVENIRS

The Swiss take pride in their traditional handicrafts, particularly those associated with Alpine culture and folklore. Handicrafts from all Switzerland, including wood carvings, ceramics, music boxes, jewellery and hand-woven textiles, linen and embroidery are available at **Heimatwerk Bern**, on Kramgasse.

A wide selection of pocket knives, particularly the multifunctional Swiss Army knives, is available at **Klötzli Messerschmiede**, on Rathausgasse.

Kunsthandwerk Anderegg, on Kramgasse, specializes in beautifully handmade toys from Switzerland and other countries.

Traditional Swiss cut-out

Fruit and vegetable stall in the market, Bärenplatz

Window display at Bucherer, a jeweller's on Marktgasse

WATCHES AND JEWELLERY

Fine jewellery and the clocks and watches that have brought Swiss craftsmanship international renown have many retail outlets in Bern. Two of the city's best clock, watch and jewellery shops are **Bucherer**, on Marktgasse, and **Gübelin**, on Bahnhofplatz.

MUSIC AND BOOKS

Having close associations with music, Bern has several excellent music stores. **Musik Müller**, in Zeughausgasse, concentrates uniquely on musical instruments. **Musikhaus Krompholz**, on Spitalgasse, also stocks a good range of CDs, as well as sheet music, musical scores and all kinds of books on music. Bern also has the largest and reputedly the best bookshop in Switzerland. This is **Stauffacher English Books**, on Neuengasse. You will find a good range of books in English here.

SHOES AND LEATHER GOODS

Leather shoes and accessories made by the internationally known Swiss shoe manufacturer **Bally** are available from a large branch of its outlets on Spitalgasse. Another major outlet for high-quality leather goods is

Hummel Lederwaren, on Marktgasse and at the train station. Stock here includes luggage, briefcases, purses and wallets, and a range of accessories, made in Switzerland and elsewhere in Europe.

CHOCOLATE

Like every other Swiss city, Bern has several shops offering tempting arrays of Swiss chocolates and other confectionery. Just two of them are **Eichenberger Tea Room**, on Bahnhofplatz, famous for its hazelnut *Lebkuchen* (spicy honey biscuits), and **Tschirren**, on Kramgasse, which has been making and selling its own chocolates for over 90 years.

DEPARTMENT STORES

Doll in traditional Swiss costume

Bern's two main department stores are **Loeb** and **Globus**, both located on Spitalgasse, on the western side of the Old Town. Their many departments stock an enormous variety of goods, and they are also known for their clothes, including designer labels, for both men and women.

DIRECTORY

MARKETS

Bundesplatz/ Bärenplatz
(Fruit, vegetables, flowers).
◻ 8am–noon Tue & Sat.

Mühleplatz
(Handicrafts).
◻ May–Oct: 3rd Sat of the month.

Münstergasse
(Meat and dairy).
◻ 8am–noon Tue & Sat.

Waisenhausplatz
(General).
◻ 8am–6pm Tue & Sat.

ART & ANTIQUES

Mäder Wohnkunst
Kramgasse 54.
Tel 031 311 62 35.

Puppenklinik
Gerechtigkeitsgasse 36.
Tel 031 312 07 71.

CRAFTS & SOUVENIRS

Heimatwerk Bern
Kramgasse 61.
Tel 031 311 30 00.

Klötzli Messerschmiede
Rathausgasse 84.
Tel 031 311 00 80.

Kunsthandwerk Anderegg
Kramgasse 48.
Tel 031 311 02 01.

WATCHES & JEWELLERY

Bucherer
Marktgasse 2.
Tel 031 328 90 90.

Gübelin
Bahnhofplatz 11.
Tel 031 310 50 30.

MUSIC & BOOKS

Musik Müller
Zeughausgasse 22.
Tel 031 311 41 34.

Musikhaus Krompholz
Spitalgasse 28.
Tel 031 328 52 11.

Stauffacher English Books
Neuengasse 25–27.
Tel 031 313 63 63.

SHOES & LEATHER GOODS

Bally
Kramgasse 55.
Tel 031 311 54 81.

Hummel Lederwaren
Marktgasse 18. *Tel 031 311 19 49.* Bahnhofshop
Tel 031 311 20 39.

CHOCOLATE

Eichenberger Tea Room
Bahnhofplatz 5.
Tel 031 311 33 25.

Tschirren
Kramgasse 73.
Tel 031 311 17 17.

DEPARTMENT STORES

Globus
Spitalgasse 17–21.
Tel 031 320 40 40.

Loeb
Spitalgasse 47–51.
Tel 031 320 71 11.

MITTELLAND, BERNESE OBERLAND AND VALAIS

These three regions occupy the western central section of Switzerland. The Mittelland, or Swiss Heartland, is a fertile area of rolling hills. While the Bernese Oberland, a massif in the heart of Switzerland, contains some of the country's most spectacular peaks, the Valais, in the south, has Switzerland's highest mountains, including the Matterhorn and the Dom.

The Mittelland, the heart of the Swiss farming industry, is made up mostly of the small canton of Solothurn and the northern part of the canton of Bern. Unlike Bern and Basel, Solothurn remained Catholic after the Reformation. By contrast, the predominantly German-speaking people of the canton of Bern embraced the Reformation and have been Protestant since the 16th century.

The southern part of the canton of Bern makes up the Bernese Oberland, a mountainous area that rises to the south of two lakes, the Thunersee and the Brienzersee. These lakes are bordered by the towns of Thun, Interlaken and Brienz. A land of natural wonders, the Bernese Oberland has some dramatically high peaks, with excellent skiing pistes, but also many gentler valleys that are ideal countryside for hiking.

The Valais, equally known as Wallis, encompasses the Rhône valley and the Pennine Alps. It is divided into two regions: Lower Valais, a French-speaking and Catholic region to the west, and Upper Valais, which is German-speaking and Protestant, to the east. The lower-lying parts of the Valais are agricultural. By contrast, its more mountainous regions, with the large international resorts of Verbier, Crans-Montana, Zermatt and Saas Fee, support a thriving year-round tourist industry.

Wooden chalets in Blatten, a village in the Lötschental, Upper Valais

◁ The majestic Matterhorn, above Zermatt, in the canton of Valais

Exploring the Mittelland, Bernese Oberland and Valais

Each of these regions is exceptionally scenic. While the area contains some of Switzerland's most historic towns, including Bern, Solothurn and Sion, it also has many natural wonders. The Thunersee and the Brienzersee, two beautiful lakes, lie at the foot of the Bernese Oberland, a paradise for skiers and hikers. The region also includes the Eiger, Monch and Jungfrau. To the south, in the Valais, lie the sunny Rhône valley and the rugged Pennine Alps, which culminate in the Matterhorn.

GETTING AROUND

As Bern has only a small airport, with relatively infrequent flights, it is best reached by train, which carries cars and travels through the Lötschberg Tunnel. The A1 motorway runs from Zürich, via Olten and Solothurn, to Bern. Bern also has motorway links with Thun and Biel/Bienne. Two routes lead south to the Rhône valley: the A6 follows the Aare valley and the A11 skirts the mountains, running west. The motorway linking Martigny with Sion and Sierre runs along the Rhône valley. Interlaken is the hub of a network of Alpine train and cable-car lines, with destinations that include the Jungfraujoch, the Schilthorn and Schynige Platte.

SEE ALSO

- **Where to Stay** pp245–8
- **Where to Eat** pp269–72

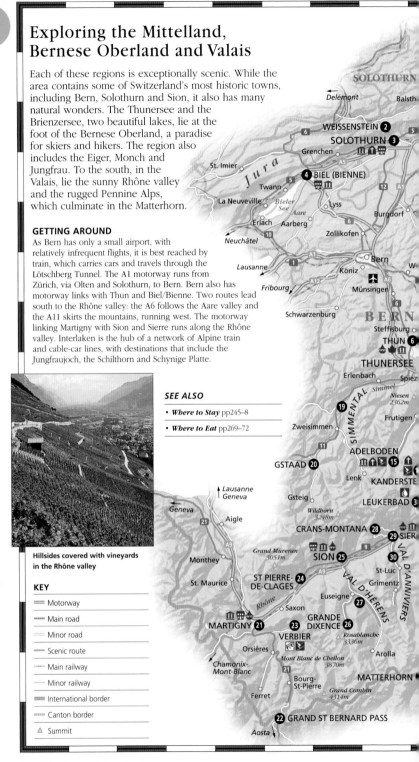

Hillsides covered with vineyards in the Rhône valley

KEY

▬▬	Motorway
▬▬	Main road
▭▭▭	Minor road
▬▬	Scenic route
▬▬	Main railway
───	Minor railway
▮▮▮▮	International border
▬▬	Canton border
△	Summit

A2
OLTEN 1
Zürich
A1
Zofingen
Luzern
Langenthal
Huttwil
Luzern
Langnau
Trubschachen
Emme
0 km 20
0 miles 20
FREILICHTMUSEUM BALLENBERG 11
BRIENZ 10
BRIENZERSEE 9
MEIRINGEN 12
Axalp
Beatenberg
8
INTERLAKEN
Faulhorn 2681m
GRINDELWALD 16
Andermatt
WENGEN 17
Eiger 3970m
JUNGFRAUJOCH 13
Gletsch
Jungfrau 4158m
Finsteraarhorn 4274m
Münster
Aletschhorn 4195m
ALETSCH GLACIER 38
Fiesch
Blatten
Rhône
BRIG 36
Simplon Tunnel
Visp
Vispa
SIMPLON PASS 37
Stalden
Simplon
Fletschhorn 3995m
SAAS FEE 35
Dom 4545m
Tasch
ZERMATT
Gornergrat 3089m
MONTE ROSA 34

View of Zermatt and the Matterhorn

Scenic alley in Sion

SIGHTS AT A GLANCE

Adelboden 15
Aletsch Glacier 38
Barrage de la Grande Dixence 26
Biel/Bienne 4
Brienz 10
Brienzersee 9
Brig 36
Crans-Montana 28
The Emmental 5
Grand St Bernard Pass 22
Grindelwald 16
Gstaad 20
Interlaken 8
Jungfraujoch 13
Kandersteg 14
Leukerbad 31
Martigny 21
Matterhorn 33
Meiringen 12
Monte Rosa 34
Mürren 18
Olten 1
Saas Fee 35
Sierre 29
The Simmental 19
Simplon Pass 37
Sion pp86–7 25
Solothurn pp72–3 3
St Pierre-de-Clages 24
Swiss Open-Air Museum Ballenberg pp80–81 11
Thun 6
Val d'Anniviers 30
Val d'Hérens 27
Verbier 23
Weissenstein 2
Wengen 17
Zermatt 32

Tour

Thunersee pp74–5 7

Olten ❶

Road map D2. 🏔 19,000. 🚊 🚌
ℹ️ Frohburgstrasse 1; 062 213 16
16. **www**.oltentourismus.ch

The small town of Olten has
a picturesque location on the
banks of the River Aare.
Pedestrian access to the old
part of the town is provided
by the Alte Brücke, a covered
bridge dating from 1802.

The Old Town is dominated
by the tall Gothic belfry of a
church that was demolished
in the 19th century. There are
many fine historic houses,
particularly on Hauptgasse and
along the Old Town's riverbank. Also of interest are the
17th-century monastery church
and the Neo-Classical Stadtkirche, dating from 1806–12
and decorated with paintings
by Martin Disteli. Many works
by this artist, together with
19th- and 20th-century paintings and sculpture, are exhibited in the **Kunstmuseum**.

🏛 **Kunstmuseum**
Kirchgasse 8. **Tel** 062 212
86 76. ⬤ Tue–Fri 2–5pm,
Sat–Sun 10am–5pm. 📷
www.kunstmuseumolten.ch

**Houses along the banks of the
Aare in Olten**

Weissenstein ❷

Road map C2. ℹ️ Solothurn,
Hauptgasse 69; 032 626 46 46.

Some of the most spectacular
views of the Mittelland can be
enjoyed from the summit of
the Weissenstein, a ridge
of the Jura that rises like a
rampart 1,284 m (4,213 ft)
high. It is situated 40 km
(25 miles) southwest of Olten
and 10 km (6 miles) north of
Solothurn. It is accessible by

road or rail to Oberdorf, from
where you can either hike to
the summit or take a chair lift
(closed on Mondays).

On the ridge is the Kurhaus
Weissenstein, a hotel with a
restaurant. The hotel is a
good base for hiking, rock-
climbing and paragliding in
summer, and for sledging in
winter. Other attractions
include a botanical garden
with plants and flowers of
the Jura, a small regional
museum, the Nidleloch, a
limestone cave, and the
Planetenweg, or Planet Trail,
a walk with a schematic
layout of the Solar System.

Solothurn ❸

See pp72–3.

Biel/Bienne ❹

Road map C3. 🏔 55,000. 🚊 🚌
🚤 ℹ️ In the train station; 032 329
84 84. 📷 Bieler Lauftage (Jun), Bieler
Seefest (Jul–Aug), Onion Market
(Oct). **www**.biel-seeland.ch

Biel, known as Bienne in
French, is the second-largest
town in the canton of Bern.
It was founded in the 13th
century, and from then until
the 19th century it was ruled
by the prince-bishops of
Basel. Biel/Bienne's principal
industry is watchmaking, its
factories producing such
leading brands as Omega and
Rolex. It is Switzerland's only
officially bilingual town: two-
fifths of its inhabitants speak
German, and the rest French.

The town is set on the
shores of the Bielersee
(or Lac de Bienne) at the
point where the River Schüss
(or Suze) flows into it.
The Old Town, which has
narrow cobbled streets and
decorative fountains, is set
on a hill. Its nucleus is a
square known as the **Ring**,
which is surrounded by fine
arcaded houses. One of
them is the house of the
guild of foresters. This
beautiful building has a
16th-century circular corner
turret topped by an onion
dome. Also on the square
is the 15th-century church

of St Benedict, with
impressive late Gothic
stained-glass windows.

At the intersection of
Burggasse and Rathausgasse,
west of the Ring, stands the
Rathaus, the Gothic town
hall, which dates from the
1530s. It is fronted by a
Fountain of Justice. The late
16th-century Zeughaus, or
arsenal, nearby is now used
as a theatre.

Biel/Bienne has several
museums and galleries. The
Museum Neuhaus contains
re-creations of 19th-century
patrician interiors, as well as
paintings and exhibits relating
to the town's history and
industries, and a section
devoted to cameras and the
cinema. The dynamic **Centre
Pasquart** stages a programme
of changing exhibitions of
contemporary art and
photography, and shows
relating to the cinema.

Foresters' guildhouse, Biel/Bienne

🏛 **Museum Neuhaus**
Schüsspromenade/Prde de la Suze 26.
Tel 032 328 70 30. ⬤ 11am–5pm
Tue–Sun. 📷 www.mn-biel.ch

🏛 **Centre Pasquart**
Seevorstadt/Faubourg du Lac 71–75.
Tel 032 322 55 86. ⬤ 2–6pm
Wed–Fri, 11am–6pm Sat–Sun. 📷

Environs
Twann, a medieval town, **La
Neuveville**, which has cobbled
streets, **Erlach**, which has a
castle, and **St Petersinsel** can
all be visited by boat from
Biel/Bienne. There are also
boat trips on the lake, with
views of vineyards on the
surrounding hillsides. A river-
boat service runs between
Biel/Bienne and Solothurn.

Schloss Burgdorf, the castle of the Zähringers, in the Emmental

The Emmental ❺

Road map C3. 🚉 🚌 🚶 *Langnau, Schlossstrasse 3; 034 402 42 52.* **www**.emmental.ch

The Emmental, the long, wide valley of the River Emme, has an outstandingly beautiful landscape of green meadows, which provide grazing for cows. The valley, which has excellent cycling and hiking routes, is also dotted with traditional wooden chalets with high roofs, eaves almost reaching to the ground and windows with decorative carvings.

The local culture of the Emmental is traditional and conservative, with a farming economy. This is also where the famous Emmental cheese is made, most of it by hand. At the **Schaukäserei** (show dairy) in Affoltern visitors can see every stage in the process of producing this holey, nutty-tasting cheese. It is also on sale in the dairy's shop and on the menu in its restaurant. Many inns along the valley also serve this highly prized local speciality.

Burgdorf is a small town in the north of the Emmental. The old part of the town, on top of a hill, has arcaded houses, a Gothic church and a castle, founded by the Zähringers in the 7th century. **Trubschachen**, a village further up the valley, has pottery workshops where the colourful local ware is made and offered for sale.

The Emmental also has the longest arched wooden bridge in Europe. Built in 1839, the Holzbrücke spans the Emme just downstream of the villages of **Hasle-Rüegsau**.

🏛 **Schaukäserei**
Affoltern. **Tel** 034 435 16 11.
⭕ 9am–5pm daily. 🈂

Thun ❻

Road map C3. 🚶 *41,000.* 🚉
🚌 🛈 *Bahnhof; 033 225 90 00.* **www**.thuntourismus.ch

The historic market town of Thun is set on the River Aare, at the northern end of the Thunersee. The origins of Thun go back to 1191, when Berthold V, Duke of Zähringen, built a castle on a hill above the river here.

Thun's Old Town spreads out beneath the castle, on the right bank of the river. Obere Hauptgasse, the main street running parallel to the river, is split into two levels. The walkway is built on the roofs of the arcaded buildings lining the street, so that pedestrians step downstairs to enter the shops below. Stepped alleys off Obere Hauptgasse lead up to the castle, **Schloss Thun**, from which there are impressive views of the town and the Bernese Oberland. Inside the castle's massive turreted keep, which looms over Thun, is a museum documenting the town's history. Other rooms in the castle contain collections of clocks, dolls and household objects, weapons and uniforms, glass and ceramics, coins and toys. The huge Knights' Hall, with an imposing fireplace, is used as a concert hall. Also on the hill is the Stadtkirche, the town's church. A short walk east of the castle and down to the river leads to the **Kunstmuseum**, which contains a large collection of contemporary and modern Swiss art.

On the left bank of the river is Schadau Park. Near the lake here stand a Neo-Gothic folly and a cylindrical pavilion, whose interior walls are painted with the **Wocher Panorama**. This visual record of daily life in Thun was painted by Marquard Wocher in 1814, and is the oldest such panorama in the world.

Detail of a fountain in Thun

♜ **Schloss Thun**
Schlossberg 1. **Tel** 033 223 20 01.
⭕ Feb–Mar: 1–4pm daily; Apr–Oct: 10am–5pm daily; Nov–Jan: 1–4pm Sun. 🈂 **www**.schlossthun.ch

🏛 **Kunstmuseum**
Hofstettenstrasse 14.
Tel 033 225 84 20. ⭕ 10am–5pm Tue & Thu–Sun; 10am–7pm Wed.
🈂 **www**.kunstmuseumthun.ch

🏛 **Wocher Panorama**
Seestrasse 45, Schadaupark.
Tel 033 223 24 62.
⭕ Mar–Oct: 10am–5pm Tue–Sun; Jul–Aug:10am–6pm daily. 🈂

Schloss Thun, from the left bank of the River Aare

Solothurn ❸

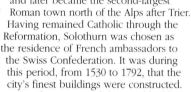

Renowned as Switzerland's most beautiful Baroque city, Solothurn is the capital of the eponymous canton. It was founded by Celts and later became the second-largest Roman town north of the Alps after Trier. Having remained Catholic through the Reformation, Solothurn was chosen as the residence of French ambassadors to the Swiss Confederation. It was during this period, from 1530 to 1792, that the city's finest buildings were constructed.

Clock on the Zytglogge

Today Solothurn is a vibrant city, with historical buildings, fascinating museums and good shopping opportunities.

Exploring Solothurn

The historic nucleus of Solothurn, on the River Aare, occupies a small area on the north bank, a short walk from the railway station on the opposite side. The Kreuzackerbrücke, which spans the river, linking the old and new towns, leads to Klosterplatz. From here, Solothurn's main historic sights, including vestiges of fortifications on the northeastern side of the town, are within easy reach.

From Solothurn boat trips depart for Biel/Bienne, and follow a particularly beautiful stretch of the Aare.

🏛 St Ursen Kathedrale

Hauptgasse. **Treasury** ⬛ *8am–noon, 2–6pm daily (to 7pm in summer).*
Built from 1763 to 1773, Solothurn's monumental Neo-Classical cathedral takes the form of a three-aisle basilica with a transept and a dome over the crossing. A bell tower rises next to the presbytery at the eastern end.

Set on a hill, the cathedral is reached by steps flanked by ornamental fountains. The two-tier façade, which shows the influence of the Italian Baroque, is faced by Corinthian columns divided by a frieze. The frieze contains figures, among which are those of the city's patron saints, Ursus and Victor, who were martyred by the Romans in Solothurn.

The cathedral's interior features elaborate stucco-work. The treasury, in the crypt, contains an interesting collection of liturgical vestments dating from the 10th century.

Baroque pulpit in St Ursen Kathedrale

🏛 Altes Zeughaus

Zeughausplatz 1. **Tel** *032 627 60 70.* ⬛ *1–5pm Tue–Sat, 10am–5pm Sun.* 🎟

The former arsenal is a large four-storey Baroque building dating from 1609–14. Above the upper storey is a crane that was used to lift heavy armoury from the ground level to the upper floors.

The arsenal now serves as a museum of militaria. It contains a large collection of swords, suits of armour and cannons, and a tank used in World War II. Of particular interest is the collection of arms and uniforms used by Swiss mercenaries who served as bodyguards to French kings. Many of these

mercenaries came from Solothurn. The third floor houses special exhibitions.

🏛 Riedholzschanze

Solothurn was fortified several times in the course of its history. The oldest walls surrounded a Roman camp, and their remains can be seen on Friedhofplatz and at Löwengasse. A later ring of walls, with gates and towers, was built in the Middle Ages. In the early 16th century the city's defences were modernized with the addition of two gates, Bieltor and Baseltor, and three towers, Buristurm, Krummturm and Riedholzturm, all of which still stand. In 1667 work on new fortifications, with bastions, began. Although these were later levelled out to make way for streets and parks, Riedholzschanze, a bastion at the northeastern corner of the old town, survives.

🏛 Kunstmuseum

Werkhofstrasse 30. **Tel** *032 624 40 00.* ⬛ *11am–5pm Tue–Fri, 10am–5pm Sat–Sun.* 🎟
This small art gallery contains some very fine works. Among its Old Master paintings are the exquisite *Madonna of Solothurn* (1522) by Hans Holbein the Younger, and *The Madonna in the Strawberries* (1425) by an anonymous artist. Most of the exhibition space is devoted to Swiss and French painting of the 19th and 20th centuries. There are landscapes by Caspar Wolf, Alexandre Calame and Giovanni Giacometti, and a dramatic depiction of William Tell

Part of the façade of the Altes Zeughaus, once the city's arsenal

For hotels and restaurants in this region see pp245–8 and pp269–72

The imposing entrance of the Rathaus

emerging from the clouds by Ferdinand Hodler *(see p54)*, and many paintings by Van Gogh, Degas, Cézanne, Matisse, and Picasso. A section is devoted to contemporary Swiss artists, including Deiter Roth, Markus Raëtz and Meret Oppenheim.

Rathaus
Rathausplatz.
Solothurn's town hall, on the east side of Rathausplatz, is in an ornate Mannerist style. The building's complex appearance is the result of work on the building having occurred in successive stages over many years.

The Gothic building that was begun in 1476 was not completed until 1711, when the town hall acquired its narrow three-part façade, with a central tower and onion domes crowning the lateral sections. The interior has a spiral staircase known as the Schnecke (Snail), which curves upwards, leading to the grand hall.

Jesuitenkirche
Hauptgasse.
Dating from 1680–89, Solothurn's Jesuit church is a magnificent example of High Baroque architecture. While the exterior is sparsely decorated, the interior glistens

The Baroque nave and high altar of the Jesuitenkirche

with frescoes and is encrusted with stuccowork by masters from Ticino.

On the high altar, which dates from the early 18th century, is a huge altarpiece by Franz Carl Stauder depicting the Assumption of the Virgin. Stones, some with Roman inscriptions, are also displayed in the church.

Zytglogge
Marktplatz.
Its lower part dating from the 12th century and its upper from the 15th, the clock tower is Solothurn's oldest surviving building. The astronomical clock was made in 1545. It contains mechanical figures, including a knight, a figure of Death and the King of Jesters, which form a procession on the hour.

VISITORS' CHECKLIST

Road map C3. 15,100. Hauptgasse 69. **Tel** 032 626 46 46. Solothurner Filmtage (Jan), Fasnacht (spring carnival), Solothurn Literary Days (May), Solothurn Classics (Jul), Chlausemäret (Dec). **www**.solothurn-city.ch

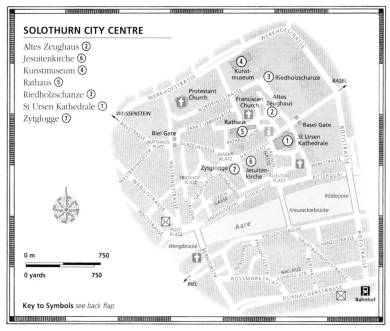

SOLOTHURN CITY CENTRE

0 m 750
0 yards 750

Key to Symbols *see back flap*

Thunersee ❼

A beautiful lake in a spectacular mountain setting, the Thunersee forms a slender arc between Thun and Interlaken in the valley of the River Aare. Some 18 km (11 miles) long and almost 4 km (3 miles) wide, the lake offers many kinds of water sports, including sailing, windsurfing, water-skiing and diving. The surrounding areas are ideal for hiking and cycling. A ferry service links the towns, villages and other places of interest on the lakeshore, and vintage steamships take visitors on tours of the lake.

Thun ①
The historic centre of Thun, still dominated by a medieval castle, was built mostly in the 12th century. The raised pavements of the upper Hauptgasse are worth a visit of their own.

Hilterfingen ②
As well as a sailing school, Hilterfingen has a mid-19th-century castle, Schloss Hünegg. It is in the Neo-Renaissance style, with Art Nouveau interiors.

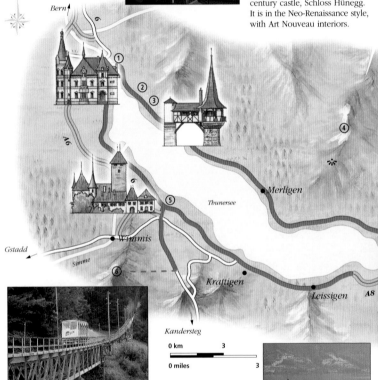

Bern

A6

Gstaad

Simme

Winmis

Thunersee

Merligen

Krattigen

Leissigen   A8

Kandersteg

0 km   3

0 miles   3

Niesen ⑥
A funicular from Mülenen takes visitors to the summit of the Niesen, which rises to 2,362 m (7,750 ft) and offers a fine view of the Thunersee and its surroundings.

Spiez ⑤
The medieval castle in Spiez is set on a spur jutting into the lake. Near the castle is a Roman-esque church with a fine Baroque interior.

Oberhofen ③
The lakeside castle here dates from the 12th century. It is now an outpost of the Bernisches Historisches Museum (see p61).

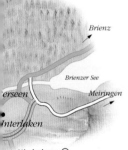

Niederhorn ④
Accessed by a mountain railway, Niederhorn offers breathtaking views of the Bernese Alps.

KEY

▬	Motorway
▮▮▮	Suggested route
▬	Suggested route
═	Other roads
═	River, lake
--	Funicular
✼	Viewpoint

The Hôtel du Lac at Interlaken and the jetty on the Brienzersee

Interlaken ❽

Road map D4. 🏔 13,500. 🚌 🚉 ℹ Höheweg 37; 033 826 53 00. **www**.interlaken.ch 🎷 Musikfestwochen (Aug).

Interlaken lies on a narrow strip of land between the Thunersee and the Brienzersee. In prehistory the isthmus between the lakes, known as the Bödeli, was inhabited by Celts. The present town owes its name to the monastery that was founded here in the 12th century. It was named Inter Lacus, meaning "between lakes" in Latin.

Today Interlaken is a popular resort that makes an excellent base for mountaineers and hikers in summer and for skiers in winter. Interlaken is also a rail junction on the route by rack railway up to the Jungfrau region (see p79), to Wengen (see p83) and beyond. A funicular also takes visitors up to the summit of the Heimwehfluh (669 m/2,195 ft).

Interlaken's popular attraction is the **Jungfrau Park**, a theme park that introduces visitors to the great unsolved mysteries of the world. It consists of several pavilions, in which elaborate displays focus on the meaning of mysterious ancient monuments, such as the pyramids of Egypt, question how the ancient Maya devised their complex calendar, and investigate the origins of religion in ancient cultures. A further section is devoted to outer space and the search for extraterrestrial intelligence.

Rugen Forest, on the south side of Interlaken, is the bucolic setting for open-air productions of Schiller's play *Wilhelm Tell*. On the opposite side of the Aare is Unterseen. The **Touristikmuseum** here documents the evolution of tourism in the Jungfrau region since the 19th century.

Environs

Alpine fauna can be seen at the zoo at **Harder**, accessible by cable car from Interlaken. **Schynige Platte**, which can be reached by rack-railway from Wilderswil, south of Interlaken, is a 2,000-m (6,564-ft) high plateau offering magnificent views of the two lakes. There is also a botanical garden here, with alpine plants and flowers.

🏛 **Jungfrau Park**
Obere Bönigstrasse 100, Interlaken. **Tel** 033 827 57 57. ◯ May–Oct: 10am–6pm daily. 🌐 www. jungfraupark.ch

🎭 **Wilhelm Tell**
Performances: late Jun–mid-Sep: Thu & Sat. Tickets via www. tellspiele.ch; 033 822 37 22, and tourist offices in the region.

🏛 **Touristikmuseum**
Obere Gasse 28, Unterseen. **Tel** 033 822 98 39. ◯ May–Oct: 2–5pm Tue–Sun. 🌐

Flower clock in front of the Kursaal in Interlaken

The small town of Brienz, at the eastern tip of the Brienzersee, with the Brienzer Rothorn in the background

Brienzersee ❾

Road map D4. 🚉 🚌 ℹ️ *Haupt-strasse 143, Brienz; 033 952 80 80.* **Boat trips on the lake** *Tel 078 611 20 12.* www.steamchen.com
Grandhotel Giessbach
***Tel** 033 952 25 25.* ◯ *Apr–Oct.*

Lying east of Interlaken and the Thuner see *(see pp74–5)*, the clear waters of the Brienzersee stretch out in a setting of forested slopes and water-falls, with majestic mountains rising in the background. Some 14 km (9 miles) long and almost 3 km (2 miles) wide at its broadest point, the Brienzersee is slightly smaller than the Thunersee and much less developed, with fewer sports centres and less boating activity. As such, it is much more appealing to anglers.

From Interlaken, places of interest around the shore can be visited by bicycle or by taking a boat trip on the lake. On the north side of the lake are the ruins of **Goldswil** castle and the village of **Ringgenberg**, where there is a small Baroque church. The small town of **Brienz** lies at the eastern tip of the lake. On the south side is Axalp, good for skiing in winter and walking in summer, and the magnificent **Giessbachfälle**, waterfalls that can be viewed from the terrace of the Grand Hotel Giessbach, reachable by a funicular.

Brienz ❿

Road map D3. 🎿 *3,000.* 🚉 🚌 ℹ️ *Hauptstrasse 143; 033 952 80 80.* www.brienz-tourismus.ch

Located at the eastern end of the Brienzersee, Brienz is the main town on the lake-shore. It is a good base not only for mountain hikers but also for anglers and water-sports enthusiasts. Axalp, nearby, has a small ski and snowboarding centre.

Being the centre of Swiss woodcarving, Brienz is full of shops selling all kinds of wooden objects. The work-shops of its renowned wood-carving school, the **Schule für Holzbildhauerei**, are open to visitors during term-time. Students can be seen at work,

Alley in Brienz, lined with traditional houses

and there is also an exhibition of their finished pieces.

Another speciality of Brienz is violin-making. The **Geigen-bauschule**, where future violin-makers learn their craft, also welcomes visitors, and there is an exhibition of instruments.

Environs

The summit of the **Brienzer Rothorn**, which rises to 2,350 m (7,710 ft) about 5 km (3 miles) north of Brienz, can almost be reached by steam-driven rack railway, which runs to 2,244 m (7,383 ft). It is one of the few still in use, though the carriages are sometimes pulled by a diesel locomotive. The 7.6-km (4.75-mile) route up the mountain passes through six tunnels. The short walk from the summit station is rewarded by breath-taking views of the Brienzer-see and the Bernese Alps.

🏛 **Schule für Holzbild-hauerei**
Schleegasse 1. *Tel 033 952 17 51.*
Exhibition ◯ *8–11:30am & 2–5pm Mon–Fri.*

🏛 **Geigenbauschule**
Oberdorfstrasse 94. *Tel 033 951 18 61.* ◯ *By prior arrangement.*

Swiss Open-Air Museum, Ballenberg ⓫

See pp80–81.

◁ **Schloss Oberhofen, the 13th-century castle on the northern shore of the Thunersee**

Meiringen ⑫

Road map D4. 🚠 *4,500.* 🚗 �
🛈 *Bahnhofplatz 12; 033 972 50 50.*

This small town lies in the heart of the Hasli valley, the Upper Aare valley east of the Brienzersee. It is a snow sports resort in winter, and a base for hiking and mountain biking in summer.

Meiringen lies near the **Reichenbachfälle**, the waterfalls chosen by the writer Arthur Conan Doyle as the scene of Sherlock Holmes' "death" after a struggle with Professor Moriarty. The **Sherlock Holmes Museum,** in the basement of a church, features a representation of Holmes' drawing room at 221B Baker Street, London. A statue of the fictional detective graces Conan Doyle Place.

Also of interest in Meiringen is the small church at the top of the town. It was built in 1684 over the crypt of an early Romanesque church. The town has two regional museums, one of which is open only in summer.

🏛 **Sherlock Holmes Museum**
Bahnhofstrasse 26. **Tel** *033 971 41 41.* ⬜ *May–Sep: 1:30–6pm Tue–Sun; Oct–Apr: 4:30–6pm Wed & Sun.* 🈂 **www.**sherlockholmes.ch

Environs

From Meiringen a funicular takes visitors to the top of the **Reichenbachfälle**. From here there is a stupendous view of the cascading waters. Equally impressive is the **Aareschlucht**, a deep gorge cut by the Aare between Meiringen and Innertkirchen.

Statue of Sherlock Holmes in Meiringen

🏞 **Reichenbachfälle**
Tel *033 972 9010.* ⬜ *early May–Jun & Sep–Oct: 9–11:45am & 1:15–5:45pm; Jul–Aug: 9am–6pm.*

🏞 **Aareschlucht**
Tel *033 971 40 48.* ⬜ *Apr–Oct: 8:30am–5:30pm. Floodlit illumination, mid-Jun–mid-Oct: 8:30am–10pm Wed–Sun.*

The Eiger, Mönch and Jungfrau, the highest peaks in the Jungfrau massif

Jungfraujoch ⑬

Road map D4. 🛈 *Höheweg 37, Interlaken; 033 826 53 00.* **www.**jungfrau.com

South of Interlaken lies the Bernese Oberland's most impressive mountain scenery, centred on a giant triple-peaked ridge: the Eiger (3,970 m/ 13,025 ft), the Mönch (4,099 m/ 13,448 ft) and the Jungfrau (4,158 m/13,642 ft). A network of rail and cable-car routes from Interlaken (*see p75)* makes it easy to travel around this area.

The best-known rail excursion (not inexpensive but a unique experience) is to the Jungfraujoch. This icy saddle, which lies just below the summit of the Jungfrau, has been dubbed the "Top of Europe", and at 3,454 m (11,333 ft) above sea level, the train station here is the highest in Europe.

As there are two different routes up to the Jungfraujoch, this excursion can easily be done as a circular journey. Trains head from Interlaken to Lauterbrunnen, where you change to the rack railway that climbs up through Wengen (*see p83)* and on further up to the dramatic station at Kleine-Scheidegg, which nestles directly beneath the famous North Face of the Eiger. Different trains head from Interlaken to Grindelwald (*see p82)*, where you again change to the rack railway, which from the other direction climbs up to Kleine-Scheidegg. From Kleine-Scheidegg, a separate line heads up to the Jungfraujoch itself. Seat reservations are recommended from April to September.

The engineering on the lower sections of the rail route, around Wengen, is impressive enough but the topmost line, above Kleine Scheidegg, is extraordinary. It runs through steep tunnels blasted out of the heart of the Eiger. At the top, which can be quite crowded, there are cafeteria-style restaurants, a post office (where mail is stamped with a unique "Top of Europe" postmark), a set of ice sculptures, and other attractions. It is, however, far more rewarding to focus on the spectacular views, eastward out to the Black Forest, in Germany, westward to the Vosges, in France, and south into Italy.

There are also opportunities for walking, although they are limited. Some trails head out across the snows. You should, however, be aware that at this altitude the air is thin, and you may feel dizzy walking up steps or exerting yourself in any way. If this happens, the best cure is to rest, then head down again.

The Eiger, a major landmark in the Bernese Alps

For hotels and restaurants in this region see pp245–8 and pp269–72

Swiss Open-Air Museum Ballenberg

From simple alpine chalets to entire farmsteads, about 100 historic rural buildings and 250 farm-yard animals fill this 66-hectare (160-acre) open-air museum. The buildings, some of wood, others of stone or brick, come from several regions of Switzerland. Carefully dismantled, they were transported and reconstructed here, most being saved from demolition. The buildings are grouped according to their area of origin, and each group is linked by paths. The museum grounds also have gardens and fields with crops and farm animals. All the buildings are authentically furnished.

★ Richterswil House
Built in 1780 at Richterswil, near Zürich, this two-family house is an example of the half-timbered buildings typical of northeastern Switzerland, particularly the Zürich area. The house was once inhabited by a vineyard-owner.

Villnachern Family House
Built of limestone in 1630, this was probably the home of a wealthy family.

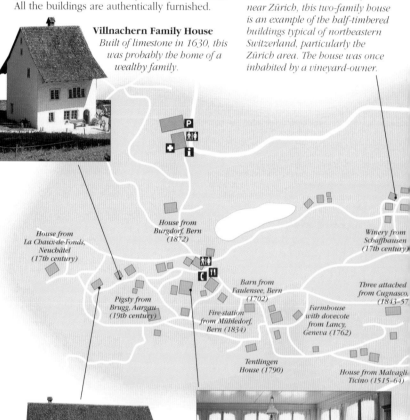

House from
La Chaux-de-Fonds,
Neuchâtel
(17th century)

House from
Burgdorf, Bern
(1872)

Winery from
Schaffhausen
(17th century)

Pigsty from
Brugg, Aargau
(19th century)

Barn from
Faulensee, Bern
(1702)

Three attached
from Cugnasco,
(1843–57)

Fire-station
from Mühledorf,
Bern (1834)

Farmhouse
with dovecote
from Lancy,
Geneva (1762)

Tentlingen
House (1790)

House from Malvagli
Ticino (1515–64)

Therwil House
Built in stone, with a wooden outbuilding, this house is typical of the architecture of the Jura. It dates from 1675.

★ Ostermundigen House
This large house was built in 1797. Although it is made of wood, the façade was painted grey to resemble stone. In the work areas of the house, the rooms are set up as exhibition galleries.

WORKSHOPS

Some of the houses at the museum have workshops where craftsmen using authentic tools and original machinery demonstrate some of the crafts and trades of Switzerland's regions. Among these crafts are

weaving, spinning, pottery, wickerwork, lace-making and cheese-making. The museum also stages fairs and festivals in which folk traditions are revived.

VISITORS' CHECKLIST

Road map D4. 🚌 🚆 Brienzwiler.
**Swiss Open-Air Museum
Ballenberg**, 3 km (2 miles) east
of Brienz. **Tel** *033 952 10 30*.
www.ballenberg.ch. **Interiors**
⬤ *early Apr–Oct: 10am–5pm daily.*
Ticket office & park ⬤ *mid-
Apr–Oct: 9am–5pm daily.* 🅱

0 m ———————————— 200

0 yards ———————————— 200

Törbel Mill House
This mill house from Valais was built in the 19th century. Since the late Middle Ages, the power of mountain streams has been used to grind grain.

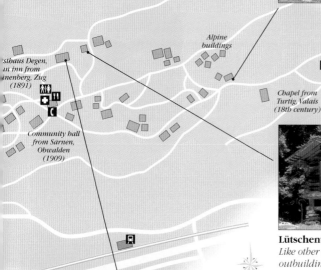

Alpine buildings

...sthaus Degen, ...n inn from ...nenberg, Zug (1891)

Community hall from Sarnen, Obwalden (1909)

Chapel from Turtig, Valais (18th century)

Lütschental Cheese Store
Like other houses and outbuildings of the Bernese Oberland, this storehouse for cheese has a ridge roof with protruding eaves and gable ends.

Brülisau House
This wooden house, typical of the architecture of eastern Switzerland, was built in 1754.

STAR SIGHTS

★ Ostermundigen House

★ Richterswil House

The parish church in Kandersteg

Kandersteg ⓮

Road map C4. 🎿 800. 🚉
🛈 *Hauptstrasse; 033 675 80 80.*
www.kandersteg.ch

The village of Kandersteg
stretches out along the valley
of the River Kander, west of
the Jungfrau massif. The
village is located near the
north entrance to the Lötschberg Tunnel, through which
trains run for 15 km (9 miles)
under the Lötschberg to
emerge at Goppenstein, in
eastern Valais. The 35-km (22-
mile) tunnel cuts 72 minutes
off the standard train journey
from Bern to nearby Zermatt.

Apart from its attractive
16th-century parish church,
Kandersteg's main interest to
visitors is as a resort. In winter,
the gentle slopes around the
village make ideal skiing pistes
for beginners. In summer the
village is a popular base for
hiking and paragliding or
simply for exploring the
stunningly beautiful lakes and
mountains in the vicinity.

The **Oeschinensee**, a small
lake surrounded by towering
cliffs, can be reached by a
chairlift from the eastern edge
of the village. Fit hikers can
walk back down to Kander-
steg. The **Blausee**, a small
boating lake surrounded by a
pine forest, is a ten-minute
drive north of Kandersteg.

The Blümlisalphorn (3,671 m/
12,044 ft) and Hockenhorn
(3,297 m/10,820 ft), two nearby peaks, offer mountaineers a
more demanding challenge.

Adelboden ⓯

Road map C4. 🚉 🏃 3,650.
*Dorfstrasse 23; 033 673
80 80.* **www.**adelboden.ch

Located at the head of
Engstligental, a wide valley,
Adelboden is an attractive
village with chalets, pleasant
streets and well-kept gardens.
The small parish church here
was built in 1433 and is of
interest for its frescoes and
stained-glass windows by
Augusto Giacometti. The
village also has an interesting
museum documenting local
history and daily life in the
Engstligental.

Adelboden is, however,
primarily a resort. With 72
ski lifts and some 210 km
(130 miles) of pistes, it is a
popular ski area, and caters
particularly well for families.
Adelboden also offers
facilities for extreme
sports as well
as ice-rinks for
skating and
curling. In summer
it is a base for
mountain biking
and hiking.

The **Engstligen-
fälle**, spectacular
waterfalls tumbling
from Engstligenalp,
4 km (3 miles)
above Adelboden,
are accessible by
cable car. There are
several hiking trails, which
lead up to higher altitudes,
including Ammertenspitz
(2,613 m/ 8,573 ft) and also
down past the falls, that can
be started from here.

**Epitaph in Adelboden's
parish church**

Grindelwald ⓰

Road map D4. 🚉 🛈 *Dorfstrasse
110; 033 854 12 12.*
www.grindelwald.ch

The road and railway line
into the mountains diverge
just south of Interlaken. One
branch continues into the
Lauterbrunnen valley, with
access to Lauterbrunnen,
Wengen and Mürren, and the
other heads east along the
Lütschen valley to Grindelwald.

Nestled beneath the giant
Wetterhorn, Mettenberg and
Eiger, this lively resort village
has long been one of the
most popular destinations in
the Alps. In winter it offers
good skiing, and in summer
excellent hiking. A one-hour
walk east of the village leads
to the trailhead for a scenic
stroll through woodland to
the awe-inspiring Oberer
Gletscher, a glacier
inching its way
down the
Wetterhorn.

Some of the
region's best hiking
trails lie in the area
around **First**, which
is served by its own
gondola. A classic
half-day route from
First gives a superb
ridge-top walk along
to the glittering
Bachalpsee tarn and
on to the summit
of the **Faulhorn** (2,681 m/
8,795 ft), where refreshment
can be found at a restaurant
and an inn. From here the
views of the sunrise and
sunset are breathtaking.

Snow-covered chalets at the resort of Wengen

Schloss Wimis, the 16th-century castle in the Nieder Simmental

Wengen ⓱

Road map C4. 👥 *1,405.* 🚉
🛈 *Dorfstrasse; 033 856 85 85.*
www.wengen.ch

The road and rail line from Interlaken terminate in Lauterbrunnen, a quiet village on the floor of the stunning Lauterbrunnen valley, the world's deepest U-shaped valley. This is classic Swiss Alpine scenery, with the sheer cliffs, waterfalls, green meadows where cows graze, and snowy peaks.

Mountain trains climb from Lauterbrunnen towards the Jungfraujoch (see p79), stopping midway at Wengen, a village of chalets and large hotels tucked on a shelf of southwest-facing pasture. Like its neighbours Grindelwald and Mürren, car-free Wengen has been a magnet for summer and winter visitors for a century or more.

Skiing and snowboarding terrain is extensive, and in summer the countryside around Wengen offers superb hiking. Trails lead down to the flowery meadows around Wengwald, and up to Männlichen (which can also be reached by cable car). From here visitors can enjoy spectacular views down over Grindelwald on one side and the Lauterbrunnen valley on the other.

Mürren ⓲

Road map C4. 👥 *350.* 🚉
🛈 *033 856 86 86.*
www.muerren.ch

From Lauterbrunnen there are two ways of reaching the small car-free village of Mürren, on the opposite side of the valley from Wengen. Both routes are spectacular. A cable car rises to Grütschalp, from where a tram takes a scenic route along the cliff-edge to reach Mürren. Alternatively, buses head along the valley-floor road from Lauterbrunnen (past a magnificent set of waterfalls at Trümmelbach) to Stechelberg, from where a cable car climbs to Mürren, perched 800m (2,625 ft) above the valley floor. The views, down the valley and up to a dazzling panorama of snowy crags, are astounding. The cable car heads further up, to the ice-bound summit of the Schilthorn (2,970 m/9,744 ft), where there is a famous revolving restaurant.

The Simmental ⓳

Road map C4. 🚉 🚌
🛈 *Rawilstrasse 3, Lenk; 033 736 35 35.* **www**.lenk-simmental.ch

The Simmental, the long valley of the River Simme, is divided into two sections. Nieder Simmental, the lower section, runs from Spiez, where the Simme enters the Thunersee, westwards to Boltigen. Here the valley veers southwards, becoming Obere Simmental, the upper section. This part stretches up to the resort and spa town of **Lenk**, near the source of the Simme.

Several villages lie along the Simmental. **Erlenbach** is the starting point for white-water rafting down the Simme. **Zweisimmen**, at the confluence of the Kleine Simme and Grosse Simme, is the trailhead of roads that run along the valley floor up towards Lenk and Gstaad. From Lenk ski lifts take hikers and skiers up to Metschberg, Betelberg and Mülkerblatten.

The Saane River near Gstaad, excellent for white-water rafting

Gstaad ⓴

Road map C4. 👥 *2,500.* 🚉 🚌
🛈 *Haus des Gastes; 033 748 81 81.*
🎪 *Hot Air Balloon Week (Jan), Swiss Open Tennis Tournament (Jul), Menuhin Festival (Jul–Sep).*
www.gstaad.ch

For one of Switzerland's smartest resorts, Gstaad is a surprisingly small village, its size out of proportion to its international fame and prestige. Lying at the junction of four valleys, Gstaad connects into a larger regional skipass network, including the Diablerets glacier.

In summer Gstaad attracts numerous visitors who come here to enjoy rock climbing, hiking, cycling, tennis and fun sports, such as rafting on the turbulent waters of the Saane.

By avoiding high-rise developments and remaining faithful to traditional Swiss-style architecture, Gstaad has maintained its romantic character. Its main street, the Promenade, is lined with shops, cafés, restaurants and art galleries. Craftsmen can be seen at work on woodcarvings and decorative paper cut-outs.

Luxuriously furnished interior of a chalet in Gstaad

Martigny ㉑

Road map B5. 🚶 *13,000.* 🚉 🚌
ℹ️ *Ave. de la Gare 6; 027 720 49
49.* **www**.martigny.com

Located at the confluence
of the Drance and the Rhône,
at the point where the latter
curves northward, Martigny
(Octodorus) was established
by the Romans in about 15
BC. Excavations have
revealed a complex of Roman
buildings, including a temple
dedicated to Minerva, baths
and an amphitheatre.

The town is dominated by
the **Tour de la Bâtiaz**, a 13th-
century fortress set on a
promontory. Other buildings
of interest in Martigny's old
district are the 15th-century
Maison Supersaxo and the
**Chapelle Notre-Dame-de-
Compassion**, built in the 1620s.

Martigny's main attraction is
the **Fondation Pierre
Gianadda**, a museum built on
the ruins of a Gallo-Roman
temple. It consists of several
collections. While the main
gallery stages important
temporary
exhibitions, the
Musée Archéo-
logique Gallo-
Romain contains
statues, coins,
pottery and bronzes
uncovered during
excavations. The
Musée de l'Auto, in
the basement, has
about 50 vintage
cars, including Swiss-made
models. A small number of
paintings, by Van Gogh,
Cézanne, Toulouse-Lautrec
and other important artists, are
shown in the more intimate
Salle Franck. Modern sculpture
fills the Parc des Sculptures, an
open area around the museum.

The mountain refuge at the Col du Grand-St-Bernard

🏛️ **Fondation Pierre Gianadda**
59 Rue du Forum. **Tel** *027 722 39
78.* ⬜ *Jun–Nov: 9am–7pm daily;
Dec–May: 10am–6pm daily.* 📷

**Roman head of a bull
in Martigny**

Environs
The small town of **St-Maurice**,
15 km (9 miles) north of
Martigny, has an Augustinian
abbey founded in 515. The
church is part of the oldest
surviving abbey north of the
Alps. Northwest of Martigny

lies the extensive Franco-Swiss
skiing area known as the
Portes du Soleil, which can
be reached via the town of
Monthey. The area comprises
12 resorts and has about 650
km (400 miles) of pistes.

Grand St Bernard Pass ㉒

Road map B5. 🚌 ℹ️ *Grand-St-
Bernard; 027 775 23 81.*
www.st-bernard.ch

Situated on the
border with Italy
at an altitude of 2,469
m (8,103 ft), the St Ber-
nard Pass, or Col du
Grand-St-Bernard, is the
oldest of all Alpine pass
routes. An isolated
nexus between
western Europe
and Italy, it has
been used since at least
800 BC. Julius Caesar came
over the pass in the 1st
century BC, followed by
Charlemagne in 800, on the
return from his coronation in
Milan, and Napoleon in 1800.

The pass is named after
Bernard of Menthon, Bishop
of Aosta, who built a hospice
for travellers here in 1049. In
recognition of his missionary
work, St Bernard was beati-
fied after his death, in the
1080s, and was later made
patron saint of the Alps.

The hospice on the pass
has been inhabited by monks
ever since and is still open to
travellers all year round. The
present building, which dates
from the 18th century, incorporates a 17th-century church,
in which a casket containing
the remains of St Bernard is
displayed. The treasury has a
collection of liturgical vessels.
There is also a museum,
**Musée et Chiens du Saint-
Bernard**, with exhibits documenting the history of the
pass since pre-Roman times
and kennels for the famous

ST BERNARD DOGS
Named after the hospice at the Grand St Bernard Pass
where they were kept by monks, these sturdy dogs, with
a body weight of up to 100 kg
(220 lb), are synonymous with
mountain rescue. Athough
the monks probably began
to breed them in the Middle
Ages, training them to sniff
out travellers lost in snow
or swallowed by avalanches,
the earliest mention of St
Bernards dates from the late
17th to early 18th centuries.
However, most rescue
work is now done
with helicopters.

St Bernard with a handler

rescue dogs. The dogs can be watched training both indoors and outdoors but no petting or playing with them is permitted.

Because of its elevation and heavy snowfalls in winter, the pass itself can be used only between mid-June and October. However, the St Bernard Tunnel, running 6 km (4 miles) under the pass, provides a year-round route between Switzerland and Italy.

🏛 Musée et Chiens du Saint-Bernard
Route du Levant 34, CP 245, Martigny.
Tel *027 720 49 20.* ⬜ *10am–6pm.*
🖥 www.museesaintbernard.ch

Verbier ㉓

Road map C5. 🏔 *2,600.* 🚌
ℹ *Place Centrale; 027 775 38 88.*
www.*verbier.ch* 🎿 *Xtreme Verbier (Mar); Verbier Festival (late Jul).*

Few Swiss resorts match Verbier in terms of its beautiful location and the range of winter activities that it offers. At an altitude of 1,500 m (4,921 ft), the resort lies on a wide plateau that opens to the south onto views of peaks in Italy, France and Switzerland alike. Just below Verbier lies a picturesque valley, the Val de Bagnes.

Verbier is part of the Four Valleys skipass area, with some 410 km (255 miles) of ski runs, including glacier pistes and extensive ungroomed terrain.

Summer sports here include golf, tennis, horse riding and mountain biking. The town is also a good starting point for hikes along the Val de Bagnes, at the head of which is a dam, the Barrage de Mauvoisin, and for climbing the mountains in the vicinity, including Pierre Avoi (2,472 m/8,113 ft), which offers a breathtaking view of Mont Blanc.

Xtreme Verbier is a winter event in which skiers and snowboarders descend steep faces studded with cliffs. In summer the town hosts the Verbier Festival, an international festival of classical music with free workshops open to everyone.

The Romanesque church at St Pierre-de-Clages

St Pierre-de-Clages ㉔

Road map B5. 🏔 *600.* 🚌 🚊
🎿 *Fête du Livre (late August).*

The tiny village of St Pierre-de-Clages is set on the southern, vineyard-covered slopes of the Rhône valley. Apart from an annual literary festival, the village's main attraction is its beautiful Romanesque church. Dating from the late 11th to the early 12th century, it originally formed part of a Benedictine priory. The rib-vaulted interior is almost entirely devoid of decoration, and this pleasing austerity is accentuated by the bare stonework of the walls and columns. The stained glass dates from 1948.

Sion ㉕

See pp86–7.

Barrage de la Grande Dixence ㉖

Road map C5. 🚌 *late Jun–mid-Oct.*
🎿 *mid-Jun–Sep: 11:30am, 1:30pm, 3pm & 4:30pm.*

The world's highest gravity wall dam and the greatest feat of modern engineering in Switzerland, the Barrage de la Grande Dixence is a hydroelectric dam 285 m (935 ft) high across the River Dixence, at the head of the Val d'Hérémence.

The Lac des Dix, a stretch of water filling the valley above the dam, is surrounded by mountains. Rising to the west is Rosablanche (3,336 m/ 10,945 ft); to the east Les Aiguilles Rouges (3,646 m/ 11,962 ft), and to the south Mont Blanc de Cheilon (3,870m/12,697 ft) and Pigne d'Arolla (3,796m/12,454 ft). A cable car runs from the foot of the dam, where there is a restaurant, up to the lake. From here you can take a boat to the Cabane des Dix, a mountain refuge, walk around the lake or go on a hike – for example, to the small resort of Arolla.

Val d'Hérémence joins Val d'Hérens (*see p88*) at the level of Hérémence. This small town is a good base for skiing on the eastern slopes of Mont Rouge and for hiking in the mountains.

Interior of the Romanesque church at St Pierre-de-Clages

Sion ⑳

The capital of the Canton of Valais, Sion (Sitten in German) is a pleasant town with a rich heritage.
It lies on a plain on the north bank of the Rhône, at the foot of two hills, each of which is crowned by a medieval castle. A Roman settlement named Sedunum was established here in the 1st century. The two castles that tower above the town are vestiges of its powerful bishopric, which ruled over Valais for centuries. In the Middle Ages Sion was also an important producer of wine and fruit, for which the fertile Rhône Valley is still renowned. Sion's Fendant wines are also highly prized.

Sion, seen from Valère, one of two hills overlooking the town

Exploring Sion
Sion's old town, with quiet cobbled streets and fine houses, is easily explored on foot. The castles can also be reached on foot, or in summer there is a tourist train via Rue des Châteaux to an area of level ground between the two hills. From here steep paths lead left to Tourbillon and right to Valère. Both hills offer panoramic views of the town and of the vineyard-covered hillsides all around.

♙ Château de Tourbillon
Tel 027 606 47 45. ☐ mid-Mar–Apr & Oct–mid-Nov: 11am–5pm daily; May–Sep: 10am–6pm daily.
Standing on the higher of the two hills, this great medieval fortress is surrounded by crenellated walls with tall square towers. The castle was built in the late 13th century as the fortified residence of Bishop Boniface de Challant. It was besieged and rebuilt on several occasions and in 1788 it was destroyed by fire. The castle itself is now in ruins, but much of the ramparts remain. The chapel, with ribbed vaulting and carved capitals, contains medieval wall paintings.

♙ Château de Valère
Church *Tel* 027 606 47 15. ☐ Jun–Sep: 10am–6pm daily; Oct–May: 10am–5pm Tue–Sun. ☐ or guided tours of choir; free entry to nave but no access during services. **Musée d'Histoire du Valais** *Tel* 027 606 47 15. ☐ Jun–Sep: 11am–6pm daily; Oct–May: 11am–5pm Tue–Sun.
Built in the 12th to 13th centuries, with a square tower, curtain wall and rampart walk, the Château de Valère is in fact a fortified church, Notre-Dame-de-Valere. It stands on the site of an 11th-century fortress and a Roman building. The impressive heights of Valeria overlooking Sion are a National Heritage Site.
Romanesque capitals and Gothic frescoes grace the interior of the church. Other notable features are the stunning 15th-century murals, 17th-century stalls and a remarkable organ. Dating from about 1430–40, it is the oldest playable organ in the world.
Next to the church stands a 12th-century building that was originally the canon's residence. It now houses the Musée d'Histoire du Valais. The museum's collection includes more than 1,000 objects, scale models and interactive displays detailing the history of Valais, from the first traces of human occupation to the present day. Sections on the prehistoric hunter-gatherers, medieval pageants of the court of the Bishop-Prince, Swiss mercenaries and the industrial 19th century trace the developments that have shaped Valais.

🏛 Musée d'Art du Valais
15 Place de la Majorie. *Tel* 027 606 46 90. ☐ Jun–Sep: 11am–6pm Tue–Sun; Oct–May: 11am–5pm Tue–Sun. ☐ www.museums-valais.ch
This art gallery occupies two 15th-century houses that were once the residence of episcopal officers. Ranging from the 17th century to the present, the collection concentrates mainly on paintings by Valais artists, including some folk art.

Notre-Dame-de-Valère, the fortified church on a hill overlooking Sion

For hotels and restaurants in this region see pp245–8 and pp269–72

Rue du Grand-Pont, with the white-fronted Hôtel de Ville

🏛 Hôtel de Ville

12 Rue du Grand-Pont. ⬤ *only for those on the Tourist Office walking tour.*

With its clocktower crowned by a cupola and lantern, Sion's 17th-century town hall stands out among other fine buildings on Rue du Grand-Pont. The town hall, which dates from 1657–65, has finely carved wooden doors at the entrance. Stones with Roman inscriptions are embedded in the walls of the hall within. Among them is a stone with a Christian inscription dating from 377, the earliest of its kind in Switzerland. The council chamber on the upper floor of the town hall has rich furnishings and decorative woodwork.

🏛 Maison Supersaxo

Rue de Conthey. ⬤ *2–5pm Mon–Fri.*

This ornate late Gothic mansion was built in about 1505 for Georges Supersaxo, the local governor. A wooden spiral staircase leads up to the grand hall, which has a wooden ceiling depicting lavishly painted in the late Gothic style. The centrepiece of the ceiling is a painted medallion by Jacobinus de Malacridis depicting the Nativity. Busts of the Prophets and the Magi fill alcoves lining the walls.

Nativity medallion in Maison Supersaxo

⛪ Cathédrale Notre-Dame du Glarier

Rue de la Cathédrale 13. **Tel** 027 322 80 66. ⬤ *7am–7pm daily; access only via the tourist office guided tour.*

Although the main part of the cathedral dates from the 15th century, it contains earlier elements, including a 12th-century Romanesque belfry

VISITORS' CHECKLIST

Road map C5. 👥 *28,000.* 🚍 🚉
ℹ️ *Place de la Planta; 027 327 77 27.* **www.**siontourisme.ch
🎵 *Festival International de Musique (Aug–Sep).*

crowned by an octagonal steeple. Interesting features of the interior include tombs of the bishops of Sion, early Baroque stalls and a wooden triptych depicting the Tree of Jesse. The Église St-Théodule, the late Gothic church just to the south of the cathedral, dates from 1514–16. The 19th-century building opposite the cathedral is the Bishop's Palace.

🏛 Tour des Sorciers

Avenue de la Gare 42.
⬤ *for private functions.*

The Witches' Tower, so named because of its conical roof, is the only remaining part of Sion's medieval fortifications. Located just north of the old town, the tower once defended the town's northwestern aspect.

SION TOWN CENTRE

Cathédrale Notre-Dame du Glarier ⑥
Château de Tourbillon ①
Château de Valère ②
Hôtel de Ville ④
Maison Supersaxo ⑤
Musée d'Art du Valais ③
Tour des Sorciers ⑦

The Pyramides d'Euseigne, striking rock formations in the Val d'Hérens

Val d'Hérens ㉗

Road map C5. 🚌 ℹ️ *Rue Principale 13, Euseigne; 027 281 28 15.* **www**.valdherens-tourisme.ch

Stretching southeast from Sion, the Val d'Hérens (Eringertal in German) reaches into the Pennine Alps. This tranquil valley has enchanting scenery and villages with wooden chalets. Women wearing traditional dress can be seen working in the fields.

A striking geological feature of the Val d'Hérens is a group of rock formations known as the **Pyramides d'Euseigne**. These jagged outcrops of rock, which are visible from the valley road, jut out of the hillside like fangs. They were formed during the Ice Age by the erosive action of wind, rain and ice. Each point is capped by a rock, which protected the softer rock beneath from erosion, so producing these formations.

The village of Evolène, 15 km (9 miles) south of the village of Euseigne, is a good base for hiking. At the head of the valley is the hamlet of Les Haudères, where there is a Geology and Glacier Centre, with an interesting museum. Beyond Les Haudères the Val d'Hérens extends into the Val d'Arolla. The road ends at the small resort of Arolla.

Crans-Montana ㉘

Road map C4. 🚠 *4,500.* 🚌 ℹ️ *027 485 04 04.* **www**.crans-montana.ch
🏌️ *European Masters Golf Tournament (Sep).*

The fashionable ski and golf resort of Crans-Montana lies on a plateau north of the Rhône valley, with a clear view of the Valais Alps to the south. In the late 19th century, as the fashion for mountain holidays grew, Crans and Montana expanded but they remain two separate villages.

Crans-Montana can be reached by road from Sion. From Sierre it is accessible either by a road that winds up through vineyards and pasture, or by funicular. This extremely sunny resort has a network of cable cars

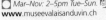

Window with flowers, a typical sight in Valais

and ski lifts, accessing over 160 km (100 miles) of pistes and the glacier of Pleine Morte, popular for cross-country skiing.

Summer activities include golf, paragliding and hot-air ballooning. A plateau lying at an altitude of 2,267 m (7,437 ft), Plaine Morte offers stunning views of the Valais Alps, with Mont Blanc to the southwest. From here mountain trails lead to Bella Lui and Bisse du Roh.

Sierre ㉙

Road map C4. 🚠 *11,000.* 🚉 🚌
ℹ️ *Place de la Gare 10; 027 455 85 35.* **www**.sierre-salgesch.ch

Located in the Rhône valley, Sierre (Siders in German) lies on the border between French- and German-speaking Valais. Enjoying an exceptionally sunny climate, it is surrounded by vineyards, and contains several historic buildings, including a 16th-century castle, the **Château des Vidomnes**. The Baroque town hall contains a small museum of pewter objects.

The local winemaking tradition is documented by the **Musée Valaisan de la Vigne et du Vin**, a wine museum whose collections are displayed in two places. One part occupies a wing of the 16th-century Château de Villa in Sierre, and the other the 16th-century Zumofenhaus in Salgesch (Salquenen in French), a village east of Sierre. The two locations are linked by a Sentier Viticole, or wine route, running for 6 km (4 miles) through villages and their vineyards, with wine-tasting stops along the way.

🏛️ **Musée Valaisan de la Vigne et du Vin**
Château de Villa, 4 Rue Ste-Catherine. *Tel 027 456 35 25.* 🕐 *Mar–Nov: 2–5pm Tue–Sun.* 🅿️ **www**.museevalaisanduvin.ch

The 16th-century Château des Vidomnes in Sierre

Characteristic wooden houses in Grimentz, Val d'Anniviers

Val d'Anniviers ⑳

Road map C4. 🚌 🛈 0848 84
80 27. www.sierre-anniviers.ch

Surrounded by the high
peaks of the Pennine Alps
and washed by the River
La Navisence, the rugged
Val d'Anniviers begins
opposite Sierre and runs
southwards up to the glaciers
of Zinal. The valley is dotted
with villages, which offer
visitors winter skiing and
summer hiking and cycling.

From Soussillon you can
make a trip to the medieval
village of **Chandolin**, which
has wooden chalets and
spectacular views. From
Vissoie it is worth going to
sun-drenched **Saint-Luc** at
1,650 m (5,413 ft) for a
breathtaking view of the Val
d'Anniviers. From Saint-Luc
you can proceed further up,
to the top of Bella Tola (3,025
m/9,924 ft).

Grimentz is a fascinating
village, full of traditional tall
wooden chalets built on the
underlying bedrock. From
here hiking trails lead up to
the Moiry dam, and the
Glacier de Moiry. The
highest-lying village in the
valley is **Zinal** at 1,670 m
(5,479 ft). This resort is a ski
centre in winter and a good
base for hiking in summer.
From Zinal it is possible to
hire a guide for the climb
to the summit of the Zinal-
Rothorn (4,221 m/13,848 ft),
the Pyramide des Besso,
Oberes Gabelhorn and
Pointe de Zinal. There are
many easier peaks for less
ambitious climbers, and
several highly scenic
rambling routes.

Leukerbad ㉑

Road map C4. 🚠 1,600. 🚌
🛈 Rathausstrasse 8; 027 472 71 71.
www.leukerbad.ch

Lying at the head of the
Dala valley, at an altitude of
1,400 m (4,595 ft), Leukerbad
(Loèche-les-Bains in
French) is one of the
highest and largest spa
resorts in Europe. The
therapeutic properties of
its hot springs, which
are rich in calcium,
sulphur and gypsum,
have been appreciated
since Roman times.

Leukerbad has
several public spa
complexes, with
indoor and outdoor
pools and many
other facilities,
including various
treatments and
rehabilitation programmes.
Leukerbad also has skiing
pistes. Above the resort, and
accessible by cable car, lies
the Gemmi Pass, on the hiking
trail to Kandersteg (see p82)
and the Bernese Oberland.

Zermatt ㉜

Road map C5. 🚠 4,200. 🚉 🚌
🛈 Bahnhofplatz 5; 027 966 81 00.
www.zermatt.ch

Nestling at the foot of the
Matterhorn (see p90) and
surrounded by mountains over
4,000 m (13,000 ft), Zermatt
is Switzerland's best-known
resort. As it is closed to
motorized traffic, Zermatt
must be reached by train
from Brig, Visp or Täsch.

A ski paradise in winter,
Zermatt is a centre of hiking
and mountaineering in
summer. Skiing on glaciers in
the vicinity is also possible all
through the summer.

The **Matterhorn Museum** in
Zermatt documents the
history of mountaineering in
the region, with a display
devoted to Edward
Whymper, who led the
first ascent of the
Matterhorn in 1865. The
small Anglican church
here was built in the
19th century for
English climbers
scaling the neighbour-
ing peaks. The town
square, surrounded
by historic houses,
features a fountain
with marmot
statues.

**Marmot on a
fountain in Zermatt**

From Zermatt a
series of lifts run to
the summit of the
Klein Matterhorn (3,883 m/
12,739 ft), and a rack railway
climbs to the Gornergrat
(3,089 m/10,134 ft) from
where there are breathtaking
views of the Matterhorn and
the Gornergletscher.

Municipal baths in Leukerbad

The Matterhorn, for daring climbers only

Matterhorn ❸❸

Road map C6. 🚏 *Zermatt,
Bahnhofplatz; 027 966 81 00.*
www.zermatt.ch

Although the Matterhorn is
not the highest mountain in
Switzerland, it is certainly the
most awesome. It straddles
the Swiss-Italian border, and
with its distinct pyramidal
peak, which reaches 4,478 m
(14,692 ft), it has become one
of Switzerland's national
symbols. Shrouded in legend,
it has claimed the lives of
several of the 2,000 people
brave enough to climb it each
summer. The best views of
the mountain are from the
centre of Zermatt *(see p89)*.

The Matterhorn (Cervino in
Italian) was first conquered
on 14 July 1865 by a team
led by the British explorer
Edward Whymper. The
expedition ended in tragedy
when three of the English
mountaineers and a Swiss
guide were killed during the
descent. Their tombs lie in
Zermatt along with those of
others who lost their lives
on the mountain.

The Matterhorn is still a
challenge for recreational
climbers. The most difficult
ascent route is on the east
face, which was not con-
quered until 1932.

Monte Rosa ❸❹

Road map C5.

Right on the international
border, Monte Rosa is
divided into Swiss and Italian
territory. Although it is not as
famous as the Matterhorn, the

Monte Rosa massif boasts the
highest peak in Switzerland
and the second-highest in the
Alps after Mont Blanc. This is
the Dufourspitze, which culminates at 4,634 m (15,203 ft).

Because of its shape, Monte
Rosa does not present as
much of a challenge to
climbers as the Matterhorn.
Situated on its Italian side,
near the summit at 4,556 m
(14,947 ft), is the Capanna
Regina Margherita, the highest
mountain shelter in Europe,
built in 1893. The Monte Rosa
massif is encircled by the
Gornergletscher, a vast
glacier; stretching lower down
are the slopes of Stockhorn
and Gornergrat, with long
pistes and many ski lifts.

Saas Fee ❸❺

Road map D5. 🏔 *1,700.* 🚌
Tel *027 958 18 58.* **www.**
saas-fee.ch 🎉 *Alpaufzug (Jun),
Älplerfest (mid-Aug).*

A village with a history
going back to the 13th
century, Saas Fee, in the
Pennine Alps, has
evolved into a resort
since the early 19th
century. It is the main
town in the Saas Valley,
through which flows the
River Saaser Vispa. Saas
Fee has a magnificent
setting at the foot of
the Dom (4,545
m/14,908 ft) and
is surrounded
by several other
tall peaks.

The resort is closed to
motorized traffic. It has many
traditional wooden chalets,
which are built on high stone

**Monument to a
guide in Saas Fee**

foundation walls. Saas Fee,
more than many resorts,
cherishes its traditional rural
culture; several local
traditions are enacted for the
benefit of visitors. These
include processions marking
Corpus Christi, cow fights
and yodelling contests, folk
festivals celebrating Swiss
National Day, and the
Alpaufzug festival in late
spring, which marks the time
when cows are taken up to
their summer pastures.
The Saaser Museum, which
is devoted to regional folk
traditions and culture,
includes the reconstruction
of a typical local house, and
a large collection of crafts
and costumes.

The view up from the
village, winter or summer,
is of snowy glaciers and
glistening crevasses. Summer
skiing is possible on the
Feegletscher (Fairy Glacier)
in the Mischabel massif.

In summer visitors have
a choice of countless trails,
ranging from easy to
demanding, leading to the
surrounding peaks or to
other sites, such as the
Mattmarksee, an artificial
lake. A cable car also runs
up to Felskinn. From here
the Alpine Metro runs to
Mittelallalin, where there
is a revolving restaurant at
3,500 m (11,480 ft).

Brig ❸❻

Road map D4. 🏔 *10,000.*
🚉 🚏 *Bahnhofplatz 1;
027 921 60 30.*
www.brig-belalp.ch

Brig is the major town
in the Upper Valais. It
lies at the crossroads of
the main Alpine routes
leading over the Sim-
plon, Furka, Grimsel
and Nufenen passes
and through the
Lötschberg Tunnel.
Located on the
Rhône, the town
takes its name from
the bridges that span
the river at this spot, where a
Roman settlement once stood.
During the 17th century, the
trade route to Italy, leading

The towers of the Stockalper Palace in Brig

CUSTOMS OF THE LÖTSCHENTAL

The Lötschental is a remote valley just east of Leukerbad (*see p89*). For centuries the valley's inhabitants were isolated from the outside world during winter, and they have retained many ancient rituals, customs and traditions. Now studied by ethnographers and cultural anthropologists, they have also become a visitor attraction. One such ancient custom is Tschäggätta, a festival that lasts from Candlemas until Shrovetide. During this time young bachelors don sheepskin coats, with the fleece on the outside, and wear grotesque masks. Masked processions are held on the last Thursday and Saturday of the carnival.

Tschäggätta mask

over the Simplon Pass, was controlled by the Stockalper family of merchants. Kaspar Jodok Stockalper von Thurm gave Brig its finest monument, a Renaissance-Baroque palace built in 1658–78. The building is set with three tall square towers crowned by cupolas known as Caspar, Melchior and Balthazar. The palace has an attractive arcaded courtyard and a chapel dedicated to the Three Kings, with an exquisite silver altarpiece made by Samuel Hornung of Augsburg. The palace houses various offices and a history museum.

Brig also has other historic buildings, town houses and churches, including the pilgrimage church in Glis, built in 1642–59.

Simplon Pass ③⑦

Road map D5. 🅸 *Simplon Dorf; 027 979 10 10.* **www**.simplon.ch

At 2,005 m (6,580 ft), the Simplon Pass is one of the most important routes between Switzerland and Italy, and between western and southern Europe. It also marks the border between the Pennine and Lepontine Alps. The route, once used by the Romans, has played an important role in trade since the Middle Ages. The strategic importance of the pass was recognized by

Napoleon, on whose orders a new road was built here in 1800–06. It is about 64 km (40 miles) long and runs from Brig, over the pass and through the village of Simplon, to the Italian town of Domodossola.

Aletsch Glacier ③⑧

Road map D4. 🅸 *Bahnhofstrasse 7, Riederalp; 027 928 60 50.* **www**.aletsch.ch

The longest glacier in the Alps, the Aletsch Glacier (or Grosser Aletschgletscher) stretches for about 23 km (14 miles) from the Jungfrau (*see p79*) to a plateau above the Rhône valley. At its widest point the glacier is 2 km (1 mile) across. Together with the Jungfrau

and Bietschhorn mountain ranges, the Aletsch Glacier has been declared a UNESCO Natural Heritage Site.

The best starting point for a hike to the Aletsch Glacier is the small mountain resort of **Riederalp**, just above the Rhône valley. It is closed to motor traffic but can be reached by cable car from Mörel.

The tourist information centre in Riederalp contains a small alpine museum with a traditional cheese dairy. Within walking distance is the secluded Villa Cassel at **Riederfurka**. The Pro Natura Zentrum Aletsch here is a scientific centre that provides information and permanent exhibitions on alpine glaciers and the environmental protection of this region.

Hikers beside the Aletsch Glacier

GENEVA

With its beautiful lakeside setting, Geneva is a cosmopolitan city whose modest size belies its wealth and importance on the world stage. French-speaking yet Calvinistic, it is a dynamic centre of business with an outward-looking character tempered by a certain reserve. It is also the European headquarters of the United Nations and the birthplace of the International Red Cross.

A city with a population of just 185,000, Geneva is the capital of the canton of the same name. Sharing 95 per cent of its border with France, the canton is joined to the rest of Switzerland only by a narrow strip of land on its north side.

Loosely bound to the Holy Roman Empire from the 9th century, Geneva was later controlled by Savoy, from which it won independence in 1536. In 1602, when the Savoyards attempted to retake the city, they were repulsed. This event is commemorated to this day by a festival known as L'Escalade (Scaling the Walls).

By the 16th century, the city of Geneva was established as a prosperous centre of trade. When Jean Calvin began to preach here, Geneva also became a stronghold of the Reformation. Known as the Protestant Rome, it attracted Protestant refugees from all over Europe, who further increased the city's wealth and boosted its cosmopolitan character. Briefly an independent republic, Geneva was annexed by France from 1798 to 1813. In 1815, the city and its canton joined the Swiss Confederation.

The seat of over 250 international organizations, mostly NGOs, Geneva is today a centre of international diplomacy. It is also the home of the European Laboratory for Particle Physics (CERN), one of the world's most advanced scientific laboratories.

International flags on the approach to the Palais des Nations, in Geneva's International Area

◁ Mausolée du Duc de Brunswick, in the style of Scaglieri's tomb in Verona, on Geneva's South Bank

Exploring Geneva

Set at the western extremity of Lake Geneva at the point where the Rhône flows away towards France, Geneva is divided by water. On the South Bank (Rive Gauche) is the 16th-century Old Town (Vieille Ville), once surrounded by walls. Plainpalais, southwest of the Old Town, is the university district, while further south is Carouge, a picturesque suburb with a population of artists. The North Bank (Rive Droite), dominated by grand quayside hotels, is Geneva's main commercial area. Further north lies the Cité Internationale, base of international organizations. Both riverbanks have pleasant green areas. From La Rade, the harbour, rises the Jet d'Eau, Geneva's famous fountain.

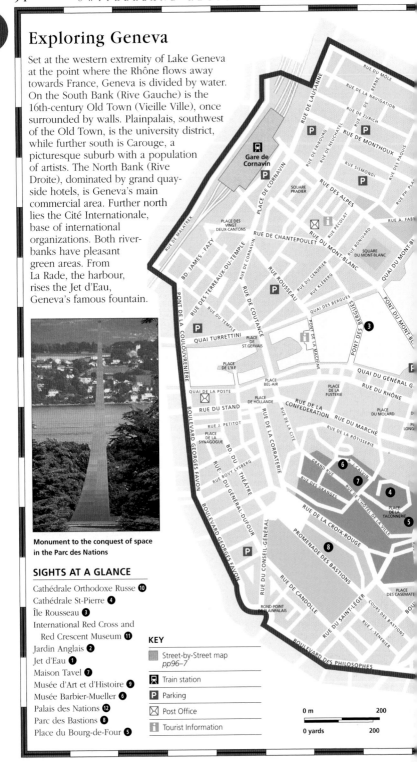

Monument to the conquest of space in the Parc des Nations

SIGHTS AT A GLANCE

Cathédrale Orthodoxe Russe ⑩
Cathédrale St-Pierre ④
Île Rousseau ③
International Red Cross and
   Red Crescent Museum ⑪
Jardin Anglais ②
Jet d'Eau ①
Maison Tavel ⑦
Musée d'Art et d'Histoire ⑨
Musée Barbier-Mueller ⑥
Palais des Nations ⑫
Parc des Bastions ⑧
Place du Bourg-de-Four ⑤

KEY

▨	Street-by-Street map *pp96–7*
🚉	Train station
🅿	Parking
⊠	Post Office
ℹ	Tourist Information

0 m — 200
0 yards — 200

SEE ALSO

• **Where to Stay** pp248–9

• **Where to Eat** pp272–3

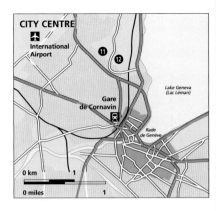

CITY CENTRE

International
Airport

11
12

Gare
de Cornavin

Lake Geneva
(Lac Léman)

Rade
de Genève

0 km   1

0 miles   1

GETTING THERE

Geneva's international airport is 6 km
(4 miles) northwest of the city. Transfer
to the city centre takes six minutes by
train and 15 minutes by bus. The Gare
de Cornavin, on the North Bank, is
Geneva's main train station. Paris is
three and a half hours from Geneva by
TGV high-speed train. From France,
Geneva can be reached via the
A40 from Chamonix or Lyon,
and via the N5 from Dijon.

PROMENADE DU LAC

QUAI GUSTAVE ADOR

JARDIN
ANGLAIS
2

QUAI DU GÉNÉRAL-GUISAN

RUE DU RHÔNE

Rade
de Genève

RUE PIERRE FATIO

RUE DE LA SCIE

RUE F. VERSONNEX

RUE DU LAC

RUE MUZY

RUE DES EAUX-VIVES

RUE MALNOIR

RUE DE LA MAIRIE

RUE DU 31 DÉCEMBRE

RUE DE MONTCHOISY

DE RIVE

RUE D'ITALIE

P

BOULEVARD HELVÉTIQUE

BOULEVARD HELVÉTIQUE

PLACE
DES
EAUX-VIVES

AVENUE PICTET-DE-ROCHEMONT

RUE DU NANT

RONO-POINT
DERIVE

RUE AMI LULLIN

CAPREFOUR
DE RIVE

RUE DES GLACIS-DE-RIVE

RUE DE LA TERRASSIÈRE

P

RUE DU MIDI

RUE FERDINAND HODLER

DALCROZE

9

LEVARD HELVÉTIQUE

EVARD HELVÉTIQUE

RUE ÉMILIE GALLAND

RUE C STURM

10

RUE ÉMILIE GOURD

PLACE
EMILE
GUVENOT

RUE DE VILLEREUSE

ROUTE DE MALAGNOU

PARC
DE MALAGNOU

CHEMIN DE ROCHES

RUE DU ST VICTOR

BONNET

ÉNEE

BOULEVARD DES TRANCHÉES

ROUTE DE FLORISSANT

AVENUE JULES CROSNIER

RUE DE CONTAMINES

RUE MICHEL CHAUVET

**Tour de l'Île, a medieval tower
on an island on the Rhône**

Street-by-Street: Old Town

Set on elevated ground on the south bank of the
Rhône, the Old Town (Vieille Ville) clusters around
the cathedral and Place du Bourg-de-Four. This
atmospheric district, whose main thoroughfare is the
pedestrianized Grand' Rue, has narrow cobbled streets
lined with historic limestone houses. While the southern limit of the Old Town is marked by the Promenade
des Bastions, laid out along the course of the old city
walls, its northern side slopes down to the quay,
which is lined with wide boulevards
and the attractive Jardin Anglais.

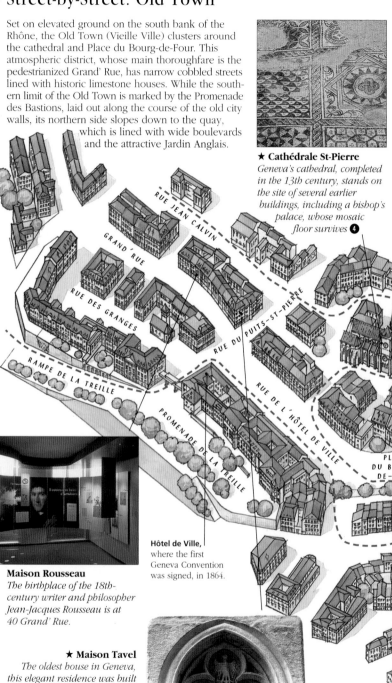

★ **Cathédrale St-Pierre**
*Geneva's cathedral, completed
in the 13th century, stands on
the site of several earlier
buildings, including a bishop's
palace, whose mosaic
floor survives* ❹

RUE JEAN CALVIN

GRAND' RUE

RUE DES GRANGES

RAMPE DE LA TREILLE

RUE DU PUITS-ST-PIERRE

RUE DE L'HÔTEL DE VILLE

PROMENADE DE LA TREILLE

PLAC
DU BO
DE-FC

Maison Rousseau
*The birthplace of the 18th-
century writer and philosopher
Jean-Jacques Rousseau is at
40 Grand' Rue.*

Hôtel de Ville,
where the first
Geneva Convention
was signed, in 1864.

★ **Maison Tavel**
*The oldest house in Geneva,
this elegant residence was built
in 1334. It is now a museum
documenting daily life in
Geneva through the ages* ❻

LOCATOR MAP

★ **Place du Bourg-de-Four**
This central square was used as a market place in the Middle Ages. It is still lined with old inns, as well as modern cafés and restaurants ❺

KEY

- - - Suggested route

STAR SIGHTS

★ Cathédrale St-Pierre

★ Maison Tavel

★ Place du Bourg-de-Four

Jet d'Eau, emblem of Geneva and Europe's tallest fountain

Jet d'Eau ❶

Off Quai Gustave-Ador.

Standing in isolation on a jetty on the south bank of Lake Geneva, the Jet d'Eau is the world's highest fountain, shooting a plume of water 140 m (460 ft) into the air, at a rate of 500 litres (113 gallons) per second and a speed of 200 km per hour (125 mph). It came into existence almost by accident.

In the late 19th century a purely functional fountain was set up to relieve excess water pressure while a reservoir system was being installed. Such was the fountain's popularity that the authorities decided to construct a permanent fountain, which became more spectacular as increasingly powerful pumps were installed. Visible from afar and floodlit after dark, the Jet d'Eau is the pride of Geneva and has been adopted as the city's emblem.

Floral clock at the entrance to the Jardin Anglais

Jardin Anglais ❷

Quai du Général-Guisan.

Laid out on the lakeside at the foot of the Old Town, the Jardin Anglais (English Garden) offers a view of the harbour, and of the buildings along the quay on the north bank. The entrance to the garden is marked by a large floral clock, the **Horloge Fleurie**. Created in 1955 as a tribute to Switzerland's clock-making tradition, it consists of eight intersecting wheels with 6,500 flowering plants. The **Monument National** nearby commemorates Geneva's accession to the Swiss Confederation in 1814.

Protruding from the lake at a point just north of the Jardin Anglais are two stones brought down by glaciers during the Ice Age. They are known as the **Pierres du Niton** (Neptune's Stones), and the larger of the two was once used as the reference point from which altitude was measured in Switzerland.

Île Rousseau ❸

Pont des Bergues.

A walkway jutting out at a right angle from the centre of the Pont des Bergues leads to a medieval bastion in the Rhône. Now known as the Île Rousseau, it is named after Jean-Jacques Rousseau (1712–78), the writer and philosopher of the Enlightenment who was one of Geneva's most distinguished citizens.

Statue of Jean-Jacques Rousseau

Rousseau, the son of a clockmaker, left Geneva at the age of 16. Although he praised the city in his writings, his views elicited the disapproval of the authorities and his books were burned. However, in 1834, 56 years after his death, a statue was installed on the bastion that now bears his name.

Cathédrale St-Pierre ❹

Built over a span of some 70 years from 1160 to 1230, with later additions, Geneva's vast cathedral is in a mixture of styles. Basically Gothic, it incorporates earlier Romanesque elements and has an incongruous Neo-Classical portal, which was added in the 18th century. In 1536 it became a Protestant church, losing most of its lavish Catholic decoration. Only the stalls and the stained glass in the chancel escaped the purge. The result, however, is a plain interior of awesome austerity. The cathedral stands on the site of a Roman temple and a complex of later buildings, part of the remains of which can be seen at the archaeological site nearby.

Calvin's Chair
Calling for a radical reform of the Church, Jean Calvin preached many sermons in the cathedral, reputedly seated in this chair.

The Nave
The groin-vaulted nave combines Romanesque and early Gothic elements. The arches are surmounted by a triforium.

Chapelle des Macchabées
This side chapel in the flamboyant Gothic style was added in the early 15th century. With later frescoes and stained glass, it is a contrast to the austere nave.

STAR FEATURES

★ Capitals

★ Stalls

Main entrance

VISITORS' CHECKLIST

Cour St-Pierre 6–8. **Archaeological site** ☐ *10am–5pm daily.* **www**.site-archeologique.ch **Church** ☐ *10am–5:30pm Mon– Sat, noon–5:30pm Sun.* 🅿️

Stained glass of St Andrew
The stained-glass windows in the presbytery are copies of the original 15th-century windows. These are on display in Geneva's Musée d'Art et d'Histoire.

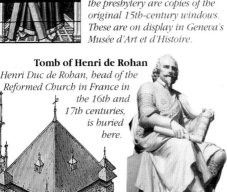

Tomb of Henri de Rohan
Henri Duc de Rohan, head of the Reformed Church in France in the 16th and 17th centuries, is buried here.

★ Capitals
Masterpieces of Romanesque and Gothic stonework, these capitals are among the few decorative features to have survived the Reformation.

★ Stalls
The stalls, with intricately carved back panels and canopy, originally stood near the choir.

Place du Bourg-de-Four, filled with café tables

Place du Bourg-de-Four ❺

Probably overlying Geneva's Roman forum, the Place du Bourg-de-Four was the city's market place in the Middle Ages. Today, graced by an 18th-century fountain and lined with 16th-century houses, art galleries and antique shops, and with busy cafés and restaurants, the square is still the hub of Geneva's Old Town.

The imposing **Palais de Justice** on the southeastern side of the square was built in 1707–12 and has been used as the city's law courts since 1860. Nearby, on Rue de l'Hôtel-de-Ville on the southwestern side of the square, stands the **Hôtel de Ville**, with a Renaissance façade. Built in the 15th century with additions in the 16th, 17th and 18th centuries, it was originally the city hall and now serves as the seat of the cantonal authorities. The ramp in the courtyard allowed cannons to be pulled up into the building and enabled dignitaries to ride their horses to the upper floors. The Tour Baudet, a tower dating from 1455 and the oldest part of the city hall, once housed the cantonal archives. On the ground floor of the Hôtel de Ville is the Alabama Room, where the Geneva Convention was signed in 1864 and where the International Red Cross was recognized as a humanitarian organization. It was also here that the League of Nations assembled for the first time, in 1920.

Opposite the Hôtel de Ville stands the **Ancien Arsenal**, a granary that became a weapons store in the 18th century.

Sculpture of a human head on the façade of Maison Tavel

Musée Barbier-Mueller ❻

Rue Jean-Calvin 10. **Tel** 022 312 02 70. ⬤ 11am–5pm daily. 📷 **www**.barbier-mueller.ch

Almost hidden away in a back street near the Cathédrale St-Pierre is this art museum with stunning works from tribal and classical antiquity. It was founded in 1977 to preserve a collection begun in 1907 by Josef Mueller and continued by his daughter Monique and her husband Jean Paul Barbier-Mueller. The beautifully displayed collection includes masks, sculptures and other artifacts from Africa, Asia and Oceania, as well as items from Greece, Italy and other parts of the ancient world.

Maison Tavel ❼

6 Rue du Puits-St-Pierre. **Musée du Vieux Genève Tel** 022 418 37 00. ⬤ 10am–6pm Tue–Sun.

This fine limestone building is the oldest house in Geneva. The Gothic façade, with three tiers of windows and a turret at one corner, is decorated with the arms of the Tavel family, who built the house, and with curious stone sculptures of animal and human heads. Although it was rebuilt after the fire of 1334 that destroyed a large part of Geneva, the earliest record of the house goes back to 1303.

The Maison Tavel now houses the **Musée du Vieux Genève**, a museum devoted to daily life in Geneva from the 14th to the 19th centuries. While the basement is reserved for temporary exhibitions, the rest of the house is filled with exhibits ranging from coins and ironwork to tiles, wooden doors and other elements of ancient houses. Twelve rooms on the second floor illustrate urban life in the 17th century. In the attic is a huge model of Geneva, made in 1850, before the city's medieval fortifications were demolished. A son-et-lumière presentation highlights points of interest on the model.

A separate section is devoted to Général Dufour (1787–1875), the son of a Genevese clockmaker who created a 1:100,000 scale topographic map of Switzerland. As commander of the Federal forces during the civil war of 1847 he managed to defeat the separatists. He was also a founder of the International Red Cross.

Equestrian statue of **Général Dufour**

Parc des Bastions ❽

Created in the 18th century, the Parc des Bastions was laid out just outside the ramparts on the south side of the city. A vast and slightly forbidding monument looms up on the eastern edge of the park. This is the **Mur de la Réformation** (or Reformation Wall), erected in 1909 to mark the 400th anniversary of the birth of Jean Calvin and the 350th anniversary of the foundation of Geneva's Academy, a famous Protestant school. The monument takes the form of a wall 100 m (330 ft) long on which stand 5-m (16-ft) statues of the four leaders of the Reformation in Geneva: Guillaume Farel; Jean Calvin; Théodore de Bèze, first rector of the Academy; and John Knox. On the pavement in front of the monument are shown the arms of Geneva between the Bear of Bern and the Lion of Scotland, symbolizing the religious alliance between these Swiss cities and Scotland. The monument is flanked by memorials to Martin Luther and Ulrich Zwingli, two other leaders of the Reformation.

Musée d'Art et d'Histoire ❾

See pp102–03.

Cathédrale Orthodoxe Russe ❿

Rue Lefort. **Tel** 022 346 47 09. ⬤ 9am–noon Tue–Fri, 9am–noon & 2–8pm Sat.

Set on a hilltop in the smart residential district of Les Tranchées, the Russian Orthodox church is visible from afar, its gilt onion domes glittering in the sun.

In the 19th century, Geneva was a popular place of residence and recreation for wealthy Russians. Among

Four leaders of the Reformation, on a monument in the Parc des Bastions

The Cathédrale Orthodoxe Russe, with distinctive gilt onion domes

them was Grand Duchess Anna Feodorovna, who funded the construction of a Russian church. Completed in 1869, it is built on the plan of a Greek cross. The interior is richly decorated in the Byzantine style, with a marble iconostasis and a gilt wooden doorway.

International Red Cross and Red Crescent Museum ⓫

17 Avenue de la Paix.
Tel 022 748 95 25. **www**.micr.org
⬜ 10am–5pm Wed–Mon. ♿

Moving and harrowing yet inspiring hope, this museum within the head-quarters of the International Committee of the Red Cross is devoted to documenting human kindness and compassion, as well as the cruelty and suffering that the Red Cross has sought to alleviate since its foundation in 1863. The building itself takes the form of a glass and concrete bunker designed in such a way that natural light illuminates the rooms. At the entrance is a group of stone figures, blind-folded and with their hands tied, symbolizing the violation of human rights.

The museum initiates visitors into contemporary humanitarian action with an exhibition organized around three zones designed by

internationally renowned architects from different cultural backgrounds: *Defending Human Dignity* (Gringo Cardia, Brazil), *Reconstructing the Family Link* (Diébédo Francis Kéré, Burkina Faso) and *Refusing Fatality* (Shigeru Ban, Japan). Within each zone, visitors firstly come to an inter-active phase where they "live through" an intense emotional experience, with the aim of raising aware-ness of an issue. Historical and background information is then provided. The "On the Spot" area shows the latest news from the field on an interactive globe.

Monument, International Red Cross and Red Crescent Museum

Palais des Nations ⓬

Public entrance: 14 Avenue de la Paix.
Tel 022 917 48 96. **www**.unog.ch
⬜ Apr–June: 10am–noon & 2–4pm daily; Jul–Aug: 10am–4pm daily; Sep–Mar: 10am–noon & 2–4pm Mon–Fri. Identification necessary. 🎫 for guided tour. 🎦

The world's largest conference centre for international peace and security, the Palais des Nations is the focal point of Geneva's international area. It was built in 1929–36 as the headquarters of the League of Nations, founded in 1920 to preserve world peace in the aftermath of World War I. In

1946, when the League of Nations was dissolved, the complex became the Euro-pean headquarters of the United Nations Organization (Organisation des Nations Unies, or ONU, in French). Some 3,000 people from all over the world work here, and the whole building is international territory. Parts of it are open to the public, with guided tours available in 15 languages. Winding through long corridors, the tours take in the **Salle du Conseil** (Council Chamber), whose walls and ceiling are decorated with allegorical paintings by the Catalan artist José Maria Sert depicting technical, social and medical advances and a vision of a future free of conflict. Visitors will also step into the **Salles des Assemblées** (Assembly Hall). With seating for 2,000, it is the largest of the UNO's 30-odd conference rooms.

The **Parc des Nations**, which surrounds the UNO, is planted with trees and decorated with sculptures, including a bronze armillary sphere donated by the United States, and a tall, tapering monument that rears up into the sky. Clad in high heat-resistant titanium, it is a tribute to the conquest of space and was donated by the former USSR (*see illustration on p94*).

Bronze armillary sphere in the Parc des Nations

Musée d'Art et d'Histoire **⑨**

The huge collection of paintings, sculpture and artefacts on display at Geneva's museum of art and history covers a timespan ranging from prehistory to the mid-20th century. While the large archaeological section contains pieces from Mesopotamia, Egypt, Greece, Rome and other ancient cultures, the displays of applied arts feature pottery, furniture, stained glass and other fine objects, as well as reconstructions of period interiors. The painting and sculpture galleries contain works ranging from the Impressionist to the Surrealist periods and beyond. Swiss artists, including those of the Geneva school, are well represented.

★ Miraculous Draught of Fishes
This painting is part of the altarpiece that Konrad Witz made for the Cathédrale St-Pierre (see pp98–9) in 1444. In the background is a view of Geneva.

Hodler's Furniture
Side chairs, armchairs, a table and a bookcase come from the set of oak furniture that Josef Hoffman, of the Vienna Workshops, designed for the 19th-century Swiss painter Ferdinand Hodler (see p54).

Ground floor

★ Statuette of Nemtynakht
This serene sculpture in hard yellow quartzite depicts a dignitary of the Middle Kingdom, dating from c.1750 BC.

Main entrance

Greek Vase
Decorated by the Master of Bari, this beautiful vase from Taranto dates from c.350 BC. It is a fine example of Greek red-figure vase-painting.

Lower ground floor

First floor

Le Quai des Pâquis à Genève

The French painter Camille Corot was a regular visitor to Geneva. He completed this view of the lake in 1863.

Ferme à Monfoucault

Rural scenes such as this one, painted in 1874, were frequently chosen as subjects by the French Impressionist painter Camille Pissarro (1830–1903).

Mezzanine

GALLERY GUIDE

The lower ground floor contains the museum's collection of antiquities. The ground floor is devoted to prehistory and the applied arts, while the mezzanine contains reconstructions of palatial rooms. The first floor contains the museum's galleries of painting and sculpture.

Le Bain Turc

Félix Vallotton (1865–1925), a Swiss artist who worked in Paris, pays homage in this 1907 painting to Neo-Classical painter Jean-Auguste-Dominique Ingres' masterpiece The Turkish Bath.

KEY

▦	Antiquities
▢	Applied arts
▢	Prehistory
▦	Reconstructed palace rooms
▢	Painting and sculpture gallery
▦	Temporary exhibitions

STAR EXHIBITS

- ★ Castle Drawing Room

- ★ Miraculous Draught of Fishes

- ★ Statuette of Nemtynakht

★ Castle Drawing Room

The drawing room of the Cartigny Castle in Geneva is reconstructed here. Dating from about 1805, it was designed and furnished in the Neo-Classical style.

ENTERTAINMENT IN GENEVA

Geneva enjoys a lively and wide-ranging cultural life. Sharing the Orchestre de la Suisse Romande with Lausanne, the city is a leading centre of classical music, and a world-class programme of concerts is staged here throughout the year. Opera and ballet, performed at several venues in the city centre, occupy an equally important place in Geneva's cultural calendar. Geneva also has an English-speaking theatre company and a renowned amateur operatic society. Film is another aspect of the city's culture, and on summer evenings open-air showings take place around the lake.

The Fêtes de Genève is the city's most popular festival. It takes place from late July to early August, when the lake-shore comes alive with concerts, colourful parades and spectacular firework displays. Other international events include the annual regatta on Lake Geneva.

Yachts at a regatta on Lake Geneva

INFORMATION/TICKETS

Geneva's daily newspaper *Le Temps* carries listings of all major entertainments in the city. Other sources of information are *Genève Agenda* and *Genève: Le Guide*, both published in French and English, and both available at the city's tourist office.

Tickets for most mainstream events can be purchased from the agencies **Ticket Corner** or **FNAC**. Tickets for plays and operas performed in English are obtainable from the **Theatre in English**. The larger department stores and supermarkets *(see p107)* such as Manor, Migros, Globus and Centre Balexert also sell tickets for most of the mainstream events taking place in the city.

CLASSICAL MUSIC, THEATRE AND DANCE

Geneva is one of Europe's leading centres of classical music. The prestigious Orchestre de la Suisse Romande, which is based in Geneva and Lausanne, gives regular concerts in the **Victoria Hall**. Another major venue for classical music is the **Grand-Théâtre de Genève**, where opera productions are staged, and where solo recitals and chamber concerts are given. The **Geneva Amateur Operatic Society** offers a programme of entertainments in English. These range from light opera and musicals to cabaret and pantomime.

Opera, jazz and classical music, as well as modern dance, are also staged at the **Bâtiment des Forces-Motrices**, a former power station on the Rhône. Free concerts take place in several of Geneva's churches throughout the year, as well as in the city's parks during the summer months.

The theatrical scene in Geneva ranges from the classic to the avant-garde. While the **Comédie de Genève** concentrates on classical productions, the **Théâtre du Grütli** specializes in experimental theatre, producing contemporary Swiss drama as well as foreign plays. Modern drama is also staged at the **Théâtre de Carouge**.

The **Théâtre des Marionettes de Genève** is a dynamic puppet theatre that puts on magical shows aimed at audiences ranging from young children to adults.

Fireworks around the lake at the Fêtes de Genève

Geneva also has a children's theatre, the **Théâtre Am Stram Gram**. Although its productions are in French,

Scene from *Romeo and Juliet* at a theatre in Geneva

English-speaking audiences can enjoy certain plays and other entertainments that are staged here. Most theatrical productions are in French. However, the **Geneva English Drama Society** stages plays in English. Each season features four productions and a series of play readings. The society also organizes workshops and other activities.

The **Fêtes de Genève**, which is held from late July to the beginning of August, is the city's principal and most popular festival. The festival's programme of indoor and outdoor events includes concerts of classical, techno and rock music, theatrical

performances and children's shows, as well as street parades. There are firework displays on the lakeshore too.

NIGHTCLUBS

Geneva's nightclub scene encompasses more than 40 cabaret venues, bars, discos and clubs. Between them they offer the full range of musical styles, from 1960s music at **La Coupole Avenue** to house and techno music at other venues. The **Organic Club**, where the entertainment includes male go-go dancing, is Geneva's most fashionable gay nightclub.

While many nightclubs are closed on Mondays, at weekends they stay open into the early hours of the morning, or until the last guest leaves.

CINEMA

As well as many small cinemas both in the city centre and in outlying districts, Geneva has a large central cinema complex, the **Pathé Balexert**. Some screenings are dubbed, but most films are shown in their original language, with French and German subtitles. In newspaper listings this is indicated by the letters *vo* (for *version originale*). French films are usually shown with English, and sometimes also with German, subtitles.

A particular pleasure for visitors to Geneva in summer are the open-air film screenings on the lakeshore. Taking place from late June to mid-August, the series is organized by **Cinélac**, and a different film is shown each night throughout the season.

Techno parade through the streets of Geneva at the Fêtes de Genève

DIRECTORY

INFORMATION/ TICKETS	MUSIC, THEATRE AND DANCE		

INFORMATION/ TICKETS

Office du Tourisme
18 Rue du Mont-Blanc.
Tel 022 909 70 00.
www.genevatourism.ch

Ticket Corner
Tel 0900 800 800.

FNAC
16 Rue de Rive.
Tel 022 816 12 30.

Theatre in English
22 Chemin des Batailles, 1214 Vernier.
Tel 022 341 5190/5192.

MUSIC, THEATRE AND DANCE

Victoria Hall
14 Rue du Général-Dufour.
Tel 022 418 35 00.

Grand-Théâtre de Genève
5 Place Neuve.
Tel 022 418 30 00.

Geneva Amateur Operatic Society
www.gaos.ch

Bâtiment des Forces-Motrices
2 Place des Volontaires.
Tel 022 322 12 20.

Comédie de Genève
6 Blvd des Philosophes.
Tel 022 320 50 01.

Théâtre du Grütli
16 Rue du Général-Dufour.
Tel 022 888 44 88.

Théâtre de Carouge
39 Rue Ancienne, Carouge.
Tel 022 343 43 43.

Théâtre des Marionnettes
3 Rue Rodo.
Tel 022 807 31 00.

Théâtre Am Stram Gram
56 Route de Frontenex.
Tel 022 735 7924.

Geneva English Drama Society
www.geds.ch

Fêtes de Genève
Tel 022 909 70 00.

NIGHTCLUBS

La Coupole Avenue
116 Rue du Rhône.
Tel 022 737 40 40.

Organic Club
4 bis Rue de la Rotisserie
Tel 022 310 14 28.

CINEMA

Pathé Balexert
27 Avenue Louis-Casaï.
Tel 090 130 20 10.

Cinélac
Port Noir.
www.cine.ch

SHOPPING IN GENEVA

Geneva has been described as a shopper's paradise. Catering for a wealthy clientele, the city's smartest shops glitter with trays of diamond-studded watches and opulent jewellery, and attract attention with seductive displays of clothes by international designers. A leading centre of the art market, the city also has many art galleries and antique shops.

Box of Swiss praline chocolates

Away from the city's smartest streets, however, are shops that offer more affordable goods, from watches at more modest prices to high-quality craft items and a variety of handmade souvenirs. Swiss specialities such as chocolate, cheese and the locally produced wines are also available. Beyond the city centre are colourful street markets selling everything from books to collectables.

Colourful display of painted cow bells in a souvenir shop in Geneva

OPENING HOURS

Most shops in Geneva are open from 8am to 6:30pm Monday to Friday, and from 8am to 4pm or 5pm on Saturday. Late opening for shops in the city centre is until 8pm on Thursdays. The only shops open on Sunday are those selling souvenirs, and supermarkets and general stores at petrol stations, at the airport and the train station.

DEPARTMENT STORES

The **Migros**, Coop, **Globus** and **Manor** supermarket chains and department stores all have large branches in Geneva. **Bon Génie** specializes in designer clothing and high-class cosmetics. One of the city's largest shopping centres is Balexert. Another large shopping centre is La Praille, near the football stadium.

MARKETS

Geneva's largest outdoor markets are held at **Plaine de Plainpalais**, southwest of the Old Town. A fruit and vegetable market takes place here on Tuesday and Friday mornings, and there are interesting flea markets all day Wednesday and Saturday, where you may be able to discover some real finds, such as old watches, furniture ranging from antique to modern, ornaments and clothes from all over the world. Lively markets are also held on Wednesday and Saturday mornings in Place du Marché, near Carouge, and in Boulevard Helvétique, in the city centre. A crafts and local produce market is held every Thursday in **Place de la Fusterie**.

WATCHES AND JEWELLERY

With its Geneva branch on Place du Molard, the **Gübelin** chain of shops offers a choice of clocks and watches by leading Swiss makers, and a range of gemstones, jewellery and pens. **Bucherer** and **Cartier**, both on Rue du Rhône, one of Geneva's smartest shopping streets, are two other upmarket watch and jewellery shops selling renowned brands.

SOUVENIRS

Geneva abounds in shops selling high-quality goods associated with Switzerland, from pen-knives and cuckoo clocks to fine linen, leather goods and a wealth of high-quality craft items, as well as a more affordable range of watches and jewellery. **Swiss Corner**, **Cadhor** and **Molard Souvenirs** are three of the best.

Swiss watch

Bookstore and antique shop at 20 Grand' Rue, in the Old Town

Logo of Rolex, a leading Swiss watchmaker

ART AND ANTIQUES

The greatest concentration of antique shops and art galleries in Geneva is along Grand' Rue, in the Old Town. While many galleries along this street are filled with expensive Old Master paintings, others specialize in more affordable types of art, such as modern paintings and graphics, and a variety of attractive prints.

The Carouge district, to the south of the Old Town, has many small specialist studios and craft shops where craftsmen can be seen at work.

BOOKS

A good range of books in English is stocked by **OffTheShelf**, on Boulevard Georges-Favon. **Payot**, on Rue Chantepoulet, is well known for stocking the largest selection of English books in French-speaking Switzerland. **Les Recyclables** on Rue de Carouge is a second-hand bookshop with a café.

CONFECTIONERY

The local chocolate manufacturer is Favarger. Its brand products may be bought in factory outlets, as well as in Mercury chain stores and the food halls of department stores. Several traditional manufacturers have their own factory outlets in various parts of the city. There are also many chocolate shops in Geneva's Old Town. Two of the best are the **Chocolaterie du Rhône** and the **Chocolaterie Stettler**, which sells such specialities as *pavés de Genève* (Genevese chocolate squares).

Chocolate rabbit

CHEESE AND WINE

A great variety of Swiss cheeses *(see pp264–5)* can be purchased in many specialist shops all over the city. Among them are **Ursula Antonietti**, on Rue de Cornavin, and **Fromagerie Bruand**, on Boulevard Helvétique. The area around Geneva is a prime wine-growing region *(see pp266–7)*. Bottled wine of an excellent quality can be bought directly from winegrowers in several villages around the city. Many outlets allow customers to sample the wines before they buy.

Colourful flower stall in a street in Geneva

DIRECTORY

DEPARTMENT STORES

Bon Génie
34 Rue du Marché.
Tel 022 818 11 11.

Globus Grand Passage
48 Rue du Rhône.
Tel 058 578 50 50.

Manor
6 Rue Cornavin.
Tel 022 909 46 99.

Migros Plainpalais-Centre
64 Rue de Carouge.
Tel 022 807 09 60.

MARKETS

Plaine de Plainpalais.
(fruit, vegetables, souvenirs)
Tue & Fri, 8am–1pm.

Plaine de Plainpalais.
(flea market)
Wed & Sat 8am–6pm.
Place de la Fusterie.
(handicrafts) Thu
8am–6:45pm.
Place de la Fusterie.
(books) Apr–Nov:
Fri 8am–6:45pm.

WATCHES AND JEWELLERY

Bucherer
45 Rue du Rhône.
Tel 022 319 62 66.

Cartier
35 Rue du Rhône.
Tel 022 818 54 54.

Gübelin
1 Place du Molard.
Tel 022 365 53 80.

SOUVENIRS

Cadhors
Rue du Mont-Blanc 11.
Tel 022 732 28 25.

Molard Souvenirs
Rue de la Croix d'Or 1.
Tel 022 311 47 40.

Swiss Corner
Rue des Alpes 7.
Tel 022 731 06 84.

BOOKS

OffTheShelf
15 blvd Georges-Favon.
Tel 022 311 10 90.
www.offtheshelf.ch

Payot
5 Rue Chantepoulet.
Tel 022 731 89 50.

Les Recyclables
53 Rue de Carouge.
Tel 022 328 23 73.

CONFECTIONERY

Chocolaterie du Rhône
3 Rue de la Confédération.
Tel 022 311 56 14.

Chocolaterie Stettler
10 Rue de Berne.
Tel 022 732 44 67.

CHEESE

Fromagerie Bruand
29 Boulevard Helvétique.
Tel 022 736 93 50.

Ursula Antonietti
1 Rue de Cornavin.
Tel 022 731 25 05.

WESTERN SWITZERLAND

A predominantly French-speaking region, western Switzerland consists of three distinct geographical areas: the mountainous terrain of the Swiss Jura in the north, the western extremity of the Mittelland plateau in the east, and the Alpine region in the southeast. Western Switzerland's geographical hub is Lake Geneva (Lac Léman), on whose banks lie Geneva, Lausanne, Vevey and Montreux.

Western Switzerland is a region of lakes and rolling hills, great cities and atmospheric medieval towns, and small villages with beautiful ancient churches. It consists of the cantons of Geneva, Vaud, Jura, Fribourg and Neuchâtel. Western Switzerland is bordered by France, but the canton of Geneva is surrounded on three sides by French territory. Western Switzerland is known as Suisse Romande, or Romandie, and it has a strong French-Swiss cultural identity.

While Geneva's high profile in global events and its role as a centre of world banking give it an international character, Lausanne, with its great cathedral and its university, is a centre of culture and intellectual life. Fribourg, straddling the River Sarine, is a bilingual town, French being spoken on the west side of the river and German on the east. The purest French in Suisse Romande is supposed to be spoken in Neuchâtel.

It was in western Switzerland, particularly in the Jura, that the country's world-famous watchmaking industry was born and where it continues to flourish today. The region is also renowned for its wines, most especially from the vineyards that border Lake Geneva. Western Switzerland also has one of the country's most memorable sights, the beautiful Château de Chillon, set serenely beside the sparkling blue waters of Lake Geneva.

The city of Fribourg, dominated by the Gothic tower of the 13th-century Cathédrale St-Nicolas

◁ The medieval Château de Chillon, set on an islet on the eastern shore of Lake Geneva

Exploring Western Switzerland

A region with a diverse landscape, western Switzerland has many atmospheric towns and internationally famous cities. The Jura mountains in the west have much to offer hikers and cross-country skiers, and the southeastern part of the region has many ski resorts. With Lake Geneva as its focal point, the centre of the region is a land of great lakes, with vineyards covering sunny hillsides. The cities of Geneva, Lausanne, Fribourg and Neuchâtel are bustling centres of industry and culture with a wealth of museums and historic buildings. By contrast, the sophisticated towns of Vevey and Montreux, situated on the shores of Lake Geneva, offer relaxation in an unequalled setting.

Escaliers du Marché, leading off Place de la Palud, in Lausanne

GETTING THERE

The main gateways to western Switzerland are Geneva's and Zürich's international airports. From Geneva, the A1 motorway gives access to the whole region. Western Switzerland is also served by a rail network. Trains depart both from Geneva's airport and from the city itself. While the main rail route runs from Geneva north to Neuchâtel and Biel/Bienne, fast trains also run along the shores of Lake Geneva to Fribourg and beyond, both northwards to Bern, and southwards via Lausanne and Montreux to Valais. Most of the rail route is extremely scenic.

Rooftops in Murten/Morat, from the town walls

Les Verrières
10
Fleurier
STE-CROIX 19
L'Auberson
GRANDSON
YVERDON-LES-BAINS
A9
Orbe
VALLORBE 17
9
ROMAINMÔTIER 16
Le Pont
La Sarraz
Lac de Joux
A1
VAUD
Le Brassus
Cossonay
Vallée de Joux
Bière
Lons-le-Saunier
Vufflens-le-Château
LAUSANNE
Jura
2
Rolle
St. Cergue
LAKE GENE
(LAC LÉMA
1
Nyon
A1
Versoix
Meyrin
Genève (Geneva)
GENÈVE
Rhône
St. Julien
Lyon
Annecy

KEY

- Motorway
- Main road
- Minor road
- Scenic route
- Main railway
- Minor railway
- International border
- Canton border
- △ Summit

For additional map symbols *see back flap*

0 km 20

0 miles 20

Belfort

Bonfol

Porrentruy

Mulhouse

Basel

Damvant

JURA

ST-URSANNE 24

25 DELÉMONT

Bassecourt

FRANCHES-MONTAGNES

Saignelégier 23

Le Noirmant

Doubs

Biel

22 LA CHAUX-DE-FONDS

LE LOCLE 20

Bern

NEUCHÂTEL

Peseux

20 NEUCHÂTEL

MURTEN (MORAT) 11

Lac de Neuchâtel

Lac de Morat

Saâne

ESTAVAYER-LE-LAC 14

12 AVENCHES

13 PAYERNE

10 FRIBOURG

La Broye

Lucens

Romont

Slâne

Rossens

Lac de la Gruyère

FRIBOURG

Bulle

Jaun

Sense

9 GRUYÈRES

Gstaad

Château d'Oex

VEVEY 3

4 MONTREUX

5 CHÂTEAU DE CHILLON

LEYSIN 7

Le Sépey

8 LES DIABLERETS

AIGLE 6

Les Diablerets 3210m

Villars-s-Ollon

Bex

Martigny

Grand Muveran 3051m

Gorge near Le Châtelot, in the Jura

SEE ALSO

SIGHTS AT A GLANCE

Fontaine de St Jacques on Planche Supérieure, Fribourg

Lausanne ❶

With an outstandingly beautiful setting on the north shore of Lake Geneva, Lausanne is one of Switzerland's finest cities. It was founded in the 1st century as a Roman lakeshore settlement but for greater safety its inhabitants later moved to higher ground on the hills above the lake. This area is now Lausanne's Old Town (Vieille Ville). It became a bishopric in the late 6th century, and its Fondation Académie was founded in 1537. Lausanne is a centre of the cultural and economic life of French-speaking Switzerland. It is also the seat of the Federal Supreme Court and the location of the International Olympic Committee's headquarters.

Detail of the 18th-century Église St-Laurent

Exploring Lausanne

A city of steep gradients, Lausanne's city centre is set on three hills that rise in tiers from the lakeshore. The hub of the city is Place St-François. To the north is the city's shopping district, centred on Rue du Bourg. Further north lies the Old Town (Vieille Ville), dominated by Lausanne's great cathedral (*see pp114–15*). The district of Bel-Air, to the west, overlooks a valley where the Flon stream once flowed. The Grand-Pont, a bridge across the valley, offers fine views of Bel-Air and of the Old Town, which rises behind it.

🏛 Tour Bel-Air and Salle Métropole

1 Place Bel-Air. **Tel** *021 345 00 29.*
Set on a steep slope, at the foot of the Old Town, the Tour Bel-Air was the first high-rise structure to be built in Switzerland. Standing 50 m (165 ft) high, the Tour Bel-Air

contains offices, residential apartments and the Salle Métropole. Completed in 1931, the building gives Lausanne's townscape a touch of metropolitan verve, while the theatre has become a cultural hub.

🏛 Église St-Laurent

Rue St-Laurent.
Less than a hundred paces from Bel-Air, amid the well-preserved houses of the Old Town, stands the Protestant Église St-Laurent. It was built in 1716–19, on the ruins of a 10th-century church. Its façade, designed by Rodolphe de Crousaz in the second half of the 18th century, is one of the few examples of Neo-Classical architecture in Lausanne.

🏛 Place de la Palud

The south side of this market square is dominated by Lausanne's town hall, a two-storey arcaded building fronted by the arms of the city. Built in the Renaissance style, it dates from the 17th century. On 10 April 1915, the official documents ratifying the establishment of the International Olympic Committee and the archives of the modern Olympic era were signed here.

Place de la Palud is a popular meeting area. A street market takes place here on Wednesdays and Saturdays,

and once a month the square is filled with a crafts fair.

At the centre of the square is the 16th-century Fontaine de la Justice, with an allegorical figure of Justice. The covered wooden stairs beyond the fountain are known as the Escaliers du Marché. They lead up to Rue Viret, from where further steps lead up to the cathedral.

The bare Gothic interior of the Église St-François

🏛 Place St-François

At the centre of this square stands the Église St-François, built in the 13th and 14th centuries as the church of the Franciscan monastery. The monastery was dissolved during the Reformation and the church stripped of its decoration. Although the façade was restored in the 1990s, the interior is disappointingly bland. The streets leading off Place St-François are among the city's smartest. Rue du Bourg, which is lined with old houses, contains upmarket jewellers' shops and boutiques, as well as bars and jazz clubs.

🏛 Musée Historique

4 Place de la Cathédrale. **Tel** *021 315 41 01.* ◯ *11am–6pm Tue–Thu, 11am–5pm Fri–Sun (Jul & Aug: also 11am–6pm Mon).* 📷
Lausanne's museum of history fills the restored rooms of the former bishop's palace, which dates from the

Figure on the Fountain of Justice

11th century. The museum's collections constitute a detailed account of the city's history from prehistory to the present day. A particularly interesting exhibit is the model of Lausanne as it was in 1638.

🛈 Lausanne Cathedral

See pp114–15.

🏛 Palais de Rumine

6 Place de la Riponne.
Musée cantonal des Beaux-Arts Tel *021 316 34 45.* ⬜ *11am–6pm Tue & Wed, 11am–8pm Thu, 11am–5pm Fri–Sun.* 🈲
Musée cantonal d'Archéologie et d'Histoire Tel *021 316 34 30.* ⬜ *11am–6pm Tue–Thu, 11am–5pm Fri–Sun.* 🈲

Wall decoration, Palais de Rumine

The imposing Neo-Renaissance Palais de Rumine, built in 1896–1906, housed Lausanne's university until the latter moved to new premises on the outskirts of the city. The building now contains the university library and five museums.

The Musée cantonal des Beaux-Arts, on the ground floor, has a fine collection of Swiss paintings from the 18th to the 20th centuries. Of

particular interest here are 19th-century landscapes of the Vaud countryside and works by François Bocion and Giovanni Giacometti, father of the more famous Alberto Giacometti.

The museum of archaeology and history, on the sixth floor, is devoted to finds made during local excavations. The exhibits range from the Bronze Age to the medieval period, and one of the finest is the gold bust of Marcus Aurelius *(see illustration on p35)*, discovered at Avenches in 1939.

The other three museums are devoted to geology, numismatics and zoology.

⚓ Château St-Maire

Place du Château. ⬤ *Closed to visitors.*
This massive brick and sandstone edifice was built in 1397–1427 as the palace of the bishops of Lausanne, who ruled the city. When they were overthrown, the chateau became the residence of new overlords, the bailiffs of Bern. The fight for the

independence of Lausanne and canton of Vaud was led by Jean Davel, who was beheaded in 1723 on the orders of the Bernese authorities. A monument to his memory stands in front of the chateau. The building is now the seat of the cantonal authorities of Vaud.

Château St-Maire, fronted by a statue of Jean Davel

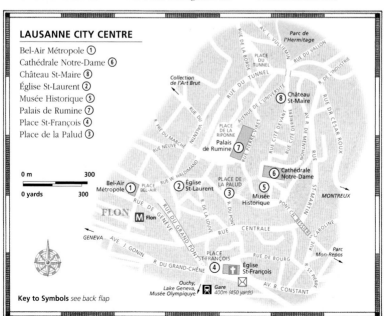

LAUSANNE CITY CENTRE

0 m 300
0 yards 300

Key to Symbols *see back flap*

Cathédrale Notre-Dame

Begun in the mid-12th century and completed in the 13th, the Cathédrale Notre-Dame in Lausanne is the finest Gothic building in Switzerland. It is built on the site of a Roman camp and overlies the foundations of Carolingian and Romanesque basilicas. With a central nave flanked by aisles, a transept over which rises a tower, an apse and an ambulatory, the cathedral's design and decoration show the influence of the French Gothic style. Consecrated by Pope Gregory X in 1275, Notre-Dame has been a Protestant cathedral since the Reformation. The top of the southwest tower commands a spectacular view of the city and Lake Geneva.

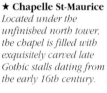

Nave
Alternating thick and slender columns line the nave. The thick columns support the central vaulting.

Stalls
Decorated with expressive figures of saints, the stalls in the Chapelle St-Maurice are masterpieces of late Gothic woodcarving.

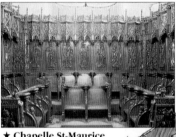

North tower, containing the Chapelle St-Maurice

★ Chapelle St-Maurice
Located under the unfinished north tower, the chapel is filled with exquisitely carved late Gothic stalls dating from the early 16th century.

Montfalcon Portal
The entrance at the west end, known as the Montfalcon Portal, is decorated with replicas of Gothic carvings dating from 1515–36.

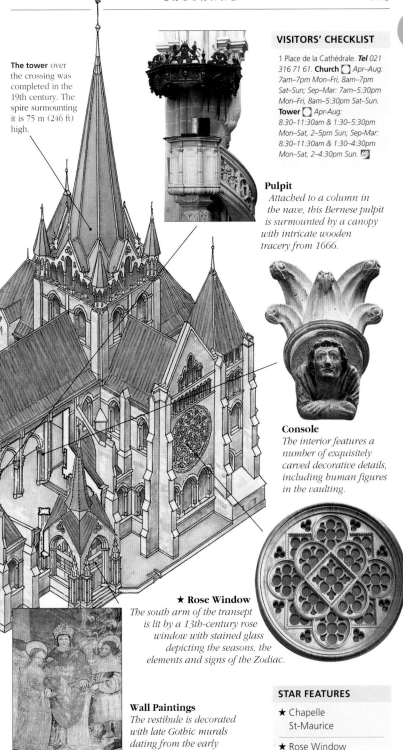

The tower over the crossing was completed in the 19th century. The spire surmounting it is 75 m (246 ft) high.

VISITORS' CHECKLIST

1 Place de la Cathédrale. *Tel* 021 316 71 61. **Church** ◯ Apr–Aug: 7am–7pm Mon–Fri, 8am–7pm Sat–Sun; Sep–Mar: 7am–5:30pm Mon–Fri, 8am–5:30pm Sat–Sun. **Tower** ◯ Apr–Aug: 8:30–11:30am & 1:30–5:30pm Mon–Sat, 2–5pm Sun; Sep–Mar: 8:30–11:30am & 1:30–4:30pm Mon–Sat, 2–4:30pm Sun. 📷

Pulpit
Attached to a column in the nave, this Bernese pulpit is surmounted by a canopy with intricate wooden tracery from 1666.

Console
The interior features a number of exquisitely carved decorative details, including human figures in the vaulting.

★ Rose Window
The south arm of the transept is lit by a 13th-century rose window with stained glass depicting the seasons, the elements and signs of the Zodiac.

Wall Paintings
The vestibule is decorated with late Gothic murals dating from the early 16th century.

STAR FEATURES

★ Chapelle St-Maurice

★ Rose Window

Beyond the city centre

West of Place St-François is the offbeat district of Flon, which is filled with art galleries, restaurants and bars. North of the Old Town stretches the extensive Parc de l'Hermitage. To the south of the city centre lies the old fishing village of Ouchy, now a popular lakeside resort and the location of the Musée Olympique.

🏛 Collection de l'Art Brut

11 Avenue des Bergières. *Tel 021 315 25 70.* 🚌 *2 from Place St-François.* ○ *Jul–Aug: 11am–6pm daily; Sep–Jun: 11am–6pm Tue–Sun.* 🗓 *(free adm 1st Sat of the month).* www.artbrut.ch

Art Brut is the name that the French painter Jean Dubuffet (1901–85) gave to art created by people living on the fringe of society, including criminals, psychotics, patients at psychiatric hospitals or other institutions, and spiritualist mediums, who had no artistic training. The ideas for art came from their own imaginations, free from established cultural influences and the history of a fine arts tradition. The originality, freshness and often indecency of Art Brut inspired Dubuffet in his search for creative expression, and in 1945 he began to amass a private collection. In 1971 he presented it to the city of Lausanne, and the Collection de l'Art Brut opened in 1976.

Only about 1,000 pieces from the present holding of about 30,000 are on display at any one time. The exhibits are laid out on four floors in converted stables at the 18th-century Château de Beaulieu, northwest of the city centre.

Ranging from paintings, drawings and painted fabrics to wood carvings, sculptures and even an illustrated novel, these extraordinary works of art have a striking force and spontaneity. Alongside each exhibit is a short biography of the artist, giving the visitor some insight into the mental attitude and personal circumstances in which these works were created.

🏛 Fondation de l'Hermitage

2 Route du Signal. *Tel 021 320 50 01.* 🚌 *3 from the main train station or* 🚌 *16 from Place St-François.* ○ *10am–6pm Tue–Sun, 10am–9pm Thu.* 🗓 www.fondation-hermitage.ch

The imposing Neo-Gothic villa set in magnificent parkland north of Lausanne was built in 1842–50 by Charles-Juste Bugnion, a wealthy banker, and donated to the city by his descendants. Now known as the Fondation de l'Hermitage, it is a gallery with a permanent collection of nearly 800 French paintings. Of particular note are the Impressionist and Post-Impressionist paintings, as well as the works of 20th-century Vaudois artists. The Fondation also stages two or three large-scale temporary exhibitions every year of the work of world-class artists.

The Parc de l'Hermitage, the extensive grounds in which the villa is set, is landscaped with exotic trees.

At its northern extremity is the Signal de Sauvabelin, a hill which rises to a height of 647 m (2,120 ft) and offers views of Lausanne and Lake Geneva, with the Alps in the background. Beyond the hill are woods and the Lac de Sauvabelin, where there is a reserve for ibexes and other alpine animals.

❧ Parc Mon-Repos

Avenue Mon-Repos.

This landscaped park, laid out in the 19th century to the southeast of the city centre, is the most elegant of all Lausanne's gardens.

It contains a Neo-Gothic tower, a Neo-Classical temple, a conservatory and a rockery with a cave and a waterfall. At the centre of the park stands an 18th-century villa, which at the time that it was built was surrounded by vineyards. The 18th-century French writer Voltaire lived in the villa during his stay in Lausanne.

Statue in Parc Mon-Repos

The villa also has associations with the Olympic Games. The Olympic spirit was resurrected by the French aristocrat Baron Pierre de Coubertin (1863–1937), who believed that sport plays an essential role in the development of citizens and nations. De Coubertin set up the International Olympic Committee (IOC) in Paris in 1894, with himself as president, and two years later the first modern Olympic Games were held in Athens. During World War I De Coubertin moved the IOC's head office to Switzerland. From 1922 until his death, the villa at Mon Repos was his residence and until the 1970s it was also the headquarters of the IOC, and the location of the first Olympics museum to be set up.

At the north end of Parc Mon-Repos stands the building of the Federal Tribunal, Switzerland's supreme court.

Le Cinema (c.1950) by Collectif d'enfants at the Collection de l'Art Brut

For hotels and restaurants in this region see pp249–51 and pp273–6

Hôtel du Château d'Ouchy, one of many lakeside hotels in Ouchy, on the outskirts of Lausanne

Ouchy

On Lake Geneva, 2 km (1 mile) south of central Lausanne, accessible by metro (M2 line).

Once a fishing village, Ouchy, on the outskirts of Lausanne, is now a popular lakeside resort. It has a beautiful setting on Lake Geneva, with views of the surrounding mountains, and a tree-lined promenade along the lakeshore. Cruises on the lake depart from here.

All that remains of the 12th-century castle that once defended the harbour is a tower, which now forms part of the Neo-Gothic Château d'Ouchy, built in the 1890s. The chateau is now a hotel and restaurant.

Several other late 19th- to early 20th-century hotels line the lakeshore. They include the Beau-Rivage Palace, a fine example of Art Nouveau architecture, and the Hôtel d'Angleterre, the house where Lord Byron stayed when he came to Lausanne and where he wrote *The Prisoner of Chillon (see pp122–3)*.

🏛 Olympic Museum
1 Quai d'Ouchy. **Tel** 021 621 65 11. ☐ Apr–Oct: 9am–6pm daily; Nov–Mar: 9am–6pm Tue–Sun (due to re-open late 2013 following renovation). 🖼 **www**.olympic.org/museum
The Olympic Museum illustrates the history of the Olympic movement, from the athletes of Ancient Greece to the modern Olympic Games. It is Switzerland's best-known museum, drawing over 200,000 visitors a year. Multimedia presentations, archive film footage, interactive equipment, photographs and postage stamps show the development of individual sport disciplines and the achievements of Olympic champions, many of whom have donated their medals to the museum.

The museum is set in parkland planted with Mediterranean trees and shrubs. The

Figures of cyclists in the Olympic Park

upper floor has a restaurant with a large terrace offering fine views of Lake Geneva and the surrounding mountains.

🏛 Musée Romain
24 Chemin du-Bois-de-Vaux. **Tel** 021 315 41 85. ☐ 11am–6pm Tue–Sun (Jul–Aug: 11am–6pm daily). 🖼 🖼 **www**.lausanne.ch/mrv
About ten minutes' walk west of Ouchy are the remains of Lousonna and Vidy, two Roman towns that flourished from 15 BC to the 4th century AD. The ruins have been excavated, and the finds that were uncovered are on display in the Musée Romain nearby.

The objects are laid out in the reconstruction of a Roman house. They include glassware and pottery, jewellery, coins and votive figures and some fine examples of classic Roman mosaics.

Entrance to the Olympic Museum in the Olympic Park

Lake Geneva (Lac Léman) ❷

Lying in an arc bordered by the Jura mountains to the west, the French Alps to the south, and the Mittelland to the northeast, Lake Geneva, known as Lac Léman in French, is the largest lake in the Alps. While most of the southern shore is French territory, the greater part of the lake lies within Switzerland. Its shores are dotted with towns and villages, many of which are the departure points of boat trips on the lake. An important stop on the Grand Tour of Europe in the 19th century, Lake Geneva attracted and inspired many Romantic writers. With the mountains reflected in its still blue waters, it is one of Switzerland's most spellbinding sights.

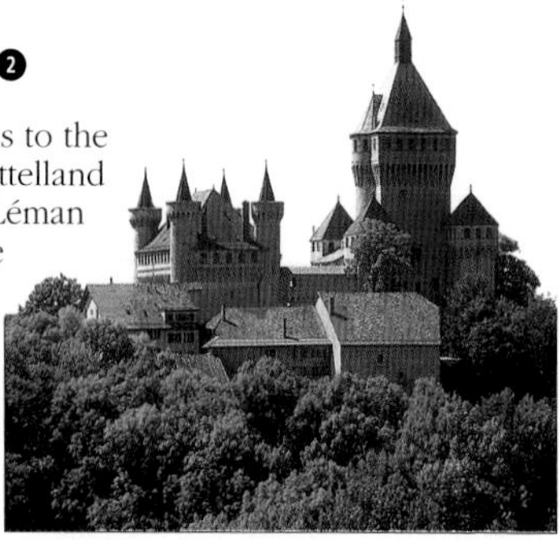

★ Vufflens-le-Château
Built in the 15th century in the North Italian style, the castle here is one of Switzerland's most magnificent Gothic fortresses. It has a turreted keep, a central courtyard and living quarters within its towers.

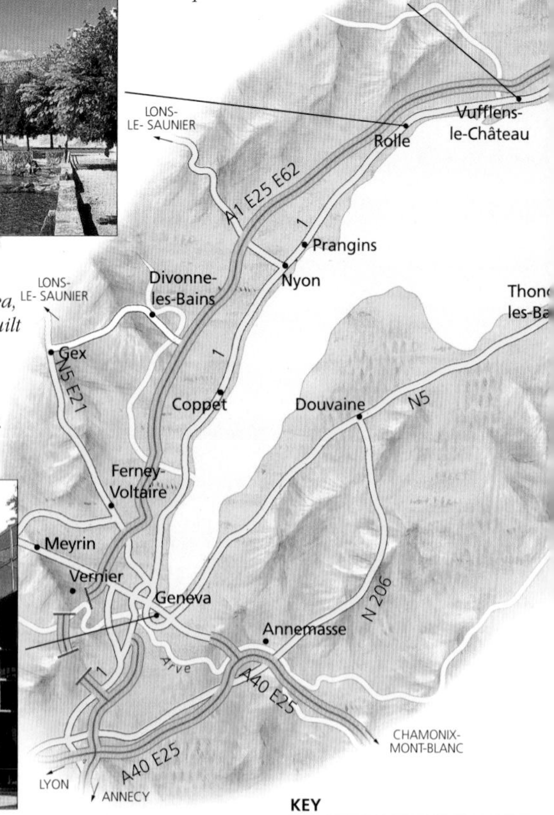

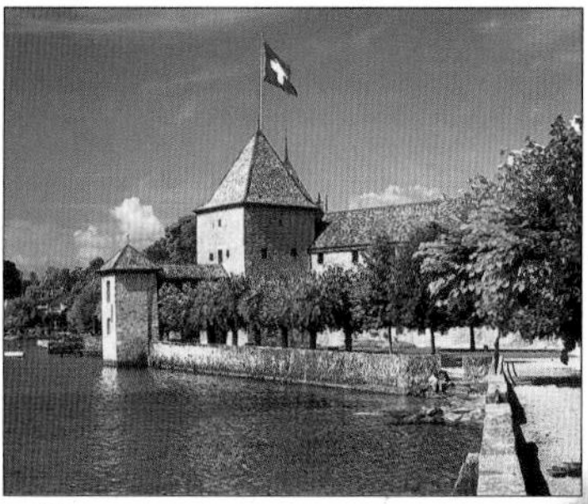

Rolle
A village at the heart of the La Côte wine-producing area, Rolle has a moated castle built by the Duke of Savoy in the 13th century. The castle is built to a triangular plan, with a tower at each corner.

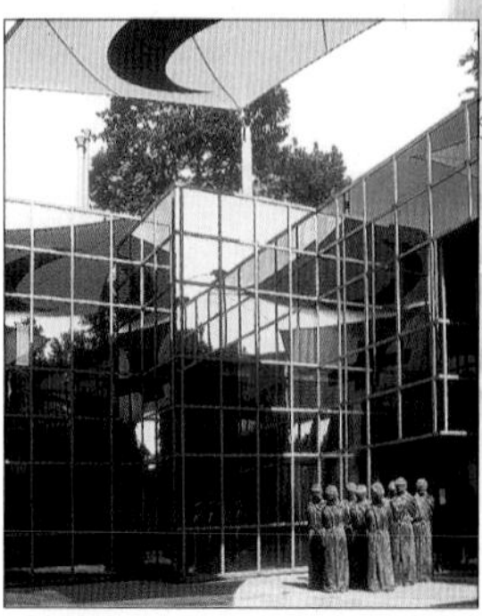

Geneva
This is the largest city on the lakeshore. The headquarters of more than 200 international organizations, Geneva has a prominent place on the world stage.

STAR SIGHTS

★ Vevey

★ Vufflens-le-Château

KEY

- Motorway
- Major road
- Minor road
- River
- Viewpoint

For hotels and restaurants in this region see pp249–51 and pp273–6

Cully

One of many scenic villages around Lake Geneva, Cully is a centre of the local wine trade. The sun-drenched hillsides above it are covered with vineyards.

VISITORS' CHECKLIST

Road map A4, B4. 🚗 🚌 ⛴
🛈 Lausanne, 60 Avenue d'Ouchy; 021 613 26 26.
www.lake-geneva-region.ch
Boat Trips: Compagnie Générale de Navigation; 0848 811 848

St-Saphorin

This romantic winemaking village has steep cobbled streets and a 7th-century church that was remodelled in the 16th century, in the flamboyant Gothic style.

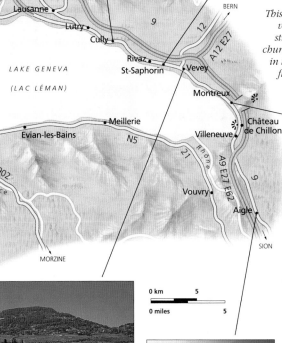

YVERDON-LES-BAINS

PAYERNE

A1 E23

A9 E62

Lausanne

Lutry

Cully

BERN

9

12

A12 E27

Rivaz

St-Saphorin

Vevey

LAKE GENEVA

(LAC LÉMAN)

Montreux

Meillerie

Château de Chillon

Evian-les-Bains

N5

Villeneuve

Rhône

21

A9 E27 E62

9

D 902

ance

Vouvry

Aigle

SION

MORZINE

0 km   5

0 miles   5

Montreux

Stretching along the lakeshore, Montreux is a cosmopolitan resort. Renowned for its music festivals, it is also an important cultural centre.

★ Vevey

This stately and traditional resort offers a choice of cultural events. It is renowned for the Fête des Vignerons, a grape-harvest festival held here every 25 years.

Aigle

At the intersection of the Ormonts and Rhône valleys, Aigle is the capital of the Chablais winemaking region. Its 12th-century castle, which contains the Musée de la Vigne et du Vin, is surrounded by vineyards.

The lakeside resort of Vevey, with mountains in the background

Vevey ❸

Road map B4. 🏔 *16,000.* 🚉 🚌
🛈 *Montreux, 5 Rue du Théâtre;*
0848 86 84 84.
www.montreux-vevey.com
🎭 *Street Artists Festival (Aug).*

With Montreux, Vevey is
one of the two best-
known holiday resorts of the
Swiss Riviera, the stretch of
land bordering the north-
western shores of Lake
Geneva between Lausanne
and Villeneuve. The region
began to develop as a centre
of tourism in the 19th
century. Known for its
sophisticated ambience,
Vevey soon attracted an
international clientele, which
included the Austrian painter
and playwright Oskar
Kokoschka, the writer
Ernest Hemingway and the
comedian Charlie Chaplin,
who spent the last 25 years
of his life in Vevey and who
was buried here in 1977.

Known in Roman times as
Viviscus, Vevey was once
Lake Geneva's main port. It
continued to flourish through
the Middle Ages and by the
19th century was the first
industrial town in the canton
of Vaud. It was here, in 1867,
that Henri Nestlé established
the powdered milk factory
that revolutionized baby foods.
Now the world's largest food
and beverage company, the
Nestlé company still has its
international headquarters
in Vevey.

The most attractive part of
Vevey is its Grande Place
(also known as Place du
Marché). On Tuesday and
Saturday mornings this huge
square is filled with a market,
and in summer regional
growers offer wine tastings.
A folk arts market is also held
here on Saturday mornings in
July and August. La Grenette
(1808), a handsome building
on the north side of the
square, was once the
town's granary.

The narrow alleys of
Vevey's historic quarter
continue to the east of
Grande Place. On Quai
Perdonnet stands a
statue of Charlot, the
French name by which
Charlie Chaplin is known
here. Le Manoir-de-Ban,
Chaplin's former home,
opens to the public as
the **Charlie Chaplin
Museum** in late
2013. To the east of
the train station
is the **Musée
Jenisch**. Besides
a large collection
of paintings and
sculpture by 19th-
and 20th-century Swiss artists,
this gallery is the home of the
Fondation Oskar Kokoschka,
which contains 800 Expressionist paintings by this
Austrian artist. The Musée
Jenisch also houses an outstanding collection of prints,
which includes not only the
largest assemblage of litho-
graphs of Rembrandt in Europe
but also works by such major
artists as Albrecht Dürer and
Jean-Baptiste Corot.

🏛 **Musée Jenisch**
2 Avenue de la Gare. **Tel** *021 925
35 20.* ⏰ *10am–6pm Tue–Sun (to
9pm Thu).* ♿

🏛 **Charlie Chaplin Museum**
Le Manoir-de-Ban. ⏰ *check the
website for the latest information.*
www.chaplinmuseum.com

Montreux ❹

Road map B4. 🏔 *20,000.* 🚉 🚌
🛈 *5 Rue du Théâtre; 0848 86 84 84.*
www.montreux-vevey.com
🎭 *Narcissus Festival (spring);
Montreux Jazz Festival (Jul).*

Often described as the jewel
of the Swiss Riviera, Montreux
is an upmarket resort that is
renowned for its annual jazz
festival. The town began to
develop as an international
tourist resort in about 1815,
and its golden age lasted until
the outbreak of World War I
in 1914. In the 19th century
the charm of the area
captivated artists, writers and
musicians, including Lord
Byron and Mary Shelley,
Leo Tolstoy and Hans
Christian Andersen.

Montreux has many
Belle Époque hotels. The
most famous of them is
the Montreux Palace
on Grand'Rue, west of
the town centre.

Opposite this hotel
is the Centre des
Congrès, a modern
conference centre.
It contains the
Auditorium Stravinsky,
a concert hall built in
1990 and dedicated
to Igor Stravinsky
(1882–1971), who
composed *The
Rite of Spring* in
Montreux.

The metal-
framed market

**Statue of Freddie Mercury
in Montreux**

hall in Place du Marché was
built in 1890 with funds
donated by Henri Nestlé,
founder of the multinational
food company. At the end of
the square, on the lakeshore,
is a statue of Freddie Mercury,
vocalist in the band Queen.
Montreux was his second
home and it was here that
he died, in 1991.

East of the statue, on the
lakeshore promenade, is a
casino rebuilt after a fire that
has entered into rock legend.
On 4 December 1971, during
a concert given by Frank Zappa
and the Mothers of Invention,
a rocket-flare was fired into
the ceiling and the building
was suddenly engulfed by
flames. As clouds of smoke
soared above the waters of

Château d'Aigle, once a bailiff's castle and now the home of a museum of wine and winemaking

the lake, Ian Gillan, of the band Deep Purple, who was watching from his hotel room, was inspired by the sight to write *Smoke on the Water*.

Château de Chillon ❺

See pp122–3.

Aigle ❻

Road map B4. 🏔 *6,500.* 🚉 🚌
🛈 *5 Rue Colomb; 024 466 30 00.*
www.aigle-tourisme.ch

Aigle is the capital of the Chablais, a wine-growing region and a major cycling centre, that lies southeast of

Wooden chalets along a street in the ski resort of Leysin

Lake Geneva and produces some of Switzerland's best wines (*see pp266–7*). Set among vineyards covering the foothills of the Alpes Vaudoises, the town is dominated by a turreted castle, the Château d'Aigle. Built in the 12th century by the Savoyards, it was severely damaged in the 15th century but was later rebuilt to serve as the residence of the region's Bernese bailiffs.

The castle now houses the **Musée de la Vigne et du Vin**, whose exhibits illustrate the age-old methods of vine-cultivation and wine-making. The 16th-century Maison de la Dîme opposite the castle contains the **Musée International de l'Etiquette**, which documents the history of wine labels over 200 years.

🏛 **Musée de la Vigne et du Vin** and **Musée International de l'Étiquette**
Château d'Aigle, Place du Château 1. **Tel** 024 466 21 30.
⏰ *Apr–Oct: 11am–6pm Tue–Sun; Jul–Aug: 11am–6pm daily.* 🎟
www.museeduvin.ch

Leysin ❼

Road map B4. 🏔 *2,700.* 🚉 🚌
🛈 *Place Large; 024 493 33 00.*
www.leysin.ch

The small village of Leysin, now a popular winter and summer resort, occupies a sun-drenched mountain

terrace with views across to the Dents du Midi and down onto the Rhône valley. Lying at an altitude of 1,260 m (4,135 ft), Leysin enjoys an unusually dry and sunny climate. Once a centre for the treatment of tuberculosis, the village later evolved into a ski resort. Cable cars carry visitors up to the Tour de Mayen (2,326 m/7,631 ft) and to Berneuse (2,037 m/6,683 ft), where there is a revolving restaurant that enables diners to admire a panoramic view of the Alps.

Les Diablerets ❽

Road map B4. 🏔 *1,300.* 🚉 🚌
🛈 *Rue de la Gare; 024 492 00 10.*
www.diablerets.ch

Set among Alpine meadows in the Ormonts valley, the small ski resort of Les Diablerets lies at an altitude of 1,150 m (3,775 ft) in the Alpes Vaudoises. Above it rise the peaks of Les Diablerets, 3,210 m (10,531 ft) high and among which lies the glacier of the same name.

There is no downhill skiing in summer, but the glacier is open and offers cross-country skiing, dog sleigh rides and the world's highest bobsleigh on rails – the Alpine Coaster. The Monster Snowpark, for freestyle skiers and boarders, opens as early as October.

Château de Chillon ⑤

This enchanting medieval castle, set on a rocky spur on the eastern shore of Lake Geneva, is one of Switzerland's most evocative sights. Built for the Dukes of Savoy, its origins probably go back to the 11th century but its present appearance dates from the 13th century. In 1536, the castle was captured by the Bernese, and from then until 1798 it was the seat of the region's Bernese bailiffs. The centre of court life, the castle was also used as a prison. Its most famous captive was François de Bonivard, imprisoned there from 1530 to 1536 for political incitement.

Heraldic Hall
This ceremonial hall is decorated with the coats of arms of the Bernese bailiffs.

Defences
Surrounded by thick walls, the castle is also defended by three semicircular turrets.

A guest room, the Camera Paramenti, and another bedchamber are located here.

Aula Nova
The former banqueting hall contains a museum, with furniture, pewter vessels, armour and weapons.

Grand Burgrave Hall
This great hall has a wooden ceiling resting on columns that support arches. The walls are richly decorated with paintings.

The covered bridge leading to the gatehouse was originally a drawbridge.

★ **Grand Ducal Hall**
*This large room,
also known
as the Aula Magna,
has chequered walls
and its original
15th-century wooden
ceiling, which is
supported by black
marble columns.*

VISITORS' CHECKLIST

Road map B4. Ave de Chillon
21. 🚉 🚌 **Tel** *021 966 89 10.*
⏱ Mar: 9:30am–5pm daily;
Apr–Sep: 9am–6pm daily; Oct:
9:30am–5pm; Nov–Feb:
10am–4pm daily. 📷
www.chillon.ch

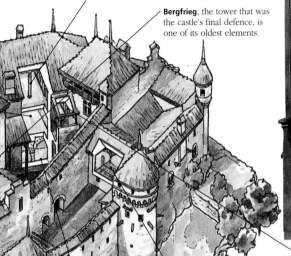

Bergfrieg, the tower that was
the castle's final defence, is
one of its oldest elements.

Ducal Chamber
*This chamber, also known
as the Camera Domini,
has a wooden beamed
ceiling and contains
Gothic furniture.*

Chapel
*The castle's chapel,
dedicated to St George,
is in the early Gothic
style, with a rib-
vaulted ceiling. The
walls and ceiling are
covered with frescoes.*

★ **Bonivard's Prison**
*The castle's vaulted
underground chambers
were once used as a
prison. François de
Bonivard, who spent six
years in captivity here,
was immortalized by
Lord Byron in*
The Prisoner of Chillon,
*a poem that he wrote
in Ouchy in 1816.*

STAR FEATURES

★ Bonivard's Prison

★ Grand Ducal
Hall

Gruyères

Road map B4. 🏠 *1,200.* 🚆 *To Pringy* 🚌 **Tel** *026 921 10 30.*
www.la-gruyere.ch

Visible from afar against the backdrop of Alpine scenery, the well-preserved medieval village of Gruyères is a popular destination for visitors, and is often crowded during the summer. As its only street is restricted to pedestrians, vehicles must be left in the parking areas below.

The village has houses dating from the 15th to the 17th centuries and is crowned by a castle, the **Château de Gruyères**. Built in the 11th century, the castle was continuously inhabited by the counts of Gruyères until the mid-16th century, when the bankrupted 19th count fled and his lands were divided between the lords of Bern and Fribourg.

In 1848, the castle was acquired by the Bovys, a wealthy Genevese family who carried out extensive and much-needed restoration. In 1939 the castle passed into the ownership of the cantonal authorities of Fribourg. It now contains a museum. Displayed in rooms with frescoes and grand fireplaces, the exhibits include 16th-century Flemish tapestries and booty taken after the Battle of Murten (1476). Delicate landscapes by the French Impressionist painter Jean-Baptiste Corot (1796–1875), who stayed at the castle, are also on view.

At **La Maison du Gruyère**, a working dairy in Pringy, at the foot of the village, visitors can watch the famous local cheese being made. The dairy also has a restaurant and a shop selling local produce.

🏰 **Château de Gruyeres**
Tel *026 921 21 02.* ⏰ *Apr–Oct: 9am–6pm daily; Nov–Mar: 10am–4:30pm daily.* 📷 **www**.chateau-gruyeres.ch

🏰 **La Maison du Gruyere**
Pringy. **Tel** *026 921 84 00.* ⏰ *Jun–Sep: 9am–7pm daily; Oct–May: 9am–6pm daily.* **www**.lamaisondugruyere.ch

Fribourg ⑩

See pp126–7.

Murten/Morat ⑪

Road map B3. 🏠 *5,000.* 🚆 🚌 ℹ️ *Französische Kirchgasse 6; 026 670 51 12.* **www**.murtentourismus.ch

The resort town of Murten (Morat in French) lies on the eastern shore of the Murten-see (Lac de Morat). It has strong historical associations. It was at Murten, on 22 June 1476, that the forces of the Swiss Confederation crushed the army of Charles the Bold, Duke of Burgundy, killing 12,000 of his soldiers, while losing only 410 of their own. According to legend, a messenger ran 17 km (10 miles) from Murten to Fribourg with news of the victory, dropping dead with exhaustion on his arrival. His sacrifice is commemorated by an annual run between Murten and Fribourg that takes place on the first Sunday in October.

View from Murten's fortified walls

The town was founded by the Zähringer dynasty in the 12th century, and is still encircled by walls dating from the 12th to the 15th centuries. Haupt-gasse, the main street through the old town, is lined with 16th-century arcaded houses with overhanging eaves. The rampart walk, reached from several points along Deutsche Kirchgasse, offers views of the Murtensee, the castle and the old town's brown-tiled houses. At the western end of the town is a 13th-century castle, with a courtyard that provides a fine view over the lake. At the eastern end stands Berntor (or Porte de Berne), a Baroque gatehouse with a clock dating from 1712. The **Musée Historique**, in a disused mill on the lakeshore, has pre-historic finds from local excavations and items relating to the Burgundian Wars.

🏛 **Musée Historique**
Ryf 4, Murten. **Tel** *026 670 31 00.* ⏰ *Apr–Oct: 2–5pm Tue–Sat, 10am–5pm Sun.* 📷

Avenches ⑫

Road map B3. 🏠 *2,000.* 🚌 ℹ️ *3 Place de l'Église; 026 676 99 22.* **www**.avenches.ch
🎭 *Opera Festival (Jul); Rock Oz'Arènes (Aug); Musical Parade (military bands); Sep).*

Originally the capital of the Helveti, the Celtic tribe that once ruled western Switzerland, Avenches was conquered by the Romans in the 1st century BC. Named

The Château de Gruyères, seat of the counts of Gruyères for 500 years

Aventicum, it became the capital of the Roman province of Helvetia. At its peak in the 2nd century AD, Aventicum was larger than the present town of Avenches. Encircled by 6 km (4 miles) of walls set with watchtowers, it supported a population of 20,000. By 260, however, much it had been razed by the Alemani, a Germanic tribe, and by 450 it had lost its importance.

Vestiges of the Roman city can still be seen to the east of the medieval town centre. The most complete of these remains is the amphitheatre, with seating for 6,000. Other features include the Tornallaz, a tower that is the only surviving part of the old city walls, the forum, the baths and a 12-m (40-ft) Corinthian column known as the Tour du Cigognier.

The **Musée Romain**, in a medieval square tower within the amphitheatre, contains an impressive display of Roman artifacts discovered during excavations at Aventicum. The exhibits range from items of daily life, such as pottery, tools and coins, to bronze and marble statues of Roman deities, mosaics and wall paintings, and a replica of a gold bust of Marcus Aurelius (*see illustration on p35*).

🏛 **Musée Romain**
Tour de l'Amphitheatre. *Tel 026 557 33 15.* ○ Apr–Sep: 10am–5pm Tue–Sun; Oct: 2–5pm Tue–Sun; Nov–Jan: 2–5pm Wed–Sun; Feb–Mar: 2–5pm Tue–Sun. 🖼

Nave of the Romanesque abbey church in Payerne

Payerne 🔞

Road map B3. 🏘 *7,000.* 🚌 🛈 *10 Place du Marché; 026 660 61 61.* **www**.payerne.ch

The small market town of Payerne, in the canton of Vaud, is distinguished by its remarkable church, one of the most beautiful Romanesque buildings in Switzerland.

The **Église Abbatiale** was built in the 11th century as the abbey church of a Benedictine monastery, of which little remains. Stripped of its decoration during the Reformation, the church's interior is bare, but this only

Knocker on the abbey church in Payerne

serves to accentuate its impressive grandeur and the contrasting colours of its soaring limestone and sandstone columns. The portico features 12th-century frescoes and one of the chapels in the apse has 15th-century Gothic paintings. There are monthly organ recitals.

🔒 **Église Abbatiale**
Tel 026 662 67 04. ○ May–Sep: 10am–noon & 2–6pm Tue–Sun; Oct–Apr: 10am–noon & 2–5pm Tue–Sun. 🖼

Estavayer-le-Lac 🔞

Road map B3. 🏘 *4,000.* 🚌 🛈 *16 Rue de l'Hôtel de Ville; 026 663 12 37.* **www**.estavayer-payerne.ch

Surrounded on three sides by the canton of Vaud, this small town on the southern shore of Lake Neuchâtel lies within an enclave of the canton of Fribourg. A popular yachting centre, Estavayer-le-Lac is also a pleasant medieval town with arcarded streets. Its focal point is the Château de Cheneaux, a fine Gothic castle that is now the seat of local government.

The **Musée des Grenouilles**, housed in a 15th-century mansion, contains an eclectic assemblage of exhibits, including kitchen implements. It also boasts an unusual curiosity, namely a collection of 108 stuffed frogs and other creatures arranged in poses that parody the social life of the mid-19th century. The scenes were created by François Perrier, an eccentric resident of Estavayer who served in the Vatican's Swiss Guard and who produced this bizarre display in the 1860s.

🏛 **Musée des Grenouilles**
Rue du Musée 13. *Tel 026 664 80 65.* ○ Mar–June: 10am–noon & 2–5pm Tue–Sun; Jul–Aug: 10am–noon & 2–5pm daily; Sep–Oct: 10am–noon & 2–5pm Tue–Sun; Nov–Feb: 2–5pm Sat–Sun. 🖼

The Roman amphitheatre in Avenches

Street-by-Street: Fribourg ⑩

With steep cobbled streets, immaculately preserved Gothic houses and numerous fountains, Fribourg (Freiburg in German) is one of Switzerland's most attractive towns. Set on a rocky peninsula within a bend of the River Sarine (Saane in German), it was founded in 1157 by Berthold IV of Zähringen, and joined the Swiss Confederation in 1481. Despite the Reformation, Fribourg remained Catholic, and a Catholic university was founded here in 1889.

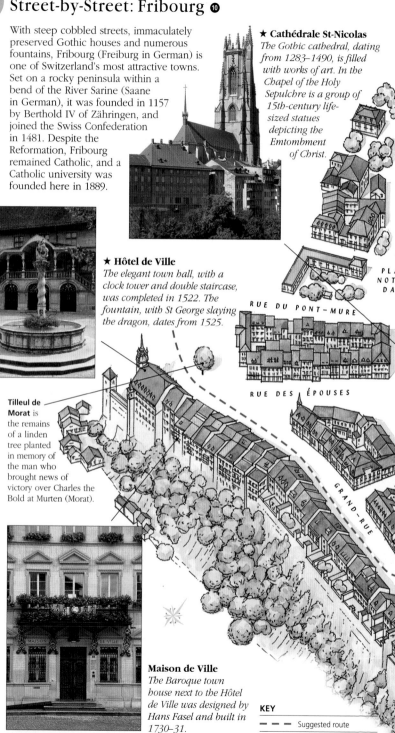

★ Cathédrale St-Nicolas
The Gothic cathedral, dating from 1283–1490, is filled with works of art. In the Chapel of the Holy Sepulchre is a group of 15th-century life-sized statues depicting the Emtombment of Christ.

PLA
NOTR
DAM

RUE DU PONT–MURE

RUE DES ÉPOUSES

GRAND–RUE

★ Hôtel de Ville
The elegant town hall, with a clock tower and double staircase, was completed in 1522. The fountain, with St George slaying the dragon, dates from 1525.

Tilleul de Morat is the remains of a linden tree planted in memory of the man who brought news of victory over Charles the Bold at Murten (Morat).

Maison de Ville
The Baroque town house next to the Hôtel de Ville was designed by Hans Fasel and built in 1730–31.

KEY
- - - Suggested route

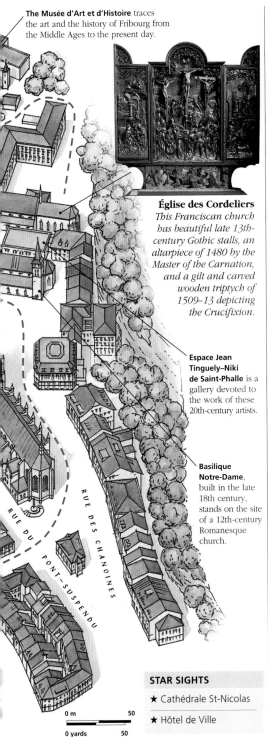

The **Musée d'Art et d'Histoire** traces the art and the history of Fribourg from the Middle Ages to the present day.

Église des Cordeliers
This Franciscan church has beautiful late 13th-century Gothic stalls, an altarpiece of 1480 by the Master of the Carnation, and a gilt and carved wooden triptych of 1509–13 depicting the Crucifixion.

Espace Jean Tinguely–Niki de Saint-Phalle is a gallery devoted to the work of these 20th-century artists.

Basilique Notre-Dame, built in the late 18th century, stands on the site of a 12th-century Romanesque church.

RUE DES CHANOINES

RUE DU PONT–SUSPENDU

0 m   50

0 yards   50

STAR SIGHTS

★ Cathédrale St-Nicolas

★ Hôtel de Ville

VISITORS' CHECKLIST

Road map B3. 🏛 *36,500.*
🚉 *1 Place Jean-Tinguely; 026 350 11 11.* **www**.fribourg tourism.ch 🎭 *Carnival (late Feb); Jazz Parade (Jul); Celebration of St Nicholas (Dec).*

Exploring Fribourg

While Fribourg's major historic sights are clustered around the cathedral, there is much else of interest in this ancient district of the town.

On Rue de Morat, north of the cathedral, is the **Éspace Jean Tinguely–Niki de St-Phalle**. This vast gallery contains kinetic sculptures by Jean Tinguely, who was born in Fribourg, and installations by his wife, Niki de St-Phalle. South of the cathedral, streets lead down to Place du Petit St-Jean, on the peninsula. **Rue d'Or**, just north of the square, is lined with Gothic houses. The peninsula is connected to the south bank of the river by the **Pont de Berne**. This wooden bridge leads to Place des Forgerons, where there is a Renaissance fountain and vestiges of fortifications.

Around Planche Supérieure, a square to the east of the peninsula, are the Église St-Jean and a museum of archaeology. From here, the Pont de St-Jean leads across the river to Neuveville, a low-lying area above which stands the town hall.

Pont de Berne, a wooden bridge across the Sarine in Fribourg

🏛 **Gutenberg Museum**
Place de Notre Dame 16. **Tel** *026 347 38 28.* ⬛ *11am–6pm Wed, Fri–Sat, 11am–8pm Thu, 10am–5pm Sun.* 📷
www.gutenbergmuseum.ch
This museum shows the history of printing and communication through language, images and text. It is housed in a restored granary dating from 1527.

The 13th-century Château d'Yverdon, focal point of Yverdon-les-Bains

Yverdon-les-Bains ⑮

Road map B3. 👥 22,000. 🚉 🚌
ℹ️ 1 Avenue de la Gare; 024 423
61 01. **www**.yverdonlesbains
region.ch

Situated at the southwestern
extremity of Lake Neuchâtel,
Yverdon-les-Bains is Vaud's
second town after Lausanne.
The Celtic settlement that
was originally established
here later became a Gallo-
Roman camp, Eburodunum,
and the Romans built thermal
baths here so as to use the
hot sulphurous springs.
Yverdon's town centre
overlies the Roman settlement.
The focal point is the
Château d'Yverdon, a
massive castle built by Peter
II of Savoy in the 13th century.
    Part of the castle now
houses a museum of local
history, with a collection of
Gallo-Roman finds and other
exhibits. A section of the
museum is devoted to the life
and work of Johann Heinrich
Pestalozzi (1746–1827), the
Swiss educational reformer
who set up a school for
deprived children in the
castle in 1805. Influenced by
the writings of Jean-Jacques
Rousseau, his revolutionary
teaching methods were based
on a flexible school
curriculum suited to the
character of each child.
    Place Pestalozzi, opposite
the castle, is dominated by
the Hôtel de Ville, the town
hall built in 1768–73 on the
site of a former market hall.
The collegiate church on the

west side of the square dates
from 1757. The arched
pediment of its Baroque
façade features an allegory of
Faith. Of particular interest to
fans of science fiction is the
Maison d'Ailleurs (House
of Elsewhere). This museum
presents temporary exhibits
related to science fiction,
utopian worlds and fantasy.
The library of 60,000 volumes
is open only to researchers.
    Yverdon's thermal baths lie
on Avenue des Bains, about
1 km (half a mile) southeast
of the town centre. The
Centre Thermal is one of
Switzerland's largest and most
modern spa centres. With
indoor and outdoor pools,
saunas and physiotherapy,
the centre is used by some
1,300 people every day.
Rich in minerals, the water
here is particularly effective
in curing respiratory ailments
and rheumatism.

♠ Château d'Yverdon
🕐 Jun–Sep: 11am–5pm Tue–Sun;
Oct–May: 2–5pm Tue–Sun. 🈶

🏛 Maison d'Ailleurs
14 Place Pestalozzi. **Tel** 024 425
64 38. 🕐 2–6pm Tue–Fri,
11am–6pm Sat–Sun. 🈶

🌊 Centre Thermal
22 Avenue les Bains.
Tel 024 423 02 32. 🕐 8am–10pm
Mon–Sat, 8am–8pm Sun & public
holidays. **www**.cty.ch

Environs
Beyond Clendy, the northern
suburb of Yverdon-les-Bains,
is a Neolithic stone circle. It
stands near the shore of Lake
Neuchâtel and is one of
several similar ancient
monuments around the lake.

Romainmôtier ⑯

Road map A4. 👥 400. 🚉 🚌 La
Porterie. ℹ️ 024 453 33 28.
www.romainmotier-tourisme.ch

The small village of
Romainmôtier, set in
beautiful wooded hills,
is worth a detour for its
remarkable abbey church.
One of Switzerland's most
beautiful Romanesque
religious buildings, the **Église
Abbatiale de Romainmôtier**
was built between the late
10th and early 11th centuries
by monks from the Abbaye
de Cluny, in France. The
interior contains fine 13th-
and 14th-century frescoes
and a medieval statue of
the Virgin. Although the
15th-century monastery
was dissolved in 1536, in the
wake of the Reformation,
the abbey church and part
of the cloister have survived.

**🛕 Église Abbatiale de
Romainmôtier**
Tel 024 453 14 65. 🕐 7am–8pm
daily.

The nave of the Romanesque Église
Abbatiale de Romainmôtier

Vallorbe ⑰

Road map A3. 👥 3,000. 🚉 🚌 ℹ️
11 Rue des Grandes-Forges; 021 843
25 83. **www**.vallorbe-tourisme.ch

This small industrial town lies
near the Franco-Swiss border.
From the Middle Ages up to
recent times, the town was an
iron-smelting centre. It was
also at Vallorbe that the
tunnel beneath the Jura was

World War II tank at the Fort de Pré-Giroud, near Vallorbe

built, thus creating the Paris–Istanbul rail route.

This is reflected in the **Musée du Fer et du Chemin de Fer** (Iron and Railway Museum), which traces the history of the Swiss iron industry, with a section that is devoted to the Swiss railways.

About 3 km (2 miles) southwest of Vallorbe are the **Grottes de Vallorbe**. These are caves with stalactites and stalagmites. The caves form a tunnel over the River Orbe, which surges through a gorge. A short distance west of Vallorbe is the **Fort de Pré-Giroud**, which was built as a surveillance post on the eve of World War II to observe the French border. Disguised as a chalet, it is a large underground bunker with space for over 100 people.

🏛 Musée du Fer et du Chemin de Fer
11 Rue des Grandes-Forges. *Tel 021 843 25 83.* ☐ Apr–Oct: 2–6pm Mon, 10am–6pm Tue–Sun; Nov–Mar: 2–6pm daily. ☐ ☐

♣ Grottes de Vallorbe
Tel 021 843 22 74. ☐ Apr–May & Sep–Oct: 9:30am–4:30pm daily; Jun–Aug: 9:30am–5:30pm daily. ☐

Grandson ⓲

Road map B3. 🏠 *2,000.* 🚊 🚌
ℹ️ *Maison de Terroirs, Rue Haute 13, 024 445 60 60.* **www.**grandson-tourisme.ch

Dominated by its great medieval castle, the town of Grandson is associated with a momentous event in the history of the Swiss Confederation. This was the defeat of Charles the Bold, Duke of Burgundy, at the Battle of Grandson on 2 March 1476.

In February 1476, the duke's army laid siege to Grandson and its castle, eventually securing the surrender of the garrison, who were put to death. However, after raising an army of 18,000, the Confederates marched on Grandson to wreak revenge on the duke and his army. Fleeing in panic, the Burgundians abandoned their arms, horses and tents, as well as the ducal treasury. The booty is now displayed in the Historisches Museum in Bern *(see p61)*.

Built between the 11th and 14th centuries, the **Château de Grandson** rises proudly from the shore of Lake Neuchâtel. It contains a model of the battlefield and a diorama illustrating the town's history from the Middle Ages to the present day. In the basement is an automobile museum with exhibits including a white Rolls Royce that belonged to Greta Garbo and Winston Churchill's Austin Cambridge car.

Capital in the Église St-Jean-Baptiste in Grandson

♣ Château de Grandson
Place du Château. *Tel 024 445 29 26.* ☐ Apr–Oct: 8:15am–6pm daily; Nov–Mar: 8:15am–5pm daily. ☐

Ste-Croix ⓳

Road map B3. 🏠 *4,500.* 🚊 🚌
ℹ️ *10 Rue Neuve; 024 445 41 42.*

Appropriately known as the Balcony of the Jura, the town of Ste-Croix lies at an altitude of 1,092 m (3,584 ft) and commands a wide view of the Alps, the Swiss Upland and the Jura mountains.

Since the early 19th century Ste-Croix has been the world capital of musical-box manufacture. Two local museums are devoted to this art. In the course of a guided tour of the **Musée du CIMA** (Centre International de la Méchanique d'Art) the guide sets in motion a mesmerizing assortment of musical boxes with performing acrobats, drummers and accordionists.

🏛 Musée du CIMA
2 Rue de l'Industrie. *Tel 024 454 44 77.* ☐ for guided tours only; call for times. ☐ ☐

Environs
The **Musée Baud**, in the village of L'Auberson, 6 km (4 miles) west of Ste-Croix, has similar exhibits. The collection was created by members of the Baud family of musical-box makers.

🏛 Musée Baud
23 Grand-Rue, L'Auberson. *Tel 024 454 24 84.* ☐ Jul–mid-Sep: 2–5pm daily; mid-Sep–Jun: 2–5pm Sat, 10am–noon & 2–6pm Sun. ☐ obligatory. ☐ **www.**museebaud.ch

One of the musical boxes in the Musée du CIMA in Sainte-Croix

Neuchâtel

Lying on the northwestern shore of Lake Neuchâtel, no more than about 20 km (12 miles) from the French border, Neuchâtel is a graceful town with a strikingly Gallic atmosphere. It is also notable for its pale yellow limestone buildings, which famously led the writer Alexandre Dumas to describe the town as looking as if it were carved out of butter. Neuchâtel, a university town, owes its wealth to its watchmaking and precision-engineering industries, which go back to the 18th century. The region is also renowned for its wines, which are celebrated each September at the Fête des Vendanges wine festival.

Église Collégiale, fronted by a statue of Guillaume Farel unveiled in 1876

Exploring Neuchâtel

Neuchâtel's graceful Old Town (Ville Ancienne) is filled with houses built of soft, yellow sandstone, and its streets have numerous fountains. While Place des Halles, the old market square, has many busy cafés, the town's smartest district lies on the lakeshore northeast of the harbour. The rampart walk around the castle walls gives you a panoramic view of the town.

⛪ Château de Neuchâtel

Rue de la Collégiale.
Tel 032 889 60 00,
🏛 Apr–Sep: 10am, 11am, noon, 2pm, 3pm, 4pm Mon–Fri, 2pm, 3pm, 4pm Sat, 2pm, 3pm, 4pm Sun.

For over 1,000 years, the castle of the lords of Neuchâtel has been the seat of authority. Today it houses the law courts and the cantonal government. While the west wing dates from the 12th century, the rest of the castle was built in the 15th and 17th centuries. The interior has been altered many times. Of particular interest, however, is the castle's Salle des États, the state room decorated with the coats of arms of the families who married into Neuchâtel's ruling dynasty.

🛐 Église Collégiale

Rue de la Collégiale. ◻ undergoing renovations until 2016, but remains open to the public.

The early Gothic collegiate church, in a combination of Romanesque and Burgundian Gothic styles, was consecrated in 1276. The Reformation was introduced to Neuchâtel by Guillaume Farel (1489–1565), who led the religious movement in western Switzerland, and in 1530 the church became a centre of Protestant worship.

It houses a Gothic tomb known as Le Cénotaphe. This memorial, dating from 1372, consists of life-sized figures of the counts of Neuchâtel arranged in pious poses. It is an outstanding example of medieval sculpture. The other elements of the tomb were added in the 15th century, some being taken from other churches.

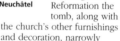

Coat of arms in the Château de Neuchâtel

During the Reformation the tomb, along with the church's other furnishings and decoration, narrowly escaped destruction at the hands of iconoclastic zealots. The commemorative plaque in the choir proclaims that the cult of images was abolished here in 1530. In accordance with the strictures of the Reformation, Farel's tomb has no monument of any kind. Neuchâtel's great reformer is, however, commemorated by a plaque in the south aisle, and by a 19th-century statue in front of the church.

🏛 Maison des Halles

Place des Halles.

The elegant turreted Renaissance market hall dates from the 16th century. Here grain was sold on the ground floor, and cloth on the upper floor. The richly ornamented eastern wall bears the coat of arms of the Orléans-Longueville family.

The influence of French culture brought to Neuchâtel by this dynasty can be seen in the Louis XIII and Louis XIV style of many of the houses in Place des Halles and in the streets around this central square.

Place des Halles, with the turreted Maison des Halles in the background

For hotels and restaurants in this region see pp249–51 and pp273–6

Hôtel de Ville

Rue de l'Hôtel de Ville.

The large Neo-Classical town hall stands in the eastern part of the Old Town, near the harbour. Completed in 1790, it was designed by Pierre-Adrien Paris, court architect to Louis XVI.

Musée d'Art et d'Histoire

Esplanade Léopold-Robert. *Tel 032 717 79 20.* 🕐 *11am–6pm Tue–Sun.*

www.mahn.ch

Neuchâtel's unusual and fascinating art and history museum is divided into three main sections. Devoted to art, the upper floor is crammed with paintings by 19th- and 20th-century Swiss artists, including Ferdinand Hodler and Albert Anker. There is also a collection of French Impressionist paintings.

The ground floor and the mezzanine are devoted to the history of the canton of Neuchâtel and to local decorative arts. The star attractions here are three automata that demonstrate the ingenuity and sophistication of 18th-century Swiss watchmakers.

The figures were made by Pierre Jaquet-Droz, a watchmaker of La Chaux-de-Fonds, and his son Henri-Louis between 1768 and 1774. Le Dessinateur (The Draughtsman) produces six different drawings, including a profile of Louis XV and a picture of a butterfly. La Musicienne (The Musician) is a young woman playing an organ. Her bosom heaves as she breathes, and she bends forward, sits up and plays several melodies, striking the keyboard with her fingers. The most sophisticated automaton is L'Écrivain (The Writer), who composes a text consisting of 40 letters, dipping his quill pen in an inkpot as he writes. He can also be made to write any phrase.

The automata are on permanent display; visitors can request a demonstration to see each of them performing.

La Musicienne, in the Musée d'Art et d'Histoire

Laténium, Parc et Musée d'Archéologie de Neuchâtel

Espace Paul Vouga, Hauterive, 3 km (2 miles) northeast of the town centre. 🚌 *1. Tel 032 889 69 10.* 🕐 *10am–5pm Tue–Sun.* 🎫
www.latenium.ch

Covering 3 hectares (7 acres), the Laténium is a large and modern museum complex that opened in 2001.

Its primary purpose is to illustrate the history of human activity and settlement in the region of Lake Neuchâtel from the end of the Ice Age to the Middle Ages. Among many fine displays, the centrepiece is the section devoted to the lakeside settlement of La Tène, which was founded by Celts in the 5th century BC. Stunning examples of Celtic metalwork and other fine objects paint a vivid picture of their lives.

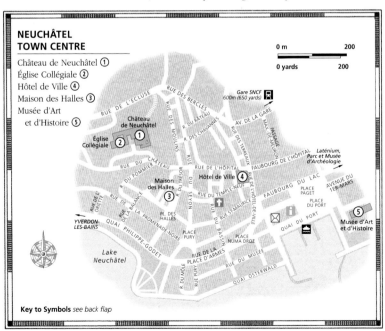

NEUCHÂTEL TOWN CENTRE

Château de Neuchâtel ①
Église Collégiale ②
Hôtel de Ville ④
Maison des Halles ③
Musée d'Art
    et d'Histoire ⑤

0 m   200
0 yards   200

Key to Symbols *see back flap*

Château des Monts, home of the Musée d'Horlogerie in Le Locle

Le Locle ㉑

Road map B3. 🚉 🚌
www.lelocle.ch

The town of Le Locle has the distinction of being the birth-place of Swiss watchmaking, and has been awarded World Heritage status by UNESCO. In 1705 the young watchmaker Daniel Jeanrichard arrived from Neuchâtel to settle in Le Locle, where he set up a workshop. The apprentices that he trained then established workshops of their own in La Chaux-de-Fonds, so launching the Swiss watchmaking industry.

The **Musée d'Horlogerie**, which is in a stately 18th-century mansion (the elegant Château des Monts) with beautiful interiors, presents a large collection of timepieces from around the world, as well as several elaborate automata.

Environs
About 2 km (1 mile) west of Le Locle are the **Moulins Souterrains du Col-des-Roches**. In use from the 16th to the 19th centuries, these underground mills were built to harness the waters of the River Biel, whose energy was used to work machinery. Having fallen into disuse, they have now been restored and their wells, waterwheels and galleries – with both permanent and temporary exhibitions – are open to visitors.

🏛 **Moulins Souterrains du Col-des-Roches**
Le Col 23. ◯ May–Oct: 10am–5pm; Nov–Apr: 2–5pm.
www.lesmoulins.ch ♿ 📷

La Chaux-de-Fonds ㉒

Road map B3. 🚶 *37,800*. 🚉 🚌
ℹ *1 Rue Espacité; 032 889 68 95.*

If Le Locle is the birthplace of the Swiss watchmaking industry, La Chaux-de-Fonds may be regarded as its cradle. The largest town in the canton of Neuchâtel, La Chaux-de-Fonds lies in the Jura at an altitude of 1,000 m (3,280 ft). Introduced to the town in the early 18th century, watchmaking was initially a cottage industry. In time it was industrialized and La Chaux-de-Fonds became the leading centre of Swiss watchmaking. The industry reached its peak in the late 18th and 19th centuries.

Carillon at the Musée International d'Horlogerie, La Chaux-de-Fonds

After it was destroyed by a fire in 1794, the town was rebuilt on a grid pattern, with long, wide avenues. It is now dotted with several modernist buildings.

La Chaux-de-Fonds' illustrious past is celebrated in the magnificent **Musée International d'Horlogerie**. The museum's collection of some 3,000 pieces from around the world illustrates the history of timekeeping from its beginnings in antiquity to state-of-the-art instruments able to record time lapses of infinitessimal fractions of a second. In purely visual terms, many of the finest pieces on display were made in La Chaud-de-Fonds during the town's apogee. Musical,

A WORLD-FAMOUS INDUSTRY

The earliest watchmaking workshops in Switzerland were established in the 17th century by Huguenot refugees who had settled in Geneva. Soon after, many other workshops were set up in the Jura, most notably at La Chaux-de-Fonds. In the 19th century, innovations in precision mechanics introduced by Abraham-Louis Breguet enabled watch-making to be industrialized, and the canton of Neuchâtel then became its leading centre. In 1967, the Centre Horloger Neuchâtelois produced the first quartz watch. This nearly led to the collapse of the Swiss watch-making industry. Now able to mass-produce cheap watches, other countries quickly gained the largest market share. However, thanks to the inexpensive and fashionable Swatch and an image update, Switzerland regained supremacy, and now produces 95 million watches a year.

Giant pocket watch as a shop sign

astrononomical, atomic and quartz clocks are also on display. The museum has audiovisual facilities, a library and a restoration workshop for antique clocks and watches. At the entrance is a tubular steel carillon that sounds every 15 minutes.

La Chaux-de-Fonds is also the birthplace of the modernist architect Charles-Édouard Jeanneret, known as Le Corbusier (1887–1965). Before he moved to Paris in 1917, Le Corbusier built several houses here, and an itinerary taking in buildings that he designed and places associated with him is available from the town's tourist office. Only one, however, is open to visitors. This is the Villa Schwob, better known as the **Villa Turque** (Turkish Villa) because of its Islamic-style features. The villa launched Le Corbusier's career and is now an office building for Ebel watches.

🏛 Musée International d'Horlogerie

29 Rue des Musées. **Tel** 032 967 68 61. **www**.mih.ch ◯ 10am–5pm Tue–Sun.

♣ Villa Turque

167 Rue du Doubs. **Tel** 032 912 31 23. ◯ 1st & 3rd Sunday of the month & by appointment.

Franches-Montagnes ㉓

Road map B2. 🚉 🚌 🛈 Saignelégier, 6 Place du 23 Juin; 032 420 47 74. 🎪 Marché-Concours (2nd weekend in Aug). **www**.juratourisme.ch

The part of the Jura mountains that lies within the canton of Jura itself are known as the Franches-Montagnes. The area received its name in the 14th century, when the prince-bishop of Basel, who owned the territory that now constitutes the canton of Jura, granted its inhabitants a *franchise*, or exemption from taxation, so as to encourage migration to this sparsely populated region.

The Franches-Montagnes lie at an altitude of 1,000–1,100 m (3,300–3,600 ft) in the

Portal of the church at St-Ursanne

southwest of the canton of Jura. With forests, pastures and picturesque low houses, this outstandingly beautiful plateau has extensive hiking trails, and cycling and cross-country skiing routes. It is also famous for horse-breeding.

The region's principal town is **Saignelégier**. Every year, in the second week in August, it hosts the Marché Concours National des Chevaux, a horse fair and horse show that draws sellers, competitors and spectators from Switzerland and eastern France.

St-Ursanne ㉔

Road map C2. 🚶 1,100. 🚌 🛈 Place Roger Schaffter; 032 420 47 73. **www**.juratourisme.ch

A charming medieval walled town with fortified gates, St-Ursanne is set in a deep canyon washed by the River Doubs. The town grew up around the hermitage that Ursicinus, a disciple of St Columba, established here in the early 7th century.

The focal point of the town is its beautiful Romanesque and Gothic **church**. It has a fine Romanesque portal, with statues of the Virgin and St Ursicinus. There is an old stone bridge across the River Doubs, on the south side of St-Ursanne, which provides a good view of the town and its setting. The bridge features a statue of St John Nepomuk, who is the little-known patron saint of bridges.

Delémont ㉕

Road map C2. 🚶 11,500. 🚉 🚌 🛈 9 Place de la Gare; 032 420 47 71. **www**.juratourisme.ch

The capital of the canton of Jura, Delémont is a quiet town with a well-preserved medieval centre. From 1212 until 1792 it served as the summer residence of the prince-bishops of Basel.

Historic buildings in the old town, which has cobbled streets and fountains, include the Château de Delémont, the prince-bishops' 18th-century mansion, the Hôtel de Ville, built in 1745 in the Baroque style, and the 18th-century Église St-Marcel, in a Rococo and Neo-Classical style. The **Musée Jurassien d'Art et d'Histoire** contains artifacts relating to local history from prehistoric times to the 18th century.

🏛 Musée Jurassien d'Art et d'Histoire

52 Rue du 23-Juin. **Tel** 032 422 80 77. ◯ 2–5pm Tue–Sun.

Façade of the prince-bishops' palace in Delémont

NORTHERN SWITZERLAND

Bordered by the Rhine to the north and the Jura to the southwest, northern Switzerland is a largely Protestant, German-speaking region with a strongly industrial economy. It consists of the half-cantons of Basel-Stadt and Basel-Landschaft in the west, Aargau in the centre, and part of the canton of Zürich in the east.

Being the most industrialized and densely populated region of Switzerland, this northern, relatively flat area is less scenic than other parts of the country. With Zürich, Switzerland's richest and most populous city, and Basel, its most industrial, northern Switzerland is noticeably less oriented towards tourism than other areas further south. However, as well as several fine historic towns, the region has a large number of world-class museums and art galleries. It is here, in Switzerland's industrial heartland, that privately acquired wealth has been translated into some of the world's most exquisite art collections.

The Rhine marks part of Switzerland's northern border and also connects this landlocked country to the sea. Set on the Rhine, Basel is Switzerland's only port, with a direct shipping link to Rotterdam and out to the North Sea.

Besides being a large industrial port, Basel is a major centre of the pharmaceuticals and chemicals industries. With the oldest university in Switzerland and the Kunst-museum, an art gallery of international standing, Basel is also one of the country's cultural capitals.

Winterthur, another of Switzerland's major industrial centres, also has a wealth of art galleries and museums. The bustling city of Zürich, in the east of the region, is Switzerland's financial capital and burgeoning centre of popular culture.

Baden's Old Town, on the west bank of the River Limmat

◁ The clock on the façade of Basel's brightly painted Rathaus

Exploring Northern Switzerland

Flanked by Basel in the west and Winterthur and Zürich in the east, this region is bordered by the Rhine to the north, while to the south lies the Mittelland. Just outside the great city and port of Basel lie the extensive remains of the Roman town of Augusta Raurica. Other focal points here include the spa resort of Baden, and the attractive towns of Zofingen and Aarau, capital of Aargau. While small towns and villages dot the landscape of vineyards in the east of the region, the industrial town of Winterthur has several exceptional art galleries. The lakeside city of Zürich is the Swiss capital of finance as well as a vibrant centre of culture.

A side altar in the monastery church at Wettingen

0 km   10

0 miles   10

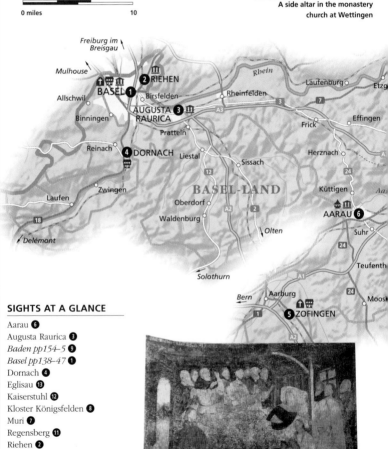

Paintings in the Reformierte Kirche in Eglisau

SIGHTS AT A GLANCE

ETTING THERE

ith international airports and rail
nks to the country's major
wns, Basel and Zürich are the
o main hubs of northern
witzerland's transport network.
otorway links from Zürich
clude the A1 north to
interthur and west to Baden,
nd the A51 to Eglisau. From
aden, the A3 runs west as far as
asel, which is also connected to
ern and western Switzerland via
e A2. The more scenic A7
llows the Rhine as far as
aiserstuhl then turns south
Winterthur.

KEY

═══ Motorway

▬▬▬ Main road

▭▭▭ Minor road

─── Scenic route

▬▬▬ Main railway

─── Minor railway

▬▬▬ International border

▬▬▬ Canton border

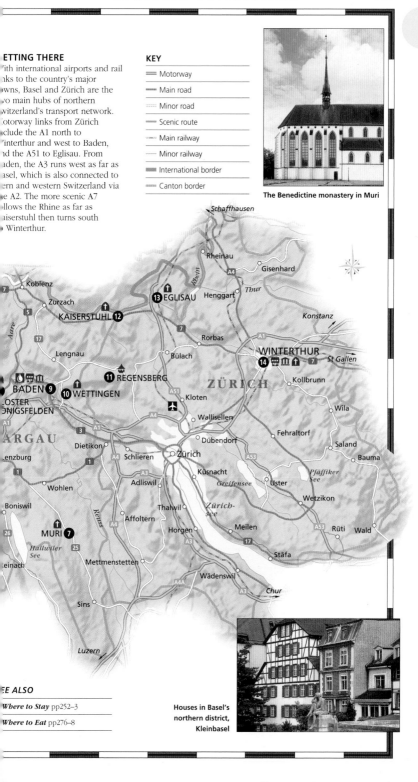

The Benedictine monastery in Muri

Schaffhausen

Rheinau

Gisenhard

Koblenz

Zurzach

KAISERSTUHL 12

13 **EGLISAU**   Henggart

Rhein   Thur

Konstanz

Rorbas

Lengnau

Bülach

WINTERTHUR

14   St Gallen

Kollbrunn

11 **REGENSBERG**

BADEN 9

10 **WETTINGEN**

Kloten

ZÜRICH

Wila

OSTER
ÖNIGSFELDEN

Wallisellen

Fehraltorf

Saland

Dietikon

Dübendorf

Bauma

enzburg

Schlieren   **Zürich**

Pfäffiker
See

Wohlen

Adliswil

Küsnacht

Greifensee

Uster

Wetzikon

Boniswil

Affoltern

Thalwil

Zürich-
see

Meilen

Rüti   Wald

MURI 7

Horgen

Hallwiler
See

Mettmenstetten

Stäfa

einach

Wädenswil

Chur

Sins

Luzern

**Houses in Basel's
northern district,
Kleinbasel**

Basel ①

The origins of the city of Basel (Bâle in French) lie in a Roman settlement, Basilia, that was established in 44 BC. Under Frankish control from the 7th century, it became part of the German empire in the early 11th century. Located at a point where the Rhine becomes navigable, it is Switzerland's only port. Basel is a major centre of commerce and industry, specializing in pharmaceuticals. The city also hosts Art Basel, the world's largest contemporary art fair, and is famous for its festivals, the largest of which are Vogel Gryff and Fasnacht, an exuberant masked carnival.

Exploring Basel
Straddling the Rhine, Basel is divided into two districts. Grossbasel (Greater Basel), on the south bank, is the oldest part of the city. On the north bank lies Kleinbasel (Lesser Basel), a largely residential area, and the Messe, the city's great conference centre.

The Spalentor seen from Spalenvorstadt

🏛 Spalentor
This monumental Gothic gate stands on the west side of the Old Town (Altstadt), at the entrance to Spalenvorstadt, a narrow alley lined with picturesque shuttered houses. Built in 1370, the Spalentor formed part of the defensive walls that once encircled Basel. The tower consists of a pair of crenellated turrets framing a square central section, which has a pointed roof laid with glazed tiles. The gate, which has wooden doors and a portcullis, is embellished with sculptures and on its west side it bears the arms of the city.

🏛 Jüdisches Museum der Schweiz
Kornhausgasse 8. *Tel* 061 261 95 14. ⏰ 2–5pm Mon & Wed, 11am–5pm Sun. 🔲
Through a variety of artifacts dating back to the 13th century, including liturgical objects and items used at religious feasts, the museum illustrates Jewish religion and customs, and the history and daily life of Jewish people. It is the only Jewish museum in Switzerland.
Basel's Jewish community of 2,000 is the second-largest in the country after Geneva's. It was in Basel that the first Zionist Congress took place, in 1897.

🏛 University
Petersplatz 1.
Founded in 1460, Basel's university is the oldest in Switzerland. Among the illustrious figures with whom it is associated are the humanist Erasmus of Rotterdam (1466–1536), the physician

Paracelsus (1493–1541), the mathematician Jakob Bernoulli (1654–1705), and the philosophers Friedrich Nietzsche (1844–1900) and Karl Jaspers (1883–1969).
The present university building is the Kollegienhaus, a great Modernist edifice on the east side of Petersplatz. It was completed in 1946. The entrance to the building is embellished with mosaics depicting the university's founders and the main hall has stained-glass windows.
Additional university buildings are located in Petersgraben and in other parts of the city. The university's botanical garden lies east of Petersplatz, beyond which is the university library.

Bust of the Basel poet J. P. Hebel (1760–1826)

🏛 Spielzeug Welten Museum Basel
Steinenvorstadt 1. *Tel* 061 225 95 95. ⏰ 10am–6pm daily. 🔲 ♿ 🔲
With more than 6,000 items laid out on four floors, the Toy Worlds Museum in Basel is the largest of its kind in Europe. Most of the exhibits date from the late 19th to the early 20th centuries, although there are also some contemporary pieces. All the doll's houses and miniature shops on display are meticulously decorated and furnished.
The collection also includes mechanical toys, teddy bears and other stuffed toys made by leading toymakers of today and yesterday.

Shuttered houses along Spalenvorstadt in the Old Town

For hotels and restaurants in this region see pp252–3 and pp276–8

🏛 Pharmaziehistorisches Museum Basel

Totengässlein 3. **Tel** *061 264 91 11.*
⏰ *10am–6pm Tue–Fri,*
10am–5pm Sat. 📷 🎫

Appropriately for a world centre of the pharmaceuticals industry, Basel has a museum devoted to the history of medicinal chemistry. Its collection includes instruments and medicines used by apothecaries

Microscope, Pharmazie-historisches Museum

through the ages and is located in the house where Erasmus and Paracelsus once lived. There are also reconstructions of a pharmacy and a laboratory.

🏛 Marktplatz

Every weekday morning Marktplatz is filled with the stalls of a produce market, and on public holidays it becomes the hub of Basel's great seasonal festivals. The square is lined with fine buildings, particularly those dating from late 19th to early 20th centuries. At its northern end is Fischmarkt, where a

fountain with statues of the Virgin and saints stands. Just to the northeast of Marktplatz is Mittlere Rhein-brücke. Near the bridge is a curious figure of a bearded man, the Lällekönig (Tongue King), which has become the symbol of Basel. It is a static replica of an amusing 19th-century mechanical figure that rolled its eyes and stuck out its tongue at the inhabit-ants of Kleinbasel, on the north bank. The original figure is in the Historisches Museum.

🏛 Rathaus

Marktplatz 9. 🎫 *available in English through the tourist office.*
The main feature of Marktplatz is the eyecatching Rathaus, the Gothic town hall whose bright red façade is decorated with allegorical figures. The central arcaded section of the building dates from 1504–21. The present façade *(see illustration on p134)* has been restored so as to re-create its

VISITORS' CHECKLIST

Road map C2. 🚩 190,000. 🚆
🚌 ℹ *Stadtcasino, Barfüsserplatz, Steinenberg 4 and in the train station; 061 268 68 68.* 🎭 *Fasnacht (late Feb); Blues Festival (Apr); Art Basel (mid-Jun); Tattoo Festival (Jul); Jazz Festival (late Aug).* **www**.basel.com

appearance as it was in about 1600. The tower and annexe date from the 19th century. The inner courtyard is painted with 16th-century (though heavily restored) frescoes.

Figure of Justice, a painting on the façade of the Rathaus

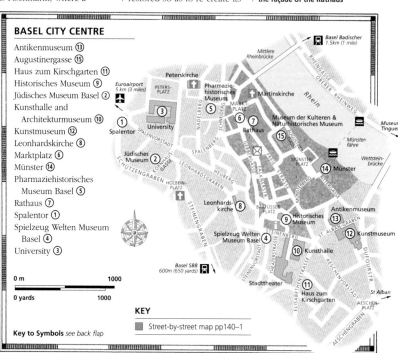

BASEL CITY CENTRE

0 m 1000
0 yards 1000

Key to Symbols *see back flap*

KEY

■ Street-by-street map pp140–1

Street-by-Street: Old Town

The nucleus of Basel's medieval Old Town, or Altstadt, lines the escarpment of the south bank of the Rhine. The hub of the Old Town is Barfüsserplatz, a buzzing square lined with cafés and crossed by trams, and its major landmarks are the Münster, Basel's great Romanesque-Gothic cathedral, and the unmistakable Rathaus, the brightly painted town hall on Marktplatz. With smart shopping streets, several churches, steep alleyways and leafy courtyards, this is Basel's busiest district. However, as many streets in the Old Town are closed to motor traffic, it is a pleasant area to explore on foot.

Mittlere Rheinbrücke
a stone bridge spanni
the Rhine, links Grossbase
on the south bar
to Kleinbasel, a district on t
north bar.

MARKTGASSE

EISENGASSE

RHEINSPRU

MARTINSGASS

MARKT–PLATZ

Martinskirche
Dating from the 14th century, this is the oldest parish church in Basel.

Marktplatz has for centuries served as a market place. It is also the hub of the city's festivals.

GERBERGASSE

FALKNERSTRASSE

★ **Rathaus**
The town hall has a brightly and elaborately painted façade and a clock surmounted by figures.

Barfüsserplatz
This square, named after the Discalced, or barefooted, Franciscans, is surrounded by buildings dating mostly from the 19th and 20th centuries.

STAR SIGHTS

★ Historisches Museum

★ Münster

★ Rathaus

KEY

 – – – Suggested route

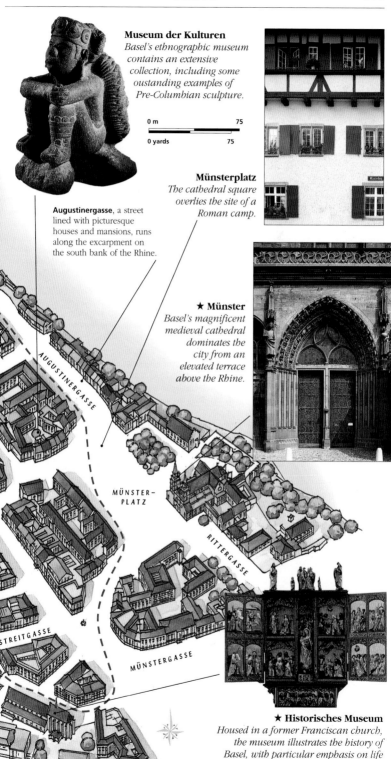

Museum der Kulturen
Basel's ethnographic museum contains an extensive collection, including some oustanding examples of Pre-Columbian sculpture.

0 m — 75
0 yards — 75

Münsterplatz
The cathedral square overlies the site of a Roman camp.

Augustinergasse, a street lined with picturesque houses and mansions, runs along the excarpment on the south bank of the Rhine.

★ Münster
Basel's magnificent medieval cathedral dominates the city from an elevated terrace above the Rhine.

AUGUSTINERGASSE

MÜNSTER–PLATZ

RITTERGASSE

STREITGASSE

MÜNSTERGASSE

★ Historisches Museum
Housed in a former Franciscan church, the museum illustrates the history of Basel, with particular emphasis on life in the city during the Middle Ages.

Exploring Basel

With over 30 museums and art galleries, ranging from the cutting-edge Kunsthalle to the venerable Kunstmuseum, Basel is one of Switzerland's most cultured cities. East of the Old Town lies St Alban-Vorstadt, a quiet district of medieval streets where it is pleasant to stroll. Opposite the Old Town, on the north bank of the Rhine, lies Kleinbasel, a prosperous suburb. At Basel's port (Hafen), downstream from the Old Town, an obelisk marks the point at which the Swiss, German and French borders meet.

The Tinguely Fountain, outside the Kunsthalle

⛪ Leonhardskirche

Kohlenberg. ☐ *9am–5pm Tue–Sat.*
The Gothic church of St Leonard overlooks the city from its hilltop location. It stands on the site of an 11th-century church, whose Romanesque crypt survives. Following the earthquake that destroyed much of Basel in 1356, the church was rebuilt in the Gothic style. The interior features 15th- and 16th-century Gothic paintings and an exquisite rood screen of 1455. The musical instruments on display in a wing of the adjoining monastery are part of the collection of the Historisches Museum.

🏛 Historisches Museum

Barfüsserplatz. **Tel** *061 205 86 00.*
☐ *10am–5pm Mon & Wed.* 🖼 📷 🔒 🛒
Occupying the Barfüsserkirche, a former Franciscan church, this fascinating museum traces the

history of Basel from Celtic times. Exhibits include wooden chests, pottery and silver-mounted vessels, Gothic, Renaissance and Baroque liturgical vessels and other items from the cathedral treasury, as well as tapestries, altarpieces and weapons.

Emblem of Basel in the Leonhardskirche

🏛 Kunsthalle

Steinenberg 7. **Tel** *061 206 99 00.* ☐ *11am–6pm Tue, Wed & Fri, 11am–8:30pm Thu, 11am–5pm Sat–Sun.* 🖼 📷 🔒 🛒
Thanks to the Kunsthalle, Basel's position at the forefront of trends in modern art is well established. One of the city's most prominent cultural institutions, the Kunsthalle hosts a continuous programme of exhibitions of the work of leading contemporary artists.
    The Kunsthalle is located opposite the Theater Basel, another institution at Basel's cultural hub. On the square

between the two buildings stands a fountain that incorporates several of Jean Tinguely's kinetic sculptures, with moving elements.

🏛 Architekturmuseum

Steinenberg 7. **Tel** *061 261 14 13.*
☐ *11am–6pm Tue, Wed & Fri; 11am–8:30pm Thu; 11am–5pm Sat–Sun.* 🖼 📷 🔒 www.sam-basel.org
The Kunsthalle also houses Basel's museum of architecture. Concentrating on the early 20th century onwards, the museum hosts temporary exhibitions of the work of Swiss architects, and of international architecture, as well as related subjects such as architectural photography and the links between art and architecture.

🏛 Haus zum Kirschgarten

Elisabethenstrasse 27–29. **Tel** *061 205 86 78.* ☐ *10am–5pm Tue–Fri & Sun, 1–5pm Sat.* 🖼 www.hmb.ch
This Rococo mansion was built in 1775–80 as the residence of J. R. Burckhardt, the owner of a silk mill. Furnished in period style, it has now been opened as a museum illustrating patrician life in the 18th and 19th centuries. On the first and second floors there are elegantly furnished drawing rooms, a dining room, a music room and a kitchen.
    The topmost floor contains a display of dolls, rocking horses and other toys. The ground floor and basement are filled with a fine collection of clocks and ceramics, including Italian faience, and of porcelain made at Meissen and other major European factories.

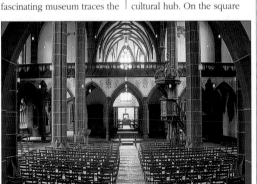

The wide nave of the Leonhardskirche

For hotels and restaurants in this region see pp252–3 and pp276–8

🏛 Kunstmuseum
See pp146–7.

🏛 Antikenmuseum
St-Alban-Graben 5. *Tel* 061 201 12
12. ◯ 10am–5pm Tue–Sun. 🖼 🗂
♿ 🖵
Basel's museum of antiquities
is devoted to the four great
early civilizations of the
Mediterranean basin, namely
those of ancient Greece, Etruria,
Rome and Egypt. The display
of Greek pieces includes a
fine collection of vases from
the Archaic to the Classical
periods, marble sculpture,
bronze figurines, pottery, coins
and jewellery. The collections
of Etruscan pottery and of
Roman and Egyptian art are
equally impressive.

🔒 Münster
See pp146–7.

♿ Augustinergasse
Naturhistorisches Museum.
Augustinergasse 2. *Tel* 061 266 55
00. ◯ 10am–5pm Tue–Sun. 🖼 ♿
Museum der Kulturen. Münsterplatz 20. *Tel* 061 266 56 00. ◯
10am–5pm Tue–Sun. 🖼 ♿ 🖵🛈
Augustinergasse is a
picturesque alley that runs
north from Münsterplatz, along
the escarpment on the south
side of the Rhine. As well as
a Renaissance fountain with a
figure of a basilisk, the street
contains several fine 14th-
and 15th-century houses.
The Neo-Classical building
at no. 2 houses the **Naturhistorisches Museum**, which
contains an extensive collection of minerals, and sections
devoted to palaeontology and
zoology. Around the corner is
the **Museum der Kulturen**,
housed in a building designed
by Basel architects Herzog and
de Meuron. This anthropology
museum presents a collection
of items from various cultures
around the world. Among the
finest pieces are wooden
reliefs from Tikal, the ancient
Mayan site in Guatemala.

♿ St Alban
Basler Papiermühle. St Alban-Tal 37.
Tel 061 225 90 90. ◯ 11am–5pm Tue–
Fri & Sun, 1–5pm Sat. ♿ 🖼 www.
papiermuseum.ch **Museum für
Gegenwartskunst.** St Alban-
Rheinweg 60. *Tel* 061 272 81 83.
◯ 11am–5pm Tue–Sun. 🖼

**The St Alban-Tor, a 13th-century
gate, in the district of St Alban**

The district of St Alban takes
its name from the church of a
former Benedictine monastery
founded on the outskirts of
Basel in the 11th century.
It is an attractive district,
with a mix of old and
modern buildings.
The canal that runs
through St Alban was
used to power the
monastery's mills.
One of these, the
**Basler Papier-
mühle**, now houses
a museum of paper,
writing and print-
ing. Visitors can
watch paper being
made by hand. The **Museum
für Gegenwartskunst**, in a
modern building a short distance from the mill, showcases
art from the 1960s to the
present day.

Kleinbasel
The first permanent bridge
over the Rhine at Basel was
built in 1226. A small fortress
was then established on the
north bank, and the settlement
that grew up around it became
part of the city in the late 14th
century. For many centuries,
Kleinbasel, as the district was
known, was inhabited mainly
by the poorer sector of the
city's population.

🏛 Museum Tinguely
Paul-Sacher Anlage 1. *Tel* 061 681
93 20. ◯ 11am–6pm Tue–Sun. 🖼
🗂 ♿ 🍴 www.tinguely.ch
This pale pink sandstone
building, designed by the
Swiss architect Mario Botta,
stands in Solitude Park, on
the banks of the Rhine. The
museum is devoted to the
work of Jean Tinguely, who is
famous for his kinetic sculptures.
Born in Fribourg in 1925, he
was educated in Basel. He
settled in New York in 1960,
but in 1968 returned to
Switzerland. where he stayed
until his death in 1991.
The nucleus of the
collection consists of
works by Tinguely
donated by his wife,
the artist Niki de
St-Phalle. These,
with many later
gifts, bequests and
purchases, trace
Tinguely's artistic
development.
While the
mezzanine contains engine-
driven contraptions that
visitors can set in motion, the
upper floor contains various
items associated with
Tinguely. The central exhibit
on the ground floor is a huge
sculpture, *Grosse Méta Maxi-
Maxi Utopia* (1987). The
museum also stages exhibitions
concentrating on individual
aspects of Tinguely's work.

Statue in Kleinbasel

The Museum Tinguely, fronted by one of the artist's sculptures

Münster

With dark red sandstone walls and a patterned roof, Basel's monumental cathedral is a conspicuous and majestic presence. The church that originally stood on the site was built in the 8th century. The present cathedral was begun in the 12th century. Partly damaged by an earthquake in 1356, it was rebuilt in the Gothic style, although elements of the earlier building were incorporated into the structure. In the 16th century, as a result of the Reformation, the cathedral was stripped of almost all its furnishings and decoration. However, some fine Romanesque and Gothic sculpture, and 14th-century frescoes in the crypt, survive. All the stained glass dates from the 19th century.

★ Crypt Paintings
The ceiling of the crypt is covered with frescoes of the life o. the Virgin and the childhood of Christ. One of the finest is thi. Nativity scene.

Stained-glass Window
The ambulatory is lit by 19th-century stained-glass windows with medallions depicting the Nativity, the Crucifixion and the Resurrection of Christ.

Carved elephants
adorn the windows of the choir.

Tomb of Queen Anna
Queen Anna of Habsburg, consort of Rudolf of Habsburg, died in 1281 and was entombed with her infant son, Karl. Their portraits appear on the lid of the sarcophagus.

STAR FEATURES

★ Crypt Paintings

★ Galluspforte

★ Panel of the Apostles

★ Galluspforte
The magnificent Romanesque portal closing the north arm of the transept dates from about 1180. The carvings depict judgment day and works of mercy.

Font
Intricately carved with figured reliefs, the font dates from 1486. It is an outstanding example of late Gothic sculpture.

VISITORS' CHECKLIST

Münsterplatz. *Tel* 061 272 91 57.
 Apr–Oct: 10am–5pm
Mon–Fri, 10am–4pm Sat,
11:30am–5pm Sun; Nov–Mar:
11am–4pm Mon–Sat, 11:30am–
4pm Sun.

The Martinsturm
terminates in a
decorative fleuron
that was com-
pleted in 1500.

The Georgsturm
features a figure
of St George. The
whiter stonework
at its lower levels
formed part of the
11th-century
church.

★ Panel of the Apostles
This late Romanesque panel in the north aisle shows six of the apostles, arranged in pairs within three arches. The panel dates from the late 11th century.

Main Portal
The sculptures on the main portal include figures of Emperor Heinrich II and his wife Kunigunde, patron saints of Basel. The emperor is shown holding a model of the cathedral.

Cloisters
The peaceful Gothic cloisters on the south side of the cathedral are filled with tombs. The walls are covered with epitaphs.

Kunstmuseum

The prestigious Kunstmuseum in Basel is said to be the world's oldest public art museum. It is the largest in Switzerland. Its collections fall into four main categories: 15th- and 16th-century paintings and drawings, including an extensive collection of German art and the largest assemblage in the world of works by Hans Holbein the Younger; 17th-century Dutch and Flemish paintings; 19th-century Swiss, German and French paintings, with works by Delacroix and Pissarro; and 20th-century art, including works by Rousseau, Picasso, Dalí and Giacometti. The courtyard is filled with sculptures, among which is Rodin's *Burghers of Calais*. In 2016, a new extension will open for large and temporary exhibitions.

Senecio
This lyrical portrait of a boy by Paul Klee dates from 1922, and is one of several works by this artist in the gallery's collection.

KEY

☐	Sculpture
▨	17th–18th-century paintings
▨	15th–16th-century paintings
☐	19th-century paintings
▨	20th-century paintings

GALLERY GUIDE
While the ground floor is reserved for temporary exhibitions, the galleries on the first floor are hung with works of the period 1400–1800 and 19th-century painting. The second floor is devoted to 20th-century art.

★ Ta Matete
The gestures of the figures in Ta Matete (The Fair), as well as the colours used in the composition, make this a powerful example of Paul Gauguin's Symbolist style. The work dates from 1892.

★ Burning Giraffe
Salvador Dalí painted this poignant Surrealist painting in 1936–7. It shows skeletal figures and a flaming giraffe set against an eerily empty landscape. It is located on the ground floor.

Main entrance

Second floor

VISITORS' CHECKLIST

St Alban-Graben 16.
Tel 061 206 62 62.
◯ 10am–6pm Tue–Sun.
📷 🚫 🍴 🛍 🏛
www.kunstmuseumbasel.ch

The Jungle
Henri Rousseau, known as Le Douanier, painted this picture in 1910, the year of his death. In the setting of a luminously painted and dream-like forest, a man is attacked by a leopard.

★ Christ in the Tomb
Painted in 1521, this unusual picture, one of the most striking by Hans Holbein the Younger, carries a strong visual and emotional charge. Dostoyevsky refers to it in his novel The Idiot.

First floor

Mermaids at Play
Arnold Böcklin, who was born in Basel, was one of the most important Swiss artists of the late 19th century. This work of Romantic fantasy is typical of his atmospheric yet rather sentimental style.

Ground floor

David Presenting Saul with the Head of Goliath
Dating from 1627, this small-scale painting of the well-known biblical story is one of Rembrandt's earlier works.

STAR EXHIBITS

★ Burning Giraffe

★ Christ in the Tomb

★ Ta Matete

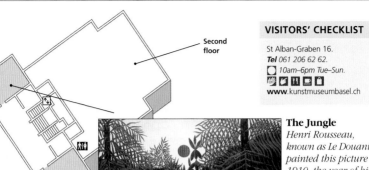
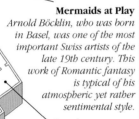

Riehen ❷

Road map C2. 🏚 20,600. 🚊 🚆
www.riehen.ch

Now almost engulfed by the encroaching outskirts of Basel, the small town of Riehen is linked to the city by a tram line. This charming place, northeast of Basel's city centre, is filled with smart villas and old country houses and has much to interest visitors.

Wettsteinhaus, the residence of a 17th-century mayor, houses the **Spielzeugmuseum**. This superb toy museum contains exhibits ranging from toy trains to board games. Also in the house are the **Dorfmuseum**, which documents daily life in Riehen in 1900, and the **Rebbaumuseum**, devoted to the local winemaking industry.

Riehen's largest museum is the exceptional **Fondation Beyeler**. It was set up by Hilda and Ernst Beyeler, art collectors who assembled some 200 pieces. These were put on public display in 1997, in a building designed by the Italian architect Renzo Piano. Most of the paintings in the collection date from the late 19th and 20th centuries. Among them are Impressionist paintings by Monet, works by Cézanne, Van Gogh, Picasso and Matisse, and canvases by Miró, Mondrian, Bacon, Rothko, Warhol and other major artists of the 20th century. A selection of arti-facts from other parts of the world, including Africa and Oceania, complements the paintings. The foundation also stages temporary exhibitions of modern art.

🏛 **Spielzeugmuseum, Dorfmuseum & Rebbaumuseum**
Baselstrasse 34. **Tel** 061 641 28 29.
⏱ 11am–5pm Mon & Wed–Sun. 🎫

🏛 **Fondation Beyeler**
Baselstrasse 101.
Tel 061 645 97 00. ⏱ 10am–6pm
Thu–Tue, 10am–8pm Wed. 🎫 ♿
🖥 🅿 www.fondationbeyeler.ch

The Goetheanum in Dornach, the world centre of anthroposophy

Augusta Raurica ❸

Road map C2. 🚊 🚌 🛳

The Roman town of Augusta Raurica lies 11 km (7 miles) east of Basel, at the confluence of the Ergolz and the Rhine. It was founded in 27 BC and at its height in about AD 200 it had a population of 20,000. By about AD 350, the town had been largely destroyed by the Alemani, a northern tribe.

Carefully excavated, Augusta Raurica is now a large and fascinating open-air museum. The site includes restored temples, amphitheatres, baths and sewers, as well as a forum and numerous houses.

Some of the many objects unearthed during excavations are displayed in the **Römermuseum**, next to the open-air excavation site. They include a hoard of silver discovered at the foot of the town's fortress. The reconstruction of a Roman house furnished with pieces found at the site illustrates daily life in the town. In the animal park, visitors can see some of the domestic animals that were kept in Roman times.

Tombstone of Dannicus in Augusta Raurica

🏛 **Römermuseum**
Giebenacherstrasse 17, Augst.
Tel 061 816 22 22. ⏱ Mar–Oct:
1–5pm Mon, 10am–5pm Tue–Sun;
Nov–Feb: 1–5pm Mon, 11am–5pm
Tue–Sun. 🎫

Dornach ❹

Road map C2. 🏚 6,300. 🚊 🚌
🛈 www.dornach-tourismus.ch

The small town of Dornach, on the southern outskirts of Basel, is the location of the world centre of anthroposophy. Founded in about 1912 by the Austrian-born social philosopher Rudolf Steiner (1861–1925), anthroposophy holds that spiritual development, nourished by myth-making and other creative activities, is of prime importance to humanity. In the development of this philosophy, Steiner was strongly influenced by the writing of the German poet Goethe.

The **Goetheanum**, a huge concrete building overlooking Dornach, is the seat of the Anthroposophical Society. Replacing the original building, which was destroyed by fire in 1922, the present Goetheanum was completed in 1928. According to the principles of anthroposophy, it has no right angles, and is regarded as being a prime example of Expressionist architecture. The interiors, completed in 1998, are decorated so as to depict anthroposophy's themes.

The centre of the building contains an auditorium with seating for 1,000 people. It is used for concerts and operas and for plays produced according to the movement's principles. The auditorium is also used for conferences on anthroposophy and for other

◁ **Blossoming cherry trees in orchards in the Fricktal region, Aargau** gatherings. The School of Spiritual Science is also here.

⚅ Goetheanum
Rüttiweg 45. **Tel** 061 706 42 42.
◷ 8am–10pm daily. ◪ Apr–Sep:
2pm Sat (in English). ◪

Zofingen ❺

Road map D2. ⛰ 11,000.
ℹ Kirchplatz 26. Tel 062 745
71 72. **www**.zofingen.ch

Zofingen, in the canton of Aargau, is a charming town whose history goes back to the 12th century. Its well-preserved old town is surrounded by a green belt laid out along the course of the former fortifications. Almost all the town's sights are clustered around three neighbouring squares, Alter Postplatz, Kirchplatz and Niklaus-Thut-Platz.

On one side of Alter Postplatz stands Alte Kanzlei, a notable Baroque building. In the centre of the square is an historic arcaded market hall that is still used for a weekly market today. Kirch-platz (Church Square) takes its name from the Stadtkirche, a parish church built in the Romanesque style and enlarged in the 15th century, when it acquired Gothic elements, and again in the mid-17th century, when the west tower, in the Renaissance style, was added. Notable features of the church's interior are its Gothic stalls and stained-glass windows.

Fountain with the figure of a knight, in Niklaus-Thut-Platz, Zofingen

The centre of Niklaus-Thut-Platz is marked by a fountain with a statue of Niklaus Thut, hero of the Battle of Sempach fought in 1386, when the Confederates routed the Austrians. Among the fine buildings surrounding the square are the Metzgern-Zunfthaus (butchers' guild house), dating from 1602, and the Baroque town hall, whose council chamber is furnished in the Neo-Classical style.

Aarau ❻

Road map D2. ⛰ 20,000.
ℹ Schlossplatz 1; 062 834 10 34.
www.aarauinfo.ch

The capital of the Canton of Aargau, Aarau has a scenic location on the River Aare. The old part of the town is built on terraces that rise steeply from the riverbank.

Aarau was granted the privileges of township in the 13th century. Part of Habsburg territory for many years, it passed to Bernese control in 1415. Briefly the capital of the Helvetic Republic (*see p39*), Aarau became the capital of Aargau in 1803. Its wealth is derived from the textiles industry.

The town's highest point is marked by Schlössli, an 11th-century castle that now houses a museum of history. Other notable buildings are the 16th-century town hall with a Romanesque tower and the Stadt-kirche, a Gothic church built in the 15th century. Some of the houses that line the narrow streets of Aarau's old districts have stepped gables and are decorated with floral motifs.

The town also has an art gallery, the **Aargauer Kunsthaus**, with a fine collection of modern paintings, and Naturama, a museum of natural history.

Decoration on a house in Aarau

🏛 Aargauer Kunsthaus
Aargauerplatz. **Tel** 062 835 23 30.
◷ 10am–5pm Tue–Wed & Fri–Sun,
10am–8pm Thu. ◪ ◪ ◪ ◪ ◪

Environs
The small town of Lenzburg, about 10 km (6 miles) east of Aarau, has an interesting castle. A museum of local history fills some of its rooms.

The castle at Lenzburg, near Aarau

For hotels and restaurants in this region see pp252–3 and pp276–8

Muri 7

Road map D2. *7,200.*
Marktstrasse 10; 056 664 70 11.
www.muri.ch

The splendidly restored Benedictine monastery in Muri constitutes this town's main attraction. **Kloster Muri** was founded by Ita von Lothringen and Count Redebot von Habsburg in 1027 and was inhabited by a community of monks until 1841. It then fell into disrepair and was gutted by fire in 1889. In 1960, after it had been meticulously restored, a small group of Benedictine monks returned to the monastery, where they ran a hospice.

The oldest surviving parts of the monastery's church include its Romanesque presbytery, crypt and transept. Some Gothic elements also survive. The main body of the church, however, is in the Baroque style. Built to an octagonal plan and crowned by a dome, it dates from the 17th century. Most of the church furnishings were made in the late 17th and 18th centuries.

The peaceful cloisters adjoining the church are the burial place of the hearts of Emperor Karl I and his wife Zita. An exhibition of paintings by the Swiss artist Caspar Wolf and items from the monastery's treasury are also on display here.

The twin-towered church of Kloster Muri

Kloster Muri
Church *until 7:30pm daily.*
Museum *Mar–Oct: Tue–Sun.*

Kloster Königsfelden 8

Road map D2. **Klosterkirche, Windisch**. *056 441 88 33.*
Apr–Oct: 10am–5pm Tue–Sun; Nov–Mar: by request.

The Franciscan Abbey of Königsfelden lies between the quaint villages of Brugg and Windisch. It was founded in 1308 by Elizabeth von Habsburg to mark the spot where her husband Albrecht I was murdered by Duke Johann of Swabia. The monastery was later given to a community of Franciscan monks and nuns of the Order of St Clare. After Elizabeth's death, building work on the abbey was continued by her daughter, Agnes of Hungary.

During the Reformation both of these religious communities were dissolved and in 1804 the monastery buildings were converted into a psychiatric hospital. When the hospital moved to new premises later in the 19th century, most of the monastery buildings were dismantled.

The church, however, survives. Built in 1310–30, it takes the form of a monumental Gothic basilica with a wooden ceiling. In the aisles are wooden panels with depictions of knights and coats of arms. The eleven large stained-glass windows in the presbytery are some of the finest in Switzerland. Made between 1325 and 1330 and restored in the 1980s, the windows show scenes from the lives of Christ, the Virgin, the Apostles and the saints.

Baroque pulpit in the church at Wettingen

Baden 9

See pp154–5.

Wettingen 10

Road map D2. *20,200.*
Seminarstrasse 54; 056 426 22 11. **www**.wettingen.ch

Set among hills bordering the scenic Limmat valley, Wettingen is a small town with a magnificent Cistercian abbey, **Zisterzienserkloster**. The monastery was dissolved in 1841, and the complex now serves as a school. Its church and the adjoining cloisters are open to visitors.

The abbey church was founded in 1227 and was remodelled several times. Although the Renaissance stalls survive, the church's interior is furnished and decorated in an extravagant Baroque style, with an ornate gilt pulpit, altars and statuary.

The Gothic cloisters, whose arcades were glazed in modern times, now contain a display of stained glass ranging from the 13th to the 17th centuries.

Zisterzienserkloster
Klosterstrasse 11. ***Tel*** *056 437 24 10.*
Church *Mar–Oct: 9am–5pm Mon–Sat.* **Cloisters**
Mar–Oct: 9am–5pm Sat–Sun.

Regensberg 11

Road map D2. *500.*

The attractive wine-growing village of Regensberg lies on a minor road off the highway running between Zürich and Waldshut, via Dielsdorf. Set on a hillside amid vineyards, it is one of the

Half-timbered houses in the village of Regensberg

best-preserved medieval villages in Switzerland. Its main square and oldest streets are lined with half-timbered houses.

The history of Regensberg goes back to 1245. The oldest building in the town is the castle's circular crenellated keep, from the top of which there is a fine view of the vineyards and countryside around. The castle itself dates from the 16th and 17th centuries and now serves as a school for children with learning difficulties. Also of interest is the early 16th-century parish church, which overlies the foundations of a medieval building.

Kaiserstuhl ⑫

Road map D2. 🛈 056 265 00 30. **www**.kaiserstuhl.ch

Lying on a gently sloping hillside on the left bank of the Rhine, on the border with Germany, Kaiserstuhl is a beautiful small medieval town. Its historic centre, which is contained within an irregular triangle, is a listed conservation area.

The upper corner of the triangle is marked by Oberer Turm (Upper Tower), a medieval bastion that once formed part of the town's fortifications. Nearby stands the Baroque Landhaus, Zur Linde. Kaiserstuhl's historic centre also contains many beautiful old houses, most of them having shuttered windows and steeply pitched roofs. Also of interest is Mayenfisch, a Baroque mansion, and a former Augustinian monastery, whose 16th-century building now accommodates the offices of the local authorities. The parish church of St Catherine has a fine pulpit and notable stalls.

From Kaiserstuhl, visitors can cross the bridge over the Rhine, arriving at Hohentengen, on the north bank, where there is a castle, Schloss Rötelen.

Oberer Turm, the medieval tower in Kaiserstuhl

Environs
The spa town of Zurzach lies about 12 km (7 miles) west of Kaiserstuhl. Of interest to visitors here is the town's historic centre, as well as museums and a castle, Schloss Zurzach, which contains a display of paintings by August Deusser. Zurzach also has two churches, the Obere Kirche, in the Gothic style, and the Verenamünster, with Romanesque and Gothic elements incorporated into later rebuilding in the Baroque style.

Eglisau ⑬

Road map E2. 🏘 4,500. 🚉 🛈 Untergass 7, 044 867 36 12. **www**.eglisau.ch

Eglisau straddles the River Rhine and is close to the German border. The town is surrounded by gentle hills covered in vineyards. Its origins go back to medieval times, when it was established at what was then a ford across the river, on an ancient route south to Zürich.

When a hydroelectric dam was built across the Rhine, the picturesque houses that once stood on the river bank were engulfed by water. Eglisau's historic covered bridge was also lost. The higher part of the old town, with its 18th-century domed church, now stands just above water level. This historic centre is filled with half-timbered houses with steeply pitched roofs. Some of the houses are decorated with colourful murals.

The belvedere behind the church offers a view of the river. Nearby, a high viaduct reminiscent of an ancient aqueduct carries a railway line past the town.

Environs
Some 10 km (6 miles) northeast of Eglisau is the small town of Rheinau. Its early 11th-century Benedictine monastery, with a fine Baroque church, is set on a sheltered bend of the Rhine.

Polychrome wall painting on a house in Eglisau

Baden ❾

One of Switzerland's oldest health resorts, Baden (meaning "Baths") is a peaceful, stately town. The therapeutic properties of its hot sulphur springs, which the Romans knew as Aquae Helveticae, have been exploited since ancient times. From the Middle Ages, Baden's location on the River Limmat contributed to its becoming an important centre of trade, and its beautiful Old Town (Altstadt) is the legacy of this historical status. Still a popular health resort with facilities for large numbers of visitors, Baden today is also a thriving industrial town, specializing in electro-mechanical engineering.

Exploring Baden

A good starting point for a stroll around Baden's Old Town is the Landvogteischloss, the castle on the east bank of the Limmat. From here, the rest of the Old Town, on the hillside to the west, is reached by crossing a wooden bridge. A short walk north along the river leads to the spa area.

🏛 Schweizer Kindermuseum

Ländliweg 7. *Tel 056 222 14 44.* ◻ 2–5pm Tue– Sat, 10am–5pm Sun. ◪
Housed in an old mansion, this museum contains a collection of toys and everyday objects that illustrate various aspects of childhood, including children's mental development and education. Young visitors are encouraged to play with many of the exhibits.

🏯 Ruine Stein

The ruins of a castle overlook the Old Town from the top of a hill, beneath which runs a road tunnel. Originating in the 10th century, the castle was rebuilt in the 13th century as an arsenal and fortress for Austrian forces, when Baden and the surrounding area were under Habsburg rule. The castle was destroyed in 1712, during conflicts between Protestant and Catholic cantons. Now surrounded by greenery, these ruins make a pleasant place for a stroll. The hilltop offers a splendid view over the River Limmat and the Old Town.

🏯 Stadtturm

This tall four-sided tower, built in the 15th century, originally guarded the entrance to the Old Town. It is set with four corner turrets and is crowned by a belfry. The tower also features a clock, which is framed by a fresco and sundial on the southern façade.

⛪ Pfarrkirche Mariä Himmelfahrt

Kirchplatz. *Tel 056 222 57 15.*
The Church of the Assumption, Baden's parish church, was built between 1457 and 1460. Although it was remodelled on several occasions, acquiring Baroque features in the 17th century and Neo-Classical elements in the early 19th, it retains its original Gothic outline, and is crowned by a pointed spire. The church treasury, with a collection of liturgical objects, is open to visitors by appointment only.

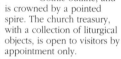

Coat of arms on the Stadtturm

The Stadthaus (town hall), north of the church, contains a beautifully restored council chamber, the Tagsatzungssaal, where Switzerland's parliament sat until 1812. Dating from 1497, the chamber is lined with fine wood panelling and stained-glass windows featuring the emblems of each of the Swiss cantons.

🏯 Holzbrücke

This picturesque wooden bridge spans the Limmat from the base of the Landvogteis-chloss. Built in 1810 to replace an earlier bridge, the Holzbrücke is an attractive single-span structure covered by a ridge roof *(see illustration on p135).*

Landvogteischloss, the Gothic bailiff's castle

♟ Landvogteischloss

Tel 056 222 75 74. ◻ 1–5pm Tue–Fri, 10am–5pm Sat–Sun. ◪ www.museum.baden.ch
The massive Gothic castle on the east bank of the Limmat was built in the 15th century, and from 1415 to 1798 was the residence of Baden's bailiffs.

The Baroque interior of the Pfarrkirche Mariä Himmelfahrt

Rooftops of Baden's Old Town

The castle keep now houses a museum of local history. Its archaeological section includes Roman pottery, coins and other objects found in and around Baden. There are also displays of weapons, religious items, traditional costumes of the Aargau region, and a set of interiors furnished and decorated in the style of successive historical periods.

A modern wing, which extends along the riverbank, contains displays of objects relating to Baden's more recent history, focusing mainly on the town's industrial development from the 19th century onwards.

Spa area

Baden's 18 thermal springs spout warm sulphur-rich waters that are especially effective in curing rheumatism and respiratory ailments.

The spa centre consists of several hotels with their own pools and wellness areas. Construction of a new public complex is underway. Designed by renowned architect Mario Bott, it is set to open in the spring of 2015. The new facility will feature thermal pools, whirlpools, saunas and solariums, as well as massage and other treatment areas.

Museum Langmatt

Römerstrasse 30. **Tel** 056 200 86 70. Mar–Nov: 2–5pm Tue–Fri, 11am–5pm Sat–Sun.

On Römerstrasse, a short walk westwards from the spa area, stands a charming villa that once belonged to the art connoisseur Sidney Brown (1865–1941). The villa was built in 1900–01; a few years later a wing was added which, like the house itself, contains an exquisite art collection.

The nucleus of the collection consists of French Impressionist

VISITORS' CHECKLIST

Road map D2. 18,400. Bahnhofplatz 1; 056 200 87 87. www.baden.ch

paintings, with works by Corot, Monet, Pissarro, Renoir, Sisley, Degas and Cézanne. The collection also includes and 18th-century Venetian townscapes, and other examples of French art, including several works by Fragonard and Watteau and paintings by Van Gogh and Gauguin. Some of the rooms contain 17th- and 18th-century French furniture.

Fountain in the gardens around the Museum Langmatt

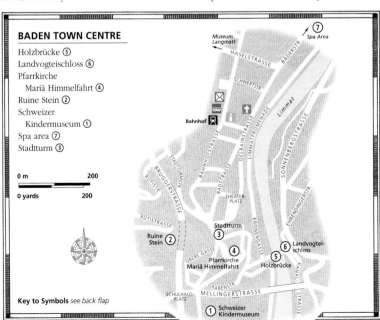

BADEN TOWN CENTRE

0 m   200
0 yards   200

Key to Symbols see back flap

Winterthur ⑭

A thriving industrial centre now associated chiefly
with textiles and mechanical engineering,
Winterthur is the second-largest town in the canton
of Zürich. Despite its industrial character, Winterthur
is a pleasant town, with many leafy streets and open
green spaces. It also has several outstanding art
galleries, the most celebrated of which contain
paintings donated by Oskar Reinhart (1885–1965),
a native of Winterthur who became a wealthy
industrialist and one of Europe's greatest art collectors.

**Marktgasse, the main street in
Winterthur's Old Town**

Exploring Winterthur

Free of motorized traffic,
Winterthur's old town centre
is pleasant to explore on foot.
A Museumbus circles the
town every hour, stopping at
each of Winterthur's principal
museums and art galleries.

🛉 Stadtkirche

🕐 10am–4pm Mon–Sat.
This Gothic parish church,
which was built on the
site of an 8th-century
shrine, dates from the
mid-13th century
and was extended
several times until
the 16th century. It
takes the form of
a vaulted basilica
with a square apse
flanked by Baroque
towers. Decorative
features of the
interior include an
organ screen, a font,
which dates from
1656, wall paintings
and fine 19th-
century stained-
glass windows.

**Stained-glass window
in the Stadtkirche**

🏛 Kunsthalle Winterthur

Marktgasse 25. **Tel** 052 267 51 32.
🕐 noon–6pm Wed–Fri, noon–4pm
Sat–Sun.
The former Waaghaus
(Weigh House) has
been converted into
a spacious exhibition
hall, the Kunstalle
Winterthur, which
organizes temporary
shows of modern art.
Marktgasse, the Old
Town's pedestrianized
main artery and its
principal shopping
street, is lined with
several other fine
historic buildings.
Among the oldest
and most attractive is
Zur Geduld (Patience House),
which dates from 1717.

🏛 Rathaus

Marktgasse 20. **Tel** 052 267 51 26.
🕐 2–5pm Tue–Sat, 10am–noon &
2–5pm Sun.
Winterthur's Neo-Renaissance
town hall was built in 1872–4
on the site of a former Gothic
structure. In 1878, the ground
floor was converted into a
shopping arcade. The upper
floors, however, have
remained intact.
The rooms here
include a stucco-
decorated Festsaal,
and former residential
quarters and offices
that now contain
two museums. On
the first floor is the
private collection of
paintings amassed
by Jakob Briner and
consisting mainly of
17th-century Dutch
Old Masters. On
the floor above is
a collection of
miniatures donated
by E.S. Kern.

**Detail on the façade
of the Rathaus**

🏛 Museum Oskar Reinhart
am Stadtgarten

Stadthausstrasse 6. **Tel** 052 267
51 72. 🕐 10am–8pm Tue,
10am–5pm Wed–Sun.
Oskar Reinhart amassed
one of the greatest private
art collections of the 20th
century. He donated part of
his collection to the town in
1951, and the rest was
bequeathed to Winterthur
after his death.
    The collection on display
in the Stadtgarten includes
works by German, Austrian
and Swiss artists of the late
18th to the early 20th
centuries. These
range from German
Romantic painting
to portraits of chil-
dren. The Swiss
artists Albert Anker,
Ferdinand Hodler
and Giovanni
Giacometti are well
represented. The
best-known works
from Reinhart's
collection hang at
Römerholz, his
villa on the edge
of the town.

🏛 Sammlung Oskar
Reinhart am Römerholz

Haldenstrasse 95. **Tel** 052 269 27
40. 🕐 10am–5pm Tue & Thu–Sun,
10am–8pm Wed.
The villa where Oskar
Reinhart lived from 1926
until his death contains about
200 works of art from his
collection. Though most of
these are French Impressionist paintings, with stunning
canvases by Manet, Degas,
Renoir and Monet, there are
also works by other major
artists such as Holbein,
Grünewald, Cranach, Poussin,
El Greco, Chardin and Goya.

**The main entrance to the
Kunstmuseum**

⛪ Kunstmuseum

Museumstrasse 52. **Tel** 052 267 51 62. ⏱ 10am–8pm Tue, 10am–5pm Wed–Sun. 🖼 🚻 ♿ 🛍 🖥

An excellent collection of 19th- and 20th-century paintings by an international span of artists fills the rooms of the Kunstmuseum.

Exhibits include paintings by Monet and Van Gogh, and Cubist works, including paintings by Picasso, as well as Surrealist works. Important painters and sculptors, such as Rodin, Hodler, Miró, Brancusi, Mondrian, Kandinsky and Alberto Giacometti are also well represented.

The building also houses a natural history museum and a museum that is designed specifically for children.

♻ Stadthaus

Stadthausstrasse 4a.
The imposing Neo-Renaissance Stadthaus houses the town's main concert hall. Built in 1865–9, it was designed by Gottfried Semper, a professor of architecture at Zürich's Technical University. Semper also designed Dresden's opera house. The Stadthaus in Winterthur is considered to be one of Gottfried Semper's finest buildings.

⛪ Fotomuseum

Grüzenstrasse 44. **Tel** 052 234 10 60. ⏱ 11am–6pm Tue & Thu–Sun; 11am–8pm Wed. 🖼 🛍 🖥

This oustanding museum is one of the finest of its kind in Europe. It occupies a spacious and

VISITORS' CHECKLIST

Road map E2. 🏠 103,000. 🚉
🚌 ℹ Train station; 052 267 67 00. 📷 Albanifest (street festival with music; Jun); Musikfest-wochen (live music; Aug–Sep).
www.winterthur-tourismus.ch

well restored warehouse about ten minutes' walk from the town centre. On view here is a comprehensive range of photographs, from the early beginnings of photography to the most recent examples of the art, by an international span of photographers. The museum also stages a programme of world-class exhibitions.

⛪ Villa Flora

Tösstalstrasse 44. **Tel** 052 212 99 66. ⏱ 2–5pm Tue–Sat, 11am–3pm Sun. 🖼 🛍 🖥 **www**.villaflora.ch
Post-Impressionist paintings collected by Hedy and Arthur Hahnloser-Bühler between 1907 and 1930 hang in the rooms of this mid-19th-century villa. Among them are fine examples of the work of the Nabis, including Bonnard and Vuillard, and of the Fauves, including Matisse and Rouault.

The Neo-Renaissance Stadthaus, designed by Gottfried Semper

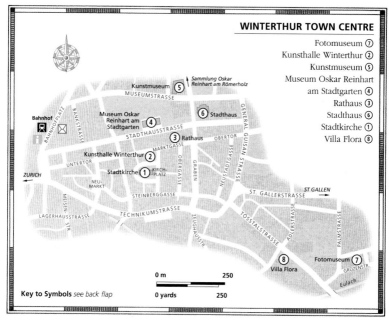

WINTERTHUR TOWN CENTRE

Fotomuseum ⑦
Kunsthalle Winterthur ②
Kunstmuseum ⑤
Museum Oskar Reinhart
am Stadtgarten ④
Rathaus ③
Stadthaus ⑥
Stadtkirche ①
Villa Flora ⑧

Kunstmuseum ⑤
Sammlung Oskar Reinhart am Römerholz
MUSEUMSTRASSE
Bahnhof
Museum Oskar Reinhart am Stadtgarten ④
STADTHAUSSTRASSE
⑥ Stadthaus
GENERAL GUISAN STRASSE
Kunsthalle Winterthur ②
③ Rathaus
MARKTGASSE
OBERTOR
OBERGASSE
NEUSTADTGASSE
Stadtkirche ①
KIRCH-PLATZ
GRABEN
ZURICH
NEU-MARKT
STEINBERGGASSE
ST. GALLERSTRASSE
ST GALLEN
LAGERHAUSSTRASSE
MEISENSTR
TECHNIKUMSTRASSE
ZEUGHAUSSTR
TÖSSTALSTRASSE
ADLERSTRASSE
PALMSTRASSE
⑧ Villa Flora
Fotomuseum ⑦
GRÜZENSTR
Eulach

0 m   250
Key to Symbols see back flap
0 yards   250

ZÜRICH

An international centre of banking and industry, Zürich is Switzerland's capital of finance and its richest city. Zürich's exuberant popular culture and vibrant arts scene also make it one of the liveliest cities in Europe. With a lakeshore setting and elegant quays, Zürich is a beautiful city, and the cobbled streets and squares of its historic centre are lined with many fine buildings.

Capital of the densely populated canton of the same name, the city of Zürich lies on the north shore of the Zürichsee at the point where the River Limmat flows north out of the lake. By the 1st century BC, a Celtic settlement, Turicum, had been established on the Lindenhof. This hill, now in the heart of the old city, was later the site of a Roman fortress. In the 9th century, a Carolingian palace was built on the Lindenhof, and a trading settlement developed at its base. Briefly under the control of the Zähringen dynasty, Zürich passed to the Holy Roman Empire in 1218 and joined the Swiss Confederation in 1351.

By the early Middle Ages, the silk, wool, linen and leather trade had already brought Zürich's merchants great wealth. However, having become too powerful, this merchant class was overthrown and replaced by guilds, who in turn held power until the late 18th century.

In the 16th century, mainly because of the activities of Ulrich Zwingli, who preached from the Grossmünster, the city's great cathedral, Zürich embraced the Reformation. Becoming rich and influential, the city then reached its apogee, only to fall into relative obscurity in the 17th and 18th centuries. In the 19th century, Zürich underwent rapid industrial growth and, thanks to Switzerland's stability and neutrality, emerged from the aftermath of both world wars as a major centre of finance. Zürich enjoys a prestigious position in international banking. It is one of the world's largest gold markets and its stock exchange is one of the most important in the world.

Zürich seen from the tower of the Grossmünster, with St Peters Kirche on the left

◁ **Monument on Bahnhofplatz to Alfred Escher, reviver of Zürich's economy in the 19th century**

Exploring Zürich

Spanned by elegant low bridges, the Limmat bisects the city as it flows north out of the Zürichsee. On the west bank is the Old Town (Altstadt), Zürich's medieval heart, dominated by the Fraumünster and St Peters Kirche. While the Old Town is now the city's commercial centre, Bahnhofstrasse, which follows the western course of the former city walls, is its smartest shopping street. On the east bank, where the Grossmünster is the principal landmark, lie the historic districts of Niederdorf and, south of Marktgasse, Oberdorf. A pleasant walk south along Utoquai leads to Zürichhorn Park, the city's largest green space.

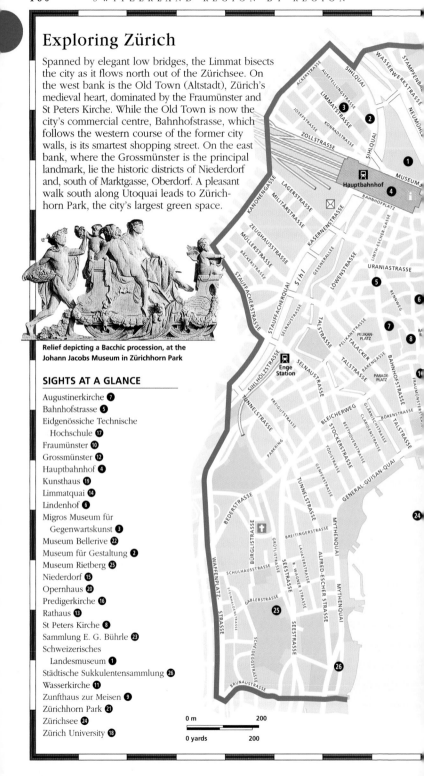

Relief depicting a Bacchic procession, at the Johann Jacobs Museum in Zürichhorn Park

SIGHTS AT A GLANCE

Augustinerkirche **7**
Bahnhofstrasse **5**
Eidgenössische Technische
    Hochschule **17**
Fraumünster **10**
Grossmünster **12**
Hauptbahnhof **4**
Kunsthaus **19**
Limmatquai **14**
Lindenhof **6**
Migros Museum für
    Gegenwartskunst **3**
Museum Bellerive **22**
Museum für Gestaltung **2**
Museum Rietberg **25**
Niederdorf **15**
Opernhaus **20**
Predigerkirche **16**
Rathaus **13**
St Peters Kirche **8**
Sammlung E. G. Bührle **23**
Schweizerisches
    Landesmuseum **1**
Städtische Sukkulentensammlung **26**
Wasserkirche **11**
Zunfthaus zur Meisen **9**
Zürichhorn Park **21**
Zürichsee **24**
Zürich University **18**

0 m   200

0 yards   200

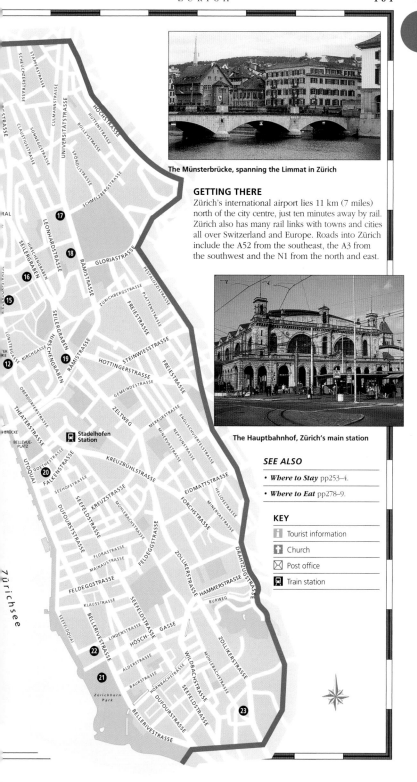

The Münsterbrücke, spanning the Limmat in Zürich

GETTING THERE

Zürich's international airport lies 11 km (7 miles) north of the city centre, just ten minutes away by rail. Zürich also has many rail links with towns and cities all over Switzerland and Europe. Roads into Zürich include the A52 from the southeast, the A3 from the southwest and the N1 from the north and east.

The Hauptbahnhof, Zürich's main station

SEE ALSO

• *Where to Stay* pp253–4.

• *Where to Eat* pp278–9.

KEY

ℹ	Tourist information
✝	Church
⊠	Post office
🚉	Train station

Schweizerisches Landesmuseum ❶

The collections of the Swiss National
Museum illustrate the country's history and
culture from prehistoric times to the present
day. The museum has outposts at locations
around the country but its headquarters
are in Zürich, which contains the largest
collection of objects illustrating the cultural
history of Switzerland. Highlights here
include artifacts from Switzerland's rich
archaeological past and a medieval
treasury. There are also reconstructions
of period interiors, as well as displays of
costume and Swiss handicrafts. Currently
undergoing renovation, the museum now
features extensive sections showcasing its
History of Switzerland, Swiss Homes and
Furnishings, and Collections galleries.

"Feather" Dress
*Among the fashion exhibits here,
including traditional costumes,
uniforms from the 17th
to the 21st century and
designer clothes,
is this modern
catwalk dress.*

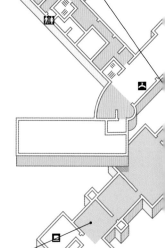

Collections Gallery
*This gallery contains a large selection of exhibits
covering Switzerland's cultural history, with displays
of many Swiss handicrafts.*

GALLERY GUIDE

*While some exhibitions have moved due to
the renovations, the ground floor contains
early history artifacts, the Collections
gallery and historic rooms. The first floor
houses the History of Switzerland gallery
and more period rooms, while the second
and third floors display the arms collections.*

Splendid Sleigh
*This hand-carved and
exquisitely painted miniature
sleigh from 1680 shows
outstanding artistry.*

Ground
floor

Main
entrance

KEY

☐ Collections gallery

☐ Tower of Arms

☐ History of Switzerland

☐ Temporary exhibitions

☐ Swiss homes and furnishings

Third
floor

Second
floor

First floor

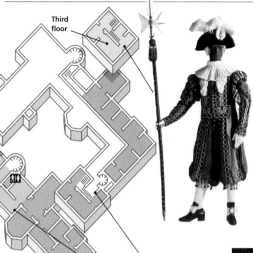

VISITORS' CHECKLIST

Road map F4. Museumstrasse 2.
Tel 044 218 65 11. ⬚ 10am–
5pm Tue–Sun (to 7pm Thu). ♿
☑ in English on request. 🔈 📷
🏠 www.landesmuseum.ch

Army Uniform
*Uniforms like this one, of
about 1720, were worn
by Louis XIV's Swiss bodyguards. From the 15th
century, Swiss mercenaries
served as royal bodyguards
at many European courts.*

★ Customer Safe
*The former Swiss People's
Bank rented out safes such
as this one in its strong
room, in which customers
could deposit personal
items of value.*

Family at Johann Caspar Lavater's Deathbed
*Antonio Orazio Moretto's painting of the 18th-
century Swiss poet and physiognomist in 1801
is representative of works of art portraying
Switzerland's historical and cultural figures.*

★ Globe
*Among the scientific instruments
on display, this globe by Jost Bürgi
(1552–1632) demonstrates an
outstanding combination of scientific
knowledge and artistic skills.*

STAR EXHIBITS

★ Customer Safe
***
★ Globe

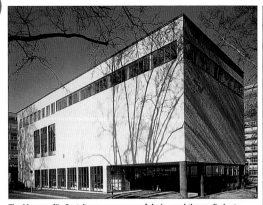

The Museum für Gestaltung, a museum of design and the applied arts

Museum für Gestaltung ②

Ausstellungsstrasse 60. **Tel** 043 446 67 67. ☐ 10am–5pm Tue–Sun (to 8pm Wed). 🎨 ☐ 🎨
www.museum-gestaltung.ch

Architecture, graphic art, industrial design and the applied arts are the main focus of the exhibitions mounted by the Museum of Design. Although it is devoted mostly to temporary exhibitions, the museum also has its own permanent collection of posters, with examples by Henri de Toulouse-Lautrec, as well as a collection of drawings dating from the 16th century.

Migros Museum für Gegenwartskunst ③

Limmatstrasse 270. **Tel** 044 277 20 50. ☐ noon–6pm Tue–Wed & Fri, noon–8pm Thu, 11am–5pm Sat–Sun. 🎨 🎨 in English on request.
www.migrosmuseum.ch

Several galleries with a dynamic programme of modern art exhibitions have made Zürich a leading international centre of modern art. One such gallery is the Migros Museum für Gegenwartskunst, which is located in the former Löwenbräu brewery. It specializes in organizing exhibitions of modern art by Swiss and foreign artists. The museum provides an interactive space for reflection and viewing the works on display.

Hauptbahnhof ④

Bahnhofplatz.

Zürich's monumental Neo-Renaissance train station is one of the city's greatest icons. Completed in 1871, it is well preserved and the original structure of the main hall is unaltered. The clean, well-kept concourse is lined with the stylish signboards of shops. Throughout the year, this space is filled with stalls, and it is also used for seasonal fairs and markets. Beneath the concourse is a modern shopping centre.

From the concourse ceiling hangs an eye-catching statue, its vibrant, almost garish colours contrasting with the sobriety of the surroundings. This is *Guardian Angel*, by Niki de St-Phalle (1930–2002), the French sculptor and wife of the Swiss installation artist Jean Tinguely.

Bahnhofstrasse ⑤

Uhrenmuseum Beyer. Bahnhofstrasse 31. **Tel** 043 344 63 63. ☐ 2–6pm Mon–Fri. 🎨 🎨
www.beyer-ch.com

Running north to south from Bahnhofplatz to the edge of the Zürichsee, Bahnhofstrasse is a long avenue that lies on the course of the medieval city's moat. Mostly pedestrianized, and with tramlines running along it, Bahnhofstrasse is Zürich's principal shopping street and the centre of its commercial activity. It is lined with upmarket shops and chic restaurants, as well as the headquarters of several major Swiss banks.

Between Bahnhofstrasse and Löwenstrasse (to the east and west) and Schweizergasse and Sihlstrasse (to the north and south) are Zürich's foremost department stores, Globus and Jelmoli. Both offer exclusive brands and upmarket cafeteria-style dining.

Beneath Beyer, a watch and jewellery shop at Bahnhofstrasse 31, is the **Uhrenmuseum Beyer**. This clock museum contains a collection of timepieces ranging from the simplest timekeeping devices, such as sundials, to elegant modern watches.

Level with Fraumünster, Bahnhofstrasse opens onto Paradeplatz on its western side. Once a military parade ground, the square is now lined with large buildings, including the headquarters of Sprüngli, the Swiss chocolatier, and of the bank Credit Suisse.

Bahnhofstrasse, Zürich's most upmarket shopping street

For hotels and restaurants in this region see pp253–4 and pp278–9

Bahnhofstrasse ends at Bürkli-platz. Facing onto the Zürich-see, this square is the departure point for boat trips on the lake.

Lindenhof ⑥

A tree-covered hill rises on the west bank of the Limmat. This is the Lindenhof, whose strategic position made it an ideal location for a Celtic settle-ment and later for a Roman fort. In the 10th century, an imperial palace stood here. Although no buildings survive, an observation platform offers a view of the surrounding rooftops and of the university buildings to the east. The hill-top also has a giant chessboard for open-air games.

The ascetically bare interior of the Augustinerkirche

Augustinerkirche ⑦

Augustinerhof 8. **Tel** 044 211 12 75. ◯ 10am–5pm Mon–Fri, noon–5pm Sat.

This beautiful, unpretentious early Gothic church was built in the late 13th century for a community of Augustinian monks. When the monastery was dissolved during the Reformation, the church was deconsecrated and stood unused for almost 300 years. The interior was restored in the 1840s and in 1847 the church was reconsecrated and taken over by Roman Catholics.

The church's present appearance is the result of remodelling carried out in 1958–9. The building takes the form of a vaulted basilica, with a small presbytery

enclosed on three sides. None of the church's historic furnishings have survived.

Augustinergasse leads to the heart of the Old Town, its winding alleys densely packed with fine old houses with oriel windows. It is full of small restaurants and cafés, as well as art galleries, antique shops and boutiques.

St Peters Kirche ⑧

St-Peter-Hofstatt 6. **Tel** 044 211 25 88. ◯ 8am–6pm Mon–Fri, 10am–4pm Sat, 11am–5pm Sun.

The most distinctive feature of the Church of St Peter is its large clockface. With a diameter of 8.7 m (28 ft), it is the largest in Europe.

The church stands on the site of a pre-Romanesque structure dating from the 9th century and of an early Romanesque church dating from about 1000. The oldest surviving vestiges are those of a late Romanesque church erected in the early 13th century. They include the simple rectangular presbytery, which is lit by a semicircular window with an intricate frame. The presbytery is crowned by a tower, the upper section of which dates from the mid-15th century.

The main body of the church dates from 1705–16. It takes the form of a galleried basilica with a striking Baroque interi-or. The dark panelling contrasts with the red columns of the nave and the brilliant white-ness of the stucco decoration.

St Peters Kirche, distinguished by the large clockface on its tower

Zunfthaus zur Meisen ⑨

Münsterhof 20. **Tel** 044 221 28 07. ◯ 11am–4pm Thu–Sun.

This elegant late Baroque house was built in the 18th century as the guild house of wine merchants. It has fine proportions, with pedimented columns dividing the façade into three sections.

The house now contains a collection of 18th-century faience and porcelain from the Schweizerisches Landes-museum (see pp162–3). While the collection features some exquisite pieces by leading European porcelain manufacturers, including Meissen and Sèvres, some of the most interesting exhibits are locally made items produced by Schooren and other Swiss manufacturers.

Zunfthaus zur Meisen, once the wine merchants' guild house

Fraumünster ⑩

Am Münsterhofplatz. *Tel 044 211 41 00.* ☐ *Nov–Mar: 10am–4pm daily; Apr–Oct: 10am–6pm daily.*

The history of the Fraumünster, or Women's Minster, goes back to 853, when King Ludwig the German made his daughter Hildegard the abbess of a convent here. The convent was dissolved during the Reformation, and the site is occupied by the Stadthaus, a Neo-Gothic building that is now used for exhibitions.

The church, however, survives. It has a mid-13th century presbytery in the late Romanesque style, an early Gothic transept and a nave that has been remodelled several times. The Neo-Gothic façade was added in 1911.

The presbytery is lit by stained-glass windows designed by Marc Chagall (1887–1985) and made in 1970. They depict biblical themes, and a different colour predominates in each. The central window, where green is the dominant colour, depicts scenes from the life of Christ. It is flanked by a blue window with a design inspired by the visions of Jacob, and by a yellow window, known as the Zion Window, featuring King David and the New Jerusalem. The orange

Window by Chagall in the Fraumünster

window in the north wall depicts the Prophets and that in the south wall, in red and navy blue, depicts the Law. Chagall also designed the rosette in the south transept, illustrating the Creation. The north transept has a window with a giant vision of Paradise created by Augusto Giacometti and installed in 1940.

The Romanesque cloisters on the south side of the church are decorated with frescoes executed by Paul Bodmer in 1923–32. They tell the story of the convent's foundation and illustrate the lives of Felix and Regula, patron saints of Zürich, and of the city's legendary links with Charlemagne. The emperor is said to have founded Zürich when he discovered the graves of Felix and Regula, who deserted a Roman legion in Valais and who were martyred for their Christian faith.

Wasserkirche ⑪

Limmatquai 31. *Tel 044 261 66 19.* ☐ *2–5pm Mon & Wed–Fri, 9am–noon Tue.*

This late Gothic church marks the spot where Felix and Regula were martyred in Roman times (see above). The Wasserkirche, meaning Water Church, owes its name to its location on an islet that is

The Wasserkirche with the adjoining Helmhaus on the left

now joined to the mainland. Built in 1479–84, the church has an austere interior. Alongside the Wasserkirche stands the Helmhaus, a former guildhall that is now used for exhibitions of modern art.

Grossmünster ⑫

Grossmünsterplatz. *Tel 044 252 59 49.* **Cloister & Church** ☐ *Mar–Oct: 10am–6pm daily; Nov–Feb:10am–5pm Mon–Sat, noon–5pm Sun.* **Tower** ☐ *Mar–Oct: 10am–5pm Mon–Sat, 12:30–5:30pm Sun; Nov–Feb: 10am–4:30pm Mon–Sat, 12:30–4:30pm Sun.* **www**.kirche-zh.ch

The tall twin towers of the Grossmünster, or Great Minster, dominate Zürich's skyline from the east bank of the Limmat. According to legend, Charlemagne founded a church here in the late 8th to early 9th century, on the graves of Felix and Regula. After they were killed at the site of the Wasserkirche, these martyrs are said to have carried their heads up the hill to the spot now marked by the Grossmünster.

Construction on the present Romanesque-Gothic basilica began in about 1100, and

Boats moored along the east bank of the River Limmat, with the Grossmünster in the background

For hotels and restaurants in this region see pp253–4 and pp278–9

the west towers were eventually completed in the late 15th century.

It was from the pulpit of the Grossmünster that the humanist Ulrich Zwingli preached the Reformation, which then spread to other cities, such as Bern and Basel. In line with reformist ideals, the minster was stripped of its furnishings and decoration, so that the interior is now almost completely bare. However, vestiges of Gothic frescoes as well as the fine Romanesque capitals of the nave survive.

The Grossmünster's large crypt contains a 15th-century statue of Charlemagne, which originally graced the south tower. (The present statue on the tower is a replica.) Other notable features of the Grossmünster are its Romanesque portal, with a bronze door (1935), and stained-glass windows by Augusto Giacometti (1932).

The Grossmünster's bronze doors, within a fine Romanesque portal

Rathaus **13**

Limmatquai 55. **Tel** 043 259 68 11.
◯ 10–11:30am Tue & Thu.

Zürich's town hall was built on piles driven into the riverbed, and the waters of the Limmat flow beneath the platform on which it stands. Replacing a medieval town hall, the present two-storey building, in the Baroque style, dates from 1694–8.

The façade is ornamented with friezes featuring masks and the windows are crowned with broken pediments filled

---

DADA

An avant-garde artistic movement, Dada was founded in Zürich in about 1916, as an anarchic reaction against the senseless carnage of World War I. The focus of the movement was the Cabaret Voltaire in Zürich and among its main exponents were Tristan Tzara, Hans Arp and Francis Picabia. Dada's essential aim was to flout convention and the traditional values of the artistic establishment, and to produce art by haphazard or absurd methods. Dada later spread to France, Germany and the United States.

A Dadaist work by Hans Arp

---

with busts. The marble doorway has gilt decoration. One of the most impressive rooms within is the grand Baroque council chamber.

Limmatquai **14**

This attractive riverside boulevard runs along the east bank of the Limmat, from Bellevueplatz in the south to the Bahnhofbrücke in the north. The most interesting stretch of Limmatquai is its southern section, in the vicinity of the Grossmünster and Rathaus. Here the boulevard is lined with guild houses, which have been converted into shops or restaurants.

Among the finest of these houses are Haus zur Saffran at no. 54, dating from c. 1720, Haus zur Rüden at no. 42, dating from the 17th century, and the adjoining Haus zur Zimmerleuten, an 18th-century building with a colourful oriel window. Most of these houses are half-timbered.

Haus zur Rüden, a 17th-century guild house on Limmatquai

Niederdorf **15**

Consisting of a dense network of cobbled alleys leading towards Limmatquai, the district of Niederdorf constitutes the heart of the Old Town's eastern section. The main artery through this historic district is Niederdorfstrasse, a pedestrianized thoroughfare that is continued by Münstergasse to the south.

Niederdorf's narrow alleys are lined with antique shops and art galleries, as well as small hotels, cafés, restaurants, beer halls and fast-food outlets.

Detail on house in Niederdorfstrasse

Predigerkirche **16**

Predigerplatz. **Tel** 044 261 09 89. ◯
10am–6pm Mon–Sat, noon–6pm Sun.

Set amid the worldly bustle of Niederdorf, this church is a haven of peace. Its origins go back to the 13th century, when it formed part of a monastery. During the Reformation, the monastery was dissolved and Predigerkirche became a Protestant church. It is now the university's main church. The building underwent much alteration. In the 17th century the nave was rebuilt in the Baroque style. The spire on the west tower, added in 1900, is the tallest in Zürich.

Eidgenössische Technische Hochschule ⑰

Rämistrasse 101. **Graphische Samm-lung der ETH** *Tel* 044 632 40 46. ☐ *10am–5pm Mon–Tue & Thu–Fri, 10am–7pm Wed.* **Thomas-Mann-Archiv** Schönberggasse 15. *Tel* 044 632 40 45. ☐ *2–4pm Wed & Sat.*

The Federal Institute of Technology, or ETH, was founded in 1855 and is now one of the most highly regarded technical colleges in Europe. It occupies a Neo-Renaissance building designed by Gottfried Semper, a prominent German architect who was also the institute's first professor of architecture.

The building is of archi-tectural interest in its own right, as is the collection of drawings and graphic art (**Graphische Sammlung**) and for the temporary exhibitions that often fill its corridors. The ETH also owns the **Thomas-Mann-Archiv**, in a building nearby. The archive is the entire literary legacy of this great German writer, who died in Zürich in 1955.

The terrace of the ETH building commands a magnif-icent view of the city. Just to the north of the ETH is the upper station of the Polybahn, a funicular that runs down to Central, a large square on the east side of the Bahnhofbrücke.

Universität ⑱

Rämistrasse 71. **Archäologische Sammlung** Rämistrasse 73. *Tel* 044 634 28 11. ☐ *1–6pm Tue–Fri, 11am–5pm Sat–Sun.*

Set on a hillside east of Niederdorf, Zürich's university buildings overlook the city. Athough the present complex dates from 1911–14, the university was founded in 1833. It is now the largest in Switzer-land, and is a prominent centre of research and higher education.

The university's collec-tion of archaeological artifacts (**Archäolo-gische Sammlung**)

Le Corbusier Haus, near Zürichhorn Park

is displayed in the adjoining building. It contains some fine Egyptian, Etruscan and Mesopotamian pieces.

Kunsthaus ⑲

See pp170–71.

Opernhaus ⑳

Falkenstrasse 1. *Tel* 044 268 64 00.

Zürich's Neo-Baroque opera house was designed by the Viennese architects Hermann Helmer and Ferdinand Fellner and completed in 1891 *(see illustration on p172)*. The elegant façade is fronted by two tiers of columns and a balcony framed by porticoes. Allegorical statues crown the roof. One of the city's most prestigious cultural venues, the Opernhaus stages a world-class programme of operas and ballets.

Statues on the façade of the Opernhaus

Zürichhorn Park ㉑

Chinagarten ☐ *mid-Mar–mid-Oct: 11am–7pm daily.* 🎨 ♿ **Atelier Hermann Haller** Höschgasse 6. *Tel* 044 383 42 47. ☐ *Jul–Sep: noon–6pm Fri–Sun.* **Le Corbusier Haus** Höschgasse 8. *Tel* 044 383 64 70. ☐ *Jun–Sep: 2–5pm Sat–Sun.* 🎨

This pleasant park to the south of the city centre stretches out beyond Utoquai, along the east shore of the Zürichsee and around the Zürichhorn, a promontory. The park contains sculptures by well-known modern artists. At the northern end stands a bronze sculpture by Henry Moore, and at the southern end a large kinetic sculpture that Jean Tinguely created for Expo 64 in Lausanne. The piece is entitled *Heureka*, and from April to October at 11.15am and 5.15pm every day its mechanism is set in motion.

In the eastern part of the park high walls enclose the **Chinagarten**. This Chinese garden, laid out in 1994, was a gift from Kunming, the Chinese city that is twinned with Zürich. It is filled with plants, buildings and objects typical of the Chinese art of creating a formal garden *(see illustration on p173)*.

The park is bordered by several interesting buildings. On Höschgasse is the **Atelier Hermann Haller**, the studio of this Swiss sculptor. Designed by Haller (1880–1950), it is a rare example of wooden Bauhaus architecture. The colourful pavilion next to it is **Le Corbusier**

Haus. Designed by Le Corbusier, it is one of the last projects that this Swiss-born architect worked on before his death in 1965. The building contains many fine examples of Le Corbusier's graphic art.

Museum Bellerive ㉒

Höschgasse 3.
Tel 043 446 44 69.
◯ *Apr–Nov: 10am–5pm Tue–Sun (to 8pm Thu); Dec–Mar: 10am–5pm Tue–Sun.*
www.museum-bellerive.ch

Specializing in the applied arts, as well as in design, decoration and crafts, the Museum Bellerive displays its permanent collection in the form of a continuous programme of temporary exhibitions. The museum's extensive holdings include furniture, tapestry, jewellery, stained glass and other pieces produced by the English Arts and Crafts Movement in the late 19th century, and Art Nouveau glass, jewellery and ceramics. The work of Swiss craftsmen and designers also figures prominently in the collections. The shop sells a great range of design objects.

Sammlung E.G. Bührle ㉓

Zollikerstrasse 172.
Tel 044 422 00 86.
◯ *by appointment only.*
www.buehrle.ch

A small but exquisite collection of Impressionist and Post-Impressionist paintings and other works of art is housed in a mansion south of Zürich-horn Park. The collection was formed by the Swiss industrialist Emil G. Bührle between 1934 and 1956 and was opened to the public after his death in 1965.

Besides paintings by Delacroix, Courbet and Corot, the collection includes little-known works by Monet, Degas, Van Gogh and Gauguin, as well as Dutch and Italian Baroque painting and fine Gothic woodcarving.

Sculpture by Henry Moore in Zürichhorn Park

The collection is open to the public by appointment only. Pending a positive vote on the expansion of Zürich's Kunsthaus, it will move to those premises for permanent display in 2017.

Zürichsee ㉔

Zürichsee Schifffahrtsgesellschaft Mythenquai 333. *Tel* 044 487 13 33.

This beautiful glacial lake stretches in a 40-km (25-mile) arc from Zürich to the foot of the Glarner Alps. The many boat trips departing from Zürich range from short trips to half- and full-day cruises, taking in several lake-shore towns and villages. The main landing stage in Zürich is at Bürkliplatz. Being unpolluted, the lake's clear waters are also safe for swimming.

Museum Rietberg ㉕

Gablerstrasse 15. *Tel* 044 206 31 31.
Villa Wesendonck & Park-Villa Rieter ◯ *10am–5pm Tue & Fri–Sun, 10am–8pm Wed–Thu.*
single charge for both villas.
www.rietberg.ch

The vast assemblage of ethnographic pieces and Oriental artifacts that make up the collections of this museum are displayed in two villas set in parkland on the west side of the Zürichsee. **Villa Wesendonck**, a Neo-Classical mansion in which the composer Richard Wagner once stayed, houses the main collection. This consists of wooden, bronze and ceramic objects from Africa, India, Tibet, China, Japan and other Southeast Asian countries. The neighbouring **Park-Villa Rieter** is devoted to Asian art. Two floors of the house are filled with changing selections of Indian, Chinese and Japanese prints and paintings.

Städtische Sukku-lentensammlung ㉖

Mythenquai 88. *Tel* 043 344 34 80.
◯ *9am–4:30pm daily.*

With more than 8,000 species of cacti, spurges, agaves, aloes and other succulents, this collection is one of the largest of its kind in Europe. Amazing succulents from every arid region of the world, from giant agaves to the tiniest cacti, are presented here in a fascinating display.

The Zürichsee, with Bürkliplatz in the left foreground and the Grössmunster in the right background

Kunsthaus ⓳

Switzerland's greatest art gallery, the Kunsthaus contains important works of art ranging from medieval religious paintings and Dutch Old Masters to Impressionist and Post-Impressionist paintings. The gallery's holdings also exemplify the major art movements of the 20th century. Highlights of this superb collection include paintings by the 19th-century Swiss artists Ferdinand Hodler and Albert Anker, the largest assemblage of the work of Edvard Munch outside Scandinavia, paintings by Marc Chagall and paintings and sculpture by Alberto Giacometti. The Kunsthaus also stages large-scale temporary exhibitions.

War
In this dramatic painting dating from 1896, Arnold Böcklin depicted war as one of the terrifying Horsemen of the Apocalypse.

GALLERY GUIDE
On the first floor, Swiss, European, American and contemporary works are exhibited. The second floor displays modern art and photography.

Second floor

First floor

KEY

☐	Swiss art
☐	Early–18th-century European art
☐	19th-century French art
☐	Photography/Sculpture
☐	19th–early 20th-century European art
☐	American art
☐	Contemporary art
☐	Temporary exhibitions

Falstaff in the Laundry Basket
Many paintings by the Swiss artist Henri Füssli were inspired by literature. This one, dating from 1792, illustrates a scene from Shakespeare's play The Merry Wives of Windsor.

Main entrance

Gro... flo...

zanine

Bird in Space
This elegant sculpture, created by Constantin Brancusi in 1925, is an abstract synthesis of the movement and apparent weightlessness of a bird in flight. Ovoid shapes typify Brancusi's mature work.

VISITORS' CHECKLIST

Heimplatz 1.
Tel 044 253 84 84.
☐ 10am–6pm Tue & Sat–Sun, 10am–8pm Wed–Fri. 🎧 📷 ⛪
www.kunsthaus.ch

Guitar on a Pedestal Table
Like this painting of 1915, many works from Pablo Picasso's Cubist period feature a guitar.

Au-dessus de Paris
The poetic imagery of Marc Chagall's paintings was inspired by his Russian Jewish origins. Floating figures, like those in this 1968 painting, are a recurring theme in his work.

★ Cabanes Blanches
Some of Vincent van Gogh's most powerful and richly expressive paintings are the views of the Provençal countryside that he painted in the final years of his tortured life.

★ The Holy Family
This tender painting by Peter Paul Rubens, dating from c.1630, is one of the most important pieces in the museum's collection of Flemish Baroque works.

STAR EXHIBITS

★ Cabanes Blanches

★ The Holy Family

ENTERTAINMENT IN ZÜRICH

The most vibrant of all Swiss cities, Zürich enjoys an extremely active, innovative and multifaceted cultural life. The Schauspielhaus offers some of the best productions in German theatre. Zürich has its own symphony and chamber orchestras. Prestigious programmes of opera, ballet and classical music take place in the Opernhaus and Tonhalle, the main concert hall. Zürich's club scene, which is concentrated in the district of Zürich West and the Industrie-Quartier, has also burgeoned, and its nightclubs are among the liveliest of any European city. With art-house cinemas, small theatres, cutting-edge art galleries and a population of artists and musicians, Zürich West has become the hub of a lively underground culture. Boisterous street festivals with parades and music are also part of Zürich's cultural life.

The Opernhaus, Zürich's main venue for ballet and opera

INFORMATION/TICKETS

Cultural events taking place in Zürich are listed in several publications. *City Guide Zürich*, published quarterly by **Zürich Tourism**, is available free from the tourist office and can also be picked up at various points in the city. The bi-monthly *Zürich in Your Pocket* can be downloaded online or found at the airport, train stations and tourist shops. German-language *Züritipp* appears as a supplement to the Friday edition of *Tages Anzeiger*, the daily newspaper, and is also available from the tourist office. The Zürich Tourism website also offers podcast MP3 downloads of nightlife information.

While tickets for the theatre, opera and classical concerts can be bought from the tourist office, tickets for most events can be bought from **Ticketcorner** or from **Starticket**. Tickets can also be purchased from the box offices of individual venues.

THEATRE, OPERA AND CLASSICAL MUSIC

Having no fewer than a dozen theatres, Zürich is a leading centre of the dramatic arts. Almost all productions are in German. Zürich's main theatre is the **Schauspielhaus**, which is known for its innovative productions. This theatre has two stages: the Schauspielhaus Pfauen, used for mainstream plays, and the Keller, where experimental theatre is staged. Other productions are staged in the main auditorium (Halle) of the **Schauspielhaus Schiffbau**, in the fashionable district of Zürich West. The Schiffbau also has a studio stage.

The **Opernhaus** is one of Europe's leading opera and ballet theatres. As tickets for its highly regarded productions sell out rapidly, booking well in advance is usually necessary. Returns are, however, sometimes available.

The Tonhalle Orchestra and Zürich Chamber Orchestra both perform regularly at the **Tonhalle**. This grand Baroque building, completed in 1895, is renowned for its excellent acoustics. Its inaugural concert, in 1895, was given in the presence of the composer Johannes Brahms.

Music festival in the courtyard of the Schweizerisches Landesmuseum

The best way to ensure you obtain tickets for concerts at the Tonhalle is to book well in advance. This is not necessary, however, for organ recitals and concerts of choral and chamber music given in many of Zürich's churches.

Participants in the August Street Parade

The Chinagarten in Zürichhorn Park

CINEMAS

Most films screened in Zürich's many cinemas are shown in their original language. The initials E/d/f in listings and on posters indicate that a film is shown in English with German and French subtitles; the letter D alone indicates that a film has been dubbed into German.

Large multi-screen complexes such as the **Abaton** and **Kino Corso** screen international blockbusters and the latest releases. **Kino Arthouse Alba** and **Xenix**, by contrast, specialize in non-commercial productions. **RiffRaff**, in Zürich West, is a four-screeen cinema complex with a bistro and bar.

Most cinemas offer cheaper tickets on Mondays.

NIGHTCLUBS

Zürich's nightclubs range from upmarket venues in the city centre to the more relaxed and innovative establishments concentrated in Zürich West. Among the smartest clubs are **Adagio**, with a medieval-style decor and jazz and rock, **Indochine**, with a Southeast Asian theme and disco,

Gun in a courtyard of the Schweizerisches Landesmusem

house and techno music, and **Kaufleuten**, with house and hip-hop music. While **Mascotte** employs internationally known DJs and hosts concerts and English-language stand-up comedy, **Labor Bar** offers the full range of musical styles. **Cabaret**, meanwhile, is a focal point of Zürich's gay scene, although it also attracts a heterosexual clientele.

LIVE MUSIC

The top live music venue in Zürich is **Rote Fabrik**, an arts complex near the lakeshore in the city's south-western suburbs. As well as staging concerts by international bands, Rote Fabrik is also an arts complex with facilities for film and theatre, and it has a bar and restaurant.

Moods, which shares the Schiffbau building with Schauspielhaus Schiffbau, is the city's foremost jazz venue, with international and local performers providing a continuous programme of all styles of jazz.

DIRECTORY

TICKET AGENCIES

Starticket
Tel 0900 325 325.
www.starticket.ch

Ticketcorner
Tel 0900 800 800.
www.ticketcorner.ch

Zürich Tourism
Hauptbahnhof.
Tel 044 215 40 00.
www.zuerich.com

THEATRE, OPERA & MUSIC

Opernhaus
Theaterplatz 1.
Tel 044 268 66 66.
www.opernhaus.ch

Schauspielhaus Pfauen
Rämistrasse 34.
Tel 044 258 77 77.
www.schauspielhaus.ch

Schauspielhaus Schiffbau
Schiffbaustrasse 4,
Zürich West.
Tel 044 258 77 77.
www.schauspielhaus.ch

Tonhalle
Claridenstrasse 7.
Tel 044 206 34 34.
www.tonhalle-orchester.ch

CINEMAS

Abaton
Heinrichstrasse 269.
Tel 0900 55 67 89.

Kino Arthouse Alba
Zähringerstrasse 44.
Tel 044 250 55 40.

Kino Corso
Theaterstrasse 10.
Tel 0900 55 67 89.

Kino Xenix
Kanzleistrasse 56.
Tel 044 242 04 11.

RiffRaff
Neugasse 57.
Tel 044 444 22 00.

NIGHTCLUBS

Adagio
Gotthardstrasse 5.
Tel 044 206 36 66.

Cabaret Club
Geroldstrasse 15.
www.cabaret.im

Indochine
Limmatstrasse 275.
Tel 044 448 11 11.

Kaufleuten
Pelikanstrasse 18.
Tel 044 225 33 00.

Labor Bar
Schiffbaustrasse 3.
Tel 044 272 44 02.

Mascotte
Theaterstrasse 10.
www.mascotte.ch

LIVE MUSIC

Moods
Schiffbaustrasse 6.
Tel 044 276 80 00.

Rote Fabrik
Seestrasse 395.
Tel 044 485 58 58.
www.rotefabrik.ch

SHOPPING IN ZÜRICH

Bahnhofstrasse, which runs north to south from Zürich's train station, is reputed to be one of the most expensive shopping streets in the world. It is lined with smart boutiques, the windows of which are filled with glittering displays of the best watches and jewellery, as well as furs, porcelain, leather goods and other luxury items. However, Zürich also has an abundance of shops offering a great variety of high-quality items that are at more affordable prices. This city is one of the best places to buy souvenirs such as excellent handcrafted work, as well as delicacies including Swiss cheeses and chocolates. Along the narrow streets in the Old Town, on the west bank of the Limmat, and the cobbled alleys of Niederdorf, on the east bank, interesting antique and souvenir shops can be found.

The multifunctional Swiss army knife

Souvenir stall with a range of handcrafted items

OPENING HOURS

Most shops in central Zürich are open from 9am to 8pm Monday to Saturday, although many shops close between 4pm and 6pm on Saturday. While some small shops and boutiques may close on Monday, many stores on Bahnhofstrasse are open on Sunday.

WATCHES AND JEWELLERY

Expensive watches by prestigious makers such as Patek Philippe and Rolex and fine jewellery by such internationally renowned designers as Cartier can be found in the upmarket shops that line Bahnhofstrasse. **Gübelin** and **Bucherer** both have branches here, as does **Swatch Store**, which offers a good range of Swiss-made though less expensive timepieces.

HANDCRAFTED ITEMS AND SOUVENIRS

One of the best outlets for high-quality handmade Swiss craft items, such as decorative glass, jewellery and ceramics, as well as Swiss designer clothing, is **Schweizer Heimatwerk**, which has several branches in the city and another at Zürich airport. **Dolmetsch**, on Limmatquai, stocks a large selection of penknives, watches and other Swiss-made items. The Schipfe district, along the River Limmat, has many handicraft shops. Other specialist handicraft shops can be found in the Niederdorf district and along Langstrasse.

LEATHER GOODS

Most of Zürich's high-class leather-goods shops are on Bahnhofstrasse. Among them is **Navyboot**, which offers shoes, belts, briefcases, handbags and wallets. Another excellent leather shop is **Lederladen**, on Schipfe, which has a fine stock of handmade items.

BOOKSHOPS

An extensive range of books in English is stocked by the **English Bookshop**, part of the Orell Füssli chain, on Bahnhofstrasse. The **Travel Bookshop**, on Rindermarkt, also stocks travel books in English, as well as maps and alpine trekking and mountaineering guides.

The upper area of the Niederdorf district contains many antiquarian bookshops, several specializing in particular subjects and many carrying selections of books in English.

ART AND ANTIQUES

The streets of Zürich's Old Town contain many interesting art and antique shops. Once a locksmith's shop, **Limited Stock**, on Spiegelgasse, has an eclectic selection of objets d'art. **Greenwich**, on Rämistrasse, stocks antique watches.

A souvenir shop, with Swiss specialities

Jelmoli, one of Zürich's leading department stores, on Seidengasse

DEPARTMENT STORES

Zürich's two major department stores are **Jelmoli**, on Seidengasse, just west of Bahnhofstrasse, and **Globus**, on Löwenplatz, also west of Bahnhofstrasse. Both stock the full range of items associated with large department stores, including designer clothes for both men and women.

Both Jelmoli and Globus also have food halls selling high-quality foods from around the world. On offer here are many Swiss delicacies and specialities, including the finest cheeses (see pp264–5) and luxury chocolates.

A popular addition to Zürich West is **Im Viadukt**, a 500-metre-long shopping area that begins at Limmatstrasse 231. It features more than 30 stores, each located beneath an arch in the railway line. Built in 1894, the railway viaduct is now a bustling urban meeting place with bars, boutiques and a market hall. Here artisans sell local specialities, such as cheeses, cured meats and baked goods, as well as international foods.

CHOCOLATE

Shops offering Switzerland's famous brands of chocolate abound in Zürich. A particularly pleasant place to sample and buy Swiss chocolate is the branch of **Confiserie Sprüngli** on Paradeplatz. Its signature chocolate is the Luxemburgerli – macaroons in a great variety of flavours sandwiched together with chocolate. The shop also has a famous café. Other high-quality *chocolatiers* can be found on Bahnhofstrasse and at Zürich airport.

Café Schober, on Napfgasse, in the heart of Niederdorf, is a confectioner's with a café that is renowned for its excellent mugs of hot chocolate. Café Schober also sells cakes.

WINE

Because they are rarely exported, Swiss wines are one of the country's best-kept secrets (see pp266–7). Zürich has several vintners featuring wines from the cantons of Zürich, Valais, Vaud, Geneva and Neuchâtel.

Two of Zürich's leading vintners are **Baur au Lac Vins**, on Börsenstrasse, and **HoferWeine**, in Zeltweg. The latter stocks over 1,500 different wines and spirits from all over the world, including a good selection of Swiss wines. Some vintners invite customers to sample certain of the wines before they buy.

Signboard of an antique shop

DIRECTORY

EASTERN SWITZERLAND AND GRAUBÜNDEN

Traversed by the Rhine, which flows through the Bodensee, eastern Switzerland is a relatively low-lying region. As well as several large towns, it has extensive rural areas with the lush pastures that help produce its famous cheeses. The high alpine region of Graubünden, to the south, is a magnet for mountaineers and winter-sports enthusiasts.

Eastern Switzerland consists of the cantons of Thurgau, Schaffhausen, St Gallen, Appenzell Ausserrhoden and Appenzell Inner-rhoden, and Glarus. The region is bordered by Germany to the north and by Liechtenstein and Austria to the east. With a majority of German- and Italian-speakers, and a small minority who speak Romansh (a language related to Latin), eastern Switzerland is officially trilingual, and religion is divided between Protestant and Catholic. The prosperity of this less populated region is based on the service industries, fruit-growing and dairy products.

East of Glarus lies the tiny principality of Liechtenstein, a vestige of the Holy Roman Empire. Although an independent country, there are no border controls.

Graubünden, bordered by Austria, Italy and Liechtenstein, occupies the southeastern corner of the country. This mountainous region corresponds to the Roman province of Rhaetia Prima. While German predominates in and around urban centres in the north of the canton, Romansh survives among the rural population. With some of the country's best ski slopes and greatest resorts, Graubünden is a major centre for winter sports, and half of its population is involved in the tourist industry. South of the Rhaetian Alps are the sunny valleys of Graubünden's Italian-speaking region.

A mountain stream and pine forest in the Parc Naziunal Svizzer, southeastern Graubünden

◁ A narrow street in Guarda, a village in the Lower Engadine

Exploring Eastern Switzerland and Graubünden

Besides several thriving towns, such as Schaffhausen and St Gallen, and the attractive medieval village of Stein am Rhein, eastern Switzerland has vast expanses of unspoilt countryside, where ancient rural traditions and ways of life continue. Further south is the peaceful Engadine valley, where the façades of historic houses have sgraffito decoration. The resorts of St Moritz, Klosters and Davos, in Graubünden, attract visitors with superb skiing, snowboarding and tobogganing, as well as hiking and mountaineering. The Parc Naziunal Svizzer, in the far southeastern corner of Graubünden, is a pristine wilderness with a network of hiking trails.

Barrels at a wine-harvest festival in Graubünden

SIGHTS AT A GLANCE

0 km   20

0 miles   20

SEE ALSO

• *Where to Stay* pp255–7.

• *Where to Eat* pp279–81.

Bridge on the route from the Julier Pass to the Engadine

GETTING THERE

The easiest way to reach eastern Switzerland is by road or rail from Zürich. Intercity rail services operate from Zürich to Schaffhausen, and to St Gallen and Liechtenstein. Rail links also connect all major towns in eastern Switzerland and Graubünden. Motorway links from Zürich include the A7 to Frauenfeld and the A1 to St Gallen. From the Bodensee (Lake Constance) the A13 runs south along the Rhine valley, passing through Liechtenstein, Bad Ragaz and Chur, where it is joined by the A3 from Zürich. Continuing southward, the A13 runs beneath the San Bernardino Pass and on towards Italy.

Cows with traditional decoration, at pasture in Appenzell

KEY

▬▬	Motorway
▬▬	Main road
▭▭	Minor road
▬▬	Scenic route
━━	Main railway
───	Minor railway
▬▬	International border
▬▬	Canton border
△	Summit
✕	Pass

Street-by-Street: Schaffhausen ❶

Capital of the canton of the same name, Schaffhausen is set on the north bank of the Rhine, 4km (3 miles) above waterfalls known as the Rheinfall. Lying at the point where boatmen unloaded their cargoes, the town was an important centre of trade from the early Middle Ages. The cobbled streets of Schaffhausen's Old Town (Altstadt) are lined with Gothic, Renaissance, Baroque and Rococo buildings, some with frescoed façades and others with graceful oriel windows. The Munot, a circular keep set on a hill to the east of the town, was built in the late 16th century, during the unrest caused by the Reformation. From the keep there is a fine view of the town and the river.

Fronwagplatz
This square, once a site of medieval markets, has two 16th-century fountains, the Metzgerbrunnen with a statue of a mercenary and the Mohrenbrunnen, with a statue of a Moorish king.

★ Rathaus
The town hall, completed in 1412 and decorated in Renaissance style, contains a beautiful council chamber.

Altes Zeughaus
The Old Armoury, in an imposing Renaissance style, is fronted by a doorway richly decorated with relief carvings.

★ Haus zum Ritter
The façade of the Knight's House is decorated with intricate Renaissance frescoes depicting aspects of knightly valour. They date from 1568–70.

Hallen für Neue Kunst is a gallery with an international collection of works of the 1960s and 1970s.

KEY

‒ ‒ ‒ Suggested route

Kirche St Johann
This parish church was founded in the 11th century and completed in the early 16th. Some of its ancient wall paintings survive.

VISITORS' CHECKLIST

Road map E2. 🏠 *34,000.*
🚌 🚆 ℹ *Herrenacker 15;
052 632 40 20.*
www.schaffhauserland.ch

0 m	50
0 yards	50

Schmiedstube
This ornate Baroque doorway, with depictions of the tools of the blacksmith's trade, fronts the Smiths' Guild House.

KIRCHHOF–PLATZ

VORDERGASSE

Museum zu Allerheiligen,
in a former monastery, has prehistoric and medieval artefacts and a collection of Swiss paintings and sculpture.

MÜNSTER–PLATZ

BAUMGARTEN–STRASSE

★ **Münster zu Allerheiligen**
The beautiful Romanesque minster, originally part of a Benedictine abbey founded in the 11th century, was completed in the mid-12th century.

Schillerglocke
The Schiller Bell in the monastery cloisters was cast in 1486. Its sound inspired the German poet Friedrich Schiller to write Song of the Clock.

STAR SIGHTS

★ Haus zum Ritter

★ Münster

★ Rathaus

The medieval town of Stein am Rhein, with Kloster St Georgen in the foreground

Rheinfall ❷

Road map E2. 🚆 🛈 *Neuhausen, Rheinfallquai 3; 052 670 02 37.*

Creating an awe-inspiring spectacle of rainbow-tinted spray, the waters of the Rhine tumble off a cataract at at Neuhausen, 4 km (3 miles) downriver from Schaffhausen. These waterfalls, known as the Rheinfall, are the largest in Europe. Although they are only 23 m (75 ft) high, they are remarkable for their width (about 150 m/492 ft) and their setting between tree-covered banks.

The best view of the falls is from **Schloss Laufen**, a turreted Renaissance castle overlooking the river from the south. From the castle, steps lead down to viewing platforms near the edge of the falls. Boat trips around the lake beneath the falls are also offered. A spectacular fireworks display is staged at the Rheinfall on National Day (1 August) each year.

Stein am Rhein ❸

Road map E2. 🏔 3,000. 🚉 🚌 🚢 🛈 *Oberstadt 3; 052 742 20 90.* **www**.steinamrhein.ch.

With many medieval half-timbered buildings and 16th-century houses whose façades are painted with frescoes, Stein am Rhein is one of the most beautiful sights in Switzerland. Founded in Roman times, this small town began to prosper and expand in the late 11th century, when the German emperor Heinrich II founded

a Benedictine monastery here. The outline of the town walls can be made out, and two of the town gates, Obertor and Untertor, still stand. Rathaus-platz, the main square, is lined with houses painted with motifs reflecting their names, such as House of the Sun or House of the Red Ox, the town's oldest tavern *(see illustration on pp8–9)*. The **Lindwurm Museum** re-creates 19th-century middle-class life over four floors of a beautifully restored house in the old town.

Overlooking the Rhine stands Kloster St Georgen, a Benedictine monastery, and its 12th-century church. The well-preserved monastery rooms, decorated in the early 16th century, now house the **Klostermuseum St Georgen**, devoted to local history.

🏛 **Lindwurm Museum**
Understadt 18. **Tel** *052 741 25 12.*
⏰ Mar–Oct: 10am–5pm daily. 📷
www.museum-lindwurm.ch

🏛 **Klostermuseum St Georgen**
Fischmarkt. **Tel** *052 741 21 42.* ⏰
Apr–Oct. 10am–5pm Tue–Sun. 📷

The riverside town of Frauenfeld, with a 13th-century castle keep

Frauenfeld ❹

Road map E2. 🏔 19, 000. 🚉 🚌 🛈 *Bahnhofplatz 75; 052 721 31 28.* **www**.frauenfeld.ch

Located on the River Murg, west of Lake Constance, Frauenfeld is the capital of the canton of Thurgau. It is a picturesque town with many attractive burgher houses in its historic centre. They include the Baliere in Kreuzplatz, a half-timbered building that is now an art gallery, and the Luzemhaus, a Baroque building that houses a museum of natural history. The origins of Frauenfeld's castle go back to the 13th century. Its restored rooms house a museum of local history.

Environs

At **Ittingen**, about 4 km (3 miles) north of Frauenfeld, is the Kartause Ittingen, a Carthusian monastery founded in the 15th century. No longer inhabited by monks, the monastery is open to visitors. As well as a hotel, a restaurant and a farm shop, the monastery also has a museum illustrating monastic life and a gallery of 20th-century Swiss painting.

Bodensee (Lake Constance) ❺

Bordered by Germany and Austria, the Bodensee (Lake Constance) marks Switzerland's northeastern frontier. The lake, which is both fed and drained by the Rhine, is 64 km (40 miles) long and 12 km (7 miles) wide. Its western and southern shores, which belong to Switzerland, are lined with small resorts that have excellent fishing and watersports facilities. Boat trips depart from several points around the lakeshore.

Gottlieben ③
In 1415 the Czech reformer Jan Hus was held prisoner in the castle here.

Schloss Arenenberg ②
In 1817, this 16th-century castle became the property of Queen Hortense, mother of Napoleon III. Empress Eugenie, his wife, bequeathed it to Thurgau in 1906, and it is now open to visitors.

0 km   10

0 miles   10

Kreuzlingen ④
The Baroque Kirche St Ulrich is Kreuzlingen's finest building. This Swiss town is now a suburb of Konstanz (Constance), over the border in Germany.

Stuttgart
A98 E54
31 E54
34
Schaffhausen
33
GERMANY
Radolfzell
33
Überlingen
Ravensburg
Meersburg
33
Konstanz
31 E54
Friedrichshafen
Leutkirch
13
Winterthur
Argen
A96 E54
Kempten
Thur
14
31 E54
Lindau
Bodensee
(Lake Constance)
13
Bregenz
❺
AUSTRIA
Lustenau
Vaduz   Feldkirch

Rorschach ❺
This attractive lakeside resort has fine 16th- to 18th-century houses.

Steckborn ①
This small town has many fine historic houses. The 14th-century waterfront castle, or Turmhof, once belonged to the abbots of Reichenau. It now contains a museum of local history.

KEY

▬	Suggested route
═	Motorway
▬	Scenic route
═	Other roads
-·-	National border
☀	View point

TIPS FOR DRIVERS

Tour length: 50 km (30 miles).
Stopping-off points: The resorts around Lake Constance offer a wide choice of hotels and restaurants.
Additional attractions: Arbon, close to the Austrian border, has many fine houses from the medieval period.

St Gallen ⑥

Capital of the canton of the same name, St Gallen is eastern Switzerland's largest town and home to a UNESCO World Heritage site. Its origins go back to 612, when Gallus, an Irish monk, chose the spot for his hermitage. A Benedictine abbey was founded here in 747 and, with the establishment of a library in the 9th century, the abbey became a centre of learning and culture. By the Middle Ages, St Gallen was already an important producer of linen, exporting fine cloth all over Europe. In the 19th century, embroidery was St Gallen's major export, and the town is still renowned for this cottage industry.

Marktplatz, once St Gallen's market square

Exploring St Gallen

While the city's focal point is its magnificent cathedral *(see pp186–7)*, its beautiful medieval centre contains many half-timbered houses and mansions with oriel windows. Most of St Gallen's museums are concentrated to the east of the Old Town (Altstadt).

🏛 Textilmuseum

Vadianstrasse 2. **Tel** 071 222 17 44. ⏲ 10am–5pm daily (to 7pm Thu). 🖼
Reflecting St Gallen's importance as a centre of the textiles industry, this museum is filled with a comprehensive array of pieces from Switzerland and abroad, illustrating the art of weaving, as well as intricate embroidery and exquisite handmade lace. Local patterns and products, and the implements that were devised to produce them, are also shown.

Statue on a fountain in St Gallen

🏛 Stiftsbibliothek

Klosterhof 6d. **Tel** 071 227 34 16. ⏲ 10am–5pm Mon–Sat, 10am–4pm Sun. 🔴 last two weeks in Aug. 🖼 book via the tourist office. **www.stibi.ch**
Although most of the abbey was destroyed during the Reformation, its important library, the Stiftsbibliothek, was spared. The main room, designed by Peter Thumb in 1758–67, is a stunning Baroque masterpiece, with elaborate Rococo decoration. The wooden floor is intricately inlaid and the ceiling decorated with stuccowork by the Gigl brothers and with trompe-l'oeil paintings by Josef Wannenmacher.
The library contains more than 150,000 books and manuscripts, including an important collection of Irish manuscripts dating from the 8th to the 11th centuries, and rare works dating from the 8th century.

🔒 St-Laurenzenkirche

Marktgasse. **Tel** 071 222 67 92. ⏲ 9:30–11:30am & 2–4pm Mon, 9:30am–4pm Tue–Sat; in summer: until 6pm Tue–Fri.
This church was originally part of the abbey complex. During the 16th century it became the main centre of the Reformation in St Gallen. The building's present Neo-Gothic appearance is the result of remodelling carried out in the mid-19th century.

🏯 Marktplatz

Once the town's main market square, Marktplatz lies on the northern side of the Old Town. The square is surrounded by fine houses dating mainly from the 17th and 18th centuries. While most of them are built of brick and have intricately painted façades, others are half-timbered and decorated with relief carving. Many also have attractive oriel windows, a feature typical of St Gallen's architecture.
On Marktgasse, the street leading off the southern side of Marktplatz, Labhart is a watchmaker's shop with a collection of musical boxes. These include some fascinating examples of Swiss ingenuity.

🏯 Waaghaus

The elongated Bohl esplanade, leading off the eastern side of Marktplatz, is dominated by the dazzlingly white façade of the Waaghaus, a weighhouse built in 1583. The building is now the seat of the city authorities, and is also used for concerts and exhibitions.

The late 16th-century Waaghaus, on Bohl

⛩ Kunstmuseum

Museumstrasse 32. *Tel 071 242 06 71.* ☐ *10am–5pm Tue & Thu–Sun, 10am–8pm Wed.*

This late 19th-century museum building is divided into two parts. One is devoted to natural history, and contains displays relating to the region's plants and animals, as well as its minerals. The other is an art gallery, with works dating mainly from the 19th and 20th centuries.

⛩ Historisches und Völkerkundemuseum

Museumstrasse 50. *Tel 071 242 06 42.* ☐ *10am–5pm Tue–Sun.*

The history of the town and region of St Gallen is the focus of the displays at this museum. Besides many archaeological pieces, there

The Natur- und Kunstmuseum

are documents, mementoes and reconstructed domestic rooms of various periods. Highlights include a scale reconstruction of St Gallen's abbey and a model of the city as it was in the 17th century. The museum also has an ethnographic collection, with Asian, African and South American artefacts.

⛩ Universität

Dufourstrasse 50. *Tel 071 224 21 11.*

The university of St Gallen is of interest for its modern architecture and its decoration. Created by innovative artists of the 20th century, the paintings and sculpture are closely integrated with the buildings' physical structure.

The main building, completed in 1963, features a ceramic frieze by Joan Miró, wall paintings by Antoni Tápies, a mosaic by Georges Braque and sculptures by Alberto Giacometti. A bronze sculpture by Jean Arp stands in the courtyard. A later building, completed in 1989, contains

several works by the painters Gerhard Richter, Josef Felix Müller and Luciano Fabro.

⛩ Kunst Halle St Gallen

Davidstrasse 40. *Tel 071 222 10 14.* ☐ *2–6pm Tue–Fri, 11am–5pm Sat–Sun.* 🖥 www.k9000.ch

This contemporary art hall sees itself as an experimental space for artists to express themselves freely. The exhibits change regularly, keeping pace with developments in the world of modern art.

⛩ Bierflaschen Museum

St Jacobstrasse 37. *Tel 071 243 43 43.* ☐ *8am–6:30pm Mon–Fri, 8am–5pm Sat.*

Switzerland's first beer bottle museum features over 2,000 bottles from 260 breweries – all empty. The well-presented exhibits are arranged by region, forming an impressive display of Swiss beer history.

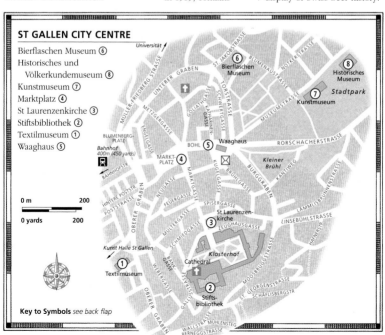

ST GALLEN CITY CENTRE

Bierflaschen Museum ⑥
Historisches und
   Völkerkundemuseum ⑧
Kunstmuseum ⑦
Marktplatz ④
St Laurenzenkirche ③
Stiftsbibliothek ②
Textilmuseum ①
Waaghaus ⑤

0 m   200
0 yards   200

Key to Symbols see back flap

St Gallen Cathedral

The Benedictine abbey was established in 747 and was at the height of its importance from the 9th to the 11th centuries. The Romanesque church and monastery, built during that period, have not survived, their only remains being the crypt containing the tombs of the abbots. The present Baroque cathedral and monastery were completed in 1767. The master architect was Johann Michael Beer von Bildstein. The interior decoration was executed by the foremost artists of the day. Such is the importance of the abbey district, with its works of art and its library (see p184), that it was made a World Heritage Site.

★ **Ceiling Frescoes**
The ceiling is decorated with dramatic frescoes by Josef Wannenmacher.

Main Altarpiece
The painting on the high altar, depicting the Assumption of the Virgin, is by Francesco Romanelli. Dating from 1645, it was later heavily retouched.

High altar

Thrones
Two thrones, made by Franz Joseph Anton Feuchtmayer and decorated by the Dirr brothers, stand among the choir stalls.

STAR FEATURES

★ Ceiling Frescoes

★ Stalls

Confessional

The sixteen Baroque confessionals in the nave are crowned with medallions featuring reliefs by Franz Joseph Anton Feuchtmayer and Anton Dirr dating from 1761–3.

VISITORS' CHECKLIST

Klosterhof 6a. **Tel** 071 227 33 81.
🕐 9am–6pm Mon–Fri (from 10am Wed), 9am–4pm Sat, 12:15–6:30pm Sun. **Lapidarium**
🕐 Jun–Oct: 2–4pm Wed & Sat.
✝ Sun 9 & 11am, 7:30pm.

Crypt

Beneath the Baroque cathedral is the Romanesque crypt of the earlier church.

Pulpit

The late Baroque pulpit, decorated with figures of the Evangelists and of angels, was made by Anton Dirr.

Main entrance

★ **Stalls**

The Baroque stalls (1763–70), made of walnut and decorated with painting and gilding, are by Franz Joseph Anton Feuchtmayer and craftsmen from his studio.

Appenzell ❼

Road map F2. 🚉 🚌 🛈 Appenzell, *Hauptgasse 4; 071 788 96 41.* **www**.appenzell.ch 🎭 *Landsgemeinde (last Sun in Apr, Appenzell).*

Surrounded on all sides by the canton of St Gallen, the region known as Appenzell consists of two half-cantons, Appenzell Ausserrhoden in the north and west, and Appenzell Innerrhoden in the south. From the 10th to the 15th centuries, Appenzell formed part of the territory owned by the abbey at St Gallen *(see p184).* Having gained its independence, Appenzell joined the Swiss Confederation in 1513.

While Appenzell Ausserrhoden, the larger of the two half-cantons, is Protestant and largely industrialized, Appenzell Innerrhoden is Catholic and markedly more bucolic, with a farming economy and a developed tourist industry. It is renowned for its cattle-breeding and its dairy products, most especially its cheeses. Along with its rural character, Appenzell Innerrhoden has strong folk traditions and a pristine natural environment.

Like many other towns in the region, **Appenzell**, capital of Innerrhoden, has a Landsgemeindeplatz, a square on which regular voting sessions are held *(see p30).* The well-preserved historic centre of this small town is

Interior of the Kirche St Mauritius in Appenzell

filled with colourfully painted wooden houses. Other buildings of interest here are the 16th-century town hall and the parish church, Kirche St Mauritius, built in the 16th century in the Baroque style and remodelled in the 19th century.

The history and culture of Appenzell is amply documented by the varied and extensive collections of the **Museum Appenzell**. These range from costumes and headdresses to embroidery and cowbells. The privately run **Museum im Blauen Haus** contains a similar, though much smaller, collection.

To the south of Appenzell lies the Alpstein massif, whose highest peak, the Säntis, rises to 2,504 m (8,218 ft). Popular with hikers and mountaineers, the Säntis can be reached by road or by cable car from Schwägalp. The summit commands an extensive panorama that takes in the Bodensee *(see p183)* and the Black Forest to the north, the Zürichsee to the southwest and the Glarner Alps to the south.

The picturesque village of **Urnäsch**, in Ausserrhoden and located northwest of the Säntis, also has a museum of local folk traditions. This is the **Museum für Appenzeller Brauchtum**,

whose collection includes reconstructed farmhouse interiors, as well as costumes and craft items. North of Urnäsch is **Herisau**, capital of Appenzell Ausserrhoden. The town has attractive wooden houses and a church with Rococo furnishings dating from 1520. A museum of local history occupies part of the town hall.

Stein, a quiet village east of Herisau, has an interesting folk museum and show dairy. While the displays at the **Appenzell Folklore Museum** illustrate the lives, culture and crafts of the local people, visitors to the **Appenzeller Showcase (Schaukäserei)** can watch cheese being made by local methods.

House in Gais, with an ornate gable

The market town of **Gais**, at the centre of Appenzell, is of interest for its colourfully painted wooden houses, many of which have ornate gables. Gais is also an excellent base for exploring the region.

The small hilltop town of **Trogen**, north of Gais, is worth a visit for its Baroque church and traditional wooden houses.

🏛 **Museum Appenzell**
Appenzell, Hauptgasse 4.
Tel 071 788 96 31. ◯ Apr–Oct: 10am–noon & 2–5pm daily; Nov–Mar: 2–5pm Tue–Sun. 🖼

Hauptgasse, the main street in Appenzell's historic district

🏛 **Museum in Blauem Haus**
Stein. *Tel 071 787 12 84.* ☐ 9am–
6pm Mon–Fri, 10am–4pm Sat.

🏛 **Museum für Appenzeller Brauchtumsmuseum**
Urnäsch. *Tel 071 364 14 87.* ☐ Apr–
Oct: 1:30–5pm daily & by arrangement.

🏛 **Appenzeller Folklore Museum**
Stein. *071 368 50 56.* ☐ Apr–Oct:
1:35–5pm Mon, 10am–noon &
1:30–5pm Tue–Sat, 10am–6pm Sun;
Nov–Mar: 10am–5pm Sun. 📷

🏛 **Appenzeller Showcase (Schaukäserei)**
Stein. *Tel 071 368 50 70.* ☐
Mar–Oct: 9am–7pm daily; Nov–Feb:
9am–6pm daily. 📷 on request.

Toggenburg **8**

Road map E3. 🚉 *Wildhaus,
Hauptstrasse; 071 999 99 11.*
www.toggenburg.org

Washed by the River Thur,
the Toggenburg is a long
valley that lies on a north–
south axis between Wil
and Wattwil, then veers
eastwards just above Alt
St Johann, where it becomes
Oberes Toggenburg. With the
Alpstein massif to the north
and Churfirsten to the south,
Oberes Toggenburg then opens
out onto the Rhine valley.

The Toggenburg has over
300 km (185 miles) of marked
hiking trails and cycling routes,
and its gentle slopes provide
excellent skiing pistes. The
valley is dotted with attractive
small towns and villages. Among
them are **Wil**, the main town,
and **Lichtensteig**, which is of
interest for its historic houses.

Wildhaus, a pleasant resort
at the eastern extremity of

**A 17th-century house in
Lichtensteig, in the Toggenburg**

Oberes Toggenburg, is the
birthplace of Ulrich Zwingli,
the leader of the Reformation
in Switzerland. The farm-
house where he was born
in 1484 is open to visitors.
Unterwasser is worth a visit
for its impressive waterfall,
the Thurwasserfälle.

Rapperswil **9**

Road map E3. 🚉 7,700. 🚏
Fischmarktplatz 1; 055 220 57 57.
www.rapperswil.ch

This small town, in the
canton of St Gallen, is set
on a promontory on the north
side of the Zürichsee.
Although the modern part of
Rapperswil has nothing of
great interest, the old district is
a pleasant place to stroll.

Behind the lakeside
promenade lie narrow streets
lined with houses fronted by
arcades, and small squares
with cafés and restaurants

that serve fresh locally caught
fish. From May to October
the air here is filled with the
delicate perfume of roses.
Known as the City of Roses,
Rapperswil has several walled
rose gardens, including one
within a Capuchin monastery
and another that is specially
designed for blind people.

Besides the 15th-century
town hall and the parish
church, Rapperswil's main
feature is its Gothic castle,
whose three forbidding towers
rise above the town. From
the castle there are views of
Zürich to the north and of the
Glarus Alps to the southwest.

Glarus **10**

Road map E3. 🚉 5,500. 🚏 *Glarus
Bahnhofstr. 23, 055 650 23 23;
Glarmerland Rätstätte A3,
Niederurnen, 055 610 21 25.*
🎭 *Landsgemeinde (1st Sun in May).*

Capital of the canton of
Glarus, this small town is
also the urban centre of
Glarnerland, an isolated and
mountainous region lying
between the Walensee and
the Klausen Pass. Largely
rebuilt after it was destroyed
by fire in 1861, Glarus is laid
out on a grid pattern and as
such is a classic example of
19th-century urban planning.
Notable buildings here
include the town hall, an art
gallery with a collection of
19th- and 20th-century Swiss
paintings, and the Neo-
Romanesque parish church
whose treasury contains a
collection of liturgical vessels.

With beautiful lakes and
valleys, the mountains around
Glarus, particularly those of
the Glärnisch massif, are popular with hikers. Many of the
slopes have excellent pistes.

Environs
South of Glarus, the main road
continues to **Linthal**, from
where a funicular ascends to
Braunwald. This tranquil car-
free resort is located on a plateau that offers superb hiking.
Beyond Linthal the road leads
through spectacular scenery
over the **Klausen Pass** (1,948
m/6,393 ft) and down to Altdorf
and Lake Lucerne (*see p224*).

High altitude ski touring in the Toggenburg

The Walensee, with the Churfirsten massif on its northern side, seen from the cable car to Tannenboden

Walensee

Road map F3.

This slender lake marks the border between the cantons of St Gallen and Glarus. About 15 km (9 miles) long and just 2 km (1 mile) across at its widest point, it lies in a steep-sided valley, with the rugged Churfirsten massif on its northern side and the Glarner Alps to the southeast. The region is also known as "Heidiland".

A railway line and the motorway linking Zürich and Chur run along the south side of the lake. Most of the towns and villages on the steep north shore are accessible only by boat or on foot. Cruises on the lake take in **Weesen**, a charming town on the western shore.

A short distance south is **Näfels**, which has a late Renaissance palace, the Freulerpalast. The building houses a museum of local history. The neighbouring town of **Mollis** contains well-preserved burgher houses and

fine 18th-century mansions. **Walenstadt**, on the lake's eastern shore, is a convenient base for exploring the surrounding mountains, taking in **Walenstadtberg**, about 8 km (5 miles) northwest of Walenstadt, and **Berschis**, 6 km (4 miles) to the southeast, where there is a 12th-century chapel decorated with frescoes.

Liechtenstein

See pp192–3.

Bad Ragaz

Road map F3. 4,580.
Am Platz 1, 081 300 40 20.
www.spavillage.ch
Maibär (spring festival, first week in May).

Bad Ragaz, set on the River Tamina, is one of Switzerland's foremost spa resorts. Its thermal springs are used to treat rheumatism and respiratory disorders, and also to promote general

health. The resort has several indoor and outdoor thermal pools. The best-known are Tamina-Therme, which are in the centre of the resort.

Bad Ragaz also has an early 18th-century parish church with Baroque wall paintings. The town hall contains a display of paintings and other graphic works of art of Bad Ragaz and its environs.

As well as skiing on the slopes of Pizol, Bad Ragaz offers golf, tennis and other sporting activities. It is also an excellent base for hiking in the surrounding hills.

Environs

About 5 km (3 miles) south of Bad Ragaz is **Bad Pfäfers**, a spa town with a beautiful Baroque church and a former Benedictine monastery that houses a local history museum.

Southwest of Bad Ragaz is the **Taminaschlucht**, a deep gorge carved out by the rushing waters of the Tamina. Also of interest is **Sargans**, with beautiful Neo-Classical buildings and a Gothic castle.

Maienfeld

Road map F3. 2,390.
Bahnhofstrasse 1; 081 330 18 00.
www.heidiland.com

The village of Maienfeld, in the hills above Bad Ragaz, is the hub of another area that has been promoted as "Heidiland". It was this region of the Swiss Alps that Johanna Spyri chose as the setting for *Heidi*, the story of an orphaned girl that

Bad Ragaz, a spa resort and base for hiking trips

For hotels and restaurants in this region see pp255–7 and pp279–81

has become a classic of children's literature.

An easy walking trail leads from Maienfeld up to the hamlet of Oberrofels. Here visitors can see Heidi's House, a wooden chalet in which the fictional surroundings of Heidi's life with her grandfather are re-created.

Chur ⑮

See pp194–7.

Arosa ⑯

Road map F4. 🚌 🚉 🚡 *2,300.*
🛈 *Poststrasse; 081 378 70 20.*
www.arosa.ch

Set in a bowl in the narrow Schanfigg valley, Arosa is one of Switzerland's most beautiful resorts. Although it lies at an altitude of 1,800 m (5,900 ft), it enjoys a gentle climate, with many days of calm, sunny weather.

The town is divided into two areas. Ausserarosa is the main resort and Innerarosa the original village. The crafts and folk art on display in the **Schanfigg Heimatmuseum** here reflect mountain life in the days before the fashion for winter sports led to its transformation.

In winter the neighbouring slopes of Weisshorn, for experienced skiers, and of Hörnli and Prätschli, for intermediate skiers, provide superb downhill pistes. There are also extensive cross-country trails, a sleigh run and an ice rink. In summer visitors can enjoy over 200

Winter sports on the slopes of the Schanfigg valley, near Arosa

Davos, with the peaks of Schatzalp and Parsenn in the background

km (125 miles) of hiking trails and mountain biking routes. There is also a golf course, and the resort's two lakes, the Obersee and Untersee, offer a variety of water sports.

🏛 **Schanfigg Heimatmuseum**
Poststrasse, Innerarosa.
Tel 081 377 33 13. ◷ *Winter: 2:30–4:30pm Tue & Fri; summer: 2:30–4:30pm Mon, Wed & Fri.*
🖳 **www**.arosa-museum.ch

Davos ⑰

Road map F3. 🚡 *10,900.*
🚉 🚌 🛈 *Promenade 67; 081 415 21 21.* **www**.davos.ch 🎿 *Swiss Alpine Marathon (Jul); Spengler Cup Ice Hockey Tournament (Dec).*

Originally a remote village, Davos developed into a health resort for tuberculosis sufferers in the 1860s, and was transformed into a winter sports resort in the 1930s. Today it is one of the largest of Swiss resorts, host to world leaders at the Davos World Economic Forum.

Davos has close associations with the German writer Thomas Mann, who came here in 1911 and was inspired to write *The Magic Mountain*. Davos is also associated with the German Expressionist painter Ernst Ludwig Kirchner, who settled here in 1917. The largest collection of his work in the world, including many of the Alpine landscapes that he painted during his years in Davos, are displayed in

Poster in the Kirchner Museum, Davos

the **Kirchner Museum**. Although a 15th-century church and 16th-century town hall survive in its old district, Davos is geared primarily to its role as a leading winter sports resort. It has some famous "off piste" powder snow runs. However, for beginners, there are several ski and snowboarding schools, and some less demanding slopes. Davos also has toboggan runs and a large natural ice rink, where ice hockey is played.

In summer visitors can enjoy golf and tennis, hiking along trails, rock climbing and trekking on horseback.

🏛 **Kirchner Museum**
Ernst Ludwig Kirchner Platz.
Tel 081 410 63 00. ◷ *late Jun–mid-Oct & early Dec–mid-Apr: 10am–6pm daily; late Oct–early Dec & mid-Apr–mid-Jun: 2–6pm daily.*
🖳 **www**.kirchnermuseum.ch

Klosters ⑱

Road map F3. 🚡 *4,000.* 🚉 🚌
🛈 *Alte Bahnhofstrasse 6; 081 410 20 20.* **www**.davos.ch

Quieter and smaller than Davos, its neighbour to the south, the discreetly chic ski resort of Klosters has an intimate atmosphere. Of the medieval monastery from which it takes its name, the only remaining trace is Kirche St Jacob, which has beautiful stained-glass windows by Augusto Giacometti. The history of the village and its development into a resort are documented by displays in the **Nutli-Hüschi**, a 16th-century chalet.

Klosters shares a skipass region with Davos, encompassing 305 km (120 miles) of ski terrain. It is suitable for a range of abilities, from beginner to experienced.

🏛 **Nutli-Hüschi**
Talstrasse. **Tel** 079 440 69 48.
◷ *Dec–mid-Apr & Jul–mid-Oct: 3–5pm Wed & Fri.* 🖳

Liechtenstein ⑫

Lying in the eastern Rhaetian Alps, Liechtenstein borders
Switzerland to the west and Austria to the east. It consists of
the estates of Schellenberg and Vaduz, which were bought
by Johann "Adam Andreas" von Liechtenstein in 1699 and
1712, and it was established as a principality in 1719. This
German-speaking country, with a population of 34,600,
is a democratic monarchy, and it has close links to
Switzerland, with which it shares an open border. It is
one of the most highly industrialized countries in the
world. The capital, Vaduz, has the air of a pleasant
provincial town and is worth a visit for its impressive
art gallery, the Kunstmuseum Liechtenstein.

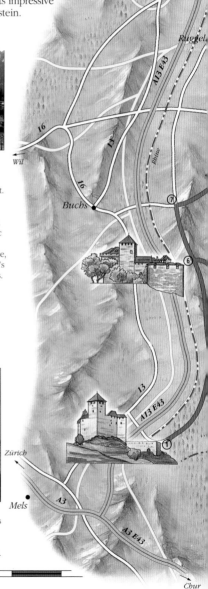

SWITZERLAND

Ruggel.

Wil

Buchs

Zürich

Mels

Chur

Triesenberg ③
This mountain village above the Rhine valley
was settled by immigrants from Valais in the
13th century. It is now a popular holiday resort.

Triesen ②
The St Mamerten
Kapelle, a Gothic
chapel with a
Romanesque apse,
is one of Triesen's
historic buildings.

Balzers ①
Burg Gutenberg, a 13th-century castle, dominates
Balzers, Liechtenstein's southernmost town.
Although the castle is not open to visitors, its
courtyard is used as a venue for cultural events.

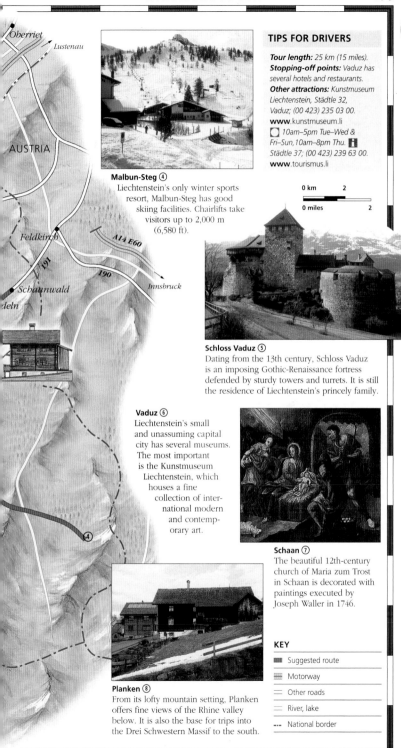

Oberriet

Lustenau

AUSTRIA

Feldkirch

191

A14 E60

190

Schaunwald

deln

Innsbruck

Malbun-Steg ④
Liechtenstein's only winter sports
resort, Malbun-Steg has good
skiing facilities. Chairlifts take
visitors up to 2,000 m
(6,580 ft).

Schloss Vaduz ⑤
Dating from the 13th century, Schloss Vaduz
is an imposing Gothic-Renaissance fortress
defended by sturdy towers and turrets. It is still
the residence of Liechtenstein's princely family.

Vaduz ⑥
Liechtenstein's small
and unassuming capital
city has several museums.
The most important
is the Kunstmuseum
Liechtenstein, which
houses a fine
collection of inter-
national modern
and contemp-
orary art.

Schaan ⑦
The beautiful 12th-century
church of Maria zum Trost
in Schaan is decorated with
paintings executed by
Joseph Waller in 1746.

Planken ⑧
From its lofty mountain setting, Planken
offers fine views of the Rhine valley
below. It is also the base for trips into
the Drei Schwestern Massif to the south.

TIPS FOR DRIVERS

Tour length: *25 km (15 miles).*
Stopping-off points: *Vaduz has*
several hotels and restaurants.
Other attractions: *Kunstmuseum*
Liechtenstein, Städtle 32,
Vaduz; (00 423) 235 03 00.
www.kunstmuseum.li
☐ *10am–5pm Tue–Wed &*
Fri–Sun, 10am–8pm Thu. ▯
Städtle 37; (00 423) 239 63 00.
www.tourismus.li

| 0 km | 2 |
| 0 miles | 2 |

KEY

▬▬ Suggested route

═══ Motorway

── Other roads

── River, lake

-·-· National border

Chur ⑮

Located at the head of the Rhine valley, Chur lies at the crossroads of ancient trade routes between the Alpine passes to the south and the Bodensee to the north. The Romans founded a settlement here in the 1st century BC, and today Chur calls itself "the oldest Swiss city". Around AD 450 it became a bishopric and prospered under the rule of prince-bishops from the 12th to the 16th centuries. With the start of the Reformation, Chur passed to the secular rule of its merchant class, becoming the capital of the canton of Graubünden in 1803.

Capital of the Bischöflicher Hof

Exploring Chur

With the Obertor, a city gate, on its western side, the Old Town clusters around Kirche St Martin. The bishop's palace and the cathedral (see pp196–7) stand to the east. The narrow streets and squares of the Old Town are quiet and pleasant to explore.

The 8th-century crypt beneath the Kirche St Luzius

🔒 Kirche St Luzius

This massive church, which is dedicated to the missionary who is said to have brought Christianity to the region, crowns a vineyard-covered hill on the east side of the Old Town. The building overlies the crypt of an 8th-century structure, which can be visited. There is also a monastery attached to the church, which houses a seminary.

🔒 Chur Cathedral

See pp196–7.

🔒 Bischöflicher Hof

Hofplatz.
The complex of buildings set on the terrace that rises to the east of the Old Town make up the bishop's palace. Founded in the 6th century on the site of a Roman fort, the palace was extended on several occasions, and its thick walls reflect the ruling bishops' need for defence. The palace's present appearance is mainly the result of remodelling in the 18th and 19th centuries. Since it is still the residence of the bishops of Chur, it is not open to visitors.

🏛 Rätisches Museum

Haus Buol, Hofstrasse 1. **Tel** 081 257 48 40. ☐ 10am–5pm Tue–Sun. 🏷 **www**.raetischesmuseum.gr.ch
The displays at this museum illustrate the history of Chur and its environs from prehistoric times to the 19th century.

Exhibits include archaeological finds from the time of the Rhaetians, who colonized the region in prehistory, and from Graubünden's Roman period. Medieval reliquaries and other precious pieces from the cathedral treasury are also displayed. Later exhibits include 17th-century furnishings and other objects. The culture and folk arts of Graubünden are also documented.

Stained-glass window by Augusto Giacometti in Kirche St Martin

🔒 Kirche St Martin

St Martinsplatz **Tel** 081 252 22 92. ☐ 8:30–11:30am & 2–5pm Mon–Fri.
The late Gothic church of St Martin was completed in 1491, replacing an 8th-century church that was destroyed by fire. Among the most notable features of its interior are the carved stalls and the three stained-glass windows created by Augusto Giacometti in 1917–19.

🎪 Obere Gasse

Chur's smartest shopping street, Obere Gasse runs from St Martinsplatz to Obertor, the Gothic city gate on the banks of the Plessur. The historic houses along the street have been converted into boutiques, restaurants and

The Bischöflicher Hof, with the cathedral on the left

cafés. On Saturday mornings in summer, a market is held in Obere Gasse and Untere Gasse.

🏛 Rathaus
Poststrasse. ◻ *By prior arrangement; 081 252 18 18.*
Built in 1465, the Gothic town hall stands on the site of an earlier building that was destroyed by fire. At ground level is an arcaded area that was once used as a marketplace. The upper floors of the town hall contain two finely decorated council chambers, one with a wooden ceiling and the other with Renaissance panelling. Both chambers have 17th-century tiled stoves.

The house at No. 57 Reichsgasse, nearby, is the birthplace of the Swiss painter Angelica Kauffmann. Born in 1741, she later moved to London, where she became a well-known portraitist and painter of mythological themes.

🏛 Regierungsplatz
Several historic buildings, now serving as the seat of the cantonal authorities, line this square on the north side of

The commemorative obelisk in the centre of Regierungsplatz

the Old Town. One of the finest is Graues Haus (Grey House), a stately three-storey residence dating from 1752.

VISITORS' CHECKLIST

Road map F3.
🏔 *37,000.*
🚉 🚻 🛈 *Am Bahnhof;*
081 252 18 18.
www.churtourismus.ch

The Vazerol-Denkmal, an obelisk in the centre of the square, commemorates the free association formed by the communes of Graubünden in the 14th century, when the local population began to organize itself against foreign domination.

Postplatz, at the northern end of Chur's Old Town

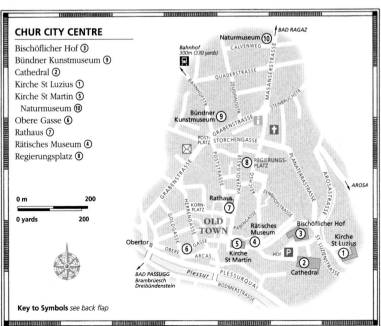

CHUR CITY CENTRE

Bischöflicher Hof ③
Bündner Kunstmuseum ⑨
Cathedral ②
Kirche St Luzius ①
Kirche St Martin ⑤
Naturmuseum ⑩
Obere Gasse ⑥
Rathaus ⑦
Rätisches Museum ④
Regierungsplatz ⑧

0 m 200
0 yards 200

Key to Symbols *see back flap*

🏛 Bündner Kunstmuseum

Postplatz. **Tel** 081 257 28 68.
🕐 10am–5pm Tue–Sun. 📷
www.buendner-kunstmuseum.ch
Chur's museum of fine arts
occupies a large Neo-
Renaissance villa dating
from 1874–5. The villa was
built for Jacques Ambrosius
von Planta, a merchant who
traded in Egypt. This
accounts for the Oriental
character of the building's
interior decoration.

Most of the paintings and
sculptures that fill the rooms
of the villa are by artists
who were either born or
worked in Graubünden
between the 18th and the
20th centuries. They include
Angelica Kauffmann,
Giovanni Segantini, Ferdinand
Hodler, Giovanni and Alberto
Giacometti and Ernst Ludwig
Kirchner. The rooms at the
back of the villa are used for
temporary exhibitions.

🏛 Bündner Naturmuseum

Masanserstrasse 31. **Tel** 081 257
28 41. 🕐 10am–5pm Tue–Sun.
📷 **www.**naturmuseum.gr.ch
This modern museum
showcases the natural
environment of Graubünden.
The well-presented displays
include a large collection of
minerals from the region's
mountains, as well as plants
and stuffed animals.

Environs

A cable car departing from
the station on Kasernenstrasse,
about five minutes' walk to
the south of Chur, carries
visitors up to the **Brambrüesch**,
at an altitude of 1,600 m
(5,250 ft). This is part of the
Dreibündenstein massif,
which has many scenic hiking
trails. Its terrain also makes it
popular with paragliders.
During the summer months,
a chair lift goes from
Brambrüesch up to
Dreibündenstein, at 2,176 m
(7,155 ft). Hiking trails from
Chur lead to Pizokel and
Calanda, at 2,806 m (9,200 ft).

The spa town of **Passugg**,
5 km (3 miles) southwest of
Chur on the road leading to
Lenzerheide, has iron-rich
mineral springs. Beyond Bad
Passugg, the road leads to the
spa region of Tschiertschen.

Chur Cathedral

Begun in 1151 and completed in the mid-
13th century, Chur's cathedral is in a mixture
of Romanesque and Gothic styles. The earliest
part of the basilica is its eastern section.
The nave, with Romanesque columns and
Gothic vaulting, and the tower, topped
by a lantern, are later elements. The
exterior was remodelled in the early
19th century, after the building was
damaged by fire. The cathedral is built
to an irregular plan, the axis of the
sanctuary and that of the nave
being out of alignment. The
cathedral's finest feature is
the renovated 15th-century
altar triptych.

Crypt Figures
*The crypt is supported by
columns with capitals in
the form of animal figures.*

★ Capitals of the Nave
*The capitals of the columns
flanking the nave are
outstanding examples
of Swiss Romanesque
stone carving.*

★ Sanctuary
*The Gothic sanctuary is
decorated with delicate
tracery and figures of saints.*

Stalls
*The intricate decorations on
the 15th-century stalls are
fine examples of late Gothic
woodcarving.*

Pulpit
*Figures of putti
and relief
carvings of
biblical scenes
adorn the
Baroque pulpit.*

VISITORS' CHECKLIST

Chur Cathedral (Kathedrale
St Mariä Himmelfahrt)
Hofplatz. **Tel** *081 258 60 60.*
☐ *8am–7pm daily.*

Frescoes
*Gothic frescoes cover
the walls of the
baptistry.*

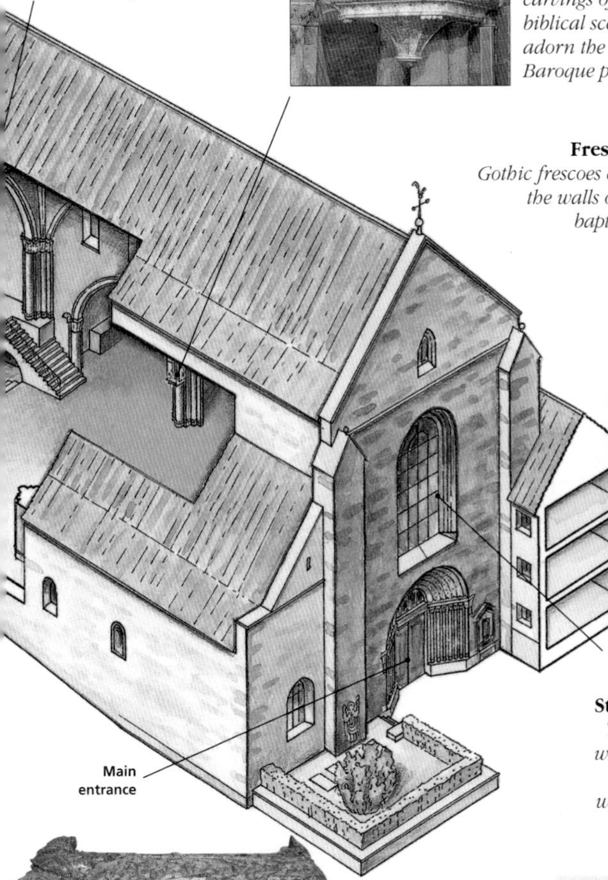

Main
entrance

Stained-glass Window
*The large stained-glass
window in the west wall
features medallions
with scenes from the life
of the Virgin.*

**Tomb of Ortileb
von Brandis**
*The Gothic tomb of
this 15th-century
bishop of Chur was
made in 1491.*

STAR FEATURES

★ Capitals of the
Nave

★ Sanctuary

Sgraffito decoration on the façade of a house in Guarda, Lower Engadine

Engadine Valley ⑲

Road map G4. ◼ *Via San Gian 30, St Moritz; 081 830 00 01.* **www**.engadin.stmoritz.ch

The Engadine Valley begins at the foot of the Rhaetian Alps, near St Moritz, and extends northeastwards as far as the Austrian border. It is named after the River Inn (En in Romansch), which runs along the valley and on into Austria, where it joins the Danube.

This deep-cut valley lies between high cliffs. It is divided into an upper, south-western section and a lower, northeastern section. The Upper Engadine (Oberengadin in German, Engiadin' Ota in Romansh), lies between the Maloja Pass and Zernez. With glaciers and snowy peaks on either side, the valley floor of the Upper Engadine lies at an altitude averaging 1,800 m (5,900 ft) and is dotted with winter sports resorts, including Pontresina and St Moritz *(see p204)*.

The Lower Engadine (Unterengadin in German, Engiadina Bassa in Romansh) lies between Zernez and Martina. Remote, unspoilt and very picturesque, this region is dotted with attractive villages set on either side of the River Inn. Many of these villages have houses with painted façades or sgraffito decoration, in which the upper layer of plaster is cut away to create a design. Particularly fine sgraffito decoration can be seen in **Guarda**, a village overlooking the River Inn. The village of **Ardez** is also notable for its painted houses, one of which is covered with a beautiful depiction of Adam and Eve in the Garden of Eden.

The principal town of the Lower Engadine is **Scuol** (Schuls in German), with a spa and a regional museum. On the opposite bank of the Inn lie the villages of **Vulpera**, which has picturesque houses and an 11th-century castle, and **Tarasp**, with a spa. Chaste Tarasp, a castle, perches on a rocky spur above the village. At **S-charl**, nearby, is a lead and silver mine that is open to visitors.

Most of the towns and villages in the Lower Engadine are good bases for exploring the Silvretta mountain range to the north and the Parc Naziunal Svizzer *(see pp202–3)* to the south.

Müstair ⑳

Road map G4. ◼ *830.* ◼ *081 858 50 00.*

Tucked away at the bottom of Val Müstair (Münstertal in German), and almost on the border with Italy, Romansh-speaking Müstair (Münster in German) takes its name from the Carolingian monastery founded here.

Founded in about AD 780, reputedly by Charlemagne, and still inhabited by a community of Benedictine nuns, the convent is one of the most ancient buildings in Switzerland.

The convent church, known in Romansh as the **Baselgia San Jon** and in German as Klosterkirche St Johann, is decorated with exceptionally well-preserved 12th- and 13th-century Romanesque

House in Ardez, in the Engadine valley, with Adam and Eve decoration

◁ **Cows at pasture in the Alpine meadows of Graubünden**

frescoes. Because of these, the church has been declared a UNESCO World Heritage Site. While the frescoes on the side walls depict scenes from the life of Christ, those in the presbytery show scenes from the life of St John. A depiction of the Last Judgment covers the west wall. Some of the frescoes have been moved to the Schweizerisches Landesmuseum in Zürich (see pp162–3). The church also contains a 12th-century statue of Charlemagne and an 11th-century relief of the Baptism of Christ. The small **museum** near the church contains Carolingian statuary and reliefs and Baroque figures.

Statue of Charlemagne in Müstair's church

🔒 **Baselgia San Jon**
Church ◻ Apr–Oct: 7am–8pm daily; Nov–Mar: 7:30am–6pm daily. **Museum Tel** 081 851 62 28. ◻ May–Oct: 9am–noon & 1:30–5pm Mon–Sat, 1:30–5pm Sun; Nov–Apr: 10am–noon & 1:30–4:30pm Mon–Sat, 1:30–4:30pm Sun. ⬚

Swiss National Park ㉑

See pp202–03.

Pontresina ㉒

Road map G4. 🏔 1,900. 🅸 Via Miastra; 081 838 83 00. **www**.pontresina.ch

The resort of Pontresina, in the Upper Engadine, lies at the foot of Val Bernina at an altitude of 1,800 m (5,900 ft). With several large hotels, it is a major resort and the base of Switzerland's leading school of mountaineering.

Among Pontresina's historic buildings is the Spaniola Turm, a Romanesque tower, and the chapel of Santa Maria. It contains Romanesque frescoes, some of which depict scenes from the life of Mary Magdalene. Exhibits in the **Museum Alpin** illustrate the history of the town and its surroundings.

Pontresina is a year-round resort. In winter the slopes of Diavolezza and Lagalb offer excellent downhill skiing. There are also many cross-country routes and snow-boarding pistes. In summer, Pontresina offers gentle walking along wooded paths in the vicinity as well as more demanding hiking and mountaineering up to the summits of Alp Ota and Munt della Bescha. The trail up Val Roseg leads to a glacier at the foot of Piz Roseg. Experienced climbers can tackle Piz Bernina, which at 4,049 m (13,289 ft) is the highest peak in the Rhaetian Alps.

🏛 **Museum Alpin**
Via Maistra. **Tel** 081 842 72 73. ◻ Mid-Jun–mid-Oct & end Dec–mid-Apr: 4–6pm Mon–Sat. ⬚

Bernina Pass ㉓

Road map G4.

At an altitude of 2,328 m (7,638 ft), the Bernina Pass (Passo del Bernina in Italian) is the highest point on the ancient route from St Moritz to Tirano, over the border in Italy. The pass marks the boundary between Romansh- and Italian-speaking Graubünden.

A road, the Berninastrasse, climbs up Val Bernina on the north side of the pass and descends Val di Poschiavo on its southern side. The pass is also served by ordinary trains

and by the Bernina Express (see p29). The breathtaking view from the pass takes in the peaks of the Rhaetian Alps to the north and Lago Bianco, an artificial lake, to the south.

Poschiavo ㉔

Road map G4. 🅸 Stazione; 081 844 05 71. **www**.valposchiavo.ch

The descent down Val di Poschiavo, the valley on the south side of the Bernina Pass, reveals a very different aspect of Switzerland. Here the climate and vegetation, as well as the culture, are Mediterranean. Buildings show an Italian influence and cypress trees and palms grow in sheltered gardens.

Poschiavo (Puschlav in German) is the main town in the valley. At its heart is the Piazza Communale, a square lined with Italianate *palazzi* and two churches, a late 15th-century Catholic church and a 17th-century Protestant church. Other notable buildings include the Casa Torre, a Romanesque tower, and the Palazzo Albricci. The so-called Spaniolenviertel (Spanish quarter) has houses painted in a colourful Moorish style.

Environs
At nearby Cavaglia are remarkable geological features known as cauldrons. These are natural wells, up to 3 m (10 ft) in diameter, that were carved into the rock by the circular action of stones and water released by a melting glacier.

The Piazza Communale in Poschiavo, lined with Italianate palazzi

For hotels and restaurants in this region see pp255–7 and pp279–81

Swiss National Park ㉑

Established in 1914, the Swiss National Park was the first national park to be created in the Alps. This pristine nature reserve covers an area of 170 sq km (66 sq miles) and its topography ranges from sheltered valleys with forests of pine and larch to flower-covered meadows and rocky, snow-covered peaks. The park is populated by ibex, chamois and deer, eagles and vultures, and colonies of marmots. Many rare plants, including edelweiss and alpine poppy, grow here. The best way to appreciate the park is to follow its well-marked hiking trails. Many of these start from parking areas off Ofenpassstrasse, the only highway through the park.

Hotel Il Fuorn ⑤
Built before the national park was established, the Hotel Il Fuorn is one of two places to stay within the park. The other is the Chamanna Cluozza, a hostel with dormitory accommodation.

Parking Area ⑥
The parking area between Punt la Drossa and the Hotel Il Fuorn offers magnificent views of Alp Grimmels and Piz dal Fuorn.

Punt la Drossa ⑦
Near the confluence of the rivers Ova del Fuorn and Spöl, Punt la Drossa is at the head of the tunnel that passes beneath Munt la Schera, emerging at the Italian border.

Susch

Zernez

Brail

Inn

Ofenpassstrasse

3,124
(10,253 ft)
Piz Nuna

VAL CLUOZZA

1882
(6174 ft)
Chamanna
Cluozza

2,836
(9,308 ft)
Piz Murter

VAL DAL DIAVEL

VAL MÜSCHAUNS

VAL SASSA

3,165
10,387 ft
Piz Quattervals

VAL TRUPCHUN

Ova Spin ⑧
On the park's western border, Ova Spin overlooks the rugged slopes of the surrounding mountains.

| 0 km | 4 |
| 0 miles | 4 |

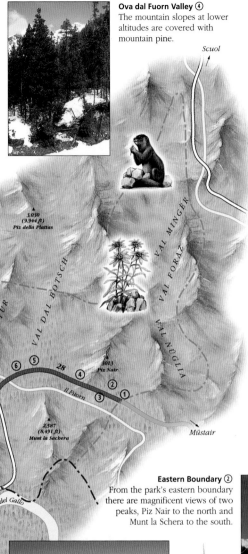

Ova dal Fuorn Valley ④
The mountain slopes at lower altitudes are covered with mountain pine.

Scuol

3,030
(9,944 ft)
Piz della Plattas

VAL MINGÈR

VAL FORAZ

VAL DAL BOTSCH

VAL NÜGLIA

6 ⑤ 28 ④ 3013
② *Piz Nair*
③ ①

Il Fuorn

2,587
(8,491 ft)
Munt la Sachera

Müstair

o del Gallo

Pass dal Fuorn	50 min

Il Fuorn	1 ¼ h
Fcla. Val dal Botsch	3 ¼ h
Tarasp Fontana	6 ½ h
Mingèr	5 ¾ h

Alp Buffalora	20 min
Munt la Schera	2 ½ h
Alp la Schera	2 ½ h
Il Fuorn	3 ¼ h

Alp Sprella	3 h
Döss Radond	4 ¼ h
Tschuccai	5 ¼ h
Sta. Maria	6 ¾ h

Alp Buffalora	20 min
Alp la Schera	2 ¼ h
Punt la Drossa	3 ¼ h

Buffalora
1968 m

Trail Signboards ③
The park has a total of 80 km (50 miles) of marked hiking trails, and for conservation reasons walkers are forbidden to step off them. The trails are open from June to October.

Eastern Boundary ②
From the park's eastern boundary there are magnificent views of two peaks, Piz Nair to the north and Munt la Schera to the south.

Pass dal Fuorn ①
Breathtaking views of the park and the Ova dal Fuorn valley stretch out below the Pass dal Fuorn (Ofenpass in German).

KEY

▬▬	Suggested route
▬▬	Scenic route
═	Other roads
═	River, lake
–·–·	Park boundary
▪▪▪	National border

Cable car to Corviglia, above St Moritz

St Moritz ㉕

Road map F4. 🚶 5,100. 🛈 Via Maistra 12; 081 837 33 33. **www.** stmoritz.ch 🚗 British Classic Car Rally (Jul).

The birthplace of winter tourism, still celebrated for its "champagne atmosphere" at 1,800 m (5,900 ft), St Moritz (San Murezzan in Romansh) lies on a sunny terrace on the north shore of the Moritzersee (Lej da San Murezzan). Surrounded by mountains, it offers superb skiing and snowboarding, and is a base for hiking and mountaineering in summer. It is also known for its curative springs, which have been exploited at least since the Middle Ages.

The town has two districts: St Moritz-Bad, the spa area on the southwestern side of the lake, and St Moritz-Dorf, on the northern side, with hotels, restaurants and boutiques.

Although little remains of the original village, St Moritz has two interesting museums. A domed building on Via Somplaz, ten minutes' walk west of St Moritz-Dorf, houses the **Giovanni-Segantini Museum**. This Symbolist painter, who spent the final years of his life in the Upper Engadine, is known for his sensitive Alpine scenes. Many are on display here, including his great triptych entitled *Birth, Life and Death*.

On Via dal Bagn, just below Via Somplaz, is the **Museum Engiadinais**, which is devoted to life in the Engadine and the history of the spa.

🏛 **Giovanni-Segantini Museum**
Via Somplaz 30. **Tel** 081 833 44 54.
🕙 10am–noon & 2–6pm. 📷

🏛 **Museum Engiadinais**
Via dal Bagn 39. **Tel** 081 833 43 33. 🕙 10am–noon & 2–5pm Sun–Fri. 📷

Sils ㉖

Road map F4. 🚶 600. 🛈 081 838 50 50. **www.**sils.ch

With houses in the traditional style of the Engadine, the charming village of Sils (Segl in Romansh) has a picturesque setting on the north shore of the Silsersee (Lej da Segl).

The village consists of two parts: Sils Baselgia, on the lakeshore, and Sils Maria, to the south. Many writers, painters and musicians have been drawn to Sils. From 1881 to 1889, Sils Maria was the summer residence of the German philosopher Friedrich Nietzsche. The house where he lived, and where he wrote *Also Sprach Zarathustra*, has been converted into a small museum, the **Nietzsche Haus**. The exhibits include photographs of the philosopher and several of his manuscripts.

IN DIESEM HAUSE WOHNTE
FRIEDRICH NIETZSCHE
WÄHREND SCHAFFENSREICHER
SOMMERMONATE 1881-1888

Plaque commemorating Friedrich Nietzsche, in Sils

🏛 **Nietzsche Haus**
Tel 081 826 53 69. 🕙 Jan–mid-Apr & mid-Jun–mid-Oct: 3–6pm Tue–Sun. 📷

Val Bregaglia ㉗

Road map F4. 🛈 Stampa; 081 822 15 55. **www.**bregaglia.ch

The western continuation of the Inn valley culminates at the Maloja Pass (1,815 m/ 5,955 ft), which marks the western boundary of the Engadine. On the western side of the pass a road winds down Val Bregaglia, one of Graubünden's Italian-speaking valleys.

Val Bregaglia, which has many scenic hiking trails and which contains extraordinary rock formations, is popular with mountaineers. It is also dotted with ruined castles and small churches. The main village in Val Bregaglia is **Vicosoprano**, which has mansions and historic law courts. Further south lies **Stampa**, birthplace of the artists Augusto Giacometti and his son Alberto. Buildings of interest in Stampa include the Casa Granda. This 16th-century palace contains a museum of local history and a display of works by Augusto and Alberto Giacometti.

The charming hamlet of **Soglio**, with narrow alleys, stone houses and *palazzi*, perches on the north side of the valley. The many hiking trails leading out of Soglio follow scenic routes both eastwards up Val Bregaglia and down towards the Italian border.

The hamlet of Soglio, on the north side of Val Bregaglia

One of the Romanesque panels in the Kirche St Martin, Zillis

Zillis 28

Road map F4. ⓘ *Poststelle Hauptstrasse, 081 661 21 73.* **www**.zillis-reischen.ch

In the village of Zillis (Ziràn in Romansh), on the east bank of the Hinterrhein, stands a small church that contains a remarkable cycle of Romanesque frescoes.

The wooden ceiling of **Kirche St Martin** (Baselgia Sontg Martegn) is covered with 153 square panels, which were painted between 1109 and 1114. While the exterior panels depict an ocean filled with sea monsters, those in the interior show scenes from the life of Christ and of St Martin. Figures of angels symbolizing the four winds fill the corners of the scheme. The history and subject matter of the frescoes, and the methods used to create them, are explained in an exhibition area within the church.

Environs
About 3 km (2 miles) south of Zillis is the **Via Mala Schlucht**, a 500-m (1,640-ft) canyon carved out by the waters of the Hinterrhein. Steps lead down to the bottom of the canyon.

🔒 **Kirche St Martin**
Tel 081 661 10 21. ⏰ *Apr–Oct: 8am–6pm; Nov–Mar: 9am–6pm.*

San Bernardino Pass 29

Road map E4. **Tel** *091 832 12 14.* **www**.sanbernardino.ch

On the great transalpine route running from the Bodensee, in the far northeast of Switzerland, down to Lake Como, in Italy, the San Bernardino is one of Europe's most important mountain passes. It lies at an altitude of 2,065 m (6,775 ft) between the Rheinwald forest to the north and the Valle Mesolcina, in the Italian-speaking region of Switzerland, to the south. Although snow usually blocks the pass from November through to May, the 7-km (4-mile) tunnel beneath it is permanently open.

The village resort of San Bernardino, on the south side of the pass, is a good base for exploring the surrounding mountains. Hiking trails lead up to the summit of Pizzo Uccello (2,724 m/ 8,937 ft), north of the village, and to Lago d'Osso, a lake 2 km (1 mile) to the south.

Mesocco 30

Road map F4. ⛰ *1,200.* **Tel** *091 822 91 40.* **www**.mesocco.ch

The picturesque stone houses of Mesocco cluster on the banks of the River Moesa, which runs along the Valle Mesolcina. This valley stretches from the San Bernardino Pass southward to Bellinzona and, although it is in the canton of Graubünden, it has strong cultural links with Ticino.

The **Castello di Misox**, a ruined fortress set on a rocky outcrop above the town, commands a stunning view of the valley and the village of Soazza (see below). Built for the counts of Sax von Misox in the 12th century, the castle was significantly extended in the 15th century and in 1480 it passed into the ownership of the Trivulizio family, from Milan. The slender campanile is a remnant of the castle complex, which was almost completely destroyed in 1526.

At the foot of the castle stands the Romanesque church of **Santa Maria del Castello**. Built in the 12th century, the church was partly remodelled in the 17th. The nave has a coffered ceiling and the walls are decorated with 15th-century murals. These depict St George and the Dragon, St Bernard of Siena, patron saint of Valle Melsocina, and scenes symbolizing the months of the year.

Environs
About 4 km (3 miles) south of Mesocco is **Soazza**, a village with an attractive 17th-century church. About 15 km (9 miles) south of Soazza is **San Vittore**, where there is an 8th-century chapel. The **Val Calanca**, which runs into Valle Mesolcina, also merits exploration for its beautiful scenery.

Campanile of Santa Maria del Castello, in Mesocco

CENTRAL SWITZERLAND AND TICINO

*T*he cradle of the swiss confederation and the birthplace of the legendary hero William Tell, central Switzerland is not only at the geographical hub but also the historical heart of the country. Beyond high mountains to the south lies Italian-speaking Ticino, a canton with its own distinctive culture and Mediterranean orientation.

Lake Lucerne and the four cantons bordering its eastern and southern shores have a unique place in Swiss history and culture. In 1291, the cantons of Schwyz, Uri and Unterwalden (now divided into the half-cantons of Obwalden and Nidwalden) swore the oath of eternal alliance that led to the formation of the Swiss Confederation. The region is suffused with historic resonance. Rütli Meadow, on the south shore of Lake Lucerne, is hallowed as the spot where the oath was sworn. The towns of Bürglen and Altdorf, in the canton of Uri, have vivid associations with William Tell. The two other cantons that make up central Switzerland are Luzern, on the west shore of the lake, and Zug.

Schwyz, Uri, Luzern and Unterwalden are known as the Waldstätte, or Forest Cantons. Central Switzerland is largely Catholic and German-speaking.

Hemmed in by the Alps to the north and bordered on almost all other sides by Italy, Ticino is a geographically, culturally and linguistically separate entity. Long ruled by the dukes of Milan, Ticino was conquered by the Swiss Confederates in the early 16th century but only joined the Confederation as a free canton in 1803. This large canton in the sunny foothills of the southern Alps is Italian-speaking and mostly Catholic, with a lifestyle that is markedly more relaxed than elsewhere in Switzerland.

The Chiesa Collegiata dei SS Pietro e Stefano in Bellinzona

◁ Sunset on Lake Maggiore, a great lake on the border between Switzerland and Italy

Exploring Central Switzerland & Ticino

With excellent transport facilities and a landscape that matches the classic image of Swiss rural life, central Switzerland is easy to explore. While to the northwest of Lake Lucerne the land is relatively flat, the area to the east and south is more mountainous. Several of the high peaks here have excellent hiking trails, and their summits offer breathtaking views. Towards Andermatt, in the northern foothills of the Alps, the terrain becomes more rugged, culminating in several high mountain passes. The route over the St Gotthard Pass leads down to the idyllic wooded valleys of northern Ticino. Further south, beyond Bellinzona, are Lake Maggiore and Lake Lugano, two of southern Ticino's most beautiful natural features.

Interior detail of the Jesuit church, Luzern

Costumed participants in Fasnacht, Luzern's carnival

Höllgrotten in Baar, to the north of Zug

GETTING THERE

With its international airport, Zürich is the gateway to central Switzerland. The region itself has an excellent network of road and rail routes. The A14 motorway connects Zürich with Luzern. From here the A2 motorway continues southeast, passing through the St Gotthard Tunnel and on into Ticino. With an airport at Lugano, Ticino can also be reached by air. Post buses, which serve many small communities, follow some very scenic routes.

KEY

══	Motorway
═ ═	Motorway under construction
──	Minor road
┄┄	Scenic route
──	Main railway
⌁	Minor railway
──	International border
▬▬	Canton border
△	Summit
✕	Pass

The scenic rail route between Realp and Gletsch

Lake Lugano ●

Nestling between steep alpine slopes, this sheltered lake is one of Ticino's most beautiful natural features. Although most of it lies in Swiss territory, its southwestern shore and northeastern branch, and a small central enclave, belong to Italy. The road bridge that crosses the lake leads up to the St Gotthard Tunnel. The best way of exploring Lake Lugano (Lago di Lugano or Ceresio in Italian) is by boat, from Lugano and several other points along the lakeshore. Fine views of the lake can be enjoyed by taking the cable car from Lugano to the summit of mountains flanking the resort.

Lugano
The lakeside resort of Lugano lies in a sheltered bay, with Monte San Salvatore to the south and Monte Brè to the east.

Monte Tamaro
The chapel on the summit of this mountain, north of Lugano, was designed by Mario Botta and decorated by Enzo Cucchi. It was completed in 1996.

★ Melide
The main attraction of Melide is the Swissminiatur, a park with 1:25 scale models of Switzerland's most notable buildings and natural features.

Morcote
The small church of Santa Maria del Sasso overlooks Morcote, one of the most attractive hamlets in Ticino.

STAR SIGHTS

★ Melide

★ Monte Brè

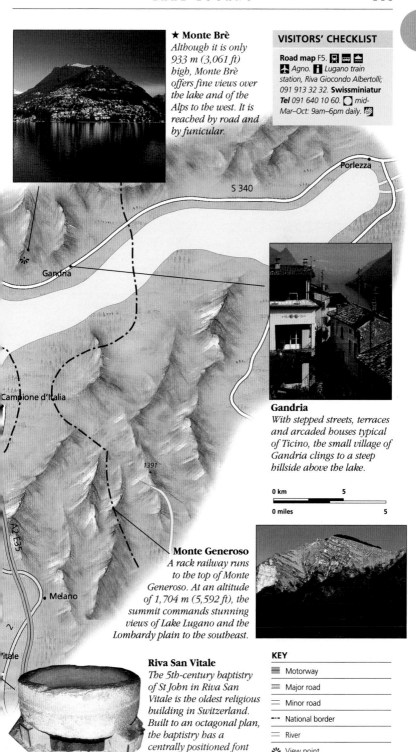

★ **Monte Brè**
Although it is only 933 m (3,061 ft) high, Monte Brè offers fine views over the lake and of the Alps to the west. It is reached by road and by funicular.

VISITORS' CHECKLIST

Road map F5. 🚆 🚌 🚢
✈ Agno. 🛈 *Lugano train station, Riva Giocondo Albertolli; 091 913 32 32.* **Swissminiatur Tel** *091 640 10 60.* ◯ *mid-Mar–Oct: 9am–6pm daily.* 📷

Porlezza

S 340

Gandria

Gandria
With stepped streets, terraces and arcaded houses typical of Ticino, the small village of Gandria clings to a steep hillside above the lake.

Campione d'Italia

0 km   5
0 miles   5

1391

Monte Generoso
A rack railway runs to the top of Monte Generoso. At an altitude of 1,704 m (5,592 ft), the summit commands stunning views of Lake Lugano and the Lombardy plain to the southeast.

Melano

Riva San Vitale
The 5th-century baptistry of St John in Riva San Vitale is the oldest religious building in Switzerland. Built to an octagonal plan, the baptistry has a centrally positioned font and 12th-century frescoes.

KEY

🛤	Motorway
▬	Major road
▬	Minor road
---	National border
▬	River
☀	View point

Street-by-Street: Lugano **❷**

Lying in a shallow inlet on the north shore of
Lake Lugano, this is the largest town in Ticino
and one the canton's great lakeside resorts. Lugano
is also a centre of finance and banking. With piazzas,
stepped streets and narrow, winding alleys, the Old
Town (Centro Storico) has an Italianate character. Its
hub is Piazza della Riforma, a square lined with tall
shuttered buildings and filled with busy pavement
cafés. Palm-fringed promenades line the quays, and
the distinctive sugar-loaf outlines of Monte Brè and
Monte San Salvatore rise to the east and south.

Palazzo Riva
*This 18th-century palace
has decorated windows with
wrought-iron balconies.*

★ **Cattedrale
San Lorenzo**
*The Renaissance
façade contains
a rose window
depicting the
Madonna and Child.*

VIA SAN LORENZO

VIA MOTTA

VIA PESSINA

VIA MAG

PIAZZA
DELLA
RIFORMA

RIVA GIOCONDO

ALBERTOLLI

Piazza della Riforma
*Filled with pavement cafés,
this spacious square is the
social and geographical hub
of Lugano's historic centre.*

Palazzo Civico
*The Neo-Classical town hall was
built in 1844–5 and features a
statue of the architect Domenico
Fontana from Melide.*

STAR SIGHTS

★ San Lorenzo

★ Villa Ciani

KEY

- - - Suggested route

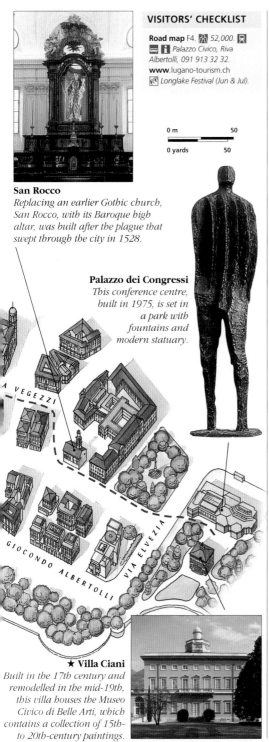

San Rocco
Replacing an earlier Gothic church, San Rocco, with its Baroque high altar, was built after the plague that swept through the city in 1528.

Palazzo dei Congressi
This conference centre, built in 1975, is set in a park with fountains and modern statuary.

★ **Villa Ciani**
Built in the 17th century and remodelled in the mid-19th, this villa houses the Museo Civico di Belle Arti, which contains a collection of 15th- to 20th-century paintings.

VISITORS' CHECKLIST

Road map F4. 🚗 52,000. 🚉
🚌 ℹ️ *Palazzo Civico, Riva Albertolli, 091 913 32 32.*
www.lugano-tourism.ch
📅 *Longlake Festival (Jun & Jul).*

0 m   50

0 yards   50

Renaissance frescoes in
Chiesa Santa Maria degli Angioli

🛐 Santa Maria degli Angioli
Piazza Luini 3. **Tel** 091 922 01 12.
This early 16th-century church, in a square southwest of the Piazza della Riforma, once belonged to a Franciscan monastery. The interior is decorated with Renaissance frescoes by Bernardino Luini and Giuseppe Antonio Petrini. Dating from the first half of the 16th century, they depict scenes from the life of Christ. The sacristy contains a small display of religious artifacts from the monastery's treasury.

🏛 Museo d'Arte
Villa Malpensata, Riva Antonio Caccia 5. **Tel** 058 866 72 14. ⏰ 9am–6pm Tue–Sun. 📷 **www**.mdam.ch
Occupying an elegant 18th-century villa, this museum conserves the municipal art collection and focuses on art of the 20th and 21st centuries. Prominent artists whose work has been exhibited at the museum include Francis Bacon, Edvard Munch, Amedeo Modigliani and Egon Schiele.

🏛 Museo Cantonale d'Arte
Via Canova 10. **Tel** 091 910 47 80.
⏰ 2–5pm Tue, 10am–5pm Wed–Sun. 📷
www.museo-cantonale-arte.ch
With a section devoted to the work of Ticinese artists of the 19th and 20th centuries, this gallery contains an interesting display of paintings depicting local peasant life. Also on view are paintings by Degas, Renoir, Turner and Klee, as well as avant-garde works by contemporary Swiss artists, and displays of sculpture and photography.

Locarno ③

With an enchanting setting at the northern tip of Lake Maggiore, Locarno lies in a wide bay in the shelter of the Lepontine Alps. It is often said to be the sunniest of all Swiss towns, and date palm, fig, pomegranate and bougainvillea thrive in its mild climate. During the Middle Ages, Locarno was the centre of a dispute between the bishops of Como and the dukes of Milan, who finally gained control of the town in the 14th century but who lost it to the Swiss Confederates in 1512. The capital of Ticino from 1803 to 1878, Locarno is now a resort that attracts visitors from north of the Alps who come to enjoy its Mediterranean climate.

Promenade Lungolago Giuseppe Motta, fringed with palms

Wall paintings at Castello Visconteo

Exploring Locarno
The old district of Locarno lies west of Piazza Grande, a short distance away from the lakeshore. It is roughly defined by Castello Visconteo, Chiesa San Francesco, Chiesa Sant'Antonio Abate and Chiesa Nuova. To the north of the old district rises the spur on which another church, the Santuario della Madonna del Sasso, is set.

🏛 Chiesa San Francesco
Via Cittadella 20.
Completed in 1572, the church of St Francis stands on the site of a 13th-century Franciscan monastery. The eagle, ox and lamb on its Renaissance façade represent Locarno's aristocrats, ordinary citizens and country-dwellers respectively. The decoration of the interior dates mainly from the 18th century.

♟ Castello Visconteo
Piazza Castello 2. **Tel** 091 756 31 80.
⬛ Apr–Oct: 10am–5pm Tue–Sun. 🏛
The origins of Castello Visconteo go back to the 12th century, when it was built for the Orelli family. In 1342 the castle came into the ownership of the Visconti, a Milanese family, who enlarged it in the late 15th century. The dovetailed crenellation of the walls and the towers dates from that period as does the ravelin, which is believed to be the work of Leonardo da Vinci. The castle was partly destroyed when the Swiss Confederates seized control of Locarno. The building's surviving wing now houses a museum of history and archaeology. The collection of Roman artifacts is particularly good.

🏛 Palazzo della Conferenza
Via della Pace.
It was in this *palazzo* that the Treaty of Locarno, drawn up between Germany and other European countries in the aftermath of World War I, was ratified in 1925.

🌳 Promenade Lungolago Giuseppe Motta
Lined with trees, plants and shrubs from around the world, this lakeshore promenade resembles the seafront boulevards of the French Riviera. The promenade leads northwards to the end of the lake and southwards towards a beach and impressive public pool.

🏛 Chiesa di San Vittore
Via Collegiata, Muralto.
The 12th-century Romanesque basilica of San Vittore stands on the site of a 10th-century church in Muralto, east of the train station. The belfry, which was begun in the 16th century but not completed until 1932, has a Renaissance relief of St Victor. The austere interior bears traces of medieval frescoes, and the crypt beneath the presbytery contains columns with carved capitals.

🏛 Piazza Grande
This rectangular paved square is the focus of life in Locarno. Along its north side are 19th-century buildings with arcades of shops, cafés and restaurants. During the International Film Festival, held for ten days in early August, the square becomes an open-air cinema.

Piazza Grande, hub of Locarno's social life

For hotels and restaurants in this region see pp257–9 and pp282–3

♙ Chiesa Nuova

Via Cittadella.

This church, also known as the new Chiesa Santa Maria Assunta, was completed in 1636, and its construction was funded by the architect Christoforo Orelli. It has a splendid Baroque interior, with sumptuous stuccowork and paintings depicting scenes from the life of the Virgin. A large statue of St Christopher graces the west front. The Palazzo Christoforo Orelli, next to the church, now serves as the canon's office.

♙ Pinacoteca Casa Rusca

Piazza Sant' Antonio. **Tel** 091 756 31 85. ◯ 10am–5pm Tue–Sun.

This elegant 18th-century residence, with an arcaded courtyard, houses Locarno's art gallery. With a permanent collection, as well as a progamme of temporary exhibitions, the gallery specializes in the work of modern and contemporary artists, many of whom have donated pieces of their work to the gallery. A highlight of the permanent collection is a display of work by Hans Arp (1886–1966), the Dadaist artist who spent the final years of his life in Locarno.

♙ Chiesa Sant'Antonio Abate

Via Sant'Antonio.

The Baroque church of St Anthony was completed in 1692 and remodelled in 1863, when the façade and dome were renewed. The high altar, dating from 1740, features a depiction of Christ's deposition from the Cross by G.A.F. Orelli.

♙ Santuario della Madonna del Sasso

◯ 6:30am–7pm daily.

The pilgrimage church of the Madonna of the Rock (Santa Maria Assunta) overlooks the town from the summit of a wooded spur. Dating from 1596, the church stands on

the site of a chapel that was built in 1487 to mark the spot where the Madonna appeared to Bartolomeo da Ivrea, a Franciscan monk. The present church is decorated with frescoes and oil paintings, notable among which is an altarpiece with the *Flight into Egypt* painted by Bramantino in 1522.

The Santuario della Madonna del Sasso

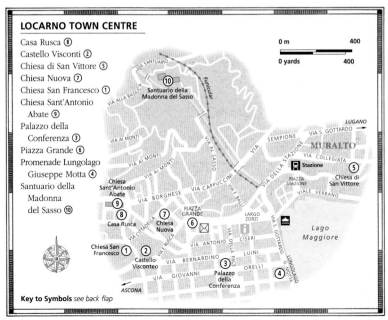

LOCARNO TOWN CENTRE

0 m 400
0 yards 400

LUGANO
MURALTO
Stazione
Chiesa di San Vittore ⑤
Santuario della Madonna del Sasso ⑩
Chiesa Sant'Antonio Abate ⑨
Casa Rusca ⑧
Chiesa Nuova ⑦
PIAZZA GRANDE ⑥
Chiesa San Francesco ①
Castello Visconteo ②
Palazzo della Conferenza ③
④
Lago Maggiore
ASCONA

Key to Symbols see back flap

Around Lake Maggiore **4**

Only the northern tip of this long, slender lake lies in Switzerland, the remaining portion curving southwards into Italian territory. Some 60 km (40 miles) long and 6 km (4 miles) wide, Lake Maggiore is hemmed in by mountains to the north, south and west. Sheltered by these mountains, this beautiful lake basks in a Mediterranean climate. Boats and hydrofoils cross the lake from Ascona, Locarno and Brissago, taking passengers all the way down to the resorts in its Italian section.

Ascona ⑤
Renowned for its mild climate and beautiful setting, this fashionable resort once attracted many artists.

Ronco ③
Set on a steep mountainside, this small town has beautiful views of the lake and of the Isole di Brissago.

Isole di Brissago ④
One of these two islands can be reached by boat from Locarno, Ascona and Ronco.

Domodossola

Tegna

⑥

⑤

③

④

13

Gerra
Gambarogno

②

①

Lake Maggiore

Brissago ②
This lakeside town is well known for its cigar factory. It is also the burial place of the Italian composer Ruggero Leoncavallo (1858–1919).

Verbania

Madonna di Ponte ①
This 16th-century Renaissance church is located in Brissago. On the high altar is a painting of the Assumption of the Virgin dating from 1569.

KEY

▬▬	Suggested route
▬▬	Scenic route
═	Other roads
═	River, lake
❄	View point

TIPS FOR DRIVERS

Tour length: 40 km (25 miles).
Stopping-off places:
Ascona and Locarno have the
widest choice of restaurants.
Other attractions: Tenero is a
very popular lakeside beach
resort at the northern tip of the
lake. ⬭ Apr–Oct: 9am–6pm
daily. 📷 🏨 091 791 00 91;
www.ascona.locarno.com

Locarno ⑥

The Santuario della Madonna
del Sasso (see pp214–15),
which towers over Locarno,
is accessible on foot or by
funicular.

Magadino ⑦

In summer, organ recitals
take place in Magadino's
Neo-Classical parish
church.

Gordola

Cugnasco

Bellinzona

Ticino

Bellinzona

0 km   5

0 miles   5

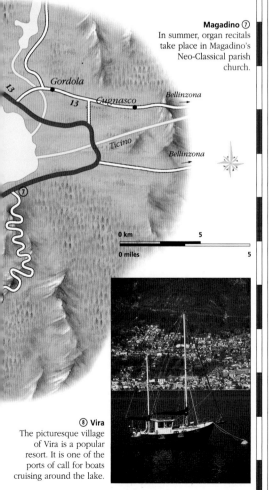

⑧ Vira

The picturesque village
of Vira is a popular
resort. It is one of the
ports of call for boats
cruising around the lake.

**A narrow alley in Ascona's
historic district**

Ascona ❺

Road map E5. 👥 5,000. 🏨 Via B.
Papio 5, 091 791 00 91.
www.ascona.locarno.com

A small fishing village for
many centuries, Ascona
developed in the early 20th
century, when it became a
fashionable health resort,
attracting writers, painters
and composers. Nearby
Monte Verita (Hill of Truth)
was established as a progressive colony around the same
time, attracting some of
Europe's leading thinkers, artists, revolutionaries and writers.

Ascona's exquisite Old Town
(Centro Storico) is a maze of
narrow cobbled streets lined
with small craft shops and art
galleries. Many of the most
picturesque of Ascona's
historic buildings, the oldest
of which date from the 14th
century, line Contrada
Maggiore. Piazza San Pietro is
dominated by the 16th-century
Chiesa dei SS Pietro e Paolo,
which has an altarpiece
painted by Giovanni Serodine,
a pupil of Caravaggio. Also
notable are the Collegio Papio,
a Renaissance building with
an arcaded courtyard, and
Santa Maria della Misericordia,
a church with 15th-century
frescoes. The Museo Comunale
d'Arte Moderna, in a 16th-
century *palazzo*, contains work
by artists associated with the
town, including Paul Klee.
Piazza Motta, a pedestrianized
lakefront promenade, is lined
with cafés and restaurants.

The village of Lionza, in the Centovalli

Centovalli ❻

Road map E5. ⓘ *Intragna; 091 780 75 00.* **www***.centovalli.ch*

The stunning Centovalli (Valley of a Hundred Valleys) is so named for the many side valleys that cut into it. The **Centovalli Railway**, from Locarno to Domodossola in Italy, takes a spectacularly scenic route up the Centovalli. On this journey of about 40 km (25 miles), the train crosses 79 bridges or viaducts over deep canyons and passes through 24 tunnels. The first part of the journey leads along the vineyard-covered Val Pedemonte and then enters more rugged country, with forests of chestnut trees.

The train stops at several villages along the route. At **Verscio**, 4 km (2.5 miles) from Locarno, there is a school of circus art, run by the famous Swiss clown Dimitri. Nearby **Intragna** has a Baroque church. **Palagnedra** has a small Gothic church decorated with 15th-century frescoes.

🚂 **Centovalli Railway**
Via Franzoni 1, Locarno.
Tel *091 751 87 31.*

Valle Maggia ❼

Road map E5. ⓘ *091 753 18 85.* **www***.vallemaggia.ch*

This deep valley runs for about 50 km (30 miles) northwest of Ascona up to Cevio. At its lower levels, the valley is wide, though as it ascends into the high Alps it becomes increasingly rugged, with forests of pine and larch. The valley is also dotted with historical buildings and churches amongst chalets and villages.

At **Maggia**, the largest village in the valley, is the 15th-century Chiesa Santa Maria delle Grazie. The exterior of this church is unremarkable but the interior is decorated with dazzling 16th- and 17th-century frescoes.

Past **Giumaglio**, where there are dramatic waterfalls, the road leads further up the valley to **Cevio**. A notable feature of this village is the 17th-century Palazzo Pretorio, its façade featuring the coats of arms of the bailiffs who successively occupied the building. Nearby stands the Palazzo Franzoni (1630), which houses a museum of regional history.

The hamlet of **Mogno** contains the serenely beautiful Chiesa di San Giovanni Battista. Designed by the Ticinese architect Mario Botta and completed in 1996, this

Detail of a fresco in the church at Brione-Verzasca

extraordinary church is built of local stone. The interior is lined with white marble and grey granite arranged in stripes and chequer patterns. Their effect is enhanced by the play of light entering through the translucent ceiling.

Val Verzasca ❽

Road map E5. ⓘ *Via Lugano 12, Bellinzona; 091 825 70 56.* **www***.ticino.ch*

Washed by the emerald waters of the River Verzasca, Val Verzasca is the smallest of the valleys lying north of Locarno. A gigantic dam near the mouth of the valley has created the Lago di Vogorno, a large artificial lake. The valley is lined with villages, whose stone houses cling to the mountainsides. **Vogorno** has a small church decorated with Byzantine

Chiesa di San Giovanni Battista at Mogno, in Valle Maggia

The Ponte dei Salti, a medieval bridge near Lavertezzo, in Val Verzasca

frescoes. Near **Lavertezzo**, the river is spanned by the Ponte dei Salti, a medieval double-arched bridge. A modern art trail, running for 4 km long (3 miles) between Lavertezzo and Brione, is lined with works by 34 Italian, Swiss and German sculptors.

At **Brione-Verzasca** is a church whose origins go back to the 13th century. Its façade is decorated with a painting of St Christopher and the interior features 15th-century frescoes. At the head of the valley lies the village of **Sonogno**, with stone houses typical of the Ticino. One of them, Casa Genardini, houses a regional museum.

Bellinzona ❾

See pp220–21.

Val di Blenio ❿

Road map E4. 🚹 *091 872 14 87.* **www**.blenio.com

This broad scenic valley, washed by the River Brenno, leads up to the Lucomagno Pass (1,916 m/6,286 ft). The road up the valley and over the pass leads into Graubünden. Val di Blenio lies in the heart of rural Ticino. It has magnificent scenery and is dotted with picturesque villages.

Biasca, at the foot of the valley, has a Romanesque church

with Gothic frescoes. Just north of Biasca is **Malvaglia**. The 16th- to 17th-century church here has a Romanesque tower and its façade features a large painting of St Christopher.

Negrentino is notable for its early Romanesque church of St Ambrose, whose tall square belfry tower can be seen from afar. The interior of the church is decorated with frescoes dating from the 11th to the 16th centuries. **Lottinga** has an interesting museum of regional history. The villages higher up the valley, such as **Olivone**, are good bases for mountain hiking.

Airolo ⓫

Road map E4. 🚹 *091 869 15 33.* **www**.airolo.ch

Located just below the St Gotthard Pass, Airolo lies at the point where the motorway and railway line through the St Gotthard Tunnel emerge. As it is by-passed by these major routes, Airolo is a quiet town and, with several hotels, it is a convenient base for exploring the valley that stretches out below. A plaque in the town

Commemorative plaque in Airolo

commemorates the 177 people who died during the tunnel's construction in the 1880s.

Environs
Valle Leventina, below Airolo, carries the motorway and main railway line that run from Zürich to Bellinzona and Lugano. The valley is dotted with small towns and villages, many of which have interesting churches. While **Chiggiogna** has a church with 15th-century frescoes, **Chironico** has a 10th-century church with 14th-century frescoes. The 12th-century church in **Giornico** is one of the finest in the Ticino. The interior is decorated with frescoes dating from 1478.

St Gotthard Pass ⓬

Road map E4. 🚹 *091 869 12 35.* **www**.passosangottardo.ch

With the Reuss Valley in the canton of Uri to the north, and the Ticino valley to the south, the St Gotthard Pass lies at an altitude of 2,108 m (6,916 ft). It is on the principal route from northern Europe to Italy.

The pass has been used since the 13th century, when a bridge was built across a gorge near Andermatt. It was only in the 19th century, when a 15-km (9-mile) road and rail tunnel was built, that the route began to carry a large volume of traffic. Because of heavy snowfall, the pass is closed in winter, usually from November to April.

The 19th-century hospice on the pass houses the **Museo Nazionale del San Gottardo**. The museum documents the history of the pass and describes the plants and animals of this high Alpine region.

Marked trails lead up to the summit of many of the surrounding peaks, including Pizzo Lucendro, and to mountain terraces from which there are splendid views.

🏛 **Museo Nazionale del San Gottardo**
Tel *091 869 15 25* 🕘 Jun–Oct: 9am–6pm daily. 🚫

Bellinzona ⑨

Because of its location in a valley on the route over the great Alpine passes, Bellinzona was a fortress town from Roman times. During the Middle Ages, the dukes of Milan built three castles here, enabling them to defend this strategically placed town and control traffic passing through the valley. The Swiss Confederates seized control of Bellinzona in the 16th century, holding the town for 300 years. After gaining its independence in 1803, Bellinzona became the capital of Ticino. Its three castles, Castelgrande, Montebello and Sasso Corbaro, have together been declared a UNESCO World Heritage Site.

Chiesa Collegiata SS Pietro e Stefano

Exploring Bellinzona
The best starting point for an exploration of Bellinzona is Castelgrande, which can be reached by taking a lift located to one side of Piazzella Mario della Valle. Steps from the castle platform wind down to Piazza Collegiata, in the heart of the Old Town, where there are several fine Renaissance buildings. A path east of the piazza leads up to Castello di Montebello. From here, a steep road leads on up to Castello di Sasso Corbaro.

♣ Castelgrande
Tel 091 825 81 45.
Museum ☐ Apr–Oct: 10am–6pm daily; Nov–Mar: 10am–5pm daily.
Castle 10am–6pm Mon, 9am–10pm Tue–Sun. 🏛
Set on a high plateau on the west side of the Old Town, this is the oldest and most impressive of Bellinzona's three castles. In the 12th century, the Roman fortress that already stood on the site was rebuilt and enlarged by the bishops of Como. The castle underwent a further phase of rebuilding after 1242, when Bellinzona was conquered by the dukes of Milan. The fortress was extended on several occasions until the late 15th century.
Today Castelgrande's main features are two square towers, the Torre Bianca (White Tower) and Torre Nera (Black Tower), which are joined by crenellated walls forming inner baileys.

The museum, in the south wing of the castle, documents the history of Bellinzona. Also on display here is a set of 15th-century painted panels from the walls and ceiling of a villa in Bellinzona.

Renaissance arcades around the courtyard of the Palazzo Civico

⚏ Old Town
Bellinzona's Old Town nestles in the wide Ticino valley, in the shadow of its great medieval castles. With Italianate squares, Renaissance buildings, and red cobblestones in its winding alleys, it is a typical Lombard town.
Among Bellinzona's many fine buildings is the Palazzo Civico, an elegant town hall with an arcaded courtyard in the Renaissance style. Other notable buildings are the **Chiesa Santa Maria delle Grazie**, a church with 15th-century frescoes depicting the Passion and Crucifixion, and the **Chiesa di San Rocco**, a Gothic church with a Baroque interior.
On Saturday mornings the Old Town is filled with colourful market stalls heaped with fresh produce, cheeses, bread, wines and local crafts.

⚓ Chiesa Collegiata dei SS Pietro e Stefano
This Renaissance monastery church, whose imposing façade is pierced by a rose window, stands at the foot of the ramparts of Castelgrande. Built originally in the Gothic style, it was rebuilt in the first half of the 16th century to plans by Thomas Rodari, the architect of Como's cathedral. The interior, in which the

Firework display over Castelgrande

For hotels and restaurants in this region see pp257–9 and pp282–3

earlier Gothic arches are preserved, is decorated with elaborate stuccowork and frescoes in a lavish Baroque style. Over the high altar is a depiction of the Crucifixion, painted by Simone Peterzano in 1658.

♣ Castello di Montebello

Tel 091 825 13 42.
Castle ○ Apr–Nov: 8am–8pm daily.
Museum ○ Apr–Oct: 10am–6pm daily. 🖼

Consisting of a 13th-century keep and a 15th-century residential palace surrounded by walls, this fortress is the most complex of Bellinzona's three castles. The crenellated walls linking Castello di Montebello, to the east of the town, and Castelgrande, to the west, created a formidable defence system across the valley.

The museum, in the keep, contains an interesting collection of archaeological artefacts from the vicinity of Bellinzona, as well as weapons and armour.

Doorway, Chiesa dei SS Pietro e Stefano

♣ Castello di Sasso Corbaro

Tel 091 825 59 06.
Castle ○ 10am–6pm Mon, 10am–10pm Tue–Sun.
Museum ○ Apr–Oct: 10am–6pm daily. 🖼

Castello di Sasso Corbaro is the most recent of Bellinzona's three fortresses. It was built in 1479 on the orders of the Duke of Milan, after the Swiss had defeated the Milanese at the Battle of Giornico, thus posing an increased threat to Ticino.

The fortress consists of a tall quadrilateral residential tower and square ramparts defended by a corner tower. The fortress is set on an elevated headland on the east side of the town, and commands wide views across the Ticino valley all the way to the northern tip of Lake Maggiore in the southwest (see pp216–17).

The museum, which is in the keep, contains displays illustrating the folk art and traditional crafts of Ticino.

VISITORS' CHECKLIST

Road map E5. 🏚 17,000.
🚌 🚉 ℹ Palazzo Civico; 091 825 21 31.
www.bellinzonaturismo.ch
📅 Rabadan (carnival; Feb).

🏛 Villa dei Cedri

Piazza San Biagio. **Tel** 091 821 85 20.
○ 2–6pm Tue–Fri, 11am–6pm Sat–Sun. 🖼 www.villacedri.ch

Set in extensive grounds, with a vineyard, this late 19th-century Neo-Renaissance villa is the town's art gallery. Its collection consists of 19th- and 20th-century paintings mainly by Swiss and Italian artists of Ticino and Lombardy. Works by the Swiss Symbolist painter Giovanni Segantini form part of the collection. Also on display is a collection of prints, including examples by Oskar Kokoschka and Alfonse Mucha.

Environs

Less than 2 km (1 mile) south of Bellinzona is **Ravecchia**. In this town is an attractive Romanesque church, the Chiesa di San Biagio, which is decorated with Gothic frescoes.

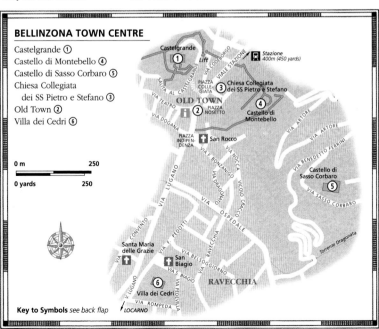

BELLINZONA TOWN CENTRE

Castelgrande ①
Castello di Montebello ④
Castello di Sasso Corbaro ⑤
Chiesa Collegiata
   dei SS Pietro e Stefano ③
Old Town ②
Villa dei Cedri ⑥

0 m   250
0 yards   250

Key to Symbols see back flap

Three Passes ⑬

The circular route over the Uri Alps traverses some of the most spectacular high Alpine scenery in Switzerland. On the route are three mountain passes: the Susten Pass, Grimsel Pass and Furka Pass, each of which mark cantonal borders. A feat of 19th-century engineering, the road twists and turns, makes tightly winding ascents and descents, crosses bridges over dramatically plunging valleys, and passes through tunnels cut into the rock. All along the route are spectacular views of snow-capped mountains, majestic glaciers and beautiful mountain lakes.

Susten Pass ⑤
On the border between the cantons of Bern and Uri, the Susten Pass lies at an altitude of 2,224 m (7,297 ft).

Innertkirchen ⑥
This small town lies at the point where routes leading down from the passes join the road heading north towards Meiringen and Interlaken.

Grimsel Pass ⑦
At an altitude of 2,165 m (7,103 ft), the pass marks the border between the cantons of Bern and Valais. On the pass is the Totensee (Dead Lake).

0 km   5

0 miles   5

Furka Pass ⑧
Lying between the cantons of Valais and Uri, the pass lies at 2,431 m (7,976 ft), with the Bernese and Pennine Alps on either side.

Gadmen

Interlaken

6-11

11

6

Guttannen

Aare

Grimselsee

Gletsch

Rhône

Brig

Furkastrasse ⑨
Built in the 1860s, this route over the Furka Pass offers spectacular views of high Alpine scenery. The Glacier Express passes through a tunnel beneath the pass.

Meienreuss Pass ④
Here a bridge spans a
deep gorge in the Meien
valley. From Wassen,
near the foot of the
valley, a road leads
to Susten.

Wassen ③
The terrace in front
of Wassen's Baroque
church is a good
vantage point for
spectacular views of
the valley below.

TIPS FOR DRIVERS

Tour length: 120 km (75 miles).
Stopping-off points: Both Andermatt and Göschennen have
small hotels and restaurants.
Other attractions: The
Handeggfall, between the Grimsel
Pass and Guttannen, are impressive
waterfalls at the confluence of
the Aare and the Arlenbach.

Göschenen ②
This town, at the northern
end of the tunnel beneath
the St Gotthard Pass, is a
good base for hiking in the
surrounding mountains.

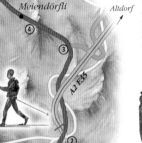

Göscheneralpsee

Andermatt ①
A skiing resort in winter and
hiking centre in summer,
Andermatt lies in the heart
of the St Gotthard Massif.
Andermatt's church contains
a beautiful Gothic font.

KEY

▦ Suggested route
▦ Scenic route
═ Other roads
═ River, lake
☆ View point

Hospental ⑩
Hospental lies at the
convergence of roads
from the north, south and
west. The 13th-century
castle that once guarded
this crossroads still
stands, although it is
now in ruins.

Frescoes on the ceiling of the chapel in Bürglen

Bürglen ⓮

Road map E3. 🏔 3,600. 🚌

This small town at the mouth of the Schächen valley is reputed to be the birthplace of William Tell, hero of Swiss legend. The supposed site of his house is marked by a chapel built in 1582. Its façade and interior are decorated with frescoes illustrating the legend of William Tell. A figure of the hero also graces an 18th-century fountain in the town.

The legend of William Tell and the place it occupies in Swiss culture and national pride are the subject of the displays in the **Tell Museum**. Consisting of chronicles and other documents, as well as paintings, sculptures and other pieces, the exhibits illustrate the legend over the 600 years of its existence.

Also of interest in Bürglen are a 17th-century wooden tavern, the **Adler Inn**, and an early Baroque church with a stucco-decorated interior and a Romanesque tower.

Environs
At **Riedertal**, 3 km (2 miles) southeast of Bürglen, is a beautiful pilgrimage chapel in the Gothic-Renaissance style. It is decorated with Gothic frescoes and contains a 14th-century Pietà, which is the object of local veneration.

🏛 **Tell Museum**
Postplatz.
Tel 041 870 41 55. ☐ May–Jun: 10–11:30am & 1:30–5pm daily; Jul–Aug: 9:30am–5pm daily; Sep–Oct: 10–11:30am & 1:30–5pm daily. 🌐 📷 www.tellmuseum.ch

Altdorf ⓯

Road map E3. 🏔 8,000. 🚌 🚉
🛈 Tellspielhaus; 041 872 80 22.
www.uri.info
🎉 Dorffest (1 Aug), Chilbi (Nov).

The capital of the canton of Uri, Altdorf is supposed to be the town where William Tell shot the apple from his son's head. The **Telldenkmal**, a 19th-century statue of Tell and his son, stands on Rathausplatz. Plays based on the Tell legend are regularly performed in the Tellspielhaus here.

Also of interest in Altdorf is the town's historic arsenal

Entrance to the arsenal in Altdorf

and the **Historisches Museum**, which illustrates the history and traditions of the canton of Uri.

🏛 **Historisches Museum**
Gotthardstrasse 18. **Tel** 041 870 19 06. ☐ May–Jun, mid-Aug–mid-Oct & Dec–early Jan: 1–5pm Wed & Sat–Sun. 🌐 www.hvu.ch

Urnersee ⓰

Road map E3. 🚌 🚉 🛈 Brunnen, Bahnhofstrasse 15; 041 825 00 40.
www.brunnentourismus.ch

The stunningly beautiful Urnersee forms the south-eastern arm of Lake Lucerne. Surrounded on all sides by high, steep-sided mountains, the Urnersee resembles a Norwegian fjord.

On an elevated promontory below Seelisberg, on the west side of the lake, is **Rütli Meadow** (Bergwiese Rütli), where the alliance between the cantons of Uri, Schwyz and Unterwalden was sworn in 1291 (see p35).

The village of **Seedorf**, at the southern extremity of the Urnersee, has a picturesque Gothic-Renaissance castle. It was built in 1556–60 and now houses a small geological museum. **Flüelen**, nearby, is the farthest port of call for the boats that sail across the lake from Luzern.

About 3 km (2 miles) north of Flüelen, on the road to Sisikon, is the **Tellsplate**, a flat rock. According to legend,

WILLIAM TELL

The legendary hero who freed Switzerland from Habsburg oppression, William Tell is supposed to have lived in the 13th century (though some historians dismiss him as a myth). Having refused to bow to imperial power, Tell was seized by the bailiff Hermann Gessler and, as a punishment, was ordered to shoot an arrow through an apple balanced on his son's head. Tell shot the apple but, after declaring his intention to kill Gessler, was condemned to prison. During the boat journey across the Urnersee, Tell escaped and later killed Gessler.

Statue of William Tell and his son in Altdorf

The Urnersee, seen from its southern shore

this is where William Tell leapt to freedom during his boat journey across Lake Lucerne, on his way to imprisonment in Hermann Gessler's castle at Küssnacht. Near the rock stands the **Tellskapelle**, a 16th-century chapel that was remodelled in the 19th century.

Brunnen, at the northern extremity of the Urnersee, is one of Lake Lucerne's largest resorts. It commands a sweeping panorama of the Urnersee, with views across the water to Rütli Meadow, on the opposite shore. Brunnen has a small Baroque chapel, the Bundeskapelle, with an altarpiece painted by Justus van Egmont, a pupil of Rubens, in 1642.

Schwyz ⑰

Road map E3. 👥 14,000. 🚌 🚉
🛈 Bahnhofstrasse 4; 041 855 59 50.
www.schwyz-tourismus.ch

This quiet town, capital of the canton of the same name, lies at the foot of the twin peaks of the Mythen. It has immense importance in Swiss history and culture.

The canton of Schwyz gave Switzerland both its name and its flag. Having sworn their mutual allegiance in 1291, the joint forces of Schwyz, Uri and Unterwalden united to defeat the Habsburgs at the Battle of Morgarten (1315). Thereafter they were known collectively as Schwyzers, and Helvetia *(see p35)* became known as Schwyzerland.

The **Bundesbriefmuseum** (Museum of Federal Charters) in Schwyz preserves a number of documents relating to important events in Swiss history. The most highly prized exhibit is the Charter of Confederation, written on parchment and stamped with the seals of the three Forest Cantons in 1291.

Schwyz's Old Town contains many 17th- and 18th-century buildings. Hauptplatz, the central square, is dominated by Pfarrkirche St Martin, a Baroque church, and by the Rathaus, the 17th-century town hall whose façade features a depiction of the Battle of Morgarten painted in 1891. The **Ital-Reding-Haus**, a mansion built in 1609, contains a suite of rooms with 17th- and 18th-century furnishings and decoration. Nearby is Haus Bethlehem, a wooden house built in 1287.

A former granary dating from 1711 houses the **Forum der Schweizer Geschichte**. This excellent museum of history illustrates daily life in Switzerland from the Middle Ages to the end of the 17th century.

Arms of Uri on the Rathaus in Schwyz

🏛 **Bundesbriefmuseum**
Bahnhofstrasse 20. **Tel** 041 819 20 64. ◷ May–Oct: 9–11:30am, 1:30–5pm Tue–Fri, 9am–5pm Sat–Sun; Nov–Apr: 9–11:30am & 1:30–5pm Tue–Fri, 1:30–5pm Sat–Sun. 📷
www.bundesbriefmuseum.ch

🏛 **Ital-Reding-Haus**
Rickenbachstrasse 14. **Tel** 041 811 45 05. ◷ May–Oct: 2–5pm Tue–Fri, 10am–noon & 2–5pm Sat–Sun. 📷
🏛 **Forum der Schweizer Geschichte**
Hofmatt. **Tel** 041 819 60 11. ◷ 10am–5pm Tue–Sun.

Vitznau ⑱

Road map E3. 👥 1,000. 🚌 🚉
🛈 Bahnhofstrasse 1; 041 227 18 10.
www.wvrt.ch

Backed by the Rigi massif, this small resort lies in a sheltered bay on the north shore of Lake Lucerne. Besides its watersports facilities, Vitznau's main attraction is as a base from which to hike through the woods and Alpine pastures of the Rigi massif.

Vitznau is also the base station of the oldest rack railway in Europe. It opened in 1871 and leads up to just below the summit of Rigi-Kulm (1,798 m/5,900 ft), the highest peak in the Rigi massif. The view from this vantage point is breathtaking. Surrounded by the waters of Lake Lucerne, and the Zugersee, the Rigi massif appears to be an island, and in clear weather the distant snow-capped peaks of the Alps are visible in the far southwest.

The northwestern shore of Lake Lucerne, between Vitznau and Weggis

Kloster Einsiedeln ⑲

The Benedictine abbey at Einsiedeln is one of the finest examples of Baroque architecture in the world. Its history goes back to 835, when Meinrad, a monk, chose the spot for his hermitage *(einsiedeln)*. In 934 a monastery was founded on the site. When, according to legend, a miracle occurred during the consecration of the church, the abbey became a place of pilgrimage. The church and monastery were rebuilt from 1704 to 1735, to a lavish Baroque design by Brother Kaspar Moosbrugger. Most of the paintings, gilding and stuccowork in the church are by the Bavarian brothers Cosmas Damian and Egid Quirin Asam.

Library
The abbey library is a fine example of the Baroque style. Only a part of the abbey's extensive collection of manuscripts is housed here.

The confessional, a chapel where pilgrims gather to make their confessions, is located in the north wing of the transept.

Interior of the Church
The spacious interior of the church is impressive. The nave is decorated with Baroque frescoes by Cosmas Damian Asam.

Well of Our Lady
As they arrive at the church, pilgrims traditionally drink the water from this well. It is crowned by a statue of the Virgin.

★ **Black Madonna**
A chapel inside the church contains the statue of a Black Madonna. This 15th century wooden figure of the Virgin with the infant Jesus is reputed to have miraculous powers.

For hotels and restaurants in this region see pp257–9 and pp282–3

★ Wall Paintings

The walls, ceiling and domes of the church are covered with frescoes and gilt stuccowork. This extraordinarily rich scheme is typical of the late Baroque style.

Organ

Bedecked with figures of putti playing instruments, the organ occupies a gallery beneath the central dome.

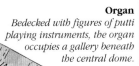

★ Grosser Saal

Lavishily decorated with paintings and stuccowork, the Grosser Saal, or Great Hall, is still used for grand receptions and official ceremonies.

Pulpit

Figures of angels and the symbols of the Four Evangelists decorate the gilt pulpit. It was designed by Egid Quirin Asam and completed in 1726.

STAR FEATURES

★ Black Madonna

★ Grosser Saal

★ Wall Paintings

Lake Lucerne and the towns of Küssnacht am Rigi and Bürgenstock seen from the summit of Pilatus

Zug ⓴

Road map E3. 🏔 *24,000.* 🚊 🚌
🚢 🛈 *Bahnhofstrasse, 041 723 68
00.* **www**.zug-tourismus.ch

Zug is set on the north-eastern shore of the Zugersee, in the wooded foothills of the Zugerberg. It is the capital of Zug, the smallest and also the richest of all Swiss cantons. Having the lowest taxation in Switzerland, Zug has become the headquarters of many multinational companies.

Substantial parts of the walls, set with towers, still encircle Zug's medieval Old Town. The focal point of the Old Town is Kolinplatz. At the centre of this square is a fountain with a statue of the knight Wolfgang Kolin, a standard-bearer of the Swiss army. Nearby stands the Gothic Rathaus, built in 1509. Also of interest is the 15th- to 16th-century Kirche St Oswald, whose portal has figures of the Virgin, St Oswald and St Michael.

The former bailiff's castle houses the **Museum in der Burg**, a museum with permanent collections of local history as well as special exhibitions. Nearby is a 16th-century granary now converted into the **Kunsthaus**, a gallery with an important collection of Viennese modern art. The **Museum für Urgeschichte** concentrates on prehistory and antiquity.

Cruises on the Zugersee depart from the harbour jetty.

RIGI-FIRST
NEUER WINTERKURORT U. SPORTPLATZ

**Poster advertising
winter sports on Rigi**

🏛 **Museum in der Burg**
Kirchenstrasse 11. **Tel** *041 728 29
70.* ☐ *2–5pm Tue–Sat, 10am–5pm
Sun.* 📷

🏛 **Kunsthaus**
Dorfstrasse 27. **Tel** *041 725 33 44.*
☐ *noon–6pm Tue–Fri, 10am–5pm
Sat–Sun.* 📷 **www**.kunsthauszug.ch

🏛 **Museum für Urgeschichte**
Hofstrasse 15. **Tel** *041 728 28 80.*
☐ *2–5pm Tue–Sun.* 📷

Küssnacht am Rigi ㉑

Road map D3. 🏔 *9,500.* 🚌 🛥
🛈 *Unterdorf 6; 041 850 33 30.*
www.hohlgassland.ch

The small town of Küssnacht am Rigi lies at the foot of the Rigi. This massif rises to the east of the Küssnachtersee, the northern arm of Lake Lucerne.

The town is a good base for hiking in the mountains and for exploring Lake Lucerne. It also offers a wide range of sports facilities.

Buildings of interest in Küssnacht's historic district include the Baroque town hall and the Kirche St Peter und St Paul. Another is the Engel Hotel, a half-timbered building dating from 1552 that has been an inn for over 400 years.

Luzern ㉒

See pp232–3.

Pilatus ㉓

Road map D3. **Pilatus Cable Car
Co.** *Kriens/Lucerne Schlossweg 1,
041 329 11 11.* **www**.pilatus.ch

The rugged outlines of Pilatus, whose highest peak reaches an altitude of 2,132 m (7,000 ft), rise on the southwestern side of Lake Lucerne. Various legends are

Houses on the waterfront in Zug's medieval Old Town

For hotels and restaurants in this region see pp257–9 and pp282–3

associated with the mountain. According to one, the body of Pontius Pilate was thrown into a lake on the mountain, and his spirit continues to haunt its heights, unleashing violent storms.

There are several convenient ways of reaching the summit of Pilatus. The first stage is a boat or train ride from Luzern to Alpnachstad, near the foot of Pilatus. From here a rack railway climbs a gradient of 48 per cent, making it the steepest cog railway in the world. From Pilatus-Kulm, the upper station, a walking trail leads up to a viewing platform on one of the mountain's peaks. In good weather it offers views of the Säntis, in the Alpstein, and of the Glarner and Berner Alps. The descent down from Pilatus-Kulm can be made either by the cog railway to Alpnachstad (runs in summer only), or by cable car down to Kriens.

Ibex on the rugged slopes of Pilatus

Hergiswil ㉔

Road map D3. 🏔 5,600. 🚉 🚌
🚤 ℹ *Seestrasse 54; 041 630 12 58*
www.hergiswil.ch

The small lakeside village of Hergiswil, on the rail route from Luzern to Stans, is worth a visit for its glassworks, the Glasi Hergiswil. The factory was established in 1817 and was saved from closure in the late 1970s by the Ticinese glassmaker Roberto Niederer. It now employs about 100 people and is the focus of Hergiswil's life.

The factory is open to visitors, who can watch glassblowers at work. Also on the premises is the **Glasi Museum**, which documents the history of the glassworks, with many photographs and hundreds of different of examples of its glassware.

🏛 **Glasi Museum**
Seestrasse 12. **Tel** *041 632 32 32.*
🕘 *9am–6pm Mon–Fri, 9am–4pm Sat.*

Stans ㉕

Road map D3. 🏔 7,300. 🚉 🚌
ℹ *Bahnhofplatz 4; 041 610 88 33.*
www.lakeluzern.ch

Capital of the half-canton of Nidwalden, Stans is a small town on the banks of the River Engelberger Aa. Above the town rises the Stanserhorn (1,900 m/6,234 ft), the summit of which can be reached from Stans by funicular and the world's first double-decker cable car with an open top.

The town's charming historic district revolves around Dorf-platz. This square is dominated by a Baroque parish church, **Pfarrkirche St Peter und St Paul**, with a Romanesque tower, the remains of an earlier church. In the centre of Dorf-platz stands a 19th-century monument to Arnold von Winkelried who sacrificed his life to help his Confederate comrades defeat the Austrians at the Battle of Sempach in 1386.

Also of interest in the town are the Höfli, a medieval turreted house that contains a museum of local history, and the Winkelriedhaus, a late Gothic building that houses a museum of local folk crafts and traditions.

Engelberg ㉖

Road map D3. 🏔 3,400. 🚉 🚌
ℹ *Klosterstrasse 3, 041 639 77 77.*
www.engelberg.ch

Within easy reach of both Luzern and Zürich, Engelberg is one of central Switzerland's main mountain resorts. It lies at an altitude of 1,000 m (3,280 ft), at the foot of Titlis, whose rocky peak reaches 3,239 m (10,627 ft) to a glacier with limited summer skiing.

The village nestles around the **Kloster**, a Benedictine monastery. Founded in the 12th century and rebuilt in the mid-18th, it has an exquisite Rococo church, built in 1735–40. The monastery, and its working cheese dairy, are open to visitors.

Engelberg has about 80 km (50 miles) of skiing pistes. It also offers tobogganing and ice-skating facilities. Marked trails in the vicinity lead past small mountain lakes and up to the summits of Titlis, Urirotstock, Schlossberg and Hutstock. There are also many cycling routes and facilities for summer sports such as paragliding. The Rotair cable car, which rotates as it travels so as to give passengers an all-round view, runs from Stand, above Engelberg, over the Titlis glacier.

The Rotair cable car from Engelberg up to Klein Titlis

Luzern ㉒

Central Switzerland's largest town, Luzern (Lucerne in French) lies on the western shore of Lake Lucerne. From its origins as a small fishing village, it grew into an important staging point when the St Gotthard Pass was opened in 1220. During the Reformation, Luzern led the Catholic resistance in Switzerland, and was long embroiled in political and religious disputes. Since the 19th century, tourism has underpinned Luzern's economy. Still attracting large numbers of visitors, the town also hosts the renowned Lucerne Festival.

Chapel Bridge, with the Wasserturm in the background

**Luzern seen from the west, with
Mount Rigi in the background**

Central Luzern

Luzern is a compact town that is easily explored on foot. The medieval Old Town (*see pp234–5*) lies on the north bank of the River Reuss and, from the train station on the south bank, it can be reached by crossing the medieval Chapel Bridge. The best view of Luzern is from the towers in the medieval fortifications that encircle the Old Town to the north. Luzern's main shopping districts are on the south bank, southwest of the train station, and in the Old Town, on the north bank.

🏛 KKL

Europaplatz 1.
With its cantilevered roof, the KKL building, or Kultur- und Kongresszentrum Luzern (Luzern Culture and Convention Centre), is a strikingly modernist glass and steel building that juts out over Lake Lucerne. It was designed by the French architect Jean Nouvel and was opened in 1998. The building contains conference halls, concert halls and theatres, and the Kunstmuseum (see below).

🏛 Kunstmuseum

KKL, Europaplatz 1. **Tel** 041 226 78 00. ○ 10am–5pm Tue & Fri–Sun, 10am–8pm Wed–Thu.
The collections of the Kunstmuseum are displayed in about 20 rooms on the topmost floor of the KKL building (see above). The gallery has a permanent collection of 18th- and early 20th-century Swiss painting, and also presents a rotating programme of exhibitions of the work of international contemporary artists.

🏛 Rosengart Collection

Pilatusstrasse 10. **Tel** 041 220 16 60. ○ May–Oct: 10am–6pm daily; Nov–Mar: 11am–5pm daily. **www**.rosengart.ch
The Rosengart Collection (Sammlung Rosengart) is a private collection of over 300 modernist paintings that was formed over several decades by the art dealers Siegfried Rosengart and his daughter, Angela. As well as 125 works by Paul Klee, the museum also has a fantastic collection of watercolours and sculptures by Pablo Picasso, many of them from the former Picasso Museum. The collection also includes Impressionist paintings, with canvases by Cézanne and Monet, and work by Chagall, Matisse and Kandinsky.

🌉 Chapel Bridge

This 14th-century covered footbridge spanning the Reuss at an angle formed part of the town's fortifications, protecting it against attack from the direction of the lake. Near the centre of the river, the bridge joins the Wasserturm, an octagonal tower that has served as a lighthouse, a prison and a treasury. In the 17th century, the bridge's roof panels were painted with scenes from the history of Luzern and episodes in the lives of St Leodegar and St Mauritius, martyrs who became the town's patron saints.

The oldest wooden bridge in Europe, Chapel Bridge (Kapellbrücke) has become the symbol of Luzern. It was partly destroyed by fire in 1993 but was rebuilt and most of its paintings restored.

The KKL building, on Luzern's waterfront

◁ **Sonlerto, a typical Alpine village in Val Bavona, Ticino**

🔒 Jesuit Church

A major landmark on the south bank of the Reuss, the great Jesuitenkirche, the Jesuit church of St Francis Xavier, was built in 1666–73, although its onion-domed twin towers were not completed until the 19th century. The Baroque interior is richly decorated with stuccowork and the ceiling paintings depict the apotheosis of St Francis Xavier.

🔒 Franziskanerkirche

Franziskanerplatz.

Dating from about 1270, this Franciscan church was built in the Gothic style, but has been much altered over the centuries. The Renaissance

Interior of the Franziskanerkirche

choir stalls, 17th-century pulpit and Baroque ceiling paintings are among notable features of the interior.

🏛 Historisches Museum

Pfistergasse 24. **Tel** 041 228 54 22.
⭕ 10am–5pm Tue–Sun. 🎫
www.hmluzern.ch

Luzern's history museum occupies the former arsenal, a Renaissance building dating from 1597. Also named the Depot, the museum has been brought up to date with interactive displays, barcodes and hand-held scanners in place of traditional information boards and audioguides.

Thousands of fascinating historical objects on display include weaponry, costumes, and folk art and crafts, as well as early advertising material from the Swiss manufacturing and tourism industries. Actors in period costume dramatize scenes from history in daily performances.

In the adjacent building is the Naturmuseum. Its displays focus on

various aspects of natural history, in particular zoology, palaeontology and geology.

♙ Spreuerbrücke

This wooden covered bridge spans the Reuss at the western edge of the Old Town. It was built in 1408 and incorporates a small chapel. The bridge's roof is lined with panels painted by Kaspar Meglinger in 1626–35. Depicting the Dance of Death, they run in sequence from the north bank and culminate with Christ's triumph over Death at the south bank.

The bridge also offers a close view of the Nadelwerk, a 19th-century device to control the river's flow.

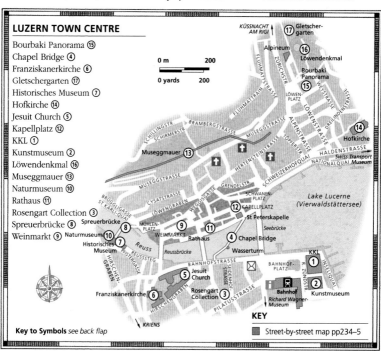

LUZERN TOWN CENTRE

KEY

⬛ Street-by-street map pp234–5

Key to Symbols see back flap

Street-by-Street: Old Town

Luzern's historic Old Town (Altstadt) is set on a shallow bend of the Reuss at the point where the river leaves Lake Lucerne. From the Middle Ages the town was defended by ramparts on its northern side and by Chapel Bridge, which spans the river on its eastern side. The Old Town's ancient layout survives, and the façades of its fine historic houses, particularly around Hirschenplatz and along Weinmarktgasse, are painted with frescoes or covered with sgraffito decoration. This historic district of Luzern is also a bustling urban centre, with plenty of shops, restaurants and cafés.

Alley near Weinmarkt
The narrow alleys off this square are lined with tall houses, some with colourfully painted shutters. Many of these houses have been converted into hotels, or contain boutiques and restaurants.

Weinmarkt
This central square, where wine was once sold, has several fine houses, many of which were guildhalls.

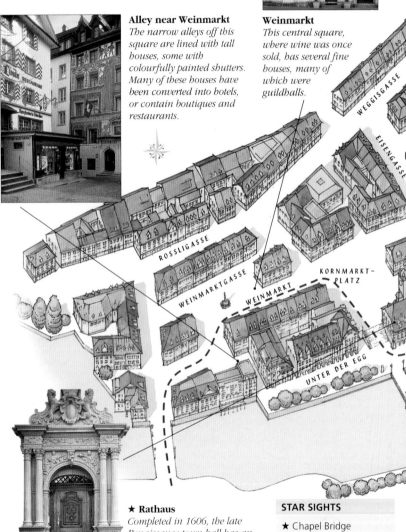

★ Rathaus
Completed in 1606, the late Renaissance town hall has an ornate façade. The main entrance is flanked by double columns.

STAR SIGHTS

★ Chapel Bridge

★ Rathaus

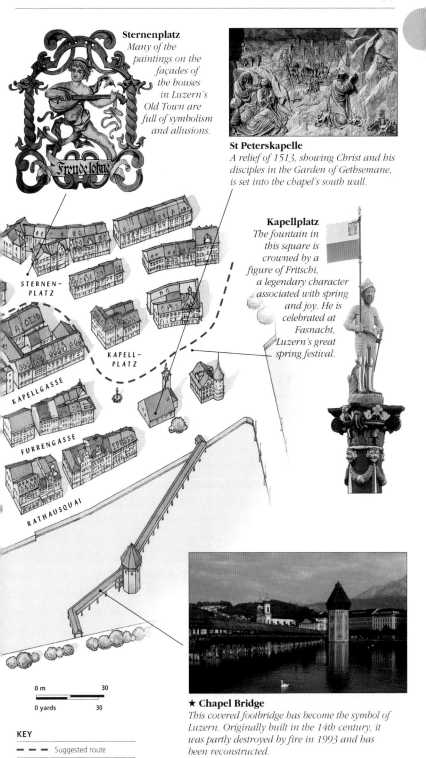

Sternenplatz
Many of the paintings on the façades of the houses in Luzern's Old Town are full of symbolism and allusions.

St Peterskapelle
A relief of 1513, showing Christ and his disciples in the Garden of Gethsemane, is set into the chapel's south wall.

Kapellplatz
The fountain in this square is crowned by a figure of Fritschi, a legendary character associated with spring and joy. He is celebrated at Fasnacht, Luzern's great spring festival.

STERNEN-PLATZ

KAPELL-PLATZ

KAPELLGASSE

FURRENGASSE

RATHAUSQUAI

0 m   30

0 yards   30

KEY

− − − Suggested route

★ **Chapel Bridge**
This covered footbridge has become the symbol of Luzern. Originally built in the 14th century, it was partly destroyed by fire in 1993 and has been reconstructed.

Exploring Luzern

One of the best views over the picturesque squares, churches, chapels and patrician houses of Luzern's Old Town is from the ramparts to the north. A pleasant walk eastwards from the Old Town leads to several other interesting buildings and museums, including the grand Renaissance Hofkirche and the Wagner Museum, dedicated to the Romantic composer. On the lakeshore further east is the fascinating Swiss Transport Museum, one of Switzerland's greatest attractions (*see pp238–9*).

🏛 Weinmarkt

Lined with historic houses, this square is one of the most attractive features of Luzern's Old Town. The Weinmarktbrunnen, a Gothic fountain in the square, is a copy of the original, which now stands in the courtyard of the Ritterscher Palast, on Bahnhofstrasse. The houses around both this square and the adjacent Hirschenplatz have painted façades, ornate doorways and oriel windows. Many of these buildings were guildhouses.

Detail of fountain in Weinmarkt

🏛 Naturmuseum

Kasernenplatz 6. **Tel** 041 228 54 11. ◯ 10am–5pm Tue–Sun. 🏷

The Natural History Museum is an easy ten-minute stroll from the Old Town, southwest across the Spreuerbrücke. With a variety of live animals and interactive displays, this is a popular choice with children and is one of the country's most family-friendly museums. Hallways are lined with stuffed animals and there is a full-time guide on hand to explain exhibits in detail. There is plenty to keep adults engaged, too, such as the impressive topographical representation of the Alps in prehistoric times. Flora and fauna from central Switzerland, including a colourful exhibit of butterflies, are displayed on rotating panels.

🏛 Rathaus

Kornmarkt 3. **Tel** 041 227 17 17. ◯ by arrangement.

The present town hall, built in a grand Renaissance style, was completed in 1606. Of the 14th-century town hall that stood on the same site, only a tower remains. The council chamber inside the building is lined with finely carved wood panelling.

🏛 Museggmauer

◯ Easter–Oct: 8am–7pm.

The Museggmauer, the well-preserved northern section of Luzern's medieval fortifications, runs for about 850 m (930 yd), from the north bank of the Reuss almost to the north shore of Lake Lucerne. The walls are set with nine towers, which were built in the second half of the 14th century. The wall walk commands fine views of the town, the river and the lake.

🏛 Kapellplatz

St Peterskapelle ◯ 7:30am–6:15pm Mon–Wed, 7:30am–9pm Thu, 7:30am–6:15pm Fri, 7:30am–5pm Sat, 8:30am–8pm Sun.

This picturesque square buzzes with life, particularly on market days. It takes its name from the Peterskapelle. This 18th-century chapel stands on the site of a 12th-century church, the earliest to be built in Luzern. The chapel contains a 14th-century Gothic crucifix.

Heraldic shield on one of the towers of the Museggmauer

⛪ Hofkirche

St. Leodegarstrasse. ◯ daily.

This collegiate church is a fine example of late Renaissance Swiss architecture. The original church, dating from the 12th century, was almost completely destroyed by fire in 1633. Only the twin towers, with pointed domes, remain and are incorporated into the present building.

The magnificent interior is decorated in the Renaissance style. Notable features include the high altar, with statues of St Leodegar and St Mauritius, patron saints of Luzern. The altar in the north aisle is graced by a depiction of the Dormition of the Virgin painted in 1500. The church also has elaborate pews, pulpit and font, and a huge organ, built in about 1640.

Painted façades of houses in the Weinmarkt square

For hotels and restaurants in this region see pp257–9 and pp282–3

The altar in the north aisle of the Hofkirche

A niche in the north tower frames a moving depiction of Christ in the Garden of Gethsemane.

🏛 Bourbaki Panorama

Löwenplatz 11. *Tel 041 412 30 30.* ◯ *Apr–Oct: 9am–6pm daily, Nov–Mar: 10am–5pm daily.* 🅰

One of the world's few surviving panoramas, this giant circular mural depicts the march of the French army through Switzerland under General Bourbaki, during the Franco-Prussian War (1870–71). In a stone building now housed in a glass shell, it is 112 m (370 ft) long and 10 m (33 ft) high, and was painted by Edouard Castres. Sound effects and a narrative (in several languages, including English) help bring the events depicted to life.

The building also contains a museum, art galleries, a cinema, bars and a restaurant.

🚩 Löwendenkmal

Denkmalstrasse.

This massive figure of a dying lion pierced by a spear is a startling monument to the Swiss Guards of Louis XVI of France. On 10 August 1792, the guards defended the Palais des Tuileries, in Paris, when it was stormed by revolutionaries. Those who survived the attack were arrested and guillotined on the night of 2–3 September.

The Löwendenkmal

The Löwen-denkmal, or Lion Monument, was carved out of the sandstone cliff face by the Danish sculptor Bertel Thorwaldsen, and it was unveiled in 1821. Reflected in the waters of a small pond, the monument has great drama and pathos.

🏛 Gletschergarten

Denkmalstrasse 4. *Tel 041 410 43 40.* ◯ *Apr–Oct: 9am–6pm daily; Nov–Mar: 10am–5pm daily.* 🅰 **www**.gletschergarten.ch

This attractive garden is an oasis of tranquillity, as well as being the setting for a fascinating natural phenomenon. In 1872 an enormous rock, complete with 32 potholes and well-sized holes, was excavated here. Formed by glacial abrasion, research showed it dated from the Ice Age. The garden was created to conserve this geological feature, which is protected by a tent-roof that allows visitors to view the rock from the sides.

The site includes an exhibition on the geological processes involved in creating the holes, a museum and the fascinating Mirror Maze of more than 90 mirrors in the style of Grenada's Alhambra.

🏛 Richard Wagner-Museum

Richard Wagner-Weg 27. *Tel 041 360 23 79.* ◯ *mid-Mar–Oct: 10am–noon & 2–5pm.* 🅰

The German Romantic composer Richard Wagner was a regular visitor to Luzern. It was here that he wrote the third act of his opera *Tristan and Isolde*. Two complete operas, *The Mastersingers of Nuremberg* and *Siegfried*, date from this period, and while he was in Luzern Wagner also started work on *The Twilight of the Gods*.

The tranquil Villa Tribschen where Wagner and his wife and son lived from 1866 to 1872 is devoted to this particularly happy period. Its rooms, with original furniture, are filled with memorabilia of the composer's life, including paintings, letters and musical instruments.

Environs

The Museum im Bellpark in **Kriens**, 3 km (2 miles) southwest of Luzern and reachable by bus, contains a collection of objects relating to photography, video and the media.

The glass pavilion of the Bourbaki Panorama

Swiss Transport Museum

Almost every mode of mechanized transport, from the earliest bicycle to the latest spacecraft, is displayed and explained at the Swiss Transport Museum (Verkehrshaus der Schweiz) in Luzern. Vintage cars and steam locomotives are part of the sections on road and rail transport, and the section on tourism showcases the ingenuity of rack railways and cable cars. Water transport, aviation and telecommunications are also documented. The section devoted to space travel includes a virtual journey through outer space and among the museum's interactive features is a flight simulator.

Rail Transport Halls
These halls have exhibits showing the history of Swiss rail transport, from the horse-drawn tram through to steam trains, cog trains and electric railways.

Krokodil
The elongated shape of this electric locomotive led to its being dubbed the Crocodile. Built in 1920, it served the route leading through the St Gotthard Tunnel.

Main
entrance

Gotthardmodell
One of the most fascinating of the museum's displays is a model that re-creates the rail route through the St Gotthard Tunnel.

KEY

☐	Railways
☐	Road transport
☐	Telecommunications
☐	Planetarium
☐	Space
☐	Air transport
☐	Water transport & tourism
☐	Hans-Erni-Museum
☐	Filmtheatre

STAR EXHIBITS

★ Aircraft

★ Cosmorama

★ Filmtheatre

★ Filmtheatre
Viewers are taken on a 40-minute film experience of new worlds, enlarging the minute and showing the large at full size.

GALLERY GUIDE

The rooms to the left of the main entrance are devoted to rail transport. Opposite the main entrance is the Road Transport Hall. The other principal rooms contain aviation and space travel exhibits. The Filmtheatre has the largest screen in Switzerland.

VISITORS' CHECKLIST

Lidostrasse 5. **Tel** 041 370 44 44.
☐ Apr–Oct: 10am–6pm daily;
Nov–Feb: 10am–5pm daily. ☐
☐ ☐ **www**.verkehrshaus.ch

Hans-Erni-Museum
A section of the museum is devoted to the abstract paintings of Hans Erni (b.1909), a native of Luzern.

Road Transport Hall
Maserati, Aston Martin, Lamborghini and Ferrari – some of the most famous sports cars of the swinging sixties are on display here.

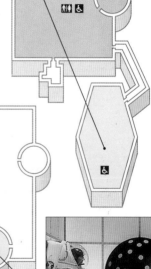

★ **Cosmorama**
As well as space suits and other equipment used by astronauts, the section on space exploration includes Cosmorama, a virtual journey through the asteroid belt.

★ **Aircraft**
This Fokker F. VII A, the oldest Swiss passenger plane still in existence, forms part of the museum's aviation section. The aircraft on display here range from microlights to supersonic military jets.

TRAVELLERS' NEEDS

WHERE TO STAY

Whether you are looking for a hotel in a city centre, at a leading winter sports resort, on the edge of a beautiful lake or in unspoiled countryside, Switzerland offers accommodation to suit all tastes and budgets. Across all categories and price ranges, Swiss hotels provide high quality and value for money, even though their prices tend to be relatively high. Cheaper options

Hotel sign in Bern

include guesthouses, to be found in some of the country's most attractive towns and villages, or a welcoming mountain inn, where you will be treated to warm Swiss hospitality. For those who enjoy the great outdoors, Switzerland has a host of well-equipped campsites in unforgettable scenery. Many farms also have rooms to let, and even give visitors the opportunity to sleep in barns, on pristine straw.

The striking lobby at the Widder Hotel in Zurich (see p255)

CHOOSING A HOTEL

The best source of information on hotels in Switzerland is the **Swiss Hotel Association**. This organization covers most types of accommodation, from luxury hotels to remote mountain inns. It also grades hotels on a scale of one to five stars, which correspond to certain standards of comfort.

Average prices range from 70 CHF for a double room without a bath in a one-star hotel, to at least 1,200 CHF for a comfortable suite in a five-star establishment. Except in the very cheapest and in the most expensive hotels, prices generally include breakfast, taxes and service. Some hotels, particularly those that are family-run, are not subject to official classification, but they are generally clean and comfortable. While many hotels have restaurants, a *hôtel garni* is an establishment that serves breakfast but no other meals.

In popular resorts, hotel prices are subject to seasonal variations. According to their location, most hotels charge the highest prices during the winter sports season or in July and August, the height of the summer season, although discounts sometimes apply for longer stays. In large towns, where hotels are more likely to rely on a business clientele, prices generally stay constant throughout the year, although special weekend rates are often available.

Hotels in many resorts offer guest cards (*Gästekarte, Kurkarte, carte des visiteurs or tessera del soggiorno*) which entitle holders to substantial discounts ranging from travel in the locality to admission to museums or swimming pools.

HOTEL CHAINS

Many hotels in Switzerland belong to international or national chains or associations. **Best Western** has

around 30 three- and four-star hotels in Switzerland. The **Swiss Quality Hotel International Group** has over 70 three- to five-star establishments in Switzerland's larger towns and cities and in the country's major holiday resorts. Hotels in this chain offer discounts to holders of the Swiss Pass (*see p305*).

The **Minotel Suisse** chain is an association of some 50 traditional family-run hotels with a rating of two to four stars. These hotels have restaurants that serve Swiss food and wine. In a less expensive price bracket are **Swiss Budget Hotels**, which has 160 hotels and other accommodation with a one-star to three-star rating. These hotels tend to be off main routes or outside the principal tourist regions but for this reason they offer good value for money. Many are in quiet, uncrowded locations.

The 27 hotels in the **Romantik** group are all independently run establishments in fine historic buildings, such as châteaux. All offer exceptionally high standards of comfort and most are in outstanding locations.

ROOMS/B&B

Guest houses and private houses advertise rooms for rent with signs reading *Zimmer frei, Chambres à louer* or *affitasi camere*. They are most likely to be found in resorts and in areas frequented by visitors.

The 3100 Kulm Hotel, with stunning views of the Matterhorn

Bed and breakfast accommodation is also becoming more widely available in Switzerland. At an average price of 40 CHF per night, both these types of accommodation offer excellent value.

HOSTELS

Switzerland has over 80 hostels, with double rooms, family rooms and dormitories. Prices range from 15 to 25 CHF per night, including breakfast, but there may be an extra charge if you don't bring your own linen. Most hostels have a television room and some serve evening meals.

SLEEPING IN STRAW

From early May until the end of October, many Swiss farms open their barns to visitors, allowing them to sleep on freshly laid straw. Charges per night are no more than about 20 CHF, which usually includes breakfast and the use of a shower. Blankets are sometimes provided, but visitors should bring their own sleeping bags.

Hotel sign in Murten

Staying on a working farm is another way of experiencing rural Switzerland at first hand. Rooms or apartments can be rented by the night or the week all year round.

MOUNTAIN INNS

Picturesque mountain inns *(Berghausen or auberges de montagne)* offer convenient overnight accommodation to hikers. As well as dormitories, many have individual rooms. Most inns also serve hot meals.

CAMPSITES

Like its hotels, Switzerland's campsites are graded on a scale of one to five stars. There are about 450, many in outstandingly beautiful locations. Most campsites are closed in winter, and many of those at higher altitudes are open only for the two or three warmest months of the year. Advance booking is recommended at any time of year.

An elegant guest room at Le Mirador Kempinski (see p250)

DIRECTORY

HOTELS

Swiss Hotel Association
Monbijoustrasse 130, Bern.
Tel 031 370 41 11.
Fax 031 370 44 44.
www.swisshotels.com

HOTEL CHAINS

Best Western Swiss Hotels
Monbijoustrasse 130, Bern.
Tel 031 378 18 18.
Fax 031 378 18 39.
www.bestwestern.ch

Minotel Suisse
Chemin Renou 2,
1005 Lausanne.
Tel 021 310 08 00.
www.minotel.com

Romantik
www.
romantikhotels.com

Swiss Budget Hotels
Monbijoustrasse 130,
Bern.
Tel 084 880 55 08.
www.rooms.ch

Swiss Quality Hotels International
Seestrasse 129, 8712
Stäfa. *Tel 044 928 27 27.*
Fax 044 928 28 28.
www.swissqualityhotels.
com

B&B

Bed and Breakfast
www.bnb.ch

HOSTELS

Swiss Backpackers
Tel 033 823 46 46.
www.swissbackpackers.ch

Swiss Youth Hostels
Schaffhauserstrasse 14,
8042 Zürich.
Tel 044 360 14 14.
Fax 044 360 14 60.
www.youthhostel.ch

SLEEPING IN STRAW

Schlaf im Stroh
Tel 041 678 12 86.
www.schlaf-im-stroh.ch

HOLIDAY FARMS

www.bauernhof-ferien.ch

Reka-Ferien
Neuengasse 15. 3001 Bern.
Tel 031 329 66 33.
Fax 031 329 66 01.
www.reka.ch

CAMPSITES

Camping and Caravaning
Bahnhofstrasse 2,
3322 Schönbühl.
Tel 031 852 06 26.
Fax 031 852 06 27.
www.swisscamps.ch

CampingNET
Grundhaldenstrasse 60,
8303 Bassersdorf.
www.camping.ch

Choosing a Hotel

Hotels have been selected across a wide price range for facilities, good value and location. All rooms have private bath, TV, air conditioning and are wheelchair accessible unless otherwise indicated. Most have Internet access, and in some cases, fitness facilities may be offsite. The hotels are listed by area. For map references, *see back endpaper.*

PRICE CATEGORIES
Price categories for a standard double room with bathroom or shower, including tax and service:

Ⓕ Under 150 CHF
ⒻⒻ 150–250 CHF
ⒻⒻⒻ 250–350 CHF
ⒻⒻⒻⒻ 350–500 CHF
ⒻⒻⒻⒻⒻ Over 500 CHF

BERN

BERN Glocke
Ⓕ
Rathausgasse 75, 3011 **Tel** *031 311 37 71* **Fax** *031 311 10 08* **Rooms** *14*
Road Map *C3*

Known by the name of Backpackers Bern, and by its older name, the Hotel Glocke, this alternative to a youth hostel is centrally located near the famous Clock Tower and a 10-minute walk from the train station. It is entirely non-smoking with free kitchen facilities and games room as well as Internet café and laundry. **www.bernbackpackers.com**

BERN Landhaus
ⒻⒻ
Altenbergstrasse 4, 3013 **Tel** *031 348 03 05* **Rooms** *10*
Road Map *C3*

Landhaus is one of the best known hotels in Bern for backpackers and young people, situated in a central location near the Bear Gardens and Old Town. The rooms are sunny and modern, with many paintings and posters. Set near the river in a quiet residential street, the hotel is itself a historic building of interest. **www.albertfrida.ch**

BERN National
ⒻⒻ
Hirschengraben 24, 3011 **Tel** *031 381 19 88* **Fax** *031 381 68 78* **Rooms** *46*
Road Map *C3*

A modest family-run hotel with a cheerful atmosphere and generous-sized rooms in a historic building very close to the main train station. Rooms with wooden floors and good views, combined with easy access to the Old Town, make this a popular hotel with budget travellers. **www.nationalbern.ch**

BERN Nydeck
ⒻⒻ
Gerechtigkeitsgasse 1, 3011 **Tel** *031 331 86 86* **Fax** *031 312 20 54* **Rooms** *12*
Road Map *C3*

Old-fashioned and imposing in exterior architecture, the Nydeck offers comfortable, spacious rooms right in the centre of Bern in the Old Town, just across from the Bear Park. This hotel is good value and ideally located for shopping and sightseeing. The restaurant serves tapas, as well as pizza and pasta dishes. **www.hotelnydeck.ch**

BERN Pension Marthahaus
ⒻⒻ
Wyttenbachstrasse 22a, 3013 **Tel** *031 332 41 35* **Fax** *031 333 33 86* **Rooms** *40*
Road Map *C3*

An inexpensive guesthouse in the leafy area of the Botanical Gardens to the north of the main train station. There is a kitchen for use of the guests, as well as free Internet access and bicycles to borrow. Rooms are good sized and excellent value for money. Reserve well in advance. **www.marthahaus.ch**

BERN Waldhorn
ⒻⒻ
Waldhöheweg 2, 3013 **Tel** *031 332 23 43* **Fax** *031 332 18 69* **Rooms** *46*
Road Map *C3*

A modern family-run pension with above average standards of furnishings and free Internet access. Waldhorn is located in a quiet suburb with good tram connections to the city centre. It is useful for visitors with cars who want to avoid driving into the city; there is free parking at the pension. Pets are welcome. **www.waldhorn.ch**

BERN Belle Époque
ⒻⒻⒻ
Gerechtigkeitsgasse 18, 3011 **Tel** *031 311 43 36* **Fax** *031 311 39 36* **Rooms** *17*
Road Map *C3*

An oasis of art and individual design in the Old Town, this hotel lives up to its name. Each guest room is unique not only in size and ambience, but furnished with Art Nouveau or Belle Époque antiques and paintings. One room even contains original works by the Swiss painter Ferdinand Hodler. **www.belle-epoque.ch**

BERN Savoy
ⒻⒻⒻ
Neuengasse 26, 3011 **Tel** *031 311 44 05* **Fax** *031 312 19 78* **Rooms** *56*
Road Map *C3*

With its mansard roof above and arcades below, the Savoy is the epitome of an elegant old-fashioned city centre hotel. The decor belongs to a somewhat earlier age, as does the high standard of service. Conference facilities have been added, and all windows have been soundproofed against city noise. **www.hotel-savoy-bern.ch**

BERN Bellevue Palace
ⒻⒻⒻⒻ
Kochergasse 3-5, 3001 **Tel** *031 320 45 45* **Fax** *031 311 47 43* **Rooms** *130*
Road Map *C3*

The Bellevue Palace is a landmark in Bern, renowned for luxury and a high standard of service. The terrace features tremendous views of the river Aare, with peaks of the Bernese Oberland in the distance. Larger than average rooms are generously furnished. A member of Leading Hotels of the World. Dogs are allowed. **www.bellevue-palace.ch**

Key to Symbols *see back cover flap*

MITTELLAND, BERNESE OBERLAND & VALAIS

BRIG Ambassador
⊞ P ⑪ ⒻⒻ

Saflischstrasse 3, 3900 **Tel** *027 922 99 00* **Fax** *027 922 99 09* **Rooms** *31*   **Road Map** *D4*

A comfortable hotel near the river, not far from the train station and the city centre, yet away from traffic. Guest rooms are of a good size, but in some cases the decor is dated, though with an old-fashioned appeal. The suites have wooden floors and oriental carpets. There is cable TV and Wi-Fi for a fee. **www.ambassador-brig.ch**

BRIG Victoria
⊞ P ⑪ ⒻⒻ

Bahnhofstrasse 2, 3900 **Tel** *027 923 1503* **Fax** *027 924 21 69* **Rooms** *37*   **Road Map** *D4*

An imposing and attractive structure with a mansard roof and balconies looking out to the Valaisan Alps, this historic hotel has some very large rooms with equally generous bathrooms. The interior furnishings are modern, and it has a well-known French dining room. **http://hotel-victoria-brig.ghix.com**

CRANS-MONTANA Grand Hotel du Golf
⊞ ⊞ P ⑪ ≋ ⊞ ⊞ ⒻⒻⒻⒻ

Allée Elysée-Bonvin 7, 3963 **Tel** *027 485 42 42* **Fax** *027 485 42 43* **Rooms** *80*   **Road Map** *C4*

Frequented by champion golfers and luxury seekers alike, the Grand is *the* golf hotel in Switzerland's top golf resort. There is a huge indoor swimming pool, beauty farm and gym facilities. The rooms all have views of the Rhone valley and Valaisan peaks. Perfectly placed for golf, the hotel also offers transport to the ski lifts. **www.ghgp.ch**

CRANS-MONTANA Royal
⊞ ⊞ P ⑪ ≋ ⊞ ⊞ ⒻⒻⒻⒻ

Rue du Pas de l'Ours, 3963 **Tel** *027 485 95 95* **Fax** *027 485 95 85* **Rooms** *54*   **Road Map** *C4*

This well-appointed modern hotel has a chalet-style exterior. Close to both golf and ski lifts, the hotel has its own park area and excellent views of the distant peaks and glaciers. The rooms are comfortably furnished, and suites feature conversation nooks and fluffy fabric sofas. Modern spa and conference facilities. **www.hotel-royal.ch**

FIESCH Fiescherhof
⊞ P ⑪ ⊞ Ⓕ

Furkastrasse, 3984 **Tel** *027 971 21 71* **Fax** *027 971 19 85* **Rooms** *27*   **Road Map** *D4*

Fiescherhof is a family-operated hotel built in the style of a chalet, with balconies for most rooms. It is located in a small, quiet village off the main road yet near ski pistes and the Aletsch glacier. The rooms are simply furnished, with small wooden tables and chairs and minimal decoration. **www.fiescherhof.ch**

GRIMSEL PASS Grimselblick
P ⑪ ⒻⒻ

Grimsel Pass, 3864 **Tel** *027 973 11 77* **Fax** *027 973 14 22* **Rooms** *10*   **Road Map** *D4*

A solid stone structure with attractive red shutters, Grimselblick is located right on the edge of the icy Totensee (Dead Sea) atop the Grimsel Pass. The rooms are small but with character, furnished in local pine. One room has a hand-carved four-poster bed with curtains. Nearby are snowshoe trails. **www.grimselpass.ch**

GRINDELWALD Parkhotel Schoenegg
⊞ ⊞ P ⑪ ≋ ⒻⒻ

Dorfstrasse, 3818 **Tel** *033 854 18 18* **Fax** *033 854 18 19* **Rooms** *49*   **Road Map** *D4*

Run by the same family for four generations, the Parkhotel Schoenegg is a quiet luxury hotel with top spa facilities, private garden and cosy reading room with wood-burning stove. There is an indoor swimming pool, a whirlpool with floor to ceiling views of the Eiger and a Finnish log sauna. Well equipped rooms. **www.parkhotelschoenegg.ch**

GRINDELWALD Grand Regina Alpin Well & Fit
⊞ ⊞ P ⑪ ≋ ⊞ ⒻⒻⒻⒻ

Dorfstrasse 80, 3818 **Tel** *033 854 86 00* **Fax** *033 854 86 88* **Rooms** *90*   **Road Map** *D4*

This majestic castle-style hotel in the village centre has spa facilities (*see p291*) with indoor and outdoor pool, sauna, and a unique "ice and glacier fountain", with ice chips for cooling off after the sauna. Luxurious suites have leather sofas and parquet floors; standard rooms have inlaid wooden ceilings. Close to Jungfrau train station. **www.grandregina.ch**

GSTAAD Bernerhof
⊞ ⊞ P ⑪ ≋ ⒻⒻⒻⒻ

Promenade, 3780 **Tel** *033 748 88 44* **Fax** *033 748 88 40* **Rooms** *45*   **Road Map** *C4*

A large chalet-style building with wooden balconies, the hotel prides itself on a casual, friendly atmosphere. It is centrally located near the train station, but free from traffic noise. Rooms have wooden floors. Playrooms for kids, jukebox, indoor swimming pool. Several restaurants, including the only Chinese in the Gstaad region. **www.bernerhof-gstaad.ch**

GSTAAD Gstaad Palace
⊞ ⊞ P ⑪ ≋ ⊞ ⊞ ⒻⒻⒻⒻⒻ

Palacestrasse, 3780 **Tel** *033 748 50 00* **Fax** *033 748 50 00* **Rooms** *104*   **Road Map** *C4*

Massive turreted fairytale palace building set in a private park with tennis courts and a swimming pool, with every possible luxury, including some of the most extensive beauty and spa facilities in Europe. There are five restaurants, 29 suites and a three-bedroom Penthouse Suite. Even the least expensive north-facing rooms measure 31 sq m (334 sq ft). **www.palace.ch**

INTERLAKEN Beatus
⊞ P ⑪ Ⓕ

Sundlauenen, 3800 **Tel** *033 841 16 24* **Fax** *033 841 16 25* **Rooms** *9*   **Road Map** *D4*

Part of the Swiss Budget Hotels chain, this white cottage-style hotel with its charming wraparound roof is just 5 km (3 miles) outside Interlaken, right on the Thunersee lake shore, with quick bus and boat connections. The rooms are all painted in white, with period French windows and sunny outlooks. **www.beatus-interlaken.ch**

INTERLAKEN Hotel du Lac

Ⓟ | ㉈ ⒫ ⒢   ⒻⒻⒻ

Höhenweg 225, 3800 **Tel** *033 822 29 22* **Fax** *033 822 29 15* **Rooms** *35*   **Road Map** *D4*

This fashionable, elegant hotel is located on the shore of the river Aare in the centre of Interlaken. Rooms are impressive in size and lavishly furnished, with views of the lake and the peaks beyond. Sightseeing and boating excursions are organized by the hotel. **www.dulac-interlaken.ch**

INTERLAKEN Victoria-Jungfrau

⒜ ⒫ Ⓟ ㉈ ⒢ ⒯ ⒣   ⒻⒻⒻⒻⒻ

Höhenweg 41, 3800 **Tel** *033 828 28 28* **Fax** *033 828 28 80* **Rooms** *212*   **Road Map** *D4*

This is one of the most majestic and impressive grand old hotels in the palace style to be found anywhere in Europe. Convenient for lake excursions, the hotel also has extensive, state-of-the-art spa (see p291) and fitness and beauty facilities. The public rooms are opulent, bedrooms generously sized and elegantly appointed. **www.victoria-jungfrau.ch**

KANDERSTEG Landgasthaus Rüdihus

Ⓟ ㉈   ⒻⒻⒻ

Hauptstrasse, 3718 **Tel** *033 675 81 81* **Fax** *033 675 81 85* **Rooms** *10*   **Road Map** *C4*

Just outside Kandersteg in fields of wildflowers with a rocky backdrop, this 250-year-old historic chalet-style farmhouse invites visitors to escape the present – there is no plastic, no steel, only old iron and wood. Some rooms have four-poster beds, and antiques are everywhere. Guests have spa and fitness privileges at the hotel Doldenhorn. **www.ruedihus.ch**

KANDERSTEG Victoria Ritter

⒫ Ⓟ ㉈ ⒢   ⒻⒻⒻ

Hauptstrasse, 3718 **Tel** *033 675 80 00* **Fax** *033 675 81 00* **Rooms** *75*   **Road Map** *C4*

One of the grandest hotels in the Bernese Oberland, now renovated and incorporating farmhouse-style period rooms in the separate Gasthaus Ritter, as well as the more traditional grand-old-hotel-style rooms in the Victoria. Tennis courts and indoor swimming pool, library and a warm welcome for children. Village-centre location. **www.hotel-victoria.ch**

LAUTERBRUNNEN Silberhorn

Ⓟ ㉈   ⒻⒻ

Alte Isenfluhstrasse, 3822 **Tel** *033 856 22 10* **Fax** *033 855 42 13* **Rooms** *35*   **Road Map** *C4*

Silberhorn is a delightful chalet-type inn not far from the train station and in the middle of the village, yet set in a large private garden. In winter a ski piste descends all the way to the hotel grounds. In summer it is peaceful, with garden dining and wildflower beds. There are excellent views of the Bernese Alps. **www.silberhorn.com**

LEUKERBAD Lindner

⒜ ⒫ Ⓟ ㉈ ⒢ ⒯ ⒣   ⒻⒻⒻ

Dorfplatz, 3954 **Tel** *027 472 10 00* **Fax** *027 472 10 01* **Rooms** *135*   **Road Map** *C4*

Part of the German Lindner chain of luxury hotels, this inn is connected to the main Leukerbad spa centre by a tunnel (see p290). There are three tiers of rooms, graded by level of luxury and corresponding to the three former hotels now amalgamated into the Lindner complex. Similarly, there are three tiers of suites. **www.lindnerhotels.ch**

LEUKERBAD Les Sources des Alpes

⒜ ⒫ Ⓟ ㉈ ⒢ ⒯   ⒻⒻⒻⒻⒻ

Tuftstrasse 17, 3954 **Tel** *027 472 20 00* **Fax** *027 472 20 01* **Rooms** *30*   **Road Map** *C4*

A charming, romantic hotel tucked away at the edge of the old village, with its own hot springs and impressive array of beauty and spa facilities. Each room is uniquely decorated and named. Each guest receives personalized letterhead stationery. Views of the cliffs and peaks from the outdoor pool. Highly recommended. **www.sourcesdesalpes.ch**

MARTIGNY Alpes & Rhone

⒫ Ⓟ ㉈   Ⓕ

Avenue du Grand-St-Bernard 11, 1920 **Tel** *027 722 17 17* **Fax** *027 722 43 00* **Rooms** *50*   **Road Map** *B5*

Unprepossessing from the exterior, this eight-storey, modestly priced city-centre hotel has a range of rooms, including family rooms and apartments – all comfortably furnished. The ski resorts of Verbier, Crans-Montana, Zermatt, Leukerbad and even Chamonix in France are all well within an hour's drive. **www.alpes-rhone.ch**

MÜRREN Alpenruh

⒫ ㉈   ⒻⒻ

Postfach, 3825 **Tel** *033 856 88 00* **Fax** *033 856 88 88* **Rooms** *26*   **Road Map** *C4*

This cosy and popular chalet-style hotel has stunning views of the Eiger and Jungfrau peaks. Set in quiet, car-free location next to the ski lifts, the Alpenruh lives up to its name "Alpine tranquillity". The hotel is furnished in a clean, modern style. Guests have access to the nearby indoor pool at the sports centre. **www.alpenruh-muerren.ch**

RIEDERALP Golfhotel Riederhof

⒜ ⒫ ㉈ ⒢   ⒻⒻ

Postfach, 3987 **Tel** *027 928 64 64* **Fax** *027 928 64 74* **Rooms** *13*   **Road Map** *D4*

This modern and well-equipped hotel with its own pitch and putt golf links, and five more courses within an hour's drive, is also on the footpath leading to the Aletsch glacier. Guest rooms have south-facing balconies with romantic views. The spa includes a swimming pool for hotel guests. **www.golfhotel-riederhof.ch**

SAAS FEE Jägerhof

⒜ ⒫ ㉈   ⒻⒻ

Obere Gasse 16, 3906 **Tel** *027 957 13 10* **Fax** *027 957 16 55* **Rooms** *15*   **Road Map** *D5*

A small, friendly, family-run hotel in the chalet style with romantic views of glaciers and crevasses. The hotel is set on a grassy hill just outside the narrow lanes of the village centre. A chalet annex offers apartments for longer stays and families. Facilities include a hot tub, solarium and sauna. Rooms are comfortable but not large. **www.hotel-jaegerhof.ch**

SAAS FEE Ferieneck Hohnegg

⒫ ㉈   ⒻⒻⒻ

Panoramaterrasse, 3906 **Tel** *027 958 10 70* **Fax** *027 958 10 99* **Rooms** *8*   **Road Map** *D5*

Set in the hills just outside the town centre, with wildflowers in summer, the timbered hotel offers both rooms and apartments. Each hotel room is unique, some with Jacuzzi bathtubs or canopied four-poster beds. There are pine-panelled ceilings and a high standard of decor overall. The apartments are in rustic chalets nearby. **www.hohnegg.ch**

Key to Price Guide *see p244* **Key to Symbols** *see back cover flap*

SION Ibis

`P` `⛊` `⛊` Ⓕ

Avenue Grand Champsec 21, 1951 **Tel** *027 205 71 00* **Fax** *027 205 71 71* **Rooms** *71* **Road Map** *C5*

This small hotel in Sion-Est is bright, modern and functional, catering mainly for business travellers. Conveniently close to the A9 highway, it is well-located for excursions to Crans Montana, Verbier and Zermatt. Services include a restaurant, bar and (charged) Wi-Fi. Good value for money. **www.ibishotel.com**

SION Du Rhône

`P` `⛊` `⛊` ⒻⒻ

Rue du Scex 10, 1950 **Tel** *027 322 82 91* **Fax** *027 323 11 88* **Rooms** *44* **Road Map** *C5*

Part of the Best Western chain of hotels, Du Rhône is modern and functional, with views of Rhône Valley and nearby peaks. Central located in a quiet area, the hotel is well equipped, with cable TV and Internet access. Medium-sized guest rooms (non-smoking available) with serviceable rather than charming decor. **www.bestwestern.ch**

SOLOTHURN Baseltor

`P` `⛊` `⛊` ⒻⒻ

Hauptgasse 79, 4500 **Tel** *032 622 34 22* **Fax** *032 622 18 79* **Rooms** *11* **Road Map** *C3*

A welcoming atmosphere with lively conversation prevails here, where the owners organize literary dinners and encourage guests to take cycling tours. This four-storey townhouse across from the cathedral was once a cannon storage facility. The restaurant has 13 Gault Millau points, and the six bedrooms added in 1992 won a design award. **www.baseltor.ch**

SOLOTHURN Die Krone

`P` `⛊` `⛊` `⛊` ⒻⒻ

Hauptgasse 64, 4500 **Tel** *032 626 44 44* **Fax** *032 626 44 45* **Rooms** *42* **Road Map** *C3*

Die Krone is said to be the country's second-oldest hotel, welcoming Napoleon as an overnight guest and, more recently, Sophia Loren and Henry Kissinger. The impressive exterior dates from the 18th century. Rooms are decorated in Louis XV or Biedermeier style, with all modern conveniences. One of Switzerland's best hotels. **www.hotelkrone-solothurn.ch**

THUN Emmental

`P` `⛊` `⛊` ⒻⒻ

Bernstrasse 2, 3600 **Tel** *033 222 01 20* **Fax** *033 222 01 30* **Rooms** *12* **Road Map** *C3*

Of immediate appeal, the exterior of this four-storey, villa-style house features green shutters and wooden porches typical of its 19th-century origins. The rooms are clean and modern, with pure white walls and black leather armchairs. Good location in the Old Town with views of Schloss Thun and the distant mountains. **www.thunisst.ch**

VAL D'ANNIVIERS Bella Tola

`⛊` `⛊` `P` `⛊` `⛊` ⒻⒻⒻ

Rue Principale, St-Luc, 3961 **Tel** *027 475 14 44* **Fax** *027 475 29 98* **Rooms** *30* **Road Map** *C5*

An exceptionally charming, award-winning family-run hotel with period furnishings, flowers and spacious rooms. Recent addition of spa and fitness facilities. Set at the edge of a medieval village with ancient barns and winding lanes, with tremendous views from the south-facing balconies. Ski bus stops right outside. **www.bellatola.ch**

VERBIER Central

ⒻⒻ

Place Centrale, 1936 **Tel** *027 771 50 07* **Fax** *027 771 50 11* **Rooms** *8* **Road Map** *C5*

A pint-sized boutique hotel in the centre of Verbier. The small rooms are decorated in neutral tones. Some rooms have balconies or feature splendid mountain views. All have Jacuzzi baths. The hotel is in the heart of the village and above Verbier's most popular stretch of bars, so not for the visitor craving silence. **www.verbiercentralhotel.com**

VERBIER Les Touristes

`P` `⛊` `⛊` ⒻⒻ

Verbier Village, 1936 **Tel** *027 771 22 47* **Fax** *027 771 21 72* **Rooms** *16* **Road Map** *C5*

Offering the best value for money in Verbier, this hotel is actually just outside the resort proper in the old village. The guest rooms are small but quaint, with old wooden panelling, though not all have en-suite bathrooms. The restaurant is famous for its cheese dishes. Ample free parking. Buses up to ski lifts. **www.hoteltouristes-verbier.ch**

VERBIER Chalet d'Adrien

`⛊` `⛊` `P` `⛊` `⛊` `⛊` ⒻⒻⒻⒻⒻ

Chemin des Creux, 1936 **Tel** *027 771 62 00* **Fax** *027 771 62 24* **Rooms** *25* **Road Map** *C5*

One of the finest hotels in this jet-set resort, completely renovated from a simple family inn. It is located next to ski lifts but an uphill hike from the town centre. There is a swimming pool, a beauty spa and an exercise room. Some bedrooms are rather small but the junior suites are luxurious and well appointed. **www.chalet-adrien.com**

VISP Visperhof

`P` `⛊` `⛊` `⛊` ⒻⒻ

Bahnhofstrasse 2, 3930 **Tel** *027 948 38 00* **Fax** *027 948 38 01* **Rooms** *35* **Road Map** *D4*

A modern hotel in the car-free district of Visp, the terminus town for the train to Zermatt. All rooms are non-smoking and have free wireless Internet access. The business-class rooms contain work desks. The decor is clean urban chic. Visperhof is convenient for day trips to nearby ski resorts, including Saas Fee. **www.visperhof.ch**

WENGEN Belvedere

`⛊` `⛊` ⒻⒻⒻ

Postfach, 3823 **Tel** *033 856 68 68* **Fax** *033 856 68 69.* **Rooms** *62* **Road Map** *C4*

Huge five-storey hotel in Art Nouveau style right by the train station in the centre of this car-free village. The rooms are comfortable and sometimes spacious, some with old wooden floors. Large family suites are also available. The Belvedere is close to ski lifts and the village centre playground, with its ice rink and skiing. **www.belvedere-wengen.ch**

WENGEN Regina

`⛊` `⛊` `⛊` `⛊` `⛊` ⒻⒻⒻⒻ

Postfach, 3823 **Tel** *033 856 58 58* **Fax** *033 856 58 50.* **Rooms** *80* **Road Map** *C4*

Regina is a period hotel in the grand old style, with iron railing balconies and white painted shutters, located in a quiet part of the village. Facilities include a beauty centre with exercise machines, massage and solarium. Bedrooms have old-fashioned floor lamps and floral bedspreads. Airy restaurant with 15 Gault Millau points. **www.hotelregina.ch**

WILDERSWIL Alpenrose   🔲 **P**   Ⓕ
Kirchgasse 72a, 3812 **Tel** *033 822 10 24* **Fax** *033 822 69 60* **Rooms** *20*   **Road Map** *D4*

Small, four-storey family-run hotel with a huge garden and views of the Bernese Oberland peaks. The exterior is not particularly characterful, but inside the rooms show flair in decoration and are larger and more generously furnished, for example with comfy sofas and period wallpaper, than generally found in this price range. **www.alpenrosehotel.ch**

ZERMATT Bahnhof   🔲   Ⓕ
Bahnhofstrasse 54, 3920 **Tel** *027 967 24 06* **Fax** *027 967 72 16* **Rooms** *17*   **Road Map** *C5*

Amazingly inexpensive for Zermatt, the Bahnhof is steeped in history and is the preferred residence of hardcore climbers and skiers. Its distinctive red shutters and wide wooden balconies are a Zermatt landmark. There are dormitories and group rooms, but also simply decorated double rooms with views of the Matterhorn. **www.hotelbahnhof.com**

ZERMATT Romantica   🔲   ⒻⒻ
Chrum 21, 3920 **Tel** *027 966 26 50* **Fax** *027 966 26 55* **Rooms** *15*   **Road Map** *C5*

This is a mountain hotel in chalet style on four floors, with stunning views and a sunny garden. The rooms are comfortable but somewhat small. On the grounds are two Valaisan mazots (200-year-old wooden cabins historically used for grain storage) converted into residences of unique romantic appeal. **www.reconline.ch/romantica**

ZERMATT 3100 Kulmhotel   🔲 🍴   ⒻⒻⒻ
Gornergrat, 3920 **Tel** *027 966 64 00* **Fax** *027 966 64 04* **Rooms** *23*   **Road Map** *C5*

As advertised, this is a "summit experience", though by no means the highest hotel in the Alps. With its two domed towers – one a working observatory – this hotel is distinctive indeed, and only accessible by cog-wheel railway. Rooms are fully equipped with modern conveniences, and the views are unbeatable. **www.matterhorn-group.ch**

ZERMATT Riffelalp   🔵🔲🍴🏊🛎🅿   ⒻⒻⒻⒻⒻ
Riffelalp, 3920 **Tel** *027 966 05 55.* **Fax** *027 966 05 50.* **Rooms** *72*   **Road Map** *C5*

Arguably the most desirable accommodation in Zermatt. Tranquillity is assured, the only way up to the hotel being by cogwheel train. The hotel complex dates back to 1884, but since total reconstruction in 2000 with a spa, indoor swimming pool and bowling alley, the hotel's rooms are among the most luxurious in the Alps. **www.riffelalp.com**

GENEVA

GENEVA Hôtel de la Cloche   🔲   Ⓕ
6 Rue de la Cloche, 1201 **Tel** *022 732 94 81* **Fax** *022 738 16 12* **Rooms** *8*   **Road Map** *A5*

A very popular bijou hotel in a quiet neighbourhood in the centre of Geneva, just behind the Quai du Mont Blanc, with the unique appeal of a 19th-century family home. Elegant stone exterior. Small but perfect rooms with parquet flooring, fireplace and balconies with wrought-iron railings. Reserve well in advance. **www.geneva-hotel.ch/cloche**

GENEVA St-Gervais   🔲   Ⓕ
20 Rue des Corps-Saints, 1201 **Tel** *022 732 45 72* **Fax** *022 731 42 90* **Rooms** *26*   **Road Map** *A5*

Inexpensive city-centre hotel within easy strolling distance of the lakeside and train station, 15 minutes from the airport. All rooms share bathroom facilities, but they do all have washbasins. Rooms vary in size according to price, all with TV and wireless Internet access. Complimentary breakfast. Cheerful atmosphere. **www.stgervais-geneva.ch**

GENEVA Comédie   🔲   ⒻⒻ
12 Rue de Carouge, 1205 **Tel** *022 322 23 24* **Fax** *022 322 23 23* **Rooms** *28*   **Road Map** *A5*

An inexpensive and friendly hotel impeccably located for quick access to Geneva's Old Town and the lakeside, and a short walk from Plainpalais underground car park. The guest rooms are light and airy, decorated with modern paintings and fresh flowers. There is also a suite. Small breakfast room. **www.hotel-comedie.ch**

GENEVA Hotel At Home   🔲   ⒻⒻ
16 Rue de Fribourg, 1201 **Tel** *022 906 19 00* **Fax** *022 738 44 30* **Rooms** *26*   **Road Map** *A5*

As the name suggests, a welcoming and casual atmosphere is cultivated at this five-storey pink structure in the heart of Geneva, a 5-minute walk from the train station. The clientele is eclectic and international. Rooms are on the small side, with clean, bare white walls and polished dark wood floors. **www.hotel-at-home.ch**

GENEVA Savoy   🔲 🍴   ⒻⒻ
8 Place Cornavin, 1201 **Tel** *022 906 47 00* **Fax** *022 906 47 90* **Rooms** *50*   **Road Map** *A5*

A downtown hotel with a reputation for above-average service and accommodation. It is located across the street from Cornavin train station, in the heart of the shopping and tourist district. All rooms have air conditioning, and some have kitchenettes. The restaurant serves breakfast, and Lebanese specialities during the day. **www.hotel-savoy.net**

GENEVA Crowne Plaza   🔵🔲**P**🍴🛎🅿   ⒻⒻⒻ
Avenue Louis-Casaï 75–77, 1216 **Tel** *022 710 30 00* **Fax** *022 710 31 00* **Rooms** *302*   **Road Map** *A5*

Luxurious and studded with facilities, this hotel next to the airport and international exhibition centre caters mostly to businessmen and convention visitors, with two separate 24-hour business centres. The spa and fitness centres are equally impressive. Basic rooms are comfortable, business suites lavish in size and appointments. **www.cpgva.ch**

Key to Price Guide *see p244* **Key to Symbols** *see back cover flap*

GENEVA Kipling 🖼 P ♿ ⓕⓕⓕ

27 Rue de la Navigation, 1201 **Tel** *022 544 40 40* **Fax** *022 544 40 99* **Rooms** *62* **Road Map** *A5*

Befitting the name, the Kipling has an Oriental flavour, with artefacts from India and China everywhere you look. Set in the heart of Geneva, with easy access to major attractions. Some rooms are stunningly furnished, all are air conditioned. Conveniences include wireless Internet access, self service laundry and a business centre. **www.manotel.com/kipling**

GENEVA L'Auberge d'Hermance 🖼 P ⏸ ⓕⓕⓕ

12 Rue du Midi, Hermance, 1248 **Tel** *022 751 13 68* **Fax** *022 751 16 31* **Rooms** *6* **Road Map** *A5*

Intimate, elegant and an escape from downtown Geneva. Tucked away in the picturesque hamlet of Hermance, the Auberge has just six romantic rooms, three of which are suites. Rooms feature original paintings, hand-painted furniture, open beams, stone walls and gorgeously tiled bathrooms. Exceptional restaurant. **www.hotel-hermance.ch**

GENEVA Hôtel Beau-Rivage 🖼 P ⏸ ♿ ⓕⓕⓕⓕⓕ

13 Quai du Mont-Blanc, 1201 **Tel** *022 716 66 66* **Fax** *022 716 60 60* **Rooms** *93* **Road Map** *A5*

Geneva's oldest family-run hotel, poised on the edge of the lake, close to all major attractions with views of the famous jet d'eau. An architectural gem, with crystal chandeliers, four-storey interior atrium with bubbling fountain, marble walls and Grecian columns. Exceptional concierge services and opulent rooms. Three apartments. **www.beau-rivage.ch**

WESTERN SWITZERLAND

AIGLE Du Nord 🖼 P ⓕⓕ

2–4 Rue Colomb, 1860 **Tel** *24 468 10 55* **Fax** *24 468 10 56* **Rooms** *19* **Road Map** *B4*

Situated in the pedestrian district of the village centre, this five-storey city-style hotel is part of the Minotel chain. Guest rooms are furnished with comfy fabric armchairs, and the hotel is friendly and appealing overall. There are coffee/tea making machines in every room. **www.hoteldunord.ch**

AVENCHES De la Couronne 🖼 P ⏸ ♿ ⓕⓕ

20 Rue Centrale, 1580 **Tel** *026 675 54 14* **Fax** *026 675 54 22* **Rooms** *12* **Road Map** *B3*

Attractive four-storey stone building with a mansard roof and red shutters in the village centre near the church. Rooms are larger than average, comfortable and tastefully decorated. Seminar and banquet facilities are located in the lofty timbered hall. The stone-vaulted wine cellar has tastings. Popular meeting place for locals. **www.lacouronne.ch**

BALLAIGUES Hôtel Croix d'Or P ⏸ ⓕ

Place du Château 1, 1338 **Tel** *021 843 26 09* **Rooms** *5* **Road Map** *A3*

This friendly, village-centre hotel offers inexpensive rooms close to the French border. Rooms are basic and clean, with shared bathrooms on the same floor. The hotel is popular with hikers and cyclists who have access to a garage to store their bikes. The price includes a good breakfast and there's a restaurant with a terrace. **www.lacroixdor.ch**

DELÉMONT Le National 🖼 P ⏸ ♿ ⓕⓕ

Route de Bâle 25, 2800 **Tel** *032 422 96 22* **Fax** *032 422 39 12* **Rooms** *27* **Road Map** *C2*

Very modern, chic, hotel in the centre of Delémont, a 5-minute walk from the train station and steps away from the historic district. Ample parking at the hotel. Rooms have a contemporary design, with fluffy white duvets. Cross-country skiing and cycle paths in the vicinity. The hotel has a highly regarded restaurant with extensive wine list. **www.lenational-hotel.ch**

ESTAVAYER-LE-LAC Le Rive Sud 🖼 P ⏸ ♿ ⓕⓕ

Rue de l'Hôtel de Ville 16, 1470 **Tel** *026 663 92 92* **Fax** *026 663 92 99* **Rooms** *13* **Road Map** *B3*

Attractive four-storey stone house, with foundations dating from the 16th century, in the medieval village centre. The interior has been tastefully decorated, and guest rooms feature shower or whirlpool bathtubs, some with timbered ceilings and views of Lake Neuchâtel. Small conference room. Gourmet restaurant and bistro. **www.lerivesud.ch**

FRIBOURG Best Western Hôtel de la Rose 🖼 P ⏸ ♿ ⓕⓕ

1 Rue de Morat, 1702 **Tel** *026 351 01 01* **Fax** *026 351 01 00* **Rooms** *40* **Road Map** *B3*

In appropriate faint rose coloured stone, this imposing 17th-century hotel is right in the centre of the Old Town, close to the cathedral. Most rooms are small and simply furnished, some with skylights. Junior suites are more spacious, with large windows and views. Dancing in the underground Cave bar goes on until 4am. **www.hoteldelarose.ch**

FRIBOURG Hôtel du Sauvage 🖼 P ⏸ ♿ ⓕⓕⓕ

12 Planche-Supérieure, 1700 **Tel** *026 347 30 60* **Fax** *026 347 30 61* **Rooms** *16* **Road Map** *B3*

"Sauvage" translates literally into "wild man", and the hotel's signature emblem is the image of a caveman holding a club. But its charm wins the Sauvage membership of the Swiss "Romantik Hotel" association. Well situated in central Fribourg, featuring charming rooms with ancient wooden ceilings and mountain-sized duvets. **www.hotel-sauvage.ch**

GRUYÈRES Hostellerie des Chevaliers 🖼 P ♿ ⓕⓕ

Route de la Cité, 1663 **Tel** *026 921 19 33* **Fax** *026 921 25 52* **Rooms** *34* **Road Map** *B4*

The hotel looks like a rambling old farmhouse, painted white and set by itself in the verdant pastures of the Gruyères countryside. Tranquil and evocative location, cyclists particularly welcome. Rooms range from the simply furnished to those with antiques and lavish colourful old fabrics covering beds and walls alike. **www.chevaliers-gruyeres.ch**

GRUYÈRES Hôtel de Ville
Route de la Cité, 1663 **Tel** *026 921 24 24* **Fax** *026 921 24 24* **Rooms** *8*   **Road Map** *B4*

Old-fashioned inn with a small outside terrace on a pedestrian-only cobblestone street in the atmospheric Old Town. The rooms are cheerful and welcoming, of average size. There is a larger junior suite and a bridal suite with antique four-poster bed. Characterful restaurant with local cheese and ham specialities. **www.hoteldeville.ch**

LA CHAUX-DE-FONDS Hôtel de la Fleur-de-Lys
13 Avenue Léopold-Robert, 2300 **Tel** *032 913 37 31* **Fax** *032 913 58 51* **Rooms** *28*   **Road Map** *B3*

Historically, a business hotel with clients in the watch-making trade, the Fleur de Lys is centrally located in La Chaux de Fonds near the train station. Rooms are of a good standard and have curtains which close off sleeping area from the sitting area. Highly regarded Italian restaurant in house.

LAUSANNE Hôtel de l'Ours
2 Rue du Bugnon, 1005 **Tel** *021 321 49 49* **Fax** *021 320 49 73* **Rooms** *20*   **Road Map** *B4*

Inexpensive city centre hotel in a bustling square with excellent tram connections. The four-storey stone building is painted pink, though faded somewhat, with a gabled roof and dormer windows, and lies within walking distance of the cathedral and museums. There is a popular Italian restaurant in house. Rooms are clean, with basic furnishings.

LAUSANNE Minotel Alagare
14 Rue du Simplon, 1006 **Tel** *021 612 09 09* **Fax** *021 617 92 55* **Rooms** *45*   **Road Map** *B4*

With its attractive exterior bedecked with the flags of many nations, this internationally minded hotel is within a 10-minute walk of the Olympic Museum and near the train station, in a quiet pedestrianized zone. Rooms are cheerful and comfortable. Japanese or Chinese breakfast available. Cable TV. **www.hotelalagare.ch**

LAUSANNE Elite
1 Avenue Sainte-Luce, 1003 **Tel** *021 320 23 61* **Fax** *021 320 39 63* **Rooms** *33*   **Road Map** *B4*

Elite is a large townhouse of pink stone with white shutters and red-striped awnings, with a large leafy garden, in the heart of downtown Lausanne between the shopping area and train station. Top rooms have views of the lake; all are non-smoking, and some have spacious balconies. Urban address with relaxed country ambience. **www.elite-lausanne.ch**

LAUSANNE Lausanne Palace & Spa
7–9 Rue du Grand-Chêne, 1002 **Tel** *021 331 31 31* **Fax** *021 323 25 71* **Rooms** *154*   **Road Map** *B4*

The epitome of the grand old Belle Époque hotel, evoking the heyday of the Swiss Riviera, with one of the most elaborately equipped spa centres in Switzerland. City centre location. Rooms range in size from 30 sq m (322 sq ft) to the 95 sq m (1,020 sq ft) Presidential Suites. Black marble bathrooms. Indoor pool. **www.lausanne-palace.ch**

LE LOCLE Jet d'Eau
Le Col 15, Le Col-des-Roches, 2400 **Tel** *032 931 46 66* **Fax** *032 931 25 41* **Rooms** *5*   **Road Map** *B3*

Attractive and inexpensive old inn set in open fields just outside Le Locle. Very quiet location, particularly welcoming for families. With its tiled gabled roof, green shutters and flower boxes, the inn offers a rural escape, but is still close to the underground mills, watch museum and other local attractions. Closed Mon & Tue. **www.jetdeau-col.ch**

LES DIABLERETS Mon Séjour
Vers-l'Église, 1864 **Tel** *024 492 14 08* **Fax** *024 492 14 17* **Rooms** *11*   **Road Map** *B4*

Within a large, modern chalet-style house, this hotel is popular with families and students seeking very inexpensive accommodation for skiing in winter and for summer hiking on the Diablerets glacier. It has double rooms as well as dormitories and a huge garden. No rooms have ensuites, but all have washbasins and bathrooms are on each floor.

LES DIABLERETS Eurotel Victoria
Chemin du Vernex, 1865 **Tel** *024 492 37 21* **Fax** *024 492 23 71* **Rooms** *101*   **Road Map** *B4*

Luxury hotel in the small family ski resort of Diablerets. Large, well furnished rooms with pine floors and clean, modern decor. Indoor swimming pool, sauna and gym with exercise machines. There is a separate wooden chalet restaurant serving Valaisan specialities as well as a gourmet restaurant in the hotel itself. **www.eurotel-victoria.ch/**

LEYSIN Classic Hotel
Route de la Cité, 1854 **Tel** *024 493 06 06* **Fax** *024 493 06 93* **Rooms** *115*   **Road Map** *B4*

The largest hotel in Leysin, modern inside and out, with complimentary shuttle service to ski pistes and sports centre, where guests have free access to the swimming pool. It is set in the centre of the village yet with open grounds and sunny views. Rooms are of average size, with standard modern furnishings. **www.classic-hotel.ch**

LUTRY Le Bourg 7
Rue du Bourg 7, 1095 **Tel** *021 796 37 77* **Fax** *021 796 37 70* **Rooms** *13*   **Road Map** *B4*

Located very close to Lake Geneva, in the heart of a beautiful old village in the Lavaux wine region, is this elegant hotel in a restored town house dating from 1520. The decor is modern, and if you like the stylish furniture and beds used in the hotel, you can even order your own. Babysitting can be arranged on request. **www.lebourg7.com**

MONT-PELERIN Le Mirador Kempinski
5 Chemin du Mirador, 1801 **Tel** *021 925 11 11* **Fax** *021 925 11 12* **Rooms** *74*   **Road Map** *B4*

Reminiscent of an elegant country manor, located in the heart of Swiss wine country on Mont-Pèlerin, surrounded by acres of vineyards. Rooms ranges from basic to gargantuan suites. A Givenchy Spa (*see p291*) has wide-ranging beauty regimes, weight loss centre, domed indoor/outdoor swimming pool and a well-equipped gym. **www.mirador.ch**

Key to Price Guide *see p244* **Key to Symbols** *see back cover flap*

MONTREUX Hôtel Villa Germaine
P ⓕ

3 Avenue Collonge, 1820 **Tel** *021 963 15 28* **Fax** *none* **Rooms** *9*   **Road Map** *B4*

A fairytale Belle Époque villa with tall chimneys, spreading stone staircases and red-striped awnings all at modest prices. Set above the lake in a quiet, wooded residential neighbourhood. Fabulous views. Some rooms have balconies. Extremely sunny, with a garden for sunbathing. The atmosphere of a private home. **www.montreux.ch/villa-germaine**

MONTREUX Fairmont Le Montreux Palace
ⓕⓕⓕⓕ

Grand-Rue 100, 1820 **Tel** *021 962 12 12* **Fax** *021 962 17 17* **Rooms** *235*   **Road Map** *B4*

One of the grandest hotels in Switzerland, with elegant Belle Époque architecture and set like a jewel along the banks of Lake Geneva. The guest rooms have been renovated and outfitted with the latest high-tech gadgets. But the decor, in warm colours, and the generous dimensions hark back to a more opulent age. **www.montreux-palace.ch**

MORGES Mont-Blanc au Lac
ⓕⓕⓕ

Quai du Mont-Blanc, 1110 **Tel** *021 804 87 87* **Fax** *021 801 51 22* **Rooms** *45*   **Road Map** *A4*

This welcoming hotel is located halfway between Geneva and Lausanne, on the lakeside promenade next to the old port area, and just a few steps from the town centre. Rooms are air conditioned and tastefully decorated. Gourmet restaurant and summer garden terrace restaurant. **www.hotel-mont-blanc.ch**

MURTEN/MORAT Le Vieux Manoir
ⓕⓕⓕⓕⓕ

18 Rue de Lausanne, 3280 **Tel** *026 678 61 61* **Fax** *026 678 61 62* **Rooms** *36*   **Road Map** *B3*

This exclusive Relais et Chateaux hotel is nestled in a magnificent park on the edge of Lake Murten, with breathtaking views. All rooms have period wallpaper. Suites with antiques and plush carpeting, some with four-poster beds. Highly rated restaurants, including the Volière, the tiniest dining room in Switzerland (*see p275*). **www.vieuxmanoir.ch**

NEUCHÂTEL Touring au Lac
ⓕ

1 Place Numa-Droz, 2001 **Tel** *032 725 55 01* **Fax** *032 725 82 43* **Rooms** *51*   **Road Map** *B3*

The exterior lacks romantic appeal, but its setting in the old port area allows for evocative views and bracing sea breezes. The rooms are comfortable, good-sized and flooded with natural light. The restaurant has an outside terrace. There is also a medium-sized conference hall with projection equipment. **www.touring-au-lac.ch**

NEUCHÂTEL La Maison du Prussien
ⓕⓕ

Rue des Tunnels 11, 2000 **Tel** *032 730 54 54* **Fax** *032 730 21 43* **Rooms** *10*   **Road Map** *B3*

This 18th-century brewery has been transformed into a luxurious, romantic hotel with an adjoining gourmet restaurant. The massive stone house is surrounded by huge trees. Guest rooms each have an individual character and unique dimensions, some with large windows and fireplaces; all have a strong romantic appeal. **www.hotel-prussien.ch**

NEUCHÂTEL Beau-Rivage
ⓕⓕⓕⓕ

1 Esplanade du Mont-Blanc, 2000 **Tel** *032 723 15 15* **Fax** *032 723 16 16* **Rooms** *66*   **Road Map** *B3*

Befitting its name, the hotel is literally on the "beautiful shore" of Lake Neuchâtel. From the upper rooms the views are stupendous. The rooms themselves are indeed elegant, with huge windows, plush furnishings and cherry wood panelling. Ultra modern spa with hammam and gym. Underground garage with valet parking. **www.beau-rivage-hotel.ch**

NYON Hotel Real
ⓕⓕⓕ

Place de Savoie 1, 1260 **Tel** *022 365 85 85* **Fax** *022 365 85 86* **Rooms** *30*   **Road Map** *A4*

This contemporary-style hotel on the lake shore, 20 minutes from Geneva airport, was constructed in white Carrara and black assoluto marble, cherry woodwork, stuccoes and Brazilian green slate. The air-conditioned rooms are generous in size, with views of the lake and Mont Blanc. Furniture was custom made for each room. **www.hotelrealnyon.ch**

ORBE Hôtel des Mosaïques
ⓕⓕ

Montchoisi 5b, 1350 **Tel** *024 441 62 61* **Fax** *024 441 15 14* **Rooms** *38*   **Road Map** *B3*

In an ideal location for visiting the Roman mosaics of Orbe and the underground cave complex at Vallorbe, and also close to the hiking trails of the Gorges of Orbe is this functional hotel with panoramic views of the Jura mountains. It is a five-minute walk to a sports centre with a swimming pool and tennis courts. **www.hoteldesmosaiques.ch**

ST-URSANNE La Couronne
ⓕ

3 Rue de 23 Juin, 2882 **Tel** *032 461 35 67* **Fax** *032 461 35 77* **Rooms** *10*   **Road Map** *C2*

This historic inn with its own fortified tower gateway lies on the edge of the Old Town. It is a three-storey stone structure, with sloping red tile roof and dormer windows. Sunny garden patio. Restaurant specializes in local variations of fondue and trout (*see p276*). Reservations essential. **www.hotelcouronne.ch**

VEVEY Vevey Hotel & Guesthouse
ⓕ

Place du Marché, 1800 **Tel** *021 922 35 32* **Fax** *021 922 35 34* **Rooms** *13*   **Road Map** *B4*

A historic five-storey stone town house by the lake, a 3-minute walk from the train station, with views of vineyards and the lake. Particularly welcoming for families, backpackers and groups. Double rooms do not have private bathrooms, but share communal ones. The wine cellar dates from medieval times. **www.veveyhotel.com**

VEVEY Hôtel des Trois Couronnes
ⓕⓕⓕⓕ

49 Rue d'Italie, 1800 **Tel** *021 923 32 00* **Fax** *021 923 33 99* **Rooms** *71*   **Road Map** *B4*

Next to the lake in central Vevey is this beautiful hotel in a grand 19th-century building with chequered stone floors, marble and plasterwork. Rooms are spacious and comfortable, and many feature balconies offering fabulous lake and mountain views. The friendly staff provide excellent service. Breakfast costs extra. **www.hoteltroiscouronnes.ch**

YVERDON-LES-BAINS Grand Hôtel des Bains

22 Avenue des Bains, 1400 **Tel** *024 424 64 64* **Fax** *024 424 64 65* **Rooms** *120* **Road Map** *B3*

A luxury grand hotel with towers and park. All deluxe rooms and suites were renovated in 2006 and have balconies, leather sofas and flat-screen TV. Hotel guests enjoy discounted rates at the Thermal Centre connected to the hotel, with thermal pools, steam baths and gym. The hotel also has its own private spa and pool. **www.grandhotelyverdon.ch**

NORTHERN SWITZERLAND

AARAU Sorellino Hotel Argovia

Kasernenstrasse 24, 5001 **Tel** *062 823 21 21* **Fax** *062 822 32 63* **Rooms** *16* **Road Map** *D2*

Comfortable four-storey hotel a 3-minute walk from the train and bus stations near the gabled Old Town. Children under 15 stay free in parents' room. Standard rooms are simple and modern, but the soccer theme room is unique, with soccer goal bedposts, corner flags and decorations from soccer stars, as well as a flat-screen TV. **www.hotelargovia.ch**

AARAU Aarauerhof

Bahnhofstrasse 68, 5000 **Tel** *062 837 83 00* **Fax** *062 837 84 00* **Rooms** *81* **Road Map** *D2*

Modern city hotel near the train station, which has the best rail connections in Switzerland. All rooms are air conditioned. Most guests are businessmen. There is a choice of standard and family rooms. Popular conference venue, with high-tech seminar facilities. Two restaurants and a nightclub. **www.aarauerhof.ch**

BADEN Atrium Hotel Blume

Kurplatz 4, 5400 **Tel** *056 200 02 00* **Fax** *056 200 02 50* **Rooms** *34* **Road Map** *D2*

This historic, characterful hotel is in a listed building dating from the 15th century. The interior features a soaring four-storey atrium with fountain, the inner courtyard filled with plants. The hotel has its own thermal spring and spa centre with sulphur baths. All rooms non-smoking and tastefully decorated. Some have parquet floors. **www.blume-baden.ch**

BADEN Du Parc

Römerstrasse 24, 5400 **Tel** *056 203 15 15* **Fax** *056 222 07 93* **Rooms** *106* **Road Map** *D2*

Part of the Best Western group, this modern business hotel built in 1989 is right across from the casino park and near the Limmat river, a 5-minute walk from the spa complex in one direction, and five minutes from the town centre in the other. Rooms are contemporary in design, and of good size. Conference rooms available. **www.duparc.ch**

BADEN Limmathof

Limmatpromenade 28, 5400 **Tel** *056 200 17 17* **Fax** *056 200 17 18* **Rooms** *10* **Road Map** *D2*

This modernized city hotel at the thermal baths site incorporates a gourmet restaurant. Rooms are cutting-edge, with designer furnishings. The historic Limmat Hall affiliated to the hotel can be hired for banquets or conferences. Novum Spa offers a full range of health and beauty treatments, gym and fitness regimes, and thermal baths. **www.limmathof.ch**

BASEL Au Violon

Im Lohnhof 4, 4051 **Tel** *061 269 87 11* **Rooms** *20* **Road Map** *C2*

This old prison was converted into a modern hotel in the Old Town with a lively French brasserie. The guest rooms were knocked together from old cells, and look into quiet inner courtyard. Other rooms have views of Old Town and cathedral. Wooden floors, comfortable and attractive accommodation. Entirely non-smoking. **www.au-violon.com**

BASEL Bildungszentrum 21

Missionsstrasse 21, 4003 **Tel** *061 260 21 21* **Fax** *061 260 21 22* **Rooms** *74* **Road Map** *C2*

Imposing and impressive stone mansion, with modern white painted rooms of larger than average size. The only hotel in the heart of Basel with its own park grounds, ensuring privacy. Special rooms for smokers and for guests with allergies. Facilities include conference rooms, two restaurants and a large covered winter garden. **www.bildungszentrum-21.ch**

BASEL Dorint An Der Messe

Schoenaustrasse 10, 4058 **Tel** *061 695 70 00* **Fax** *061 695 71 00* **Rooms** *171* **Road Map** *C2*

Located next to the trade show centre, across from the Musical Theatre, and only 10 minutes by tram from the city centre. The Euro Airport and Badischer Bahnhof (train station) are also within easy reach. This modern hotel offers comfortable rooms, and ten apartments with kitchenette and sofa bed. **http://hotel-basel.dorint.com**

BASEL Rochat

Petersgraben 23, 4051 **Tel** *061 261 81 40* **Fax** *061 261 64 92* **Rooms** *50* **Road Map** *C2*

An architectural delight in Basel's Old Town near the university and hospital. It dates from the 19th century but was constructed to look like a medieval fortified house. The restaurant has a high, carved ceiling. Rooms are simply furnished in a modern style. Air conditioning available. **www.hotelrochat.ch**

BASEL Euler

Centralbahnplatz 14, 4002 **Tel** *061 275 80 00* **Fax** *061 275 80 50* **Rooms** *66* **Road Map** *C2*

Built by Abraham Euler-Brunner in the vicinity of the new Basel Railway Station in 1865, the Hotel Euler reflects its origins in the Belle Époque and the early days of the Railway Age. The rooms and suites have been refurbished in an Oriental style and all have air conditioning. The restaurant offers terrace dining in summer. **www.hoteleuler.ch**

Key to Price Guide *see p244* **Key to Symbols** *see back cover flap*

BASEL Hotel Krafft

⚋ 🔳   ⓕⓕⓕ

Rheingasse 12, 4058 **Tel** *061 690 91 30* **Rooms** *48*   **Road Map** *C2*

This elegant hotel on the banks of the Rhine offers an excellent location for exploring the old town. The rooms are bright and airy with wooden floors and light furnishings. The eclectic restaurant serves gourmet produce, while the wine bar serves cheeses and salamis with a large selection of wines served by the glass or bottle. **www.krafftbasel.ch**

BASEL Merian am Rhein

🔳 🅿 ⚋   ⓕⓕⓕ

Rheingasse/Greifengasse 2, 4058 **Tel** *061 685 11 11* **Fax** *061 685 11 12* **Rooms** *63*   **Road Map** *C2*

In the heart of Basel along the Rhine, a 10-minute walk from the train station, this hotel is part of the Best Western group. Standard rooms are comfortably furnished; business class, junior suite and suites also available. Each room has an espresso coffee machine. Summer terrace restaurant, gourmet dining room and café specializing in fish. **www.hotel-merian.ch**

BASEL Radisson

🔳 🅿 ⚋ ♒ 🔳 🔳   ⓕⓕⓕ

Steinentorstrasse 25, 4001 **Tel** *061 227 27 27* **Fax** *061 227 28 28* **Rooms** *206*   **Road Map** *C2*

This city hotel geared to business clientele is a 5-minute walk from the train station and shopping district. The modern rooms (all air conditioned) are stylish. Suites, junior suites and a wheelchair-accessible room are also available. Health club includes indoor swimming pool, saunas, steam room and gym. Extensive conference facilities. **www.radissonblu.com**

BASEL Teufelhof

🔳 🅿 ⚋   ⓕⓕⓕ

Leonhardsgraben 47–49, 4051 **Tel** *061 261 10 10* **Fax** *061 261 10 04* **Rooms** *33*   **Road Map** *C2*

Very special art- and entertainment-themed twin hotels. The Art Hotel has eight exceptional rooms of varying sizes and a suite. The Gallery Hotel has 24 rooms and suites. Every two years, both hotels are redecorated by local artists. Superb restaurant and in-house theatre. **www.teufelhof.com**

BASEL Les Trois Rois

🔳 🅿 ⚋ 🔳   ⓕⓕⓕⓕⓕ

Blumenrain 8, 4001 **Tel** *061 260 50 50* **Fax** *061 260 50 60* **Rooms** *101*   **Road Map** *C2*

Classic example of the grand old city hotel, completely refurbished in 2006, in Basel's Old Town, by the Rhine. Every room is furnished in Art Deco style; many have balconies overlooking the river. Guests have a choice of dining in the French and Italian restaurants or the brasserie. **www.lestroisrois.ch**

MURI Ochsen

🔳 🅿 ⚋   ⓕⓕ

Seetalstrasse 16, 5630 **Tel** *056 664 11 83* **Fax** *056 664 56 15* **Rooms** *11*   **Road Map** *D2*

A charming old hotel in red stone with white shutters and gabled roof with dormer windows. Right in the village centre, yet detached with open space around, ensuring quiet. Rooms are very bright, painted in white, and modern looking. There is a covered garden restaurant with old farmhouse furniture, as well as three dining rooms. **www.ochsen-muri.ch**

WINTERTHUR Krone

🔳 🅿 ⚋ 🔳   ⓕⓕ

Marktgasse 49, 8400 **Tel** *052 208 18 18* **Fax** *052 208 18 20* **Rooms** *40*   **Road Map** *E2*

Advertising itself as a "symbiosis of the old and new", the Krone retains the charm of an old city hotel with its imposing stone façade. Inside, the renovated rooms are modern and comfortable – and all are non-smoking. Set in the heart of the old town pedestrian zone with shops, museums and theatres close by. **www.kronewinterthur.ch**

WINTERTHUR Park Hotel Winterthur

♒ 🔳 🅿 ⚋   ⓕⓕ

Stadthausstrasse 4, 8402 **Tel** *052 265 02 65* **Fax** *052 265 02 75* **Rooms** *73*   **Road Map** *E2*

A smart, modern business-class hotel in central Winterthur, close to the station and to the old town's shops and restaurants. It offers a range of room standards and prices, all with bright interiors and free soft drinks in the mini bar. Top floor rooms have balconies and splendid views. Live piano music on Friday and Saturday evenings. **www.phwin.ch**

WINTERTHUR Wartmann

🔳 🅿 ⚋ 🔳   ⓕⓕ

Rudolfstrasse 15, 8400 **Tel** *052 260 07 07* **Fax** *052 213 30 97* **Rooms** *72*   **Road Map** *E2*

Attractive city hotel run by the fourth generation of the Wartmann family. It has an enviable location across the street from the train station and only a 15-minute drive from Zurich airport. More than half of the rooms have air conditioning. Steps away from shopping district, with a fitness centre next door. **www.wartmann.ch**

WINTERTHUR Banana City

🔳 🅿 ⚋ 🔳   ⓕⓕⓕ

Schaffhauserstrasse 8, 8400 **Tel** *052 268 16 16* **Fax** *052 268 16 00* **Rooms** *101*   **Road Map** *E2*

Modern steel and glass ten storey hotel popular with businessmen. The 200 m (640 ft) curved building bears the local nickname "the banana". There are 72 larger than average rooms in the Classic wing, some with kitchenettes, and 29 air conditioned rooms in the Premier section, including five business suites. **www.bananacity.ch**

ZÜRICH

ZÜRICH City Backpacker/Hotel Biber

🔳   ⓕ

Niederdorfstrasse 5, 8001 **Tel** *044 251 90 15* **Rooms** *16*   **Road Map** *E2*

Inexpensive central hostel with some caveats: none of the rooms have private bathrooms and all guests must check in before 10pm. Located in the heart of the Old Town pedestrian zone, with parking at nearby public garages. Rooms are clean and comfortable. Guests have free use of the communal kitchen. **www.city-backpacker.ch**

ZÜRICH Zic Zac Rock-Hotel
🔲 🍴   Ⓕ

Marktgasse 17, 8001 **Tel** *044 261 21 81* **Fax** *044 261 21 75* **Rooms** *51*   **Road Map** *E2*

This centrally located hotel, near the train station, Old Town, and night-time hotspots, has colourful decor and clean, simple rooms – each named after a rock star. Its main clientele is young people. The hotel houses two restaurants, the Dörfli advertised as "the eldorado of rock musicians" and an upmarket Indian restaurant. **www.rockhotel.ch**

ZÜRICH Hirschen
🔲 🅿 🍴   ⒻⒻ

Niederdorfstrasse 13, 8001 **Tel** *043 268 33 33* **Fax** *043 268 33 34* **Rooms** *27*   **Road Map** *E2*

A guesthouse since the 14th century, parts of this building date back more than 800 years. Its attractions include an old well and a restored wine cellar. The white-painted rooms retain an old-fashioned appeal despite being updated with Wi-Fi. The hotel is close to the train station and shopping district in the heart of the town. **www.hirschen-zuerich.ch**

ZÜRICH Otter
🔲 🍴   ⒻⒻ

Oberdorfstrasse 7, 8001 **Tel** *044 251 22 07* **Fax** *044 251 22 75* **Rooms** *16*   **Road Map** *E2*

Once an old tavern, this modestly priced city centre hotel near the Lake of Zurich has a small outdoor café and a trendy restaurant popular with young locals. The rooms have been renovated to high standards, including four-poster beds and parquet floors, though none has a private bathroom. One apartment has a shower and kitchenette. **www.hotelotter.ch**

ZÜRICH X-tra Hotel
🔲 🍴   ⒻⒻ

Limmatstrasse 118, 8005 **Tel** *044 448 15 95* **Fax** *044 448 15 96* **Rooms** *43*   **Road Map** *E2*

One of Switzerland's best-known budget hotels, with an eye and ear for youth culture. Music events are regularly scheduled and rooms feature abstract paintings in bright colours. The building itself harks back to the concrete heyday of the Bauhaus period. Not all rooms have private bathrooms. Facilities include a self-service laundry. **www.x-tra.ch**

ZÜRICH Lady's First
🔲 🅿 🍴 🛏   ⒻⒻⒻ

Mainaustrasse 24, 8008 **Tel** *044 380 80 10* **Fax** *044 380 80 20* **Rooms** *28*   **Road Map** *E2*

Owned and operated by a team of five women, this unusual fashion hotel is aimed towards women. Although the "modern man" is welcomed, he is not permitted on the upper floors, which house a spa, recreation rooms and terrace. The hotel occupies an elegant 19th-century townhouse with exceptional decor. Rose garden. **www.ladysfirst.ch**

ZÜRICH Sorell Hotel Rütli
🔲 🛏   ⒻⒻⒻ

Zähringerstrasse 43, 8021 **Tel** *044 254 58 00* **Fax** *044 254 58 01* **Rooms** *58*   **Road Map** *E2*

The traditional stone exterior and cobbled pavement suggest an old-fashioned city hotel. The standard rooms with wooden floors and modern decor do not prepare the guest for the 12 extraordinary "City Rooms", each wildly spray-painted by graffiti artists for the ultimate in urban chic. Parking nearby. **www.rutli.ch**

ZÜRICH Romantik Hotel Florhof
🔲 🅿 🍴   ⒻⒻⒻⒻ

Florhofgasse 4, 8001 **Tel** *044 250 26 26* **Fax** *044 250 26 27* **Rooms** *35*   **Road Map** *E2*

Elegant and captivating, this small boutique hotel in a historic building has an evocative garden featuring an 18th-century fountain and a fig tree. It has a central location in very quiet area close to the university and art museum. The two top floor suites are particularly attractive. Highly rated for standards of service. **www.florhof.ch**

ZÜRICH Savoy Baur en Ville
🔲 🅿 🍴 🛏   ⒻⒻⒻⒻ

Am Paradeplatz, 8022 **Tel** *044 215 25 25* **Fax** *044 215 25 00* **Rooms** *112*   **Road Map** *E2*

Majestic and imposing as the historic building is, the Savoy likes to call itself "the small grand hotel". There are several elegant restaurants. Rooms are tasteful and comfortable. There are fully equipped conference facilities, including a dark-panelled chamber with chandeliers fit for a board meeting. **www.savoy-zurich.ch**

ZÜRICH Baur au Lac
🔲 🅿 🍴 🛏 🛏   ⒻⒻⒻⒻⒻ

Talstrasse 1, 8001 **Tel** *044 220 50 20* **Fax** *044 220 50 44* **Rooms** *120*   **Road Map** *E2*

Impeccable location right in the heart of the city, on the lake and steps away from the Bahnhofstrasse, yet secluded in its own private park. Services include a rooftop gym with views, business centre and beauty treatments. No two rooms in the hotel are alike. Despite the opulence, a comfortable, homey ambience prevails. **www.bauraulac.ch**

ZÜRICH Dolder Grand Hotel
🔲 🔲 🅿 🍴 ♨ 🛏 🛏   ⒻⒻⒻⒻⒻ

Kurhausstrasse 65, 8032 **Tel** *044 456 60 00* **Fax** *044 456 60 01* **Rooms** *173*   **Road Map** *E2*

This landmark hotel opened in 1899 as a place of relaxation for the people of the city. Set in a private forest just a five-minute train ride from Zürich, it offers luxurious rooms, amazing views and every facility guests could wish for, including an exclusive heath spa and a vast ice rink in winter. Prices reflect the luxury on offer. **www.thedoldergrand.com**

ZÜRICH Eden au Lac
🔲 🅿 🍴   ⒻⒻⒻⒻⒻ

Utoquai 45, 8008 **Tel** *044 266 25 25* **Fax** *044 266 25 00* **Rooms** *50*   **Road Map** *E2*

This palatial lakeside hotel has a beautiful 19th-century façade. The Art Nouveau building is a listed monument. Inside all rooms have been redesigned and each is air conditioned and furnished in a different style. Deluxe suites are huge. The gourmet restaurant is a trip back in time, with crystal chandeliers and plush velvet curtains. **www.edenaulac.ch**

ZÜRICH Hotel zum Storchen
🔲 🍴 🛏   ⒻⒻⒻⒻⒻ

Weinplatz 2, 8001 **Tel** *044 227 27 27* **Fax** *044 227 27 00* **Rooms** *67*   **Road Map** *E2*

A Zürich institution, this hotel in an iconic pink building overlooks the Limmat and is just two minutes away from the shops on Bahnhofstrasse and the nightlife of the Niederdorf. Renowned for its excellent service, the Hotel zum Storchen has been serving guests for more than 650 years. Comfortable rooms have old town or river views. **www.storchen.ch**

Key to Price Guide *see p244* **Key to Symbols** *see back cover flap*

ZÜRICH Widder
Rennweg 7, 8001 **Tel** *044 224 25 26* **Fax** *044 224 24 24* **Rooms** *49*   **Road Map** *E2*

Unusual, wildly popular luxury hotel spread out over eight former historic townhouses in the Augustiner Quarter. Very high reputation for service. No two rooms are remotely alike. Some have old hand-carved oak furnishings and four-poster beds, others have hanging steel staircases and hip leather furniture. Latest high-tech gadgets. **www.widderhotel.ch**

EASTERN SWITZERLAND & GRAUBÜNDEN

APPENZELL Adler
Adlerplatz, 9050 **Tel** *071 787 13 89* **Fax** *071 787 13 65* **Rooms** *21*   **Road Map** *F2*

An architecturally captivating hotel in the town centre, next to the old bridge over the river Sitter, with a traditional gabled roof and bright yellow shutters. Comfortable rooms, standard furnishings in most. Museum-like suite with ceramic oven and antiques. There is a dining terrace on the main street. **www.adlerhotel.ch**

APPENZELL Romantik Hotel Säntis
Landesgemeindeplatz 3, 9050 **Tel** *071 788 11 11* **Fax** *071 798 11 10* **Rooms** *37*   **Road Map** *F2*

Old-fashioned chalet-style hotel in the town centre, with parking nearby, this is part of the Romantik Hotels association. Charmingly furnished – some rooms have four-poster beds, others have contemporary leather sofas and armchairs, and flower patterned wallpaper. Suites have open-beamed ceilings. Sauna and seminar facilities. **www.saentis-appenzell.ch**

AROSA Quellenhof
Aeussere Poststrasse, 7050 **Tel** *081 377 17 18* **Fax** *081 377 48 18* **Rooms** *18*   **Road Map** *F4*

One of Arosa's oldest family inns, with a typical Graubünden café-bar much frequented by locals. The five-storey building has balconies with wooden railings. The spacious rooms have wood-panelled ceilings. There is a large sunny breakfast room with panoramic views. In summer, you can dine on the balcony terrace. **www.quellenhof-arosa.ch**

AROSA Waldhotel National
Postfach, 7050 **Tel** *081 378 55 55.* **Fax** *081 378 55 99* **Rooms** *94*   **Road Map** *F4*

Large luxury hotel in park above the village of Arosa, with views of the mountains. The Aqua Silva spa features Switzerland's first Kelosauna – a log cabin sauna using orange-scented dry heat at 90° C (112° F) – and a swimming pool and herb room. There are four restaurants, with frequent theme evenings. **www.waldhotel.ch**

BAD RAGAZ Sorell Hotel Tamina
Am Platz 3, 7310 **Tel** *081 303 71 71* **Fax** *081 303 71 72* **Rooms** *44*   **Road Map** *F3*

Grand hotel in the centre of the spa resort with underground parking. The rooms are spacious and tastefully furnished, some with parquet floors and period decor. The hotel does not have its own spa and thermal spring, but is just a 5-minute walk from the resort's communal spa facilities. There are also two restaurants. **www.hotel-tamina.ch**

BAD RAGAZ Grand Hotel Quellenhof
Pfäferserstrasse 8, 7310 **Tel** *081 303 30 30* **Fax** *081 303 30 33* **Rooms** *106*   **Road Map** *F3*

A sterling example of a grand old hotel transformed into a modern masterpiece. It was rebuilt from the ground up in 1996 and subsequently awarded Gault Millau hotel of the year. Personal butler service is available. Sumptuous rooms, 97 junior suites, Royal suite with grand piano. Thermal spa, golf course, gambling casino. **www.resortragaz.ch**

BIVIO Post
Julierroute, 7457 **Tel** *081 659 10 00* **Fax** *081 659 10 01* **Rooms** *47*   **Road Map** *F4*

Old coaching inn in the centre of Bivio, just over the Julierpass from St Moritz. Comfortable and characterful accommodation frequented in the past by the former Shah of Iran and his family. Excellent centre for ski touring. Sauna, steam room and a wood-panelled "chimney room" salon. Apartments available. **www.hotelpost-bivio.ch**

CHUR Posthotel
Poststrasse 11, 7002 **Tel** *081 255 84 84* **Fax** *081 255 84 85* **Rooms** *42*   **Road Map** *F3*

In the heart of the pedestrianized Old Town, this hotel is part of the Choice Hotels chain. It is located near shops and restaurants, and just a 7-minute walk from the train station. There is no parking at the hotel but off-site parking can be arranged. Buffet breakfast included in price of room. All rooms are non-smoking. **www.comforthotelpost.ch**

CHUR Romantik Hotel Stern
Reichsgasse 11, 7000 **Tel** *081 258 57 57* **Fax** *081 258 57 58* **Rooms** *65*   **Road Map** *F3*

An elegant city hotel with 300 years of tradition, part of Swiss Historic and Romantik Hotels associations. The owner offers free pickup from Chur station in a vintage Buick limousine. Rooms renovated to a high standard, with characterful Cembra pine panelling. The "Bündner" restaurant features Graubünden dishes and local wines. **www.stern-chur.ch**

DAVOS Hotel Weisses Kreuz
Dorfplatz, Hauptstrasse 72, 7482 **Tel** *081 407 11 61* **Fax** *081 407 11 71* **Rooms** *25*   **Road Map** *F3*

In a great location in the centre of a charming village, this hotel is popular with both visitors and locals. The rooms are simple and the bathrooms small, but the mountain views are fantastic and there is a warm welcome from the family who run the hotel. The charming, wood-panelled *stuevetta* offers fine dining. **www.weisseskreuz-berguen.ch**

DAVOS Morosani fiftyone
    🏂 P   ⓕⓕⓕ
Promenade 50, 7270 **Tel** *081 415 55 00* **Fax** *081 415 55 01* **Rooms** *24*   **Road Map** *F3*

One of the Morosani family group of hotels, fiftyone offers funky rooms with plenty of design details but does away with the usual extras to reduce the room prices. Most of the rooms have two queen-size beds and sleep up to four people. Guests can use the facilities at nearby Morosani hotels and the ski lifts are a short walk away. **www.morosani.ch**

DAVOS National
    🏂 P 🍴   ⓕⓕⓕ
Obere Strasse 31, 7270 **Tel & Fax** *081 415 10 10* **Rooms** *65*   **Road Map** *F3*

A large luxury hotel set in its own quiet private park, with a garden terrace in summer. It's a short walk to the town centre, and there is a bus to the ski lifts. Hotel guest card gives free access to the train between Klosters and Davos, as well as discounts for skating, riding and tennis. Comfortable, cosy rooms. Closed Oct–early Dec. **www.national-davos.ch**

DAVOS Schatzalp
    🏂 🍴   ⓕⓕⓕⓕ
Bobbahnstrasse 23, 7270 **Tel** *081 415 51 51* **Fax** *81 415 52 52* **Rooms** *92*   **Road Map** *F3*

Featured in Thomas Mann's *The Magic Mountain*, the Art Nouveau Schatzalp is spectacularly situated 300 m (1,000 ft) above Davos on a sunny terrace at the tree line. The only access is by funicular. The hotel's Alpinum Schatzalp is a beautiful botanical garden with 3,000 species of alpine plants. **www.schatzalp.ch**

KLOSTERS Bargis
    P 🍴   ⓕⓕ
Kantonstrasse 8, 7252 **Tel** *081 422 55 77* **Fax** *081 422 55 05* **Rooms** *10*   **Road Map** *F3*

Within a 200-year-old "barn" style farmhouse, situated just five minutes outside the chic resort of Klosters on the road to Davos, this is an unusually inexpensive accommodation. It offers a choice of self-catering apartments or double rooms and is very quiet. Home cooking is served family style at a big table. **www.bargis.ch**

KLOSTERS Vereina
    🌊 🏂 P 🍴 🍽 🍸   ⓕⓕⓕ
Landstrasse 179, 7250 **Tel** *081 410 27 28* **Fax** *081 410 27 27* **Rooms** *25*   **Road Map** *F3*

Completely refurbished in 2000, the Vereina retains Old World charm. Extensive spa facilities include indoor swimming pool, hot tub and steam rooms as well as saunas. Public rooms feature high ceilings, chandeliers and plush fabric armchairs. There are 14 new suites, lavishly decorated and up to 90 sq m (970 sq ft) in size. **www.vereinahotel.ch**

RAPPERSWIL Jakob
    🏂 🍴   ⓕⓕ
Hauptplatz 11, 8640 **Tel** *055 220 00 50* **Fax** *055 220 00 55* **Rooms** *20*   **Road Map** *E3*

Located in the heart of the old city, this hotel's rooms are light and airy, with white-painted walls. There is a cigar lounge with a wide selection of Havanas and a bistro for light meals as well as a separate wine bar featuring 150 varieties from around the world. **www.jakob-hotel.ch**

SCHAFFHAUSEN Parkvilla
    🏂 P 🍴 🍸   ⓕⓕ
Parkstrasse 18, 8200 **Tel** *052 635 60 60* **Fax** *052 635 60 70* **Rooms** *25*   **Road Map** *E2*

A four-storey manor house in stone with a high-tech glass elevator appended to the outside. Inside is a Louis XVI salon with crystal chandelier. Guest rooms are individually decorated, some with marble bathrooms and elaborate wallpaper. There are family apartments with oriental rugs and large suites with four-poster beds. **www.parkvilla.ch**

SCHAFFHAUSEN Fischerzunft
    🏂 P 🍴   ⓕⓕⓕ
Rheinquai 8, 8200 **Tel** *052 632 05 05* **Fax** *052 632 05 13* **Rooms** *12*   **Road Map** *E2*

A luxury Relais and Chateaux hotel with an Asian theme situated in the Old Town with views of the Rhine. Standard rooms are decorated in plush fabric wallpaper with matching curtains and furniture. There is a gourmet restaurant serving Asian specialities as well as European fare (*see p280*), and an extensive wine cellar. **www.fischerzunft.ch**

SCHWÄGALP Berghotel
    🏂 P 🍴   ⓕⓕ
Schwägalp, 9107 **Tel** *071 365 66 00* **Fax** *071 365 66 01* **Rooms** *30*   **Road Map** *F3*

This wooden chalet-style hotel is situated at 1,325 m (4,347 ft) in open sunny fields. There are dorm rooms for families or groups as well as individual rooms from the simple to the elaborately furnished. Access is by ski lift, and in winter you can ski from and to the hotel. In summer there is a large outdoor dining and sunbathing garden. **www.saentisbahn.ch**

SCUOL Crusch Alba
    🏂 P 🍴   ⓕⓕ
Clozza 246, 7550 **Tel** *081 864 11 55* **Fax** *081 864 90 12* **Rooms** *17*   **Road Map** *G3*

Characterful old stone house near the train station, with good access to ski lifts. Rooms are somewhat small but lovingly decorated in old wood. Stone floors and low-beamed ceilings evoke a Swiss storybook ambience. There are several dining rooms and the inn is a local meeting place with a cheerful atmosphere. **www.crusch-alba.ch**

ST GALLEN Hotel Metropol
    🏂 🍴 🛗   ⓕⓕⓕ
Bahnhofplatz 3, 9001 **Tel** *071 228 32 32* **Rooms** *32*   **Road Map** *F2*

In a city centre location, opposite the station, Hotel Metropol is well placed for visiting the city's sights or meeting business clients. Bright and airy rooms are well equipped and modern, with wood flooring, white walls and colourful accents. Staff are friendly and a generous breakfast buffet is served. **www.hotel-metropol.ch**

ST GALLEN Einstein
    🏂 P 🍴   ⓕⓕⓕⓕ
Berneggstrasse 2, 9001 **Tel** *071 227 55 55* **Fax** *071 227 55 77* **Rooms** *113*   **Road Map** *F2*

Advertised as St Gallen's leading hotel, the Einstein has an elegant exterior and is located in the heart of the historic UNESCO Abbey district. The name has no connection to the famous physicist. Rooms are strikingly elegant, marble floors and bathrooms abound. There are 14 suites, with superb views of the abbey. **www.einstein.ch**

Key to Price Guide *see p244* **Key to Symbols** *see back cover flap*

ST MORITZ Laudinella ☒☒☒☒☒ ⓕⓕⓕ

Via Tegiatscha 17, 7500 **Tel** *081 836 00 00* **Fax** *081 836 00 01* **Rooms** *204*   **Road Map** *F4*

Unassuming from the exterior the hotel is, as advertised, full of surprises within. Public rooms are impressive, and the fifth-floor spa area with sauna, steam room and fitness machines has exceptional views. Solar panels provide hot water. In addition to four traditional dining rooms there is a take away. Ideal for lakeside views and walks. **www.laudinella.ch**

ST MORITZ Badrutt's Palace ☒☒☒☒☒☒☒ ⓕⓕⓕⓕⓕ

Via Serlas 27, 7500 **Tel** *081 837 10 00* **Fax** *081 837 29 99* **Rooms** *165*   **Road Map** *F4*

One of the world's most historic and feature-laden hotels. The distinctive tower, with a rectangular box of rooms stuck to the side, is unique. The hotel has its own ski school, and guests are requested to wear suits or formal dress after sundown. The variety and opulence of room decor beggars belief. **www.badruttspalace.com**

ST MORITZ Grand Hotel Kronenhof ☒☒☒☒☒☒☒ ⓕⓕⓕⓕⓕ

Pontresina, 7504 **Tel** *081 830 30 30* **Fax** *081 830 30 31* **Rooms** *114*   **Road Map** *F4*

In a beautiful 19th-century building with grandiose public rooms, this luxurious hotel is relaxed and friendly too. Rooms and suites are spacious and offer the ultimate in comfort, while the superb spa has an indoor pool and baths with breathtaking mountain and glacier views. One of its restaurants has 16 Gault Millau points. **www.kronenhof.com**

STEIN AM RHEIN Adler ☒☒☒ ⓕⓕ

Rathausplatz 2, 8260 **Tel** *052 742 61 61* **Fax** *052 741 44 40* **Rooms** *25*   **Road Map** *E2*

In the heart of the Old Town along the Rhine, this historic inn is decorated on the outside with a number of modern and ancient frescoes. Its stone lintels are further adorned with flowers. Inside there are two *Stube* café bars typical of the region and popular with locals. Rooms are simply furnished with modern character. **www.adlersteinamrhein.ch**

STEIN AM RHEIN Rheinfels ☒☒ ⓕⓕ

Rhigass 8, 8260 **Tel** *052 741 21 44* **Fax** *052 741 25 22* **Rooms** *17*   **Road Map** *E2*

This historic building dating back to 15th century lies in the heart of the Old Town. Some rooms feature antique furniture, plush carpeting and sofas. The hotel has a large terrace along the Rhine – convenient for boat trips – banqueting halls and a restaurant famous for its fish. It also has its own boat with sleeping cabins. **www.rheinfels.ch**

VADUZ Park Hotel Sonnenhof ☒☒☒☒☒ ⓕⓕⓕⓕ

Mareestrasse 29, 9490 **Tel** *00423 239 02 02* **Fax** *00423 239 02 03* **Rooms** *29*   **Road Map** *F3*

Part of the Relais & Chateaux group, this luxury hotel features a gourmet restaurant (see p281). The beautifully furnished rooms are spacious and individually designed with many featuring sumptuous fabrics and paintings. Located on the edge of Vaduz, the hotel is set in its own grounds and has spectacular views. **www.sonnenhof.li**

CENTRAL SWITZERLAND & TICINO

AIROLO Forni ☒☒☒ ⓕⓕ

Via Stazione, 6780 **Tel** *091 869 12 70* **Fax** *091 869 15 23* **Rooms** *20*   **Road Map** *E4*

Forni has a light grey stone façade with white shutters, with a streetside terrace under yellow awnings and a large sun terrace above. Family-operated for nearly a century, the hotel was small but pleasantly furnished rooms, some with wrought-iron balconies looking out over the mountains. The restaurant is highly rated. **www.forni.ch**

ALTDORF Höfli ☒☒☒☒ ⓕⓕ

Hellgasse 20, 6460 **Tel** *041 875 02 75* **Fax** *041 875 02 95* **Rooms** *34*   **Road Map** *E3*

A traditional Uri guesthouse with five storeys and a large sloping roof. Rooms are in the rustic old house or in the newer annexe, where dimensions are somewhat larger than in the original inn. There are also business rooms equipped with working area, and conference facilities for seminars. Buses connect to nearby skiing areas. **www.hotel-hoefli.ch**

ANDERMATT Drei Könige & Post ☒☒☒☒ ⓕⓕ

Gotthardstrasse 69, 6490 **Tel** *041 887 00 01* **Fax** *041 887 16 66* **Rooms** *21*   **Road Map** *E4*

This is the principal hotel in Andermatt, with a fitness centre including a large thermal whirlpool bath, saunas and a solarium. A historic coaching inn on the St Gotthard route, the hotel is located in the village centre within walking distance of ski lifts and the train station. Rooms are of a good size and well decorated. **www.3koenige.ch**

ANDERMATT (HOSPENTAL) Gasthaus St Gotthard ☒☒ ⓕⓕ

Gotthardstrasse, 6493 **Tel** *041 887 12 66* **Fax** *041 887 05 66* **Rooms** *6*   **Road Map** *E4*

A picture postcard Swiss hotel, in the tiny village of Hospental a few minutes from Andermatt, next to an ancient stone bridge. Skiers can ski right to the door. The dining room is a museum of old guesthouse charm. Rooms vary in degree of modernization: some have hand carved wooden ceilings and wall panelling. **www.hotel-gotthard.ch**

ASCONA Romantik Hotel Castello Seeschloss ☒☒☒☒ ⓕⓕⓕ

Piazza Motta, 6612 **Tel** *091 791 01 61* **Fax** *091 791 18 04* **Rooms** *45*   **Road Map** *E5*

A charming family-run hotel in the heart of Ascona with lovely views over Lake Maggiore. Rooms vary in size and decor, the most distinct being the ones in the medieval tower, where one room comes complete with a spiral staircase. Guests can enjoy drinks and meals in the pretty lakeside garden, and there's a swimming pool. **www.castello-seeschloss.ch**

BECKENREID Boutique Hotel Schlussel 🏤 **P** 🍴 ⓕⓕⓕ

Oberdorfstrasse 26, 6375 **Tel/Fax** *041 622 03 33* **Rooms** *12* **Road Map** *D3*

This 19th-century boutique hotel has a very attractive galleried façade – in raspberry pink. Bright, spacious rooms feature free-standing baths and are decorated in neutral tones with plenty of warm wood and crisp white linen. The restaurant emphasises local, seasonal produce.

BELLINZONA Hotel Internazionale 🏤 **P** 🍴 🍴 ⓕⓕ

Viale Stazione 35, 6500 **Tel** *091 825 43 33* **Fax** *091 825 46 46* **Rooms** *63* **Road Map** *E5*

Located opposite the train station, this hotel is well situated for the centre and walks to Castelgrande. Rooms are comfortable and feature modern decor; some have balconies. The popular family-run restaurant serves both local and Italian dishes, and staff are friendly. Reserved parking is located nearby. **www.hotel-internazionale.ch**

BRUNNEN Seehotel Waldstätterhof 🛁 🏤 **P** 🍴 🍴 ⓕⓕⓕⓕ

Walstätterquai 6, 6440 **Tel** *041 825 06 06* **Fax** *041 825 06 00* **Rooms** *105* **Road Map** *D3*

Perhaps the only hotel in the world to have hosted both Queen Victoria and George Bush senior, this is a magnificent five-storey hotel with a mansard roof, right on the water's edge. It has its own boat dock, park and extravagant views. Spa facilities and comfortable rooms. Bargains on ski, biking and spa packages. **www.waldstaetterhof.ch**

CENTOVALLI (INTRAGNA) Stazione "Da Agnese" 🖥 🏤 **P** 🍴 🍴 ⓕⓕ

Via Cantonale, 6655 **Tel** *091 796 12 12* **Fax** *091 796 31 33* **Rooms** *10* **Road Map** *E5*

This family inn, locally renowned for its cuisine, lies in the centre of this small village known for its narrow streets and artistic workshops. The inn has bucolic surroundings, in a sparsely inhabited wooded valley. Rooms are cheerful and comfortable, from tiny to average. Furnishings are rustic, with some original artworks. **www.daagnese.ch**

EINSIEDELN Sonne 🏤 **P** 🍴 ⓕ

Hauptstrasse 82, 8840 **Tel** *055 412 28 21* **Fax** *055 412 41 45* **Rooms** *30* **Road Map** *E3*

This stone hotel is well situated in the Kloster square with imposing views. All rooms are non-smoking with wireless Internet access. Reasonably sized and comfortable, the rooms are excellent value for money, especially considering the impeccable location. Sonne has a friendly and welcoming atmosphere. **www.hotel-sonne.ch**

ENGELBERG Schweizerhof 🏤 **P** 🍴 🍴 ⓕⓕ

Dorfstrasse 42, 6390 **Tel** *041 637 11 05* **Fax** *041 637 41 47* **Rooms** *38* **Road Map** *D3*

Engelberg's landmark hotel, over a century old, bristles with iron balconies and a metal dome topping one tower. It is a period hotel with quirky charm and generous dimensions, especially in the old-fashioned bathrooms. All the rooms are non-smoking, and most have good views. Sauna, gym, garden and solarium. **www.schweizerhof-engelberg.ch**

HERGISWIL Seehotel Pilatus 🏤 **P** 🍴 🍴 🍴 ⓕⓕⓕ

Seestrasse 34, 6052 **Tel** *041 632 30 30* **Fax** *041 632 30 31* **Rooms** *70* **Road Map** *D3*

This hotel is right on the shores of Lake Lucerne, with a huge tree-shaded summer garden and its own boat docks. Other facilities include a scuba-diving centre, indoor swimming pool, sauna and conference facilities. Public areas have been redesigned, but some rooms are decorated in rather dated furnishings. **www.pilatushotel.ch**

KUSSNACHT AM RIGI Du Lac Seehof 🏤 **P** 🍴 ⓕⓕ

Seeplatz 6, 6403 **Tel** *041 850 10 12* **Fax** *041 850 10 22* **Rooms** *14* **Road Map** *D3*

This attractive historic hotel, right on the lake with views of mountain peaks, has dormer windows and a turret on one side of the four-storey stone structure. There is a boat dock and a large garden. Some rooms have ornate ceilings; all are sunny and comfortable. **www.du-lac-seehof.ch**

LOCARNO Esplanade 🛁 🏤 **P** 🍴 🍴 🍴 ⓕⓕⓕ

Via Delle Vigne 149, Minusio, 6648 **Tel** *091 735 85 85* **Fax** *091 735 85 86.* **Rooms** *75* **Road Map** *E5*

Esplanade is a majestic pink stucco hotel with a red-tile roof and large recessed balconies, surrounded by palm trees and overlooking Lake Maggiore with looming views of the mountains. Facilities include a spa with saunas, steam room and beauty treatments. Outdoor pool and garden, and well-equipped gym. All rooms air conditioned. **www.esplanade.ch**

LOCARNO Hotel Dell'Angelo 🏤 **P** 🍴 ⓕⓕⓕ

Piazza Grance, Viccolo della Motta 1, 6601 **Tel** *091 751 81 75* **Fax** *091 751 82 56* **Rooms** *55* **Road Map** *E5*

Historic building located on the Piazza Grande, just a short walk from the station and the lake. The guest rooms have stone floors with oriental carpets. There is a pizzeria with a wood-burning oven. Guests can enjoy the sunbathing terrace, or the quiet reading room with leather armchairs. **www.hotel-dell-angelo.ch**

LOCARNO Belvedere 🏤 **P** 🍴 🍴 🍴 ⓕⓕⓕⓕ

Via ai Monti della Trinita 44, 6600 **Tel** *091 751 03 63* **Fax** *091 751 52 39* **Rooms** *81* **Road Map** *E5*

This hotel in a former 16th-century palazzo lies on a sunny hill overlooking Locarno and Lake Maggiore. The public rooms have marble and frescoed ceilings. Large garden for dining, games or sunbathing and an outdoor pool. Four restaurants, including an outdoor grotto. Spa with indoor pool, gym, sauna and solarium. **www.belvedere-locarno.ch**

LUGANO Hotel Ibis 🏤 **P** ⓕⓕ

Via Geretta 7, 6900 **Tel** *091 986 19 09* **Fax** *091 986 19 19* **Rooms** *70* **Road Map** *E5*

Located in Lugano-Paradiso, a short bus ride or walk from the lake and city centre, the Hotel Ibis is a good budget option for Lugano. Rooms are compact, but comfortable, modern and equipped with air conditioning, flat-screen TVs and Wi-Fi. A hearty breakfast buffet is served and there is also a bar. **www.ibishotel.com**

Key to Price Guide *see p244* **Key to Symbols** *see back cover flap*

LUGANO Pestalozzi

Piazza Indipendenza 9, 6901 **Tel** *091 921 46 46* **Fax** *091 922 20 45* **Rooms** *55*   **Road Map** *E5*

An old-fashioned family-run hotel in the city centre, set back from the lake, with rooms for groups and students without ensuite bathrooms. Renovated rooms have bathrooms and views of the lake, and are comfortable and homey. There is a large conference room and a popular restaurant with Ticino specialities. **www.pestalozzi-lugano.ch**

LUGANO Villa Castagnola Au Lac

Viale Castagnola 31, 6906 **Tel** *091 973 25 55* **Fax** *091 973 25 50* **Rooms** *88*   **Road Map** *E5*

An imposing and elegant return to the days of the old grand hotels, this former estate of Russian nobility is now a five-star hotel. It has two sumptuous gourmet restaurants, a sprawling subtropical park and gardens with swimming pool, tennis courts, fitness centre and beauty spa. **www.villacastagnola.com**

LUZERN Cascada

Bundesplatz 18, 6003 **Tel** *041 226 80 88* **Fax** *041 226 80 00* **Rooms** *66*   **Road Map** *D3*

A very popular business hotel, just a 4-minute walk from the train station. Waterfalls (cascades) are the hotel's signature theme, and the tastefully decorated rooms feature contemporary art depictions of waterfalls. Lively Spanish restaurant, with frequent appearances by South American bands. Wireless Internet access throughout the hotel. **www.cascada.ch**

LUZERN Hotel Ibis Styles

Fridenstrasse 8, 6004 **Tel** *041 418 48 48* **Fax** *041 418 48 18* **Rooms** *115*   **Road Map** *D3*

Located in the historic centre of Luzern, a 10-minute walk from the train station, this Ibis hotel is a great value option from which to explore the sights of Luzern and the lake. Guest rooms feature fun, modern decor with lots of white and bright accent colours. The restaurant serves both local and international dishes. **www.ibishotels.com**

LUZERN Art Deco Hotel Montana

Adligenswilerstrasse 22, 6002 **Tel** *041 419 00 00* **Fax** *041 419 00 01* **Rooms** *62*   **Road Map** *D3*

This historic hotel overlooks Lake Lucerne. Each room is a unique Art Deco experience, with furniture, paint colours and tiles chosen to complement the theme, which extends to the bathrooms. A funicular delivers guests from the lakeside right into the hotel lobby. Two towers with suites. **www.hotel-montana.ch**

LUZERN Wilden Mann

Bahnhofstrasse 30, 6000 **Tel** *041 210 16 66* **Fax** *041 210 16 29* **Rooms** *50*   **Road Map** *D3*

A characterful hotel dating from the 16th century, Wilden Mann has carvings depicting the local myth of the "wild man". It has an elegant exterior, tastefully modernized rooms and an emphasis on making guests feel at home. The celebrated restaurant serves modern European cuisine. Member of Romantik Hotels association. **www.wilden-mann.ch**

SCHWYZ Wysses Rössli

Hauptplatz 3, 6430 **Tel** *041 811 19 22* **Fax** *041 811 10 46* **Rooms** *27*   **Road Map** *E3*

Impressive five-storey historical building with a mansard roof, set in the town centre of Schwyz, with a car park in front. Handsome banquet and seminar rooms, comfortable accommodation, and two restaurants. Good base for hiking the Swiss Trail, exploring caves in the Muota Valley, and the Lake of the Four Cantons region. **www.roessli-schwyz.ch**

STANS Engel

Dorfplatz 1, 6370 **Tel** *041 619 10 10* **Fax** *041 619 10 11* **Rooms** *18*   **Road Map** *D3*

In the village centre, on the main street, lies this white four-storey traditional inn with gabled roof. The interior has been decorated with considerable flair and in stark post-modern themes. Each room is unique, even in colour scheme, and each has mountain views. Full access for disabled. Small garden terrace. **www.engelstans.ch**

VITZNAU Hotel Rigi

Seestrasse, 6354 **Tel** *041 399 85 85* **Fax** *041 399 85 86* **Rooms** *35*   **Road Map** *E3*

A friendly, family-run hotel with its main selling points being the lakeside location and its proximity to Vitznau's cogwheel railway. Rooms vary in size and standard, with those in the annexe being larger and more modern. The restaurant menu features fish from the lake and there is a terrace for summer dining. **www.rigi-vitznau.ch**

WEGGIS Garni Hotel Frohburg

Seestrasse 21, 6353 **Tel** *041 392 00 60* **Fax** *041 392 00 66* **Rooms** *12*   **Road Map** *D3*

This small garden hotel on the lake has exceptional views of the Alps and the Lake of the Four Cantons. All the rooms have balconies. Water-skiing and tennis courts are nearby, as is a boat dock. Rooms are modern and simple. There is no restaurant at the hotel itself, but several are located within walking distance. **www.frohburg.ch**

WEGGIS Seenhof du Lac

Gotthardstrasse 4, 6353 **Tel** *041 390 11 51* **Fax** *041 390 11 19* **Rooms** *22*   **Road Map** *D3*

In the heart of Weggis and an easy stroll to the boat dock is this attractive family-run hotel in a 19th-century villa. It offers bright, modern guest rooms, many featuring fantastic lake and mountain views, although the public rooms are somewhat dated. There's a good restaurant with a lakeside terrace. **www.hotel-du-lac.ch**

ZUG Ochsen

Kolinplatz 11, 6301 **Tel** *041 729 32 32* **Fax** *041 729 32 22* **Rooms** *48*   **Road Map** *E3*

This city centre hotel within walking distance of the major attractions has a charming ambience. The comfortable, non-smoking rooms have fresh flowers, and there is an Internet corner for guests. The bar has contemporary art with stained-glass windows and the restaurant has an ancient beamed ceiling. **www.ochsen-zug.ch**

WHERE TO EAT

There is a great variety of restaurants in Switzerland, which reflects the country's cultural and regional diversity. While large cities such as Zürich and Geneva have top-class restaurants that serve international cuisine, the great majority of Swiss restaurants are relatively small, family-run concerns. These convivial establishments generally offer wholesome, filling dishes that reflect local rural traditions and that are prepared using local farm produce. Many lakeside and riverside

Coat of arms on a restaurant in Fribourg

restaurants all over the country specialize in dishes featuring delicious locally caught fish.

Switzerland also has a great number and variety of small, more informal establishments. While German Switzerland has the *Stübli*, French Switzerland has the *rôtisserie* and *brasserie*. In Ticino the choice ranges from the classic *pizzeria* to the *trattoria* and *osteria*. South of the Alps, you are also likely to dine outdoors, in a sunny town square or informally at a table set outside a *grotto*.

A self-service restaurant in a department store

TYPES OF RESTAURANTS

In Switzerland, restaurants serving international cuisine are located almost exclusively in the larger cities. The typical Swiss restaurant, by contrast, is a homely establishment serving a range of local dishes that vary according to the region.

In the German-speaking regions of Switzerland, a restaurant is sometimes called a *Beiz* or *Gasthaus*. Pleasant meals can also be enjoyed in *Kneipe*, which serve a small selection of hot dishes in addition to beer. The rustic *Stübli* often specialize in one type of dish, such as the hearty and warming *Rösti*, fondue or *raclette (see p262)*.

As well as restaurants, French-speaking regions of Switzerland have *rôtisseries*, which specialize in serving grilled food. Its more humble version is the *brasserie*, which serves buffet meals at lunchtime, and in the evenings turns into a restaurant with waiter service.

Some wine bars, called *caveaux* in French and *Weinstübli* in German, also serve meals, as do some beer taverns *(Bierstübli)*. *Spunte*, or bars in German-speaking Switzerland, serve mainly beer. *Bars*, their counterparts in French-speaking Switzerland, serve coffee and alcoholic drinks but rarely offer food.

In the Italian-speaking canton of Ticino, one of the most popular establishments is the *pizzeria*. Other types of Italian restaurants include the simple *osteria* and the slightly more formal *trattoria*. Another simple restaurant is the *grotto*, meaning "cave", a cosy rustic tavern, where meals are usually served outdoors. Ticino is also

well-endowed with ice-cream parlours *(gelateria* or *cremeria)*.

Inexpensive meals, which are of an excellent quality for the price, are offered in the self-service buffets of chain supermarkets and department stores, including Migros, Coop and Manor. These buffets, with filling soups, freshly made salads, pasta dishes and vegetarian fare, are open all day. Once found only in larger towns, fast-food outlets, and even sushi bars, are making inroads, though the Swiss tend to prefer their own cuisine and remain slow to adopt foreign tastes.

Smoking in restaurants is banned in all of Switzerland's cantons, as is smoking in public places, including bars and shopping malls. It is also prohibited on trains throughout the country.

The stylish Hiltl restaurant in Zurich (see p278)

Many restaurants are closed one day a week. This is their "rest day" *(Ruhetag, jour de repos, jour de fermeture* or *giorno de chiusura).*

MEALS

Depending on the region, breakfast may either be quite substantial or consist simply of a light, appetizing snack. In Ticino, for example, it may consist only of coffee and a croissant. Elsewhere, particularly in German Switzerland, breakfast can be considerably more filling, consisting of muesli, rye bread or crusty bread, salami and cured meats, cheese and eggs, washed down with fruit juice, tea or coffee.

All over Switzerland, lunch is served between noon and 2pm (almost all restaurants stop serving by 2:30pm). For many Swiss, this is the main meal and most restaurants offer a hearty dish of the day *(Tagesteller, plat du jour* or *piatto del giorno),* with more than one course and general-ly excellent value for money.

Evening meals are served between 6:30 and 9pm, depending on the region. The more expensive restaurants, particularly those in large towns, stay open until 10pm or later.

MENUS

In restaurants in larger towns, as well as in holiday resorts and areas that attract large numbers of foreign visitors, the menu *(Karte, carte* or *carta)* is written in French or German (or both), and very often also in English. A few restaurants have separate menus printed in English. In smaller towns and in rural or remote areas, menus are written in German, French or Italian only.

Menus are often presented with an additional list of seasonal dishes. Almost all establishments display their menus, with prices, outside the premises.

A restaurant with outdoor tables on Zürich's Bahnhofstrasse

PRICES AND TIPPING

Restaurant meals in Switzerland tend to be relatively expensive. The average price of a dish of the day with salad is 12–22 CHF. A fish main course can cost around 35–45 CHF. A plate of soup or a salad costs around 8 CHF. The average price of a fondue for two people is about 30 CHF. By contrast, the price of a meal in the self-service restaurant of a department store is typically no more than 15–20 CHF. The price of a glass of local wine ordered with a meal is 3–4 CHF. A third of a litre of beer costs roughly the same. The price of a cup of coffee or a soft drink is rarely less than 3 CHF.

Restaurant sign in Thun

Restaurants in the most popular tourist spots or in particularly attractive locations generally charge a little more for their services.

Most restaurants also add a cover charge, which includes bread, per person. At all restaurants a 15 per cent service charge is included in the final total. Tipping is therefore officially unnecessary. However, it is still customary to round the bill up, or to add a few francs to the total.

CHILDREN

In Switzerland, meals out are treated as a family occasion and it is not unusual to see small children in restaurants, even late at night. Most restaurants provide high chairs and offer a special children's menu. Many restaurants also have toilets with baby-changing facilities.

VEGETARIANS

Although meat features prominently in Swiss cuisine, menus in restaurants some-times include a selection of vegetarian dishes, as well as a variety of vegetables and salads. Self-service restaurants often include a range of vege-table-based dishes. Food aller-gies and intolerances are less well understood in rural areas.

Stunning view of the Bernese Oberland from Piz Gloria *(see p270)*

The Flavours of Switzerland

With a few notable exceptions, the traditional recipes of most Swiss regions are "borrowed" from the adjoining countries to which they are linguistically linked. This makes for very distinctive local cuisines – dishes and palates change every dozen miles travelled. With no coastline, a shortage of flat arable land and a short growing season, Swiss cuisine does a great deal with limited resources. Although the Swiss have exported their taste for melted cheese to every corner of the globe, healthy eating has become a prime consideration. Freshwater fish, such as trout and perch, appear on many menus, and organic foods are in high demand.

Swiss chocolate

Restaurant in the Valais offering traditional wood-fired raclettes

FRENCH-SPEAKING SWITZERLAND

Influenced by France, but creatively independent, franco-phone Switzerland has a distinctive cuisine. Summer foods celebrate the short but intense growing season. Apricots are a particular speciality of the Rhône valley. Berries of all types abound, preserved in jams or

baked in open pastry cases. Game, from roasted wild boar to stewed marmot, fills the autumn table. The latter is a rather greasy dish of Alpine squirrel that is seldom served to tourists. Winter foods are filling, and meals like *fondue* and *raclette* are long and convivial to while away the dark evenings. Cheese and dried meat dishes are served with a flat bread that can be kept in

attics for months at a time. In Alpine villages, loaves of dense rye bread suited to this long storage were baked in communal ovens. The Swiss claim to have around 300 varieties of bread.

GERMAN-SPEAKING SWITZERLAND

Until recent times by far the most prosperous region of Switzerland, the Teutonic

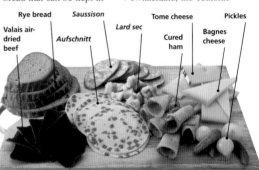

Rye bread   Saussison   Tome cheese   Pickles
Valais air-dried beef   Aufschnitt   Lard sec   Cured ham   Bagnes cheese

Generous platter of a typical *Assiette Valaisanne*

REGIONAL DISHES AND SPECIALITIES

Switzerland has produced several very simple dishes of enormous appeal. All are consumed daily by the Swiss, and devoured with gusto by millions of tourists. The French regions are the homeland of hearty cheese dishes such as *fondue* and *raclette*. *Rösti* is the national dish of the German-speaking regions, its popularity defining the linguistic and culinary border (called the *röstigraben*). Müsli was invented by Swiss-German Dr Bircher-Benner. *Birchermüsli* uses plenty of chopped fresh fruits and nuts and is softened with water, juice or milk. It is often eaten as an evening meal, as well as for breakfast, in the north. Nuts, as well as top-quality Swiss chocolate, feature in desserts and cakes.

Birchermüsli

Fondue *is a bubbling pot of Emmenthal, Gruyère and white wine sauce into which bread cubes are dunked.*

Visitors to a bakery stall in Lugano Market, Ticino

cantons (administrative regions) favour a cuisine heavy in meats, especially pork and sausages; hearty soups; savoury and sweet dumplings; and delicious, calorie-laden cakes and pies. Swiss-German bread tends to be darker and saltier than breads in French- or Italian-speaking cantons. Soft pretzels are sold everywhere in German-speaking areas, yet are almost impossible to find elsewhere in the country. Portion sizes, at home and in restaurants, are noticeably more generous in the north of the country. Offal, pigs' knuckles and trotters, and plates with six different kinds of meat, topped with sauerkraut and potatoes, make a Swiss-German diner very happy indeed, whereas French-speakers and visitors might be overwhelmed.

TICINO

Everything that's missing in the mountains and cold plains that dominate most of Switzerland is to be found in sunny Ticino, and many Swiss take their holidays here.

Cow in the lush summer pastures of the Swiss Alps

The cuisine is heavily influenced by that of Lombardy and Piedmont, the closest Italian provinces. Fresh fish from the lakes, pasta, polenta, gnocchi and risotto are typical Ticino dishes. The diet is rich in fresh fruits and vegetables. Porcini mushrooms are commonly used in risotto, while braised beef accompanies polenta. Beef, pork and veal are the main meats. On a more indulgent note, this is one of the best places in Switzerland to eat ice cream and, unique to the region, *torta di pane* is a rich, cake-like dessert made from stale bread, grappa, amaretti (almond biscuits), dried fruits and pine nuts.

ON THE MENU

Bernerplatte Smoked meats, sausages, bacon and pork with sauerkraut.

Croûte au fromage (Käseschnitte) Bread, soaked in white wine, covered with cheese, then baked. May be topped with fried egg or ham.

Filet de cerf Swiss mountain deer (served only in autumn).

Filets de perche Lake perch fillets, fried in butter, with lemon and parsley.

Gelato alla farina bona Ice cream made with roasted maize flour, speciality of Ticino.

Zupfa Braided bread served at breakfast on Sundays.

Raclette *cheese is melted by the fire or under a grill and scraped onto boiled potatoes served with pickles.*

Rosti *uses grated potatoes fried in butter and firmed into a cake, which is then fried again on both sides.*

Engadiner Nusstorte *is a shortcrust pastry pie filled with pieces of walnut mixed with caramel and honey.*

Swiss Cheeses

Switzerland is justly renowned for its cheeses, which range in taste from mild and nutty to rich and spicy. Cheese is a way of life in Switzerland. Thinly sliced, it is eaten for breakfast and is the basic ingredient or garnish of many dishes. It is also tossed into salads and is savoured at lunch or dinner as a delicacy in its own right. Half of Switzerland's milk yield goes into the making of cheese. One of the country's greatest exports, it is also an important part of the Swiss economy.

Poster for Appenzeller cheese

Cheeses in cold storage

ORIGIN OF CHEESE

Cattle have been raised and pastured in Switzerland since about 2,000 BC. In this mountainous country, expanses of arable land are naturally very limited. By contrast, Switzerland's lush Alpine meadows are ideal for keeping livestock. Milk and milk products formed the basis of the staple diet of Switzerland's mountain-dwellers, and in winter were necessary for their survival.

With the advent of roads, and more importantly of railways, linking the villages of remote mountain regions with the rest of the country, Alpine cheeses found new markets. Cheese-making also spread to the lower valleys.

Until the 15th century, most Swiss cheeses were soft. Hard cheeses gradually became more popular. Being riper, they kept better than soft cheeses, and could therefore be transported over longer distances.

CHEESE PRODUCTION

The cheese-making process involves five basic stages. First the milk is poured into large steel vats and heated to 30–36° C (86–96° F). A starter-culture, a liquid containing bacteria, is added to the milk. This causes the milk to turn sour. With the addition of an enzyme, such as rennet or pepsin, the milk forms a curd, a custard-like substance containing whey. When the curd is heated to 39–54° C (102–130°F), the whey separates from the curd.

Rounds of cheese

The whey is drained off and the curd is salted, packed into moulds and pressed to extract more whey. The curd is then shaped into blocks or circular slabs and left to mature, first in brine, where a rind forms on the cheeses, and later in a cold store, where the cheeses are regularly turned to maintain an even texture and prevent the moisture content from pooling.

The maturing, or ripening, process ranges from a few days to several months, or even years, depending on the type of cheese. The longer the ripening period, the harder the cheese.

The cheese-making season starts in early spring and continues until late autumn, coinciding with the growth of the most nourishing grass. Most Swiss cheeses are produced by small family-run businesses, of which there are about 1,000. Most of them rely on mechanized methods and sophisticated modern equipment. However, in some high Alpine regions, cheeses are still handmade entirely by traditional methods. Such cheeses, known as *Bergkäse, Alpkäse, fromage des alpes or formaggio di alpe*, are highly acclaimed.

Some cheese dairies are open to visitors. Among them are the Appenzeller Schaukäserei in Stein (see p188) and La Maison du Gruyère, at Pringy, just outside Gruyères (see p124).

Heating and stirring milk in a vat in a modern cheese factory

TYPES OF CHEESE

There are more than 400 varieties of Swiss cheese, each with its own individual texture, flavour and aroma. Each also reflects German, French or Italian traditions, and is used in different ways: either eaten thinly sliced, made into fondue or *raclette*, or grated onto pasta dishes.

Vacherin Fribourgeois *is a medium-soft cheese produced exclusively in the canton of Fribourg. It is used primarily to make fondue.*

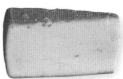

Appenzeller *is a highly aromatic cheese produced in northeastern Switzerland. The length of time it is ripened affects its taste. A black label indicates a well-matured variety, with a strong taste.*

Gruyère *is a hard cheese with a distinctive texture and flavour. Whereas a young Gruyère has a mild flavour, described as* doux, *a highly matured one has an intense flavour and is described as* salé. *Gruyère is made in western Switzerland.*

Tête de Moine, *meaning "monk's head", was first made by monks in the 12th century. Soft and light, it has a strong flavour which is best appreciated when the cheese is cut into slivers. Tête de Moine, also known as Bellelay, is made in the Jura.*

Emmental, *the most popular of all Swiss cheeses, is mild, with a nutty flavour, and large holes. This cheese is made in Emmental and throughout the central lowlands of German-speaking Switzerland. Emmental, which is exported worldwide, is one of the best cheeses to use for making fondue.*

Raclette *has a rich, spicy flavour and, because it melts easily, it is widely used for making the dish known as raclette, hence its name. This is one of the most popular cheeses in Switzerland. Although it originated in Valais, raclette is now made throughout Switzerland.*

Sbrinz *is a dry cheese with an intense flavour, similar to Parmesan. It is grated and sprinkled over dishes, or thinly sliced and served as a dessert cheese. Originating in Brienz, in the Bernese Oberland, Sbrinz is now made throughout central Switzerland. It is matured for up to three years.*

Tilsiter *is a creamy cheese with a delicate flavour. It is named after Swiss émigrés in Tilsit, Prussia, who devised the recipe in the 19th century and returned with it to Switzerland. Tilsiter is now made in eastern Switzerland.*

RETAIL AND EXPORT

Switzerland's annual cheese production amounts to over 150,000 tonnes, just over half of which is exported. By far the most popular varieties worldwide are Emmental, known as the King of Cheeses, and Gruyère.

Many of Switzerland's cheese dairies have shops where their own cheeses are offered for sale. A wide range of locally produced cheeses, including some of the most highly prized varieties, can also be found on market stalls all over Switzerland.

Some larger towns have specialist cheese shops, which stock the widest range of Swiss cheeses. Supermarkets also sell good-quality cheeses, either pre-packed or cut to order from a chilled counter.

Most Swiss cheeses are made with raw milk, which gives them their distinctive flavour. Those made with pasteurized milk are labelled accordingly. The more mature a cheese, the more expensive it is likely to be.

A variety of cheeses on display in a shop window, Stein am Rhein

What to Drink in Switzerland

Beer mat

Swiss wines are almost unknown outside their country of origin as they are rarely imported. Although vineyards are found throughout Switzerland, the best are those in the cantons of Valais and Vaud, particularly on the sheltered hillsides around Lake Geneva. Switzerland also has over 100 large and small breweries, which between them produce dark beers, light ales and lagers, also mostly for domestic consumption. Coffee, sometimes served with cream, and tea, which is usually served black, are popular hot drinks. Unique to Switzerland is Rivella, a soft drink made with whey.

Poster advertising Swiss wines

Rivella, made with whey

Valser mineral water

Caotina, a chocolate drink

NON-ALCOHOLIC DRINKS

Meals are frequently accompanied by still or sparkling mineral water from Switzerland's own mineral springs. The best-known brands include Valser, Henniez, Fontessa, Passugger and Aproz. A popular sweet, fizzy and refreshing drink is Rivella, which is made with lactoserum, a by-product in the cheese-making process *(see p264)*. Four different kinds of Rivella are available: original (with a red label), with a reduced sugar content (a blue label), with green tea (a green label) and dairy-free (a yellow label). Caotina is a smooth, flavoursome chocolate drink.

HOT DRINKS

Coffee, served in many guises, from creamy cappuccino to pungent espresso, is the most popular hot drink in Switzerland. Coffee served with a dash of liqueur or fruit-flavoured vodka is known in German as *Kaffe fertig*, and in Italian as *caffè corretto*. Tea is less widely drunk than coffee but, served ice-cold (as *Eistee, thé froid* or *te freddo*), it is particulary refreshing on hot summer days. Mint tea and Alpine herb infusions are also popular. Ovomaltine, a malted powder added to hot milk, and hot chocolate are warming and restorative winter drinks. Ovo Drink is a ready-mixed Ovomaltine and milk drink.

A malted drink, made with hot milk

Ovomaltine and milk drink

Bottled beer from Chur

Canned lager

Bottled beer from Basel

BEER

The most popular type of beer in Switzerland is a light, German-style beer with an alcohol content of 4.2 to 5.5 percent. Strong beers, with a 6 percent alcohol content, include *weizen* (wheat) and *alt* (dark) varieties. Dominant brands include Feldschlösschen, made in the Basel region, Calanda from Chur, Rugenbräu from Interlaken and Cardinal from Fribourg. Draught beer is usually served in measures ranging from 1 to 5 decilitres. The most common are the 3-decilitre *Stange* (about half a pint) and the 2-decilitre *Herrgöttli* (just over a third of a pint).

Label of the dark Calanda beer

WHITE WINE

The most popular Swiss white wine is the delicate, freshly-scented Fendant from Valais, traditionally served with fondue and *raclette* or drunk as an aperitif. From around Lake Geneva come the well-balanced wines of the Lavaux region, the delicate and refreshing wines of La Côte, and the intensely aromatic wines of the Chablais. This region, as well as Neuchâtel, also produces the light and subtle Chasselas wine, which is served with white meat and cheese and as an aperitif.

Sylvaner, in eastern Switzerland, is also renowned for its white wines. Having a subtle aroma and intense flavour, they are served with fish or asparagus. Chardonnay is produced mainly around Geneva and in Valais. It is served with fish and seafood.

Swiss Blanc from Rheinau Abbey

Pinot Gris from Neuchâtel

Fendant, a Chasselas from Valais

Mont-sur-Rolle Grand Cru de La Côte

RED WINE

One of the most common Swiss red wines is the subtle Dôle, made from a blend of Gamay and Pinot Noir grapes. This is closely followed by the Pinot Noir wines. Both often come from Valais and are ideal with red and white meats and cheese. The vineyards around Lake Geneva produce the light Salvagnin and Gamay wines, which are often served with red meat and hot hors-d'oeuvres. The Lake Neuchâtel region also produces Gamay, which goes well with poultry, veal and cheese. From eastern Switzerland comes Blauburgunder, a fine accompaniment to poultry. Typical of Ticino is Merlot, a ruby-red wine with a subtle aroma. It is excellent with red meat or risotto.

Syrah from the Geneva region

Merlot from Ticino

Pinot Noir from Zürich

Dôle from the Sion region

SPIRITS AND LIQUEURS

A proportion of the fruit grown in Swiss orchards is used to make a variety of spirits and fruit liqueurs. The most popular spirits include kirsch, made from cherries, and Williams, made from William pears. In the French-speaking regions of Switzerland, *pruneau* is distilled from plums, and in Ticino, *grappa* is distilled from the skins, stalks and pips of grapes. *Betzi*, made in German-speaking regions, is a brandy made from a mixture of fruit. Other Swiss spirits and liqueurs are made from apples, quinces, plums, apricots, cherries, raspberries or herbs. A meal often ends with a glass of brandy, to aid digestion, and a dash of spirits may be added to coffee. Liqueur, such as kirsch, is sometimes added to fondue.

Williamine pear brandy

Grundbacher plum spirit

Grappa from Ticino

Apple spirit from Zug

Choosing a Restaurant

The restaurants in this guide have been selected across a wide range of price categories for their good value, exceptional food and/or interesting location. This chart lists the restaurants by region, starting with Bern. The entries are listed in alphabetical order within each price category. For map references, *see inside back cover.*

PRICE CATEGORIES
Price categories for a three-course meal for one person, including tax and service but without wine:

Ⓕ Under 30 CHF
ⒻⒻ 30–60 CHF
ⒻⒻⒻ 60–90 CHF
ⒻⒻⒻⒻ 90–120 CHF
ⒻⒻⒻⒻⒻ Over 120 CHF

BERN

BERN Grotto-Ticino-Pizzeria
Ⓕ
Breitenrainplatz 26, 3014 **Tel** *031 331 96 77*　　　　**Road Map** C3

An inexpensive and popular restaurant next to the Breitenrainplatz tram stop with a wide range of dishes, from Ticino specialities like gnocchi and polenta to pizzas and non-Italian local Bernese favourites like *Bärner Platte* and *rösti*. Particularly tasty is the *pappardella al noci*, butterfly-shaped pasta with a nut pesto. Sidewalk terrace in summer.

BERN Tibits
Ⓕ
Bahnhofplatz 10, 3011 **Tel** *031 312 91 11*　　　　**Road Map** C3

A Swiss vegetarian fast-food chain that serves good-quality healthy sandwiches, salads, soups, snacks and desserts. Open 7 days a week from 6:30pm until late. Food is self-service and priced by weight. No reservations needed. A great option for those on a budget.

BERN Altes Tramdepot Brauerei
ⒻⒻ
Grosser Muristalden 6, 3006 **Tel** *031 368 14 15*　　　　**Road Map** C3

As the name indicates, this restaurant is located in an old tram station, very close to the Bear Gardens. Beer is brewed twice a week right on site in the middle of the restaurant. There is a charming summer terrace with good views of the Old Town. Asian-influenced dishes are cooked in a huge wok.

BERN Arlequin
ⒻⒻ
Gerechtigkeitsgasse 51, 3011 **Tel** *031 311 39 46*　　　　**Road Map** C3

Under the arcades, right in the centre of the Old Town and among the most expensive and smartest shops, the Arlequin is an inexpensive alternative eatery frequented by intellectuals. The interior is small but full of character. The house speciality is *gasse-filet*, a kind of beef steak cut up into cubes with herb butter. Closed Sun, Mon.

BERN Brasserie Bärengraben
ⒻⒻ
Grosse Muristalden 1, 3006 **Tel** *031 331 42 18*　　　　**Road Map** C3

Steps away from the Bear Gardens and by the Nydeggbrücke bridge, this former customs house offers typical Bernese fare at moderate prices. Large windows fill the dining room with light. And there is a conservatory-style annexe as well as a very popular summer garden. Desserts are a speciality. Reservations are generally required.

BERN Fischerstuebli
ⒻⒻ
Gerberngasse 41, 3011 **Tel** *031 311 53 67*　　　　**Road Map** C3

A laid-back, attractive and popular restaurant and bar in Matte, close to the Aare. The menu isn't extensive but features a good variety of dishes including pasta, fish, meat and vegetarian options. The curries are particularly popular with locals. In summer, guests can dine on the pretty terrace.

BERN Goldener Schlüssel
ⒻⒻ
Rathausgasse 72, 3011 **Tel** *031 311 02 16*　　　　**Road Map** C3

Located in a medieval building, the "Golden Key" is said to be exactly 99 steps from Bern's famous Clock Tower. Inside there is considerable atmosphere in the dark interior with old wooden floors and low, heavily beamed ceilings. Traditional Bernese fare is the trademark, drawing a regular crowd of locals, and the desserts are particularly scrumptious.

BERN Harmonie
ⒻⒻ
Hotelgasse 3, 3011 **Tel** *031 313 11 41.*　　　　**Road Map** C3

A highly regarded traditional Bernese establishment popular with tourists and locals alike, just a few steps from the Clock Tower in the old town. Fondues are the speciality. The kitchen is gleaming state-of-the-art stainless steel and ceramic tiles. Wooden walls and floors inside, with a low ceiling but good natural lighting. Closed Sat, Sun.

BERN Kabuki
ⒻⒻ
Bubenbergplatz 9, 3011 **Tel** *031 329 29 19*　　　　**Road Map** C3

One of Switzerland's oldest and most renowned Japanese restaurants, the Kabuki remains moderately priced, simple in decor, and immensely popular. Sushi, sashimi and tempura are most in demand, but worth ordering is *Tempura Udon* – thick Japanese wheat flour noodles in a mildly spicy broth with jumbo prawns in a light batter.

Key to Symbols *see back cover flap*

BERN Schmiedstube
Road Map C3

*Schmiedenplatz 5, 3011 **Tel** 031 311 34 61*

Situated in the heart of the Old Town in a former guildhall with impressive decor, this *Stube* recreates the atmosphere of an old Bernese inn. The menu changes according to the season, fresh ingredients dictating the daily specials. Special menus for children. Closed Sun.

BERN Spaghetti Factory
Road Map C3

*Kornhausplatz 7, 3011 **Tel** 031 312 54 55*

Cheerful, relatively cheap and welcoming to children, this restaurant is generally filled to overflowing with a young and voluble crowd. As the name suggests, pasta dishes are the speciality, with over 20 varieties on the menu. Wide choice of antipasto and salads, as well as some of the best ice cream in Bern. Open until 2:30am Sat.

BERN Terrasse and Casa
Road Map C3

*Dalmaziquai 11, 3000 **Tel** 031 350 50 01*

Two adjacent restaurants on the river in the heart of Bern. Terrasse sits above the weir, with an impressive outdoor location and huge wooden decking. Open all day, every day, Terrasse is popular for snacks or drinks and Sunday brunch. Bistro-style Casa serves Mediterranean inspired fare. Closed Sat lunch and Mon.

BERN Gourmanderie and Petit Moléson
Road Map C3

*Aarbergergasse 24, 3011 **Tel** 031 311 44 63*

A restaurant with a high reputation for its Bernese and Alsace cuisine, only five minutes' walk from the Parliament buildings. It is popular with tourists, not least due to its helpful English-speaking staff, as well as with Swiss politicians. On offer are organic produce, seasonal specialities and many vegetarian dishes. Good wine list. Closed Sun.

BERN Jack's Brasserie
Road Map C3

*Bahnhofplatz 11, 3001 **Tel** 031 326 80 80*

The name suggests a French bistro, but the cuisine is Bernese all the way, in terms of the generous size of the helpings and in the preponderance of cooked meats with sauerkraut and potatoes, although sea bass and sole menière are also highly recommended. The brasserie, in the Schweizerhof hotel, is sometimes called the Stadt restaurant by locals.

BERN Kornhauskeller
Road Map C3

*Kornhausplatz 18, 3000 **Tel** 031 327 72 72*

A treat for the eyes as much as for the palate, the cellar dining room of the Kornhaus features dramatic, soaring vaulted arches painted with frescoes. In the past the Kornhaus fulfilled many functions, including a grain storage facility. Restored to its glory, the cellar is now immensely popular with tourists.

BERN Wein & Sein
Road Map C3

*Münstergasse 50, 3001 **Tel** 031 311 98 44*

Expensive, somewhat eccentric Michelin-starred gourmet restaurant with immense flair in presentation. It offers only a fixed menu, evenings only, and you choose your wine from a bin at one end of the cellar dining room. Menu varies according to season. Extremely hip, and hard to get into. Reserve well in advance. Closed Sun and Mon.

MITTELLAND, BERNESE OBERLAND & VALAIS

BREITEN OB MOREL Taverne
Road Map D4

*Breitenstrasse 1, 3983 **Tel** 027 927 10 22*

A simple guesthouse in the UNESCO heritage area of the Aletsch glacier, yet with a local reputation for good food at modest prices. Chef Albert Jossen offers "surprise menus" of gourmet standard, using local game and fish. The standard menu offers old favourites but also some unusual items, like sauerkraut soup with prawns. Closed Nov.

CRANS-MONTANA Helvetia Intergolf
Road Map C4

*Route de la Moubra 8, 3963 **Tel** 027 485 88 88*

Elegant restaurant in a spa hotel. The main restaurant is decorated in a light, airy modern style. The emphasis is on French and Italian cuisine. The large windows provide good views of the Rhône Valley and surrounding peaks. There is a separate *carnozet*, a typical Valaisan room where cheese and dried meat dishes and regional wines are served.

CRANS-MONTANA Pas de l'Ours
Road Map C4

*Rue Pas de l'Ours, 3963 **Tel** 027 485 93 33*

One of the most elegant and rewarding dining experiences in any Swiss ski resort. There is a less formal bistro area in the old wooden chalet as well as the main dining room. Both feature seasonal and local ingredients, presented with a Provencal flair. The chalet has wood and stone decor dating from the 17th century. Closed Sun evening.

GRACHEN Restaurant Taverne
Road Map C5

*Rue Principal, 3925 **Tel** 027 9561612*

A small family hotel on the road from Visp to Zermatt, with an old-fashioned but cosy dining room. In addition to raclette served directly from the wood fire and a choice of fondues, the menu includes seasonal specialities such as game and delicious homemade desserts. Wines come from the Valais region. The terrace offers mountain views.

GSTAAD Charly's Tea-Room
Promenade 76, 3780 **Tel** *033 744 15 44*　　　**Road Map** *C4*

This is the hangout of Gstaad's jet-set crowd. Few people can resist the pastries and cakes, hot chocolate with whipped cream and choice coffees that have made Charly's an institution in this pampered resort. Après ski here is a scene of furs and subdued whispers. Sandwiches and light meals are also served.

GSTAAD Chesery
Lauenstrasse, 3780 **Tel** *033 744 24 51*　　　**Road Map** *C4*

The name refers to the building's origins in cheese making, prior to its restoration in 1962 by the Aga Khan. Now this charming old chalet is home to one of the best chefs in the Alps, Gault Millau cook of the year in 2005 Robert Speth. The spectacular menu changes seasonally and ranges across the world in terms of taste sensations.

INTERLAKEN El Azteca
Jungfraustrasse 30, 3800 **Tel** *033 822 71 31*　　　**Road Map** *D4*

A lively and colourfully decorated Mexican restaurant in the Hotel Blume, a historic building right in the centre of Interlaken in the pedestrian zone. Live music on weekends. The menu covers all the Mexican standards, with special attention to fajitas: chicken, beef, pork and king prawns. The guacamole is first-rate. Closed Wed afternoon.

INTERLAKEN Pizzeria Piz Paz
Bahnhofstrasse 1, 3800 **Tel** *033 822 25 33*　　　**Road Map** *D4*

Right in the town centre, this is one of the most popular meeting places in Interlaken for backpackers and tourists looking for a good meal at a modest price. The menu covers all the standard pizzas as well as pasta dishes and some specialities from Ticino. Be sure to leave room for the ice cream desserts. Closed Mon.

INTERLAKEN Schuh
Höheweg 56, 3800 **Tel** *033 888 80 50*　　　**Road Map** *D4*

An Interlaken institution since the beginning of the 19th century, the "Grand Restaurant Schuh" to give its full title, is deservedly renowned for its chocolates, many of which are unique concoctions. But the dining room menu ranges into the Orient, with Chinese and Thai dishes, as well as Swiss-German terrain with *rösti* and raclette.

LAUTERBRUNNEN Schützen
Dorfstrasse Fuhren, 3822 **Tel** *033 855 30 25*　　　**Road Map** *C4*

Traditional chalet building in the town centre near the tourist office. There is a typical *Stuebli* – a cosy wood-panelled room for eating fondue and raclette, as well as summer garden and heated winter terrace with first-rate views of the Bernese peaks. A wide range of *flammenkuchen* and cheese fondues is served.

MARTIGNY L'Olivier
Avenue du Grand-Saint-Bernard 72bis, 1920 **Tel** *027 722 18 41*　　　**Road Map** *B5*

At the crossroads of the mountain roads to Verbier and Chamonix, the Restaurant L'Olivier in the Hotel Forum is still somewhat confusingly known as Le Gourmet. By any name, a visit here is a culinary treat. The menu is dictated by the season. A good selection of wines from the Valais region is available.

RIEDERALP Tenne
Art Furrer Resort, 3987 **Tel** *027 928 44 88*　　　**Road Map** *D4*

The Tenne is the premier gourmet restaurant in this complex of hotels and spa facilities. In keeping with the emphasis on health and fitness, the menu is dictated by the changing seasons and the availability of garden-fresh produce. The decor is farmhouse style, with chintz curtains and old wood everywhere. Open from mid-Dec to Apr.

RIEDERALP Derby
Sportplatzweg, 3987 **Tel** *027 927 10 33*　　　**Road Map** *D4*

An old wooden chalet in this small village in the Aletsch glacier region. The dark wood interior, typical of canton Valais, is surprisingly enlivened in the bar by bright wall paintings of jazz singers. The menu is traditional and the wines are local. There is live music each evening during the skiing season. Closed May and Nov.

SAAS FEE Mittelallalin
Metro-Alpin, 3906 **Tel** *027 957 17 71*　　　**Road Map** *D5*

At 3,500 m (11,480 ft) this is the world's highest revolving restaurant, and the combination of the thin air with the revolving scenery can be disconcerting. The views are unbeatable. The food is surprisingly good, and moderately priced, for an attraction of such elevation. There is also a non-revolving self-service cafeteria downstairs.

SAAS FEE Waldhotel Fletschhorn
Oberdorf, 3906 **Tel** *027 9572131*　　　**Road Map** *D5*

A highly regarded gastronomic restaurant with 18 Gault Millau points, just outside the village, about a 20-minute walk uphill. The cuisine is French, and the alpine lamb is a special treat. The cellar contains 30,000 bottles, with an emphasis on the wines of canton Valais. Chef Markus Neff also offers two-day cookery courses.

SCHILTHORN Piz Gloria
Schilthorn, 3825 **Tel** *033 856 21 56*　　　**Road Map** *C4*

The first revolving restaurant in Switzerland (*see p261*), constructed for the James Bond film *On Her Majesty's Secret Service* in 1969. At 2,970 m (9,742 ft) the views of the Bernese Oberland are stupendous. Skiers who want to get an early crack at the pistes can arrange with most Mürren hotels to take their complimentary breakfast at Piz Gloria.

SION Brasserie Le Lucus

Avenue de la Gare 11, 1950 **Tel** *027 322 22 82*
Road Map C5

An attractive and congenial family-run brasserie on a quiet street in the pedestrian area, ideal for sitting outside and watching the world go by. The typical brasserie menu features steaks with french fries and sandwiches, supplemented with local game in season and made all the more tasty by the home-made bread baked on the premises.

SION L'Enclos de Valère

Rue des Châteaux 18, 1950 **Tel** *027 323 32 30*
Road Map C5

A welcoming inn on the eastern edge of Sion just under the castle walls, with a lovely garden terrace offering great views of the castle and the Rhône valley vineyards. There is an ambitious and extensive menu, mostly French dishes ranging from duck to shellfish specialities. Extensive list of Valais wines, but little other choice. Closed Sun and Mon.

SOLOTHURN Baseltor

Hauptgasse 79, 4500 **Tel** *032 622 34 22*
Road Map C3

Highly recommended and unusual restaurant. The owners share their predilection for culture by organizing heavily subscribed "literary dinners". The impressive Baroque building was once used to store cannons, but has since been renovated lovingly. The imaginative menu ranges all over the world: Mediterranean, Asian and Swiss dishes.

TORBEL Bergrestaurant Moosalp

Moosalp, 3923 **Tel** *027 952 14 95*
Road Map C5

A mountain restaurant somewhat out of the way, but worth visiting for its authentic preparation of fondues and raclette. The raclette cheese is melted on an open fire, adding a hint of wood-smoke flavour. Also worth trying is the "assiette Valaisan" plate of local dried meats. The restaurant is located above the Rhône valley, near Visp.

VERBIER Marlenaz

Route de Marlenaz, 1936 **Tel** *027 771 54 41*
Road Map C5

The only restaurant in Verbier with honest, uncontrived rustic charm in truly rural setting. It is a ten-minute drive up winding, narrow dirt roads from the resort to the quiet forest and garden surrounded by huge boulders. The *croute au fromage* is highly recommended but there is a full menu of beef, lamb and other standard fare. Attentive service.

VERBIER Millénium

Rue Medran, 1936 **Tel** *027 771 99 00*
Road Map C5

High gastronomic standard, an innovative menu and good value for money. All the meats are particularly good but the ostrich is outstanding. Some dishes have a Pacific Rim influence. Millénium is located conveniently just a few steps above the main square. The clientele tends to be young and affluent. Several celebrity sightings.

VERBIER Sonalon

Route de la Marlène 110, 1936 **Tel** *027 563 35 30*
Road Map C5

Perched just above the traffic congestion of the resort in an ancient farming hamlet, with a huge wooden sundeck and charming garden, the Sonalon is the favourite restaurant of Verbier residents. Fabulous views. Regional ingredients dominate the menu, which includes local Valaisan specialities.

VISP Le Bristol

Kantonsstrasse 28, 3930 **Tel** *027 946 33 23*
Road Map D4

A wide variety of Italian dishes, including an interesting range of pizzas and pasta. The dining room is spacious and airy, decorated in a simple, even spartan, modern style with large red floor tiles and small wooden tables covered with green and red tablecloths. Italian and Swiss wines. Closed Mon; Sun morning.

WENGEN Da Sina

Dorf, 3823 **Tel** *033 855 31 72*
Road Map C4

An unpretentious and enjoyable Italian restaurant in the centre of Wengen, one of the least expensive and best-value eateries in the village. Very popular with tourists and young people working in the resort. The food is tasty and the service is prompt. The menu consists mostly of pizzas and pasta. Limited wine list.

WILDERSWIL La Cabane

Obereigasse 29, 3812 **Tel** *033 822 84 14*
Road Map D4

One of two restaurants attached to a 1970's style motel set in the open countryside near the resort of Wilderswil. The Cabane offers "modern Swiss cuisine", which translates to a variety of meats and vegetables. The other restaurant, the Lunette, is more casual. In summer there are animated barbeques on the terrace, which offers great views.

ZERMATT Le Mazot

Dorf, 3920 **Tel** *027 966 06 06*
Road Map C5

One of Zermatt's less expensive and most welcoming small restaurants, located in the village centre near the river. The family-run inn specializes in lamb, fed on pastures under the Matterhorn, grilled on an open wood fire. Fondues are also popular. There is an admirably extensive wine list, including Spanish, Italian, French and Swiss choices.

ZERMATT Zum See

Zum See, 3920 **Tel** *027 967 20 45*
Road Map C5

One of the most highly regarded mountain restaurants in the Alps, with an ever changing menu. In summer, mountain berries and vegetables from the garden right outside the old chalet add a wonderful freshness to the menu. In winter the rustic hut is filled to the rafters with skiers in the know. Closed May to early Jun and end Oct to Nov.

ZERMATT Alexandre
Riffelalp Resort, 3920 **Tel** *027 966 05 55*   ⓕⓕⓕⓕ
                                                              Road Map *C5*

This is the gourmet restaurant of the Riffelalp (*see p248*), a luxury resort above Zermatt accessed only by railway. There are two other restaurants, one serving Valaisan cheese dishes, the other dedicated to passing skiers and hikers. The Alexandre has the decor and menu of a top Parisian restaurant, with the added attraction of unbeatable views.

ZERMATT Le Gourmet-Alpenhof
Hotel Alpenhof, 3920 **Tel** *027 966 55 55*   ⓕⓕⓕⓕ
                                                              Road Map *C5*

Highly regarded gourmet restaurant with 15 Gault Millau points. The restaurant is in the Hotel Alpenhof, right on the river and halfway between the train station and the Sunegga underground funicular building. The aptly named Gourmet is an oasis of elegance, with impeccable service and a menu typical of a grand French restaurant.

GENEVA

GENEVA Chez ma Cousine
6 Place Bourg-du-Four, 1201 **Tel** *022 310 96 96*   ⓕ
                                                              Road Map *A5*

Part of a popular chain of three restaurants in the Geneva area. This one is in the heart of the Old Town, near the cathedral. The very inexpensive menu consists of chicken, grilled or in a Thai or Indian style, or salad. Inside, the tables are small and space is scarce. Choice of five wines. Take-away available.

GENEVA Bistrot du Bœuf Rouge
Rue Alfred-Vincent 17, 1201 **Tel** *022 732 75 37*   ⓕⓕ
                                                           Road Map *A5*

A gastronomic restaurant at the top of its game masquerading as a small family bistro. The cooking is heavily influenced by the Lyons region of France, sauces for example definitely savoury and substantial. Many Swiss wines are on the list, as are impeccable vintages from France: Louis Latour for burgundies and choice northern Rhone wines. Closed Sat and Sun.

GENEVA Brasserie des Halles de l'Ile
1 Place de l'Ile, 1204 **Tel** *022 311 08 88*   ⓕⓕ
                                                           Road Map *A5*

Right in the middle of the Rhône river not far from the famous jet d'eau, with exceptional views and the tranquillity found only on such a car-free island, this charming restaurant serves a choice of tapas or à la carte menus. On week-ends, there is also a popular brunch menu. There are DJ sets on weekend evenings.

GENEVA Café de Paris
Rue du Mont-Blanc 26, 1201 **Tel** *022 732 84 50*   ⓕⓕ
                                                           Road Map *A5*

A short stroll from the lake, the Café de Paris is a venerable Geneva institution, famous for being written up as having only one item on the menu: entrecôte steak with chips, green salad, and the eponymous still secret butter sauce first developed in 1930. Short list of a dozen Swiss and French wines.

GENEVA La Veranda
20 rue des Alpes, 1211 **Tel** *022 906 97 77*   ⓕⓕ
                                                           Road Map *A5*

This is the restaurant of the 19th-century Hotel International and Terminus. The restaurant is in a stone building in a large garden. In summer there is ample space for outdoor dining as well. The sunny and airy interior, even in winter, makes a pleasant escape from the city streets. Wide ranging menu with many salads, pizza, fish and meat dishes.

GENEVA Pied de Cochon
4 Place du Bourg de Four, 1204 **Tel** *022 310 47 97*   ⓕⓕ
                                                         Road Map *A5*

Very well frequented bistro in the centre of Geneva, open every day of the year, with a small outdoor area in summer. As the name suggests, the menu features *pied de porc* (stuffed pig's trotter). But the range of tastes also extends to fish from Lake Geneva, poultry dishes and the bistro standard steak and chips.

GENEVA Riverside
19 Rue du Rhône, 1204 **Tel** *022 311 32 00*   ⓕⓕ
                                                           Road Map *A5*

This small bistro, accessed by the corridor of an indoor shopping arcade, has a small terrace with great views of the river and Lake Geneva. The menu runs from sandwiches and lunchtime specials of the day to hamburgers and local perch. It's a popular meeting point for expatriates working in Geneva. Closed Sun.

GENEVA Vieux-Bois
12 Avenue de la Paix, 1201 **Tel** *022 919 24 26*   ⓕⓕ
                                                           Road Map *A5*

A rare opportunity to test chefs in the making. The Vieux-Bois is the working laboratory of Switzerland's famous hotel school L'École Hôtelière de Genève. So all the cooks and waiters are dedicated students, attentive and keen to please. Prices are also far lower than at other restaurants of this quality. Lovely summer garden.

GENEVA Café de la Gare
2 rue Montbrillant, 1201 **Tel** *022 733 77 84*   ⓕⓕⓕ
                                                           Road Map *A5*

Despite its name, this French brasserie is not in the train station but instead located in the Hotel Montbrillant, just behind the station. It is famous for its lavish Art Deco painted glass ceiling. The dark wood panelling is typical of a real Parisian brasserie, and so is the menu, ranging from beef bourguignon to grilled meats with sauerkraut.

Key to Price Guide *see p268*   **Key to Symbols** *see back cover flap*

GENEVA L'Entrecôte Couronée   🔲   ⓕⓕⓕ
5 rue des Pâquis, 1201 **Tel** *022 732 84 45*   **Road Map** *A5*

Small, intimate bistro in downtown Geneva run by Genevans for Genevans. The wine list emphasizes wines from canton Geneva and the restaurant has been awarded a certificate for its exploitation of local meats and produce. Genuinely charming interior with retro style wooden floors and period tables. Try the steak with butter sauce. Closed Sun.

GENEVA Le Rouge et le Blanc   🔲🔲🔲   ⓕⓕⓕ
27 Quai des Bergues, 1201 **Tel** *022 731 15 50*   **Road Map** *A5*

At Le Rouge et le Blanc, market produce is used to create a seasonal menu of traditional French dishes with a light and inventive touch. The sommelier, who is one of the owners, transmits his passion for wine to his guests. At 5pm the restaurant becomes a wine bar and tapas can be ordered. There are views of the Jet d'Eau from the terrace.

GENEVA Les Armures   🔲🔲   ⓕⓕⓕ
1 Rue de Puits-St-Pierre, 1204 **Tel** *022 310 34 42*   **Road Map** *A5*

An atmospheric restaurant with a terrace in a historic 17th-century mansion in the heart of old Geneva, next to the medieval arsenal. As the name suggests, old suits of armour and ancient swords are dotted around the building for decoration. There are two air-conditioned dining rooms, one for fondues and the other French in theme.

GENEVA Thaï Phuket   🔲   ⓕⓕⓕ
Avenue de France 33, 1202 **Tel** *022 734 41 00*   **Road Map** *A5*

A Michelin-rated Thai restaurant considered among the best of the Asian eateries in Geneva, but by no means the most expensive. Located near the botanical gardens in the UN neighbourhood. Unexpectedly perhaps, there is an extensive wine list of French bordeaux crus. Fantastic aquarium with tropical fish.

GENEVA Tsé Yang   🔲🔲   ⓕⓕⓕ
19 Quai Du Mont Blanc, 1201 **Tel** *022 732 50 81*   **Road Map** *A5*

This is one of the most highly regarded Chinese restaurants in Geneva, housed in the Grand Hotel Kempinski. The views are spectacular, the service is attentive and there is a casual but smart atmosphere (dress code is smart casual). Waiters are happy to advise guests unfamiliar with the more esoteric items on the menu. The Szechuan dishes are recommended.

GENEVA Du Parc des Eaux-Vives   🔲🔲🔲   ⓕⓕⓕⓕ
82 Quai Gustave Ador, 1211 **Tel** *022 849 75 75*   **Road Map** *A5*

This historic château houses both a brasserie and a superbly elegant fine dining room, both renovated in 2003, in the grounds of a leafy park of the same name near Lake Geneva. Said to have the most beautiful summer dining terrace in Geneva. Classic French cuisine. Great Simmental beef, Paulliac lamb. Two Michelin stars. Closed Sun and Mon.

GENEVA La Réserve   🔲🔲🔲   ⓕⓕⓕⓕ
301 Route de Lausanne, 1293 **Tel** *022 959 59 59*   **Road Map** *A5*

Three different dining rooms offer considerable variety in this striking restaurant, part of a luxury spa hotel set in its own leafy park. The Tsé Fung dining room serves traditional Chinese dishes, with some spicy Szechuan items. Le Loti has a Mediterranean theme, good for fish. And the Spa Room is dedicated to light, healthy and nutritious cuisine.

GENEVA Auberge du Lion d'Or   🔲🔲🔲   ⓕⓕⓕⓕⓕ
5 Place Pierre-Gautier, Cologny, 1223 **Tel** *022 736 44 32*   **Road Map** *A5*

On the east bank of Lake Geneva just minutes from the city centre, both bistro and restaurant offer great views from the terrace as well as from the huge picture windows. Open-air dining in summer. High standard of French cuisine, one Michelin star. Exhaustive collection of wines from the Geneva region. Closed Sat and Sun.

WESTERN SWITZERLAND

AIGLE San Remo   🔲🔲🔲   ⓕⓕ
Chemin du Châtelard 23, 1860 **Tel** *024 466 34 68*   **Road Map** *B4*

French and Italian cuisine, with a dash of Spanish influence added by proprietor and chef Jesus Dominguez. Fresh, home-made pastas with imaginative fillings. The service is particularly friendly, and quick. There is also a good selection of children's dishes, and high chairs are provided. Pets are welcome, if on a leash. Closed Sun.

AVENCHES Des Bains   🔲🔲🔲   ⓕⓕⓕ
Route de Berne 1, 1580 **Tel** *026 675 36 60*   **Road Map** *B3*

Situated just outside the medieval town between the château and the Roman baths, Des Bains has a well-balanced and eclectic menu with local perch filets, beef from South Africa and lentil ragout. Menus for children. Well chosen wine list, with some exemplary Bordeaux vintages and great wines from Chile.

BONCOURT Lion d'Or   🔲🔲   ⓕⓕ
6 Route du Jura, 2926 **Tel** *032 475 52 10*   **Road Map** *B2*

A hotel restaurant in the rolling hills of Jura at the very western edge of the Swiss frontier, with good views from the terrace. It is popular with locals but little frequented by tourists. The menu offers good value, with fondues, fried carp and *potence* – cubes of beef steak hung on a metal rack and set aflame at the table. Closed Mon.

BRENT Le Pont de Brent
ⒷⒷⒷⒷⒷ

Route de Blonay 4, 1817   **Tel** *021 964 52 30*   **Road Map** *B4*

A gourmet Michelin-starred restaurant with chef Stéphane Décotterd at the helm, second-in-command to legendary predecessor Gérard Rabaey. Standards have been maintained so expect exceptional French cuisine, a first-class wine list and impeccable service. Diners are allowed to bring their dogs. Closed Sun and Mon.

BULLE L'Ecu
ⒷⒷ

Rue Saint-Denis 5, 1630   **Tel** *026 912 93 18*   **Road Map** *B4*

Seldom visited by tourists but with a local reputation for good-value food with an emphasis on regional products such as wild mushrooms, game and waterfowl from the nearby lake, fresh lake perch and river pike. Casual ambience, which extends to the waiters' delivery of various courses. Closed Mon and Tue.

CAUX Plein-Roc
ⒷⒷ

Rochers-de-Naye, 1824   **Tel** *021 963 74 11*   **Road Map** *B4*

At the top of Rochers-de-Naye at 2,045 m (6,708 ft) overlooking Lake Geneva and the Swiss and French Alps. Good Swiss and French cuisine, just short of "gourmet". There is also a self-service cafeteria. The summit restaurant is reached by cog wheel railway from Montreux. There is a garden of alpine flowers and a children's zoo with marmots.

CHAMBESY Plage du Reposoir
ⒷⒷ

222 Route de Lausanne, 1292   **Tel** *022 732 42 65*   **Road Map** *A5*

This beach restaurant offers a wide variety of snacks, as well as buffets where an entire pig is roasted, pasta, pizza and local specialities like filet of perch. There is a large verdant lawn and big umbrellas. It has a family atmosphere, with many activities for children and evenings with music. Parking for two boats. Good views. Closed Oct–Mar.

CRISSIER Restaurant de l'Hôtel de Ville
ⒷⒷⒷⒷⒷ

1 Rue d'Yverdon, 1023   **Tel** *021 634 05 05*   **Road Map** *B4*

Still remembered as *the* temple of cuisine, often described as the best restaurant in the world and presided over by Frédy Giradet who retired in 1996, this old town hall restaurant continues to live up to its reputation under chef Benoit Violier. Exquisite French cuisine, classic but imaginative and inspirational. Reservations essential. Closed Sun and Mon.

CULLY Auberge du Raisin
ⒷⒷⒷ

1 Place de l'Hôtel-de-Ville, 1096   **Tel** *021 799 21 31*   **Road Map** *B4*

Situated in the scenic village of Cully, in the Lavaux wine region, is the Auberge du Raisin. Housed in a charming 16th-century building, the restaurant serves fish from the lake and other local specialities alongside a good choice of local Lavaux wines. The interior is cosy with large wooden tables and there are two terraces for summer dining.

DELÉMONT Du Midi
ⒷⒷ

10 Place de la Gare, 2800   **Tel** *032 422 17 77*   **Road Map** *C2*

In the same family for more than a century, this city centre restaurant opposite the railway station includes a bistro, restaurant and gourmet dining room. All three are inspired by local Jura seasonal ingredients. The gourmet restaurant features shellfish and seafood, imaginatively presented. Good selection of wines. Closed Tue evening and Wed.

DELÉMONT Le Mexique
ⒷⒷ

Route du Vorbourg 142, 2800   **Tel** *032 422 13 33*   **Road Map** *C2*

The name is entirely misleading, the cuisine being a mix of Ticino and Italian specialities and nothing to do with Mexico. Near the railway station, to the north of Delémont in the Jura hills near the Vorbourg chapel, this charming white villa in a quiet residential area offers tremendous views and a large garden with swings for kids. Closed Mon.

FRIBOURG De l'Epée
ⒷⒷ

Planche Supérieure 39, 1702   **Tel** *026 322 34 07*   **Road Map** *B3*

A popular restaurant and bistro attractively decorated with original artwork in the city centre with good views of the Old Town. Typical French bistro cooking, with grilled meats and hearty portions. Special menus for children, and high chairs are provided. Awarded 13 Gault Millau points. Outdoor terrace in summer. Closed Sun and Tue evening.

FRIBOURG L'Aigle-Noir
ⒷⒷⒷ

10 Rue des Alpes, 1700   **Tel** *026 322 49 77*   **Road Map** *B3*

The Black Eagle is perched on a hill with superb views over the Old Town and towards the Jura. There is a terrace for summer dining. The decor features an old carved wood ceiling and chandelier. The restaurant is a popular meeting place and has 14 Gault Millau points. Regional dishes include fondues and dried meats. Closed Sun and Mon.

FRIBOURG Le Pérolles
ⒷⒷⒷⒷ

Bd de Pérolles 18 A, 1700   **Tel** *026 347 40 30*   **Road Map** *B3*

Le Pérolles has a longstanding reputation as one of the best restaurants in French-speaking Switzerland, with prices to match. In an unprepossessing building in the business district, it has a modern dining room with modernist art works. French cuisine with local ingredients. Save space for the cheese tray, which comes after the meal.

GRUYÈRES Le Chalet du Gruyères
ⒷⒷⒷ

Rue de Bourg, 1663   **Tel** *026 921 34 34*   **Road Map** *B4*

In an historic setting, in the Old Town under the ramparts of the castle, the Chalet is a former mill. An ideal place to sample fondue, made with the choicest selections of freshly ground gruyère cheeses – each cheese differing in flavour according to which part of the mountain the cows are grazed upon. Raclettes and grilled meats also served.

LA CHAUX-DE-FONDS La Pinte Neuchâteloise ⓕⓕ

8 Rue Grenier, 2300 **Tel** *032 913 20 30* **Road Map** *B3*

Something between a bistro and a pub, in the centre of the city, this vibrant place is always packed with locals enjoying the modest prices and generous helpings. Traditional wood decor. The menu focuses on Jura and regional Swiss dishes such as *fondue au fromage*, *tripes à la neuchâteloise*, *röstis* with various meats and *croutes au fromage*. Closed Sun.

LAUSANNE La Table d'Edgard ⓕⓕⓕⓕ

Grand Chêne 7-9, 1002 **Tel** *021 331 31 31* **Road Map** *B4*

At the Michelin-starred dining room of the luxurious Lausanne Palace & Spa hotel (*see p250*), each table is set into a recessed nook, for guaranteed privacy. The menu is traditional French cuisine. There are fine views of the lake and Lausanne. Superb wine list. There is also a brasserie decorated with dark wood. Closed Sun and Mon.

LAUSANNE (OUCHY) La Croix d'Ouchy ⓕⓕⓕ

Avenue d'Ouchy 43, 1006 **Tel** *021 616 22 33* **Road Map** *B4*

A highly regarded gourmet restaurant on the outskirts of Lausanne close to the lake. The menu offers French and Italian cuisine with good vegetarian choices. Service can be slow, but the risottos are sublime and the *escalopines au miel et citron* (escalope with honey and lemon) is also superb, as is the ravioli with black truffle. Sunny terrace.

LE NOIRMONT Restaurant Georges Wenger ⓕⓕⓕⓕ

2 rue de la Gare, 2340 **Tel** *032 957 66 33* **Road Map** *B2*

One of the most highly regarded restaurants in Switzerland, with two Michelin stars, is tucked away in a romantic castle-like hotel in the rolling hills of the Jura. Here there is a genuine passion for local, fresh ingredients such as morel mushrooms, lime blossoms and pine honey. The impressive wine cellar has 30,000 bottles. Closed Mon and Tue.

LES DIABLERETS Auberge de la Poste ⓕⓕ

Rue de la Gare, 1865 **Tel** *024 492 31 24* **Road Map** *B4*

This hotel restaurant in the centre of Diablerets has a dining room decorated in old wood with carved ceilings, with great panoramic views. The menu consists mostly of regional dishes: fondues, *croutes au fromages* and large steaks grilled on stone slabs. Friday evenings in winter there are folklore dinners with special menus and accordion music.

MONTREUX Palais Oriental ⓕⓕⓕ

6 Quai Ernest-Ansermet, 1820 **Tel** *021 963 12 71* **Road Map** *B4*

A Montreux landmark, the Palais Oriental is entertaining and exotic, with its ornate Islamic carpets (for sale) and metal work. It is a good spot to take afternoon tea. The meals are somewhat pricey, but there is an authentic range of Iranian, Moroccan, Lebanese and Egyptian cuisine. The restaurant is right on the shores of Lake Geneva.

MORAT/MURTEN Le Vieux Manoir ⓕⓕⓕ

18 Rue de Lausanne, 3280 **Tel** *026 678 61 61* **Road Map** *B3*

Dining at the Vieux Manoir is an indulgence of the senses. The setting is romantic and tranquil, the views of Lake Murten breathtaking. The cuisine is modern with an Asian touch, with attention to the seasons, and marvellously presented. In addition to the classic dining room there is an aviary room, said to be the smallest dining room in Switzerland.

NEUCHÂTEL Pinte de Pierre-à-Bot ⓕⓕ

Pierre-à-Bot 106, 2000 **Tel** *032 725 33 80* **Road Map** *B3*

Set in open countryside outside Neuchâtel with good views. The interior is simple but hospitable, with lots of old wood but no pretence. There is a huge garden, with a small lake and water slides for children in summer. The menu is inexpensive but imaginative, with grilled meats, seafood, a large selection of fondues, and Swiss wines.

NEUCHÂTEL Beau-Rivage ⓕⓕⓕ

1 Esplanade du Mont-Blanc, 2001 **Tel** *032 723 15 23* **Road Map** *B3*

This is the restaurant of the magnificent Beau-Rivage hotel on the lake of Neuchâtel (*see p251*), with panoramic views. Diners can enjoy the elegant setting and varied cuisine that blends the traditional with the new. A speciality is ham from Vaumarcus. Sunday brunch is very popular, reservations required.

NEUCHÂTEL Le Cardinal Brasserie ⓕⓕⓕ

9 Rue du Seyon, 2000 **Tel** *032 725 12 86* **Road Map** *B3*

A lively brasserie, in no way related to the biggest beer brewers in the French-speaking part of Switzerland, who have the same name and a brasserie in Fribourg. With enchanting period decor, it said to be the most beautiful brasserie in the region. Far higher standard of cuisine than normal for a brasserie. Highly recommended. Closed Sun.

NYON Café du Marché ⓕⓕⓕ

Rue du Marché 3, 1260 **Tel** *022 362 49 79* **Road Map** *B3*

For decades the home of La Pinte Vaudois, famous throughout the region, this historic building now houses the Café du Marché. The cuisine is simple and international with seasonal specialities. On Saturdays, the British chef serves up a popular brunch. Closed Sun and Mon.

PAYERNE Auberge de Vers-chez-Perrin ⓕⓕ

Vers-chez-Perrin, 1551 **Tel** *026 660 58 46* **Road Map** *B3*

A small country hotel 2 km (1 mile) east of Payerne with three tastefully decorated dining rooms concentrating on the "cuisine of the south", which covers Italy, France and Spain. Meats are cooked over fires fuelled with vine stocks. Enjoy ham from Spain and risottos from Italy. You are invited to descend into the cellar to choose your wine.

PEREFITTE Etoile   Ⓕ Ⓕ

Gros Clos 4, 2742 **Tel** *032 493 10 17*   **Road Map** *C2*

A family-run restaurant with attractive, modern decor. The menu is extensive and features fresh, seasonal produce and brasserie-style dishes, such as grilled organic chicken, fish and steak. Traditional dishes complement more innovative offerings. There's a children's menu and very well-priced set menus of three courses. Closed Sun.

PORRENTRUY Des Trois-Tonneaux   Ⓕ Ⓕ

16 Rue des Baîches, 2900 **Tel** *032 466 13 17*   **Road Map** *C2*

An old-fashioned, simple town-centre bistro nonetheless renowned throughout the Jura for its home-made *gâteau au fromage*, a savoury speciality not to be confused with American-style "cheesecake". There is a wide range of vegetarian dishes, mostly cheese-based, and a good selection of Swiss wines. Popular with locals. Closed Sun and Tue.

SAIGNELEGIER Café du Soleil   Ⓕ Ⓕ

14 Rue du Marché-Concours, 2350 **Tel** *032 951 16 88*   **Road Map** *B2*

In the hills above the verdant Jura village of Saignelégier, this is the restaurant of a regional cultural centre which promotes painting, jazz, theatre and design. The restaurant also has an artistic flair and a menu that features regional cuisine made with local organic produce. There are many vegetarian dishes. Playroom for kids. Closed Mon evening.

ST-URSANNE Du Bœuf   Ⓕ Ⓕ

60 Rue de 23 Juin, 2882 **Tel** *032 461 31 49*   **Road Map** *C2*

A simple country inn with a local reputation for hospitality and good home cooking at moderate prices. The whitewashed exterior with green shutters and flowerboxes in every window gives a cheery air. Despite the name, beef is not the main item on the menu, rather there are many vegetarian options, as well as a succulent lamb with fennel.

ST-URSANNE La Couronne   Ⓕ Ⓕ

3 Rue de 23 Juin, 2882 **Tel** *032 461 35 67*   **Road Map** *C2*

Historic restaurant in a fortified tower gateway, with a stone paved garden patio for outside dining. Cheese dishes feature widely on the menu, with some unusual variations on the basic fondue recipe. Fresh trout is also a speciality. Another treat is *potence flambée au whisky*, small cubes of beef hung from a metal rack and then set alight.

YVERDON-LES-BAINS Crêperie l'Ange Bleu   Ⓕ

11 Rue du Collège, 1400 **Tel** *024 426 09 96*   **Road Map** *B3*

A small but very popular crêperie open most nights until 11:30pm and drawing a lively young crowd of students. The crêpes and *galettes* (waffles) come with a wide assortment of fillings and sauces. There are also salads and snacks, such as hot dogs and cheese on toast. Friendly service and very low prices. Closed Mon.

NORTHERN SWITZERLAND

AARAU Rendez-vous   Ⓕ Ⓕ

Bahnhofstrasse 4, 5000 **Tel** *062 822 52 23*   **Road Map** *D2*

A traditional Swiss restaurant in the very centre of Aarau, close to the train station. Highly rated by locals for its good value for money. Game is a speciality in season. Very casual atmosphere. The restaurant does not serve alcohol. Ample outdoor parking and dining outside on the terrace in summer. Closed Sun.

BADEN Schwyzerhüsli   Ⓕ Ⓕ

Badstrasse 38, 5400 **Tel** *056 222 62 63*   **Road Map** *D2*

Almost always filled with an exuberant crowd, especially later in the evening, this restaurant and its brasserie are a local institution in Baden. The old house with its red shutters has a large terrace for summer dining. The brasserie serves snacks and grills. Fondues are most in demand in the main dining room, the Stübli.

BADEN (DÄTTWIL) Pinte   Ⓕ Ⓕ

Sommerhaldenstrasse20, Dätwili, 5405 **Tel** *056 493 20 30*   **Road Map** *D2*

This gourmet restaurant in a quiet village outside Baden, with charming gardens and an exceptional menu from chef Patrick Troxler, has earned a Michelin star and 17 Gault Millau points. Extensive wine list. Lovely Bacchusstube dining room with widely spaced tables. Steaks, tartare and other classics. Modestly priced lunch menus.

BASEL Acqua Osteria   Ⓕ

Binningerstrasse 14, 4051 **Tel** *061 564 66 66*   **Road Map** *C2*

Very trendy hangout for the young and hip in Basel. The ambience, menu and even the coffee are exclusively Italian. The building is a converted water-pumping facility, with high ceilings, subdued lighting and bistro decor. There is a bar and a lounge with comfy sofas. Good selection of inexpensive Italian wines. Closed Sun and Mon.

BASEL Gifthüttli   Ⓕ Ⓕ

Schneidergasse 11, 4051 **Tel** *061 261 16 56*   **Road Map** *C2*

The dining room is appealingly decorated with traditional wood panelling and the atmosphere is relaxed. There are seven varieties of *cordon bleu* (escalope with cheese and ham), the fad food of Swiss German youth. The streetside terrace is a popular spot in warm weather. Good wines.

Key to Price Guide *see p268* **Key to Symbols** *see back cover flap*

BASEL Bel Etage at Teufelhof   🏠 🍷   ⓕⓕⓕ

Leonhardsgraben 47-49, 4051 **Tel** *061 261 10 10*   **Road Map** *C2*

The exciting restaurant of the eccentric Teufelhof hotel and cultural centre. Here you will find a high standard of cuisine, based on local garden produce and meat, and often the menus are set in themes to complement the theatre productions held in the hotel. Nothing frozen or pre-cooked is allowed. Good wine list with over 450 vintages.

BASEL Goldenen Sternen   🚶 🍷   ⓕⓕⓕ

St. Alban-Rheinweg 70, 4052 **Tel** *061 272 16 66*   **Road Map** *C2*

The oldest restaurant in Basel (and one of the oldest in Europe), dating from the 15th century, with old-fashioned decor and standards of service. Tables are laid with starched white linen and sterling silver. A loyal clientele of locals. Wide range of Swiss German specialities as well as international fare like grilled meats. The wine list is impressive.

BASEL Kohlmanns   🍷   ⓕⓕⓕ

Steinenberg 14, 4001 **Tel** *061 225 93 93*   **Road Map** *C2*

Located in the heart of the old town at Barfüsserplatz, this restaurant with a dark wood interior offers a menu of high-quality local dishes such as *tarte flambée* with Alsatian cheese and pears or *schupfnudeln* (potato noodles) with smoked Basel sausage and Riesling *sauerkraut*. Leave room for one of the mouthwatering desserts. Closed Mon.

BASEL Stucki   ♿ 🏠 🍷   ⓕⓕⓕⓕⓕ

Bruderholzallee 42, 4059 **Tel** *061 361 82 22*   **Road Map** *C2*

One of the most highly regarded restaurants in Switzerland, with 17 Gault Millau points, a Michelin star and membership in Les Grandes Tables du Monde. Creative French cuisine, three dining rooms and a spacious garden. There are over 500 vintage wines to choose from. Reservations are required well in advance. Closed Sun and Mon.

DORNACH Schlosshof   🚶 ♿ 🏠   ⓕⓕ

Schlossweg 125, 4143 **Tel** *061 702 01 50*   **Road Map** *C2*

Medium-priced restaurant renowned for its fantastic panoramic views and superior cuisine. Pets and children are welcome. Schlosshof is only three minutes' walk from the medieval ruins in Dornach. In summer there are barbecues in the leafy garden, in autumn local game is featured and in winter there is a special *rösti* for each day of the week.

EGLISAU Landgasthaus Fähre   🚶 🍷   ⓕⓕ

Rheinsfelderstrasse 47, 8192 **Tel** *043 422 57 30*   **Road Map** *E2*

The menu varies seasonally. April, for example, introduces white French asparagus and the colder winter months are fuelled by the grilled meats and sauerkraut of the Bärner Platte. Small but eclectic wine collection, featuring wines from South Africa, Sardinia, Switzerland and the Americas. Closed Mon and Tue except in summer.

GATTIKON Smoly   ♿ 🏠 🍷   ⓕⓕⓕⓕⓕ

Sihlhaldenstrasse 70, 8136 **Tel** *044 720 09 27*   **Road Map** *E2*

A Michelin-starred restaurant, Smoly has been in the Smolinsky family since the 1970s, now with son Gregor in the kitchen. Classic French cuisine and an excellent wine list. Eat in one of three elegant dining rooms or outside on the summer terrace. Closed Sun and Mon.

KAISERSTUHL Kaiserstuhl   🚶 ♿ 🏠   ⓕⓕ

Brünigstrasse 232, 6078 **Tel** *041 678 11 89*   **Road Map** *D2*

Kaiserstuhl is a family-run lakeside restaurant and hotel in a small village between Luzern and Interlaken. The theme is simplicity and relaxation in nature. The menu features fresh fish and *pot au feu*, for a minimum of two persons. The speciality is various meats cooked *cordon bleu* style with a choice of ten fillings.

LIESTAL Bad Schauenburg   ♿ 🏠 🍷   ⓕⓕⓕⓕ

Schauenburgerstrasse 76, 4410 **Tel** *061 906 27 27*   **Road Map** *C2*

Acclaimed cuisine in this country-estate garden setting attracts a clientele consisting of local village residents and Basel business professionals. Casual meals are served in the lounge *(Gaststube)*, while gourmet cuisine and an elaborate period decor are on offer in the salon. There are superb views when dining outside on the veranda.

MURI Moospintli   🚶 ♿ 🏠   ⓕ

Dorf, 5630 **Tel** *056 675 53 73*   **Road Map** *D2*

Extremely friendly and casual café with a large garden, welcoming to children. Pastries, sandwiches and desserts make up the completely alcohol-free menu. Organic brunch with bacon, eggs, cheeses, fruit salads and dried meats is served every Sunday morning from Easter until the autumn.

RIEHEN Han Mongolian Barbecue   🚶 ♿   ⓕⓕ

Baselstrasse 67, 4125 **Tel** *061 641 54 55*   **Road Map** *C2*

Part of a worldwide franchise chain, with seven branches in Switzerland, Han offers fast food and friendly service at low prices. You are encouraged to mix dishes and choose how much of each you want by instructing the grill man. Each dish comes with a sweet and sour appetizer and Mongolian soup.

WADENSWIL Engel   🚶 ♿ 🏠   ⓕⓕⓕ

Engelstrasse 2, 8820 **Tel** *044 780 00 11*   **Road Map** *E3*

A small hotel and restaurant right on the shores of Lake Zürich with its own boat landing and huge garden. There are two dining rooms, one with parquet floors and curving white walls with panoramic views, the other a more cosy *Stübli* in old red wood and antique furniture. Fresh fish and Swiss German dishes predominate.

WETTINGEN Sternen
⊞ 🍴 ⓕⓕⓕ

Klosterstrasse 9, 5430 **Tel** *056 427 14 61* **Road Map** *D2*

A charming and historic guesthouse on the monastery peninsula of the Limmat river, advertising itself as the oldest hotel in Switzerland, has its origins as a pub from the year 750. The cuisine is regional, with good vegetarian options. The interior is all carved wood and stone pillars. Garden with views of the cloisters.

WINTERTHUR Restaurant Pearl
🍴 ⓕⓕⓕ

Marktgasse 49, 8400 **Tel** *052 208 18 18* **Road Map** *E2*

In Winterthur city centre, this smart, minimalist-styled gourmet restaurant at the Hotel Krone serves a menu of both Mediterranean and Asian dishes for which chef Denis Ast has accrued 16 Gault Millau points. There is an extensive winelist featuring top-class European wines. Closed Sun and Mon, although group dinners can be arranged.

ZOFINGEN Schmiedstube
🏃 ♿ ⊞ 🍴 ⓕⓕ

Schmiedgasse 4, 4800 **Tel** *062 751 10 58* **Road Map** *E2*

An attractive old building set in its own cobbled courtyard with a garden and an atmospheric terrace for summer dining. The menu concentrates on meat dishes, particularly veal. There is a widespread collection of European wines, particularly from Italy and Spain; many in half bottles. Closed Sat evening and Sun.

ZÜRICH

ZÜRICH Ban Song Thai
ⓕⓕ

Kirchgasse 6, 8001 **Tel** *044 252 33 31* **Road Map** *E2*

Zürich's most celebrated Thai restaurant and arguably the best in the country, is located near the cathedral. There are only a dozen or so tables, but the interior is entirely non smoking. Organic beef is featured, and the entire menu is guaranteed free of MSG. Slowly rotating ceiling fans cool things down when the triple chilli dishes get too hot.

ZÜRICH Bodega Española
🎵 ⓕⓕ

Münstergasse 15, 8001 **Tel** *044 251 23 10* **Road Map** *E2*

A longstanding favourite with locals and tourists alike, this authentic Spanish restaurant on two floors stays open until midnight. The Sala Morisca on the ground floor is smoky and atmospheric, with a strolling guitar player, and serves tapas. Upstairs coats of arms and strings of onions and garlic serve as decor. The paella is renowned.

ZÜRICH Fribourger Fonduestuebli
♿ ⓕⓕ

Rotwandstrasse 38, 8004 **Tel** *044 241 90 76* **Road Map** *E2*

One of Zurich's best loved fondue restaurants. Diners are served in a wood-panelled dining room complete with prints and antiques. A good-value traditional menu that includes puddings the kids will love and a good range of kirsch. Closed Jun–Aug and not open for lunch from Apr to Sep.

ZÜRICH Hiltl
🏃 ♿ ⓕⓕ

Sihltrasse 28, 8001 **Tel** *044 227 70 00* **Road Map** *E2*

Cited in the Guinness Book of World Records as the oldest vegetarian restaurant in Europe, Hiltl dates from 1898. The restaurant is near the Paradeplatz tram stop. An imaginative and extensive menu, with lots of organic produce. No meat dishes at all. Buffet of Indian dishes and salad buffet. You pay by the weight of your plate.

ZÜRICH Josef
ⓕⓕ

Gasometerstrasse 24, 8005 **Tel** *044 271 65 95* **Road Map** *E2*

Hip and trendy once again after a design makeover by local DJ Rockmaster K. Atmospheric candlelit bar with posters of movie stars. The restaurant has shiny foil wall covering and tightly packed tables. The interesting menu makes no distinction between starters and main courses. Pick and mix concept. Great chocolate cake with cream.

ZÜRICH Lily's Stomach Supply
🍽 ⓕⓕ

Langstrasse 197, 8005 **Tel** *044 440 1885* **Road Map** *E2*

This bargain basement eatery with take out and home delivery is extremely popular with the young. It's located in an area with many night spots. Lily's does convenience fast food with a conscience, using many organic ingredients. The menu is "pan Asian" and only available in German, but the staff are happy to translate.

ZÜRICH Reithalle
🍽 🏃 ♿ ⊞ ⓕⓕ

Gessnerallee 8, 8001 **Tel** *044 212 07 66* **Road Map** *E2*

This former stables and riding hall retains the old wood pillars and beamed ceilings of a barn. It's a cool hangout for young Zürichers, with attitude to match. You sit at long, wooden communal tables inside or at picnic table in the large summer garden. Quite a varied menu, many vegetarian choices. Great chocolate cake with whipped cream.

ZÜRICH Brasserie Lipp
ⓕⓕⓕ

Uraniastrasse 9, 8001 **Tel** *043 888 66 66* **Road Map** *E2*

A real French brasserie with oysters, seafood and steaks in a *belle époque* ambience. The atmosphere is lively and the brasserie houses the only entry to the Jules Verne Panoramabar, an Art Deco observation platform for the best views in Zürich, with good cocktails, too.

ZÜRICH Helvetia Bar
👤♿ ⒻⒻⒻ

Stauffacherquai 1, 8004 **Tel** *044 297 99 99*   ***Road Map*** *E2*

Perhaps not the place for a quiet, romantic dinner, the Helvetia Bar (also known as the Helvti Bar) is generally jammed to the rafters with a jovial local crowd. All the same, it serves decent French bistro classics and Swiss fare at reasonable prices in a good location. The Helvetia's popularity means it is advisable to book ahead.

ZÜRICH King's Kurry
🍴 ⒻⒻⒻ

Freyastrasse 3, 8004 **Tel** *043 268 48 28*   ***Road Map*** *E2*

An authentic Indian restaurant serving some of the tastiest and spiciest curries in Zürich. The short menu features tandoori starters and dishes from around India accompanied by naan breads. The original restaurant is now part of a chain of takeaways expanding throughout the city. Closed Sunday.

ZÜRICH Ristorante Cinque
♿🍴🍷 ⒻⒻⒻ

Langstrasse 215, 8005 **Tel** *044 272 46 30*   ***Road Map*** *E2*

This genuine Italian restaurant close to the Hauptbahnhof has a bric-a-brac heavy interior that is rustic and cosy. Homemade pasta is the order of the day, but the meat and fish dishes are also popular with the locals. Diners can enjoy their meals on a pleasant terrace in summer. Closed Sat lunch, Sun and Mon.

ZÜRICH Sala of Tokyo
🍴 ⒻⒻⒻ

Limmatstrasse 29, 8005 **Tel** *044 271 52 90*   ***Road Map*** *E2*

Sala was the first sushi bar to open in Switzerland in 1983. The small, intimate restaurant still serves laquered trays of fresh, tasty sushi and sashimi in a location that is conveniently close to the Hauptbahnhof. The menu also features yakitori, teriyaki and tempura dishes. Takeaways are also available. Closed Sun and Mon.

ZÜRICH Kronenhalle
👤🍷 ⒻⒻⒻ

Rämistrasse 4, 8001 **Tel** *044 262 99 00*   ***Road Map*** *E2*

An unmissable Zürich institution, as compelling for its interior as for its cooking. The dark-panelled walls contain original artwork from Picasso, Matisse and Braque. The restaurant is always filled with locals, as well as tourists. Swiss German dishes vie with French classics on the menu, and portions are generous. The chocolate mousse is famous.

ZÜRICH Rico's Kunststuben
♿🍴🍷 ⒻⒻⒻⒻ

Seestrasse 160, 8700 **Tel** *044 910 17 15*   ***Road Map*** *E2*

A favourite haunt of gourmets, who frequently claim this is the best restaurant in Switzerland. It stands just outside Zürich in the pretty lakeside village of Küsnacht. Impeccable experimental dishes justify the restaurant's two Michelin stars and 18 Gault Millau points. Closed Sun and Mon.

ZÜRICH Rigiblick
🍴🍷 ⒻⒻⒻⒻ

Germaniastrasse 99, 8044 **Tel** *043 255 15 70*   ***Road Map*** *E2*

A superb gourmet restaurant and bistro, not very well known, in a fortress-like building in a wooded area. The dining room "Spice", in keeping with the light and creative Pan Asian-influenced cooking, is of contemporary design, with wooden floors and ample space between tables. Very clean and airy. Inspired cuisine. Closed Sun and Mon.

ZÜRICH Zunfthaus zum Rüden
🍷 ⒻⒻⒻⒻ

Limmatquai 42, 8001 **Tel** *044 261 95 66*   ***Road Map*** *E2*

The architecture is stunning, but the menu is even more compelling. The "House of the Hounds", as the name translates, has a Gothic dining hall with an 11 m (36 ft) high curved wooden ceiling, and dark wood wainscoting. French cuisine dominates the menu, with special attention to game, vegetables and mushrooms as they come into season.

ZÜRICH Restaurant Mesa
🍷 ⒻⒻⒻⒻⒻ

Weinbergstrasse 75, 8006 **Tel** *043 321 75 75*   ***Road Map*** *E2*

A visit to this elegant restaurant with two Michelin stars and 18 Gault Millau points is a real culinary experience. The menu changes weekly, with the seven-course tasting menu and matching wines coming highly recommended. Excellent service and great attention to detail make for a memorable meal. Closed Sun and Mon.

EASTERN SWITZERLAND & GRAUBÜNDEN

APPENZELL Appenzell
👤♿🍴 ⒻⒻ

Am Landsgemeindeplatz, 9050 **Tel** *071 788 15 15*   ***Road Map*** *F2*

Located in the Appenzell Hotel, with its own pastry shop on the premises. The breakfasts are accordingly superb, as are afternoon teas. The dining room is of museum quality: carved wood ceiling, parquet floors, antique tables. The menu is moderately priced, the cooking modern, based on fresh ingredients. Good vegetarian choices. Kids' menus.

ARBON Braukeller Frohsinn
👤🍴 ⒻⒻ

Romanshornerstrasse 15, 9320 **Tel** *71 447 84 84*   ***Road Map*** *F2*

A large half-timbered hotel and restaurant with its own on-site brewery. There is a beer cellar serving sausages, snacks and steaks. Aside from the separate bistro, there is also the fine dining fish restaurant, which serves meats and vegetarian dishes, too. All the restaurants use organic ingredients wherever possible. Closed Mon.

AROSA Gspan

Dorf, 7050 **Tel** *081 377 14 94*

Road Map *F4*

Chalet-style hotel and restaurant with a summer garden and terrace with great views. The menu has some interesting Graubünden dishes, such as various kinds of dumplings. There is a small wine collection, mostly Swiss wines with a few Italian and French. There is also an old rustic hut on the grounds where grilled meats are the speciality.

BAD RAGAZ Gasthof Loewen

Loewenstrasse 5, 7310 **Tel** *081 302 13 06*

Road Map *F3*

In an elegant building dating from the early 1800s, Gasthof Loewen has a fresh white and wood interior and a pretty riverside garden. It offers Swiss and European cuisine with an emphasis on seasonal produce and locally-sourced ingredients. The winelist is well priced and the choice of grappas and other liquors is impressive. Closed 3 weeks in Oct.

CHUR Va Bene

Gäuggelistrasse 60, 7000 **Tel** *081 258 78 02*

Road Map *F3*

Situated in the city centre, this restaurant serves Mediterranean and Swiss dishes with considerable culinary flair to an enthusiastic clientele. Diners are mostly locals, but it is attracting an increasing number of tourists. The airy and attractive Art Deco dining room leads to an open-air terrace. Open 365 days a year.

DAVOS La Carretta

Talstrasse 2, 7270 **Tel** *081 413 32 16*

Road Map *F3*

An Italian restaurant in Davos Platz serving a wide range of home-made pasta with imaginative fillings and Swiss-styled dishes. Try the saltimbocca alla Romana. In addition to many Swiss wines there is a comprehensive collection of Italian wines at various price levels, including hard to find Abruzzi vintages. Great desserts as well.

GLARUS Schützenhaus

Schützenhausstrasse 55, 8750 **Tel** *055 640 10 52*

Road Map *E3*

A historic restaurant on the southern edge of Glarus with two dining areas. The entire building is accessible by wheelchair. The spacious bistro *(Stube)* has polished wooden floors. The renovated main dining room retains an antique feel. Simple, inexpensive home cooking with local specialities like noodles and dumplings. Closed Mon and Tue.

KLOSTERS Rustico

Landstrasse 194, 7250 **Tel** *081 410 22 88*

Road Map *F3*

A Swiss-influenced menu with an occasional nod to Asian cuisine is on offer at this family-run hotel restaurant. Elegant dishes such as monkfish medallion or veal steak in a rich porcini sauce are available alongside hearty no-nonsense sausage and fries in onion gravy or cheese and egg on toast.

KREUZLINGEN Zum Blauen Haus

Hauptstrasse 138, 8280 **Tel** *071 688 24 98*

Road Map *F2*

On the eastern edge of town, this attractive 18th-century villa isn't really blue, as its name suggests, but white with blue crisscrossed timber supports. The house speciality is meats, or prawns, grilled over an open wood fire. The restaurant prides itself on the collection of 30 different single malt whiskies. Live piano music evenings. Closed Sun.

POSCHIAVO Ristorante Albrici

Famiglia Zanolari, 7742 **Tel** *081 844 01 73*

Road Map *G4*

In a 17th-century building featuring whitewashed walls, stone and wood, is this friendly, family-run hotel restaurant. It offers excellent quality, good-value meals, including Neapolitan-style pizzas made in a genuine wood-burning oven and regional specialities such as *pizzoccheri* (a type of short tagliatelle). There is outside dining in a pretty piazza.

RAPPERSWIL Villa Aurum

Alte Jonastrasse 23, 8640 **Tel** *055 220 72 82*

Road Map *E3*

Restored city centre villa dating from the 19th century, with a large shady garden for summer dining. The formal dining room has parquet floors and large windows, while the atmospheric cellar dining area has huge vaulted rooms. The cuisine focuses on local organic seasonal products. Good mix of fish, meat and vegetarian offerings. Closed Sun and Mon.

RORSCHACH Aqua Fine Dining

Churerstrasse 28, 9400 **Tel** *071 858 39 80*

Road Map *F2*

The fine dining room of the lakeside Seerestaurant Rorschach, five minutes from the port, has frequent theme evenings, such as Italian night and retro 1960s evenings. In the same building are the Regatta Lounge and Café Lago, and there is a huge summer beer garden on the lake shore as well as a theatre building and a brewery.

SCHAFFHAUSEN zum Adler

Vorstadt 69, 8200 **Tel** *052 625 55 15*

Road Map *E2*

A comfortable *Gasthaus* atmosphere, with good home cooking and a loyal local clientele, situated in the heart of the Old Town. Several inexpensive set menu options (including kids' menus) and a good choice of house wines at modest prices. Plenty of fish and vegetarian items, or try the speciality: beef, lamb and pork filets with the famous house sauce.

SCHAFFHAUSEN Schlössli-Wörth

Rheinfallquai, Neuhausen, 8212 **Tel** *052 672 24 21*

Road Map *E2*

Splendid gourmet restaurant in a tower with views of the famous Rheinfall. The chef describes his cooking as "experimental with an element of fantasy". The presentation is imaginative, indeed. Succulent fish, vegetarian menu. Children have their own menu and playroom, and on Sunday afternoons there is a teacher to watch over them.

Key to Price Guide *see p268* **Key to Symbols** *see back cover flap*

SCHAFFHAUSEN Fischerzunft   ⓕⓕⓕⓕⓕ

Rheinquai 8, 8200 **Tel** *052 632 05 05*   **Road Map** *E2*

An exceptional gourmet restaurant on the banks of the Rhein (*see p256*). André Jaeger has twice been named chef of the year by Gault Millau and awarded 19 points. The restaurant is both a Relais et Châteaux member and one of the Grandes Tables du Monde. Tasting menu only. Lovely terrace, lavishly decorated dining room, vast wine cellar.

SCUOL Nam Thai   ⓕⓕ

Im Bogn Engiadina, 7550 **Tel** *081 864 81 43*   **Road Map** *G3*

One of the few authentic Asian restaurants in this region of the Engadine. Fairly upmarket with a wide range of dishes, including some spicy Szechuan items. Experienced connoisseurs should ask for the real thing, because otherwise these spicy dishes are moderated in taste so as not to overwhelm the taste buds of more delicate diners.

SILS-FEXTAL Chesa Pool   ⓕⓕ

Dorf, 7514 **Tel** *081 838 59 00*   **Road Map** *F4*

Worth the 20-minute hike from Sils-Maria on the road outside St Moritz, this 400-year-old guest house in the car-free hamlet of Fextal offers utter tranquillity. Only local organic items are used in the kitchen. There is a good wine cellar with local wines. Twice a day the hotel ferries guests back and forth to Sils.

ST GALLEN Tres Amigos   ⓕⓕ

Hechtgasse 1, 9004 **Tel** *071 222 25 06*   **Road Map** *F2*

A lively and inexpensive fast-food franchise serving Mexican food exclusively, and extensively. Everything from tortilla chips to burritos and enchiladas and fajitas. Interesting desserts, such as *helado borracho*, a lemon sorbet with tequila. Wines from Mexico, Spain and South America and a good choice of Mexican beers.

ST GALLEN Schoren   ⓕⓕⓕ

Dufourstrasse 150, 9000 **Tel** *071 999 09 09*   **Road Map** *F2*

A popular eatery, known for its roasted meats and elegant but cosy feel. There are several dining areas and a winter terrace. Good choice of fish dishes, and the grilled lamb is superb. Americans will be delighted to know that the Schoren's apple pie comes loaded with a scoop of vanilla ice cream on top, just like in the USA.

ST MORITZ Hanselmann   ⓕⓕ

Via Maistra 8, 7500 **Tel** *081 833 38 64*   **Road Map** *F4*

An institution in St Moritz, and not to be missed by anyone with a sweet tooth. Famous for its Engadine *Nusstorte* (nut cakes), Hanselmann's is also a kind of monument to how things used to be done. The pastries, chocolates and truffles are superb. Light meals are also served. Good place for spotting celebrities.

ST MORITZ Mathis Food's La Marmite   ⓕⓕⓕⓕ

Corviglia, 7500 **Tel** *081 833 63 55*   **Road Map** *F4*

La Marmite is where the concept of haute cuisine at high altitude was first conceived. The interior, inside the lift station building at Corviglia, is not lavish, but the menu is heaped with caviar and truffles, with at least one dish priced at over CHF 400. Far more modestly priced dishes, like the beef stroganoff, are always available, however.

ST MORITZ (CHAMPFER) Talvo by Dalsass   ⓕⓕⓕⓕⓕ

Via Gunels 15, Champfèr, 7512 **Tel** *081 833 44 55*   **Road Map** *F4*

An exceptional gourmet restaurant with 18 Gault Millau points and Michelin-starred Martin Dalsass at the helm. Located in the middle of an old farming village outside St Moritz, the Talvo (hayloft) menu is indescribable, and always changing, with fresh seafood every day from Milan.

STEIN AM RHEIN Restaurant Adler   ⓕⓕⓕ

Rathausplatz 2, 8260 **Tel** *052 742 61 61*   **Road Map** *E2*

In the historic centre of this scenic village, the Adler has one of the most impressive façades. The restaurant serves high quality, regional food and the wine list is varied, with plenty of bottles under 50 CHF. Reserve a table on the outdoor terrace in the warmer months.

STEIN AM RHEIN Rheingerbe   ⓕⓕⓕ

Schifflände 5, 8260 **Tel** *052 741 29 91*   **Road Map** *E2*

A historic 16th-century building, once a tannery, houses this elegant hotel restaurant with a riverbank terrace offering lovely views. Fresh ingredients from local farms, and fresh fish, are the mainstay of the menu. The presentation is stunning and there is a good choice of regional wines. Reserve early to get a good spot on the terrace.

VADUZ Sonnenhof   ⓕⓕⓕ

Mareetstrasse 29, 9490 **Tel** *0423 239 02 02*   **Road Map** *F3*

Under chef Hubertus Real, this Michelin-starred restaurant in the Hotel Sonnenhof (see p257) serves some of the best food in the country. Food is modern European and daily lunch menus are very well priced. The restaurant is elegantly furnished while the outside terrace has spectacular mountain views. Closed Sat lunch.

WEINFELDEN Pulcinella im Schwert   ⓕⓕⓕ

Wilerstrasse 8, 8570 **Tel** *071 622 12 66*   **Road Map** *E2*

Highly regarded small Italian restaurant near the train station in the middle of Weinfelden. It is seldom visited by tourists, but has a local reputation for modest prices and lovingly prepared Italian and local specialities, including home-made pasta. There is a decent wine list of local and Swiss wines, and some Italian. Closed Sun and Mon.

CENTRAL SWITZERLAND & TICINO

ALTDORF Goldener Schlüssel ⛓ ⛓ ⛓ ⓕⓕⓕ
Schützengasse 9, 6460 **Tel** *041 871 20 02* **Road Map** *E3*

The Golden Key has two dining rooms in an 18th-century building in Altdorf. It is one of the best known gourmet restaurants in the area, with 13 Gault Millau points. The extensive wine list ranges across Europe, but not to the Americas or Australia. The large whisky collection, however, knows no such boundaries. Closed Sun and Mon.

ASCONA Piazza au Lac ⛓ ⛓ ⓕⓕ
Lungolago Motta 29, 6612 **Tel** *091 791 11 81* **Road Map** *E5*

Amazingly good value, this small restaurant in the hotel of the same name serves pizzas and pasta as well as a variety of Mediterranean and Ticino dishes. The polenta is particularly good. The restaurant is situated in a pedestrian zone right by the lake shore. The terrace has great views. Good desserts, and very good ice cream.

BECKENRIED Panorama Berggasthaus Klewenalp ⛓ ⛓ ⛓ ⓕⓕ
Postfach, 6375 **Tel** *041 620 29 22* **Road Map** *D3*

A large mountain restaurant, with ample room for groups, at the top of the ski lift system. There are large sun terraces both in summer and winter. The menu offers typical mountain fare, from fondues to meat platters. There are regularly scheduled fairs and music events at the restaurant, including jazz, country and western and rock evenings and weekends.

BELLINZONA Cantinin del Gatt ⛓ ⓕⓕ
Vicolo al Sasso 4, 6500 **Tel** *091 825 27 71* **Road Map** *E5*

An opportunity to taste Ticinese dishes in this beautiful vaulted dining room at the heart of the canton's capital. Dishes featuring seasonal, locally-sourced ingredients are presented with flair. Try the rabbit with wild garlic, risotto flavoured with saffron and courgette, or wild boar and polenta. Closed Sun and Mon in summer; 3 weeks end Jul to mid-Aug.

BURGENSTOCK Tintoretto ⛓ ⛓ ⓕⓕ
Burgenstock, 6363 **Tel** *041 612 90 16* **Road Map** *D3*

Just one of several restaurants in the resort, Tintoretto serves Mediterranean inspired food with regional Italian specialities and wine tasting available on the last Friday of the month. The views of Lake Lucerne from the sun terrace and elevated dining room are spectacular. Open all day in the skiing season. Closed Nov–mid-Mar.

EINSIEDELN Linde ⛓ ⛓ ⛓ ⛓ ⓕⓕⓕ
Klosterplatz Schmiedenstrasse 28, 8840 **Tel** *055 418 48 48* **Road Map** *E3*

This restaurant with attentive service and a gourmet menu, awarded 14 Gault Millau points, is located in an imposing stone hotel in the town centre. Lovely dining room with wooden floors covered in Oriental rugs, carved wood ceiling. Known for handmade pasta and fresh fish dishes and a good range of vegetarian gourmet items. Closed Wed.

ENGELBERG Hotel Bänklialp ⛓ ⛓ ⛓ ⓕⓕ
Postfach, 6390 **Tel** *041 639 73 73* **Road Map** *D3*

Restaurant in a chalet-style hotel on the edge of the village surrounded by forest. There are five dining rooms, each with a different character but all serving Swiss specialities like fondues and *rösti*. There are frequent musical evenings with accordion music and folk singing. The wine list concentrates on Swiss, Austrian and Spanish offerings.

KUSSNACHT AM RIGI Engel ⛓ ⛓ ⓕⓕ
Hauptplatz 1, 6403 **Tel** *041 850 92 17* **Road Map** *D3*

Imaginative and strikingly presented cuisine. The building is a museum of antiques and carved wood. Of the three dining rooms, one dates back more than 450 years and the other over 660 years. The restaurant has many theme menus geared to the seasons or holidays. Cooking courses are regularly held here.

LOCARNO Casa del Popolo ⛓ ⛓ ⛓ ⓕⓕ
Piazza Corporazioni, 6600 **Tel** *091 751 12 08* **Road Map** *E5*

An inexpensive yet attractive and characterful restaurant in the pedestrian zone of the Old Town. The prices and quality of the food ensure a good crowd of Locarno citizens every night of the week. Perfectly prepared pasta, *filets de peche* and the house speciality *carpaccio de cheval*. The outside dining area is popular; reservations recommended.

LOCARNO La Cittadella Trattoria ⛓ ⛓ ⓕⓕⓕ
Via Cittadella 18, 6600 **Tel** *091 751 58 85* **Road Map** *E5*

This restaurant occupies two floors in a rose-coloured stone building in the heart of the Old Town in a quiet pedestrian zone. Downstairs the trattoria has a wood-burning pizza oven, and seafood is the theme. Upstairs in a more elegant dining room, fish and shellfish are more elaborately prepared. Closed Mon.

LUGANO Colibrí ⛓ ⛓ ⓕⓕ
Via Aldesago 91, Aldesago, 6974 **Tel** *091 971 42 42* **Road Map** *E5*

Hotel restaurant on Monte Brè, 15 minutes by tram or car from downtown Lugano. Sublime panoramic views, and an outdoor terrace overlooking the lake. Prices are modest and the cuisine is unpretentious, as is the restaurant decor. Daily fixed menu as well as wide choice of vegetarian dishes. Closed Jan and Feb.

Key to Price Guide *see p268* **Key to Symbols** *see back cover flap*

LUGANO (CASSARATE) Arté

Viale Castagnola 31, 6906 **Tel** *091 973 48 00* **Road Map** *E5*

At Lugano's only Michelin-starred restaurant (in the Grand Hotel Villa Castagnola), diners can enjoy a changing exhibition of contemporary art and sculpture while feasting on chef Frank Oerthle's lake fish and seafood specialities. Also on offer are excellent wines and breathtaking views over Lake Lugano. Closed Mon.

LUZERN Gennaro

Töpferstrasse 5, 6002 **Tel** *041 410 26 64* **Road Map** *D3*

In the heart of the Old Town, with an outdoor paved terrace covered by an awning, Gennaro is open until 11pm every evening. The specialities include the Luzern *Kügelipastete*, a kind of *vol-au-vent* dish first brought to Switzerland in the Middle Ages by Spanish mercenaries, and seafood of all kinds. Take-away is also available.

LUZERN Hofgarten

Stadthofstrasse 14, 6006 **Tel** *041 410 88 88* **Road Map** *D3*

This historic half-timbered building houses a hotel as well as a restaurant. The extensive vegetarian menu features homemade pasta stuffed with organic vegetables and tofu with a chilli sauce. There is a large winter garden with 60 seats as well as sunny summer dining area. Books and drawing materials are provided to keep children occupied.

LUZERN La Terrazza

Metzgerrainle 9, 6400 **Tel** *041 410 36 31* **Road Map** *D3*

Specializing in Italian fare that includes pizza, risotto, bruschetta and pasta, this is a popular and good-value riverside restaurant. The modern decor contrasts stylishly with the high ceilings and vaulted alcoves. The tables are set fairly close together, but this intimacy proves popular with the young, local crowd.

LUZERN Old Swiss House

Löwenplatz 4, 6002 **Tel** *041 410 61 71* **Road Map** *D3*

This landmark half-timbered house in the city centre near the Lion Monument has fabulous decor, with oil paintings and a wooden interior. The innovative cuisine is impeccably presented, deserving its 15 Gault Millau points. The *Wienerschnitzel* simply cannot be missed. Wine cellar with 30,000 bottles includes Château Mouton Rothschild from 1911 onwards.

RIGI KALTBAD Bergsonne

Postfach, 6356 **Tel** *041 399 80 10* **Road Map** *D3*

This old-fashioned sprawling mountain hotel and restaurant lies just above the car-free village, and guests can request transport by the restaurant's electric taxi. Tremendous views. There are four dining areas, 15 Gault Millau points, and fresh ingredients from local farms. Fish is a favourite. Inspiring presentation and fine wines.

SCHWYZ Adelboden

Schlagstrasse, Steinen, 6422 **Tel** *041 832 12 42* **Road Map** *E3*

A historic 18th-century family guesthouse in the hamlet of Steinen near the Lauerzer lake, just a few minutes' drive from downtown Schwyz. The cuisine is of a high standard with 18 Gault Millau points and two Michelin stars. Traditional French haute cuisine incorporating regional influences. Closed Sun and Mon; end Jul–mid-Aug.

STANS Cubasia

Stansstaderstrasse 20a, 6370 **Tel** *041 619 71 71* **Road Map** *D3*

An unusual restaurant, housed within an otherwise uninspiring hotel in the centre of Stans. The cuisine is a spicy mix of Chinese and Cuban, usually found only in New York or Miami, and fostered by Chinese chefs fleeing Cuba during the Castro regime. The Havana noodles are great. Lively music and hearty food.

VAL DI BLENIO Acquacalda

Strada del Lucomagno, 6718 **Tel** *091 872 26 10* **Road Map** *E5*

The restaurant of the Centro Ecologico UomoNatura (Man and Nature Ecological Centre), at the far end of a remote wooded valley, has a simple but attractive glassed-in dining terrace. Here you'll find healthy dishes of fresh trout with local herbs, risotto with porcini mushrooms, and cakes made from mountain berries. Organic products from local farmers.

VERSCIO Grotto Pedemonte

Stradon, 6653 **Tel** *091 796 20 83* **Road Map** *E5*

In the village of Verscio, ten minutes from Centovalli train stop, is this popular restaurant in a stone building. Outside there are granite tables, fig trees and mountain views. The menu features regional dishes such as polenta, pasta, and cured and grilled meats. Cold dishes served between lunch and dinner. Closed Wed (spring and autumn); Nov–Mar.

WEGGIS Annex

Hertensteinstrasse 34, 6353 **Tel** *041 392 05 05* **Road Map** *D3*

The primary gourmet restaurant of the Relais et Châteaux Park Hotel Weggis, with 16 Gault Millau points and one Michelin star. A tempting blend of traditional French and harmonious Asian and Mediterranean inspiration. There are two other restaurants. Immense attention to detail: the tableware, for example, was specially designed by Versace. Closed Tue.

ZUG Liguria

Fischmarkt 2, 6300 **Tel** *041 729 81 46* **Road Map** *E3*

This used to be the well-known Hecht am See. It has been renovated, but keeps the same views of the Zugsee. The theme of the menu is pasta and fish, the one home made and the other freshly caught – and both changing according to the season. The wine list is strictly Italian, including bottles from Sardinia and Sicily.

SPORTS AND OUTDOOR ACTIVITIES

The Swiss are among the fittest, healthiest and most active people in the world. There is something in the Swiss air that makes you want to go outside and play. The first winter tourists (Brits in St Moritz in 1864) did exactly that – they grabbed sledges local farmers used for hauling wood and invented the sports that have evolved into luge

Colourful hot air balloon

and bobsleigh Olympic events. Swiss sports are all about participating, rather than watching. Whatever you do there is almost always a spectacular view of cool pine forests, tiny alpine lakes or the sun glistening on a glacial tier of ice. You can feel secure knowing that Swiss guides are at the top of their professions.

Sledging near Klosters village in Graubünden

WINTER SPORTS

Sledging (sledding) is the oldest winter sport in Switzerland, and still one of the most popular with Swiss families. Even resorts with no skiing have sledge runs, some open at night. Grindelwald has a sledge run 15 km (9 miles) long (see p82). Variations on traditional sledging include snowtubing, where oversized inner tubes are used, and snow rafting, where a rubber boat slides down a prepared piste.

Snowshoeing has become a popular sport, especially among families and with hikers who can now access winter paths and pastures. Mountain guides also lead more ambitious treks, often to remote valleys. Snowshoers should always check local avalanche conditions before heading off marked trails.

Almost every Swiss village has an outdoor ice-skating rink, with shrieks of children conveying a winter carnival

atmosphere. Most resorts also have spacious indoor rinks used for figure skating and hockey games. Curling, a kind of bowls on ice, is taken seriously, especially since the Swiss women's team won a silver medal at the 2006 Winter Olympics. In resorts like Davos and Wengen, holidaymakers are encouraged to join in hockey and curling matches with pick-up teams.

Switzerland is not short on spectator sports, either. And naturally St Moritz, the birthplace of winter holidays, leads the world. Nowhere else has an annual gourmet festival with banquets on ice, as well as horse racing, cricket, polo and golf tournaments all conducted on the frozen lake (see p33). Children especially love the dog-sled races, held across Switzerland, where teams of huskies mush through snowy forest trails.

Climbing artificial ice towers or frozen waterfalls, an ice axe in each hand and crampons

to kick out footholds, is burgeoning in Switzerland. The world championships have been held in Saas Fee on three occasions (see p90).

Uniquely refreshing is the sport of ice diving at Lake Lioson, 1,900 m (6,232 ft) above Lake Geneva in canton Vaud. Here, divers in wet suits and scuba tanks drop through a hole in the frozen lake, and swim with the fish.

CLIMBING

With mountains like the Matterhorn and the Eiger, Switzerland attracts climbers of every ability from all over the world. Rock climbers, in their skimpy shorts and ballet-slipper-like shoes, are relative newcomers compared to mountain climbers with their mania for "bagging" summits higher than 4,000 m (13,000 ft). It was actually the British, not the Swiss, who were the first mountain

Rock climbing in the Swiss Alps, with clear blue skies and sunshine

Summer hiking along a beautiful alpine lake

climbers. Edward Whymper famously conquered the Matterhorn in 1865 *(see p90).*

Rock climbing (also called free climbing), with its technical bias for inching up sheer walls with almost invisible finger and toe-holds, has spawned a fad for indoor climbing walls, now found everywhere in Switzerland.

Summit-seekers, in all weathers and seasons, will find Swiss guides ready to teach and accompany them on routes from Ticino to the Jura to the famous peaks of the Bernese Oberland, Valais and Graubünden. Crampons, ice axes, harnesses and other gear are all available for hire in mountaineering resorts.

HIKING

No nation offers such a variety of hiking environments, so well signposted and integrated into the national system of postal buses *(see p307),* which reach even the remotest hamlet. Tourist offices organize theme hikes, such as identifying mushrooms, collecting butterflies, touring vineyards and walking from gourmet restaurant to gourmet restaurant. On some hikes, mules or llamas will carry your baggage.

From flat strolls through parkland to risky ledges (often with steel cables for attaching a safety harness to) and glacier crossings, Switzerland has over 60,000 km (38,000 miles) of marked trails. In summer, resorts operate ski lifts to provide easy access to high pastures, from where many hikes begin.

In summer it is possible to walk right across the rooftop of the Alps, from Saas Fee in Switzerland to Chamonix in France, even taking in Aosta in Italy. First accomplished by the British in the early 20th century, this itinerary is called the *Haute Route.* Hikers sleep in high altitude refuges built by the Swiss Alpine Club *(see p289).* Each one is a day's march apart.

Hikers should ensure their insurance covers helicopter rescue, and leave word with innkeepers or the local tourist office of their route and estimated return time.

SKY SPORTS

The only way to fully appreciate the vast size and splendour of Switzerland's wilderness of glaciers, peaks and blue ice crevasses is to see it from the air. Hour-long

sightseeing flights in small planes or helicopters, from Bern, Zürich or Sion airports, are surprisingly inexpensive.

Hot-air balloons cannot fly over the Alps, but the views are still enchanting, as is the flying experience itself. There are more than 500 balloons and 50 flight centres in Switzerland. Château d'Oex has a microclimate ideal for balloon flights *(see p33).* Crans-Montana, Verbier and Davos have all held balloon festivals.

Paragliding in the alpine air is unique, both because of the exceptional thermal lift and the enormous vertical descents that are possible. Flying as a passenger is also tremendous fun, and no experience is required. Various schools also offer holiday courses in which you can work towards the internationally recognized Swiss paragliding licence.

WATER SPORTS

With its alpine lakes, glacier-fed rivers and majestic waterfalls, Switzerland is a natural playground for water sports. Swiss sailors stunned the world in 2003 and 2007, when the Swiss yacht *Alinghi* won the America's Cup. Sailing boats, steam-powered paddle wheel excursion boats, dinghies, canoes and kayaks all set forth on the blue water lakes of Geneva, Constance and Neuchâtel, and down the rivers Rhône and Rhine.

Paragliding over snow-covered mountains in the Bernese Oberland

Windsurfing – a popular sport on Swiss lakes

Every lake has its summer swimming *plage* (beach). The rivers host innovative water sports like "hydro-speed" (a hybrid of free swimming and rafting) as well as traditional rafting, water-skiing and floating down quiet stretches in oversized inner tubes.

Windsurfing is also popular, the smaller lakes providing ideal learning centres. Aqua parks with slides and spouts also abound. In Bern, each summer evening the burghers hike a few miles up the river Aare, then plunge into the swift current to float back to town, a tradition dating back to medieval times.

CYCLING

Both mountain bikes and racing cycles are available for rent almost everywhere in Switzerland, not least at many train stations *(see p307)*. There are nine national bike routes on paved roads totalling 3,300 km (2,000 miles). In addition there are numerous off-road routes over mountain passes and through deserted hamlets.

For pure fun, especially for the less fit and family groups, there is downhill-only mountain biking. In summer, Swiss ski resorts modify the ski lifts to carry cycles up to 3,000 m (10,000 ft) or more. From these heights dirt roads and grassy tracks meander down through fields of wildflowers to the valley floor below. More adventurous cyclists can take the specially prepared hard-core itineraries

with jumps and expert-only trails skirting cliffs. To protect the environment and separate family hikers from cyclists, some resorts limit cyclists to specially marked trails.

ADVENTURE SPORTS

Bungee jumping and canyoning (descending ravines by jumping cliffs and sliding over rocks) remain popular high-adrenaline sports. The bungee jump from the Verzasca Dam near Locarno is cited as one of the biggest in the world, at 220 m (722 ft). But now there are new ways to fly down canyons, tethered at all times to a steel security cable.

At Saas Fee's Fairy Gorge and Grindelwald's Spider Highway holidaymakers with no experience can zip across networks of steel cables and swing out over dizzying heights in perfect safety.

A similar experience flying across a lake near Engelberg is called the "flying fox". Many resorts also have networks of rope bridges strung high in the treetops called *sentiers suspendus* or suspended pathways.

Exploring caves with a professional guide is also fun. Two of the world's ten biggest caves are in Switzerland: the Hoelloch system in Schwyz and the Muttee in canton Bern.

LEISURE SPORTS

Among the many reasons for golfing in the scenic Swiss Alps, consider that any drive on the high altitude championship course at Crans-Montana, home of the European Masters tournament, will travel 20 m (65 ft) further than at home. Many courses offer spectacular views of lakes and mountains.

Tennis courts (both outdoor and indoor) are dotted all over Switzerland, as you would expect in the home country of Roger Federer, the Swiss ace. Most surfaces are red clay or "synthetic grass", both much easier on the knees than the hard courts commonly found in North America.

Horse riding is an ideal way to see parts of the Swiss countryside that are otherwise ignored. A unique breed of horse, the Franches-Montagnes from Jura, is exceptionally easy to ride and train, the perfect horse for excursions *(see p133)*.

Mountain biking in the Swiss Alps

DIRECTORY

WINTER SPORTS

Cresta Tobogganing Club
Via Ruinatsch 9,
7500 St Moritz.
Tel 081 832 20 52.
www.cresta-run.com

Ice Diving Lake Lioson
Restaurant du Lac Lioson,
1862 Les Mosses.
Tel 024 491 11 44.
www.lesmosses.ch

Pradaschier Toboggan Ride
Postfach,
7075 Churwalden.
Tel 081 356 22 07.
www.pradaschier.ch

Snowtubing
Tourist Office,
1862 La Lécherette.
Tel 024 491 14 66.
www.lesmosses.ch

St Moritz Polo Club
Via Maistra 24,
7500 St Moritz.
Tel 081 839 92 92
www.polostmoritz.com

Swiss Alpine Guides
Postfach 29,
3800 Interlaken.
Tel 033 822 60 00.
www.swissalpineguides.ch

Swiss Guides
Case Postale, 1936 Verbier.
Tel 079 446 22 89.
www.swissguides.com

Swiss Ice Skating Instructors Association
In der Brunnmatt 1,
8103 Unterengstringen.
Tel 079 679 03 17.
www.selv.ch

Swiss Skating Association
Haus des Sportes, Postfach
606, 3000 Bern 22.
Tel 031 382 06 60.
www.skating.ch

Swiss Sled Dog Association
Mühleschwendi,
6314 Unteraegeri.
Tel 041 750 94 75.
www.schlittenhundesport
klub.ch

CLIMBING

Bergschule Uri Mountain Reality
Postfach 141,
6490 Andermatt.
Tel 041 872 09 00.
www.bergschule-uri.ch

Swiss Alpine Club
Monbijoustr. 61,
3000 Bern 23.
Tel 031 370 18 18.
www.sac-cas.ch

Swiss Indoor Climbing Walls
www.indoorclimbing.com

Swiss Mountain Guides Association
Hadlaubstrasse 49,
8006 Zürich.
Tel 044 360 53 66.
www.4000plus.ch

Swiss Rock Guides
www.swissrockguides.
com

HIKING

Adrenaline Mountain Guides
Case Postale 54,
1936 Verbier.
Tel 027 771 74 59.
www.guides-verbier.com

Eurotrek
Dörflistrasse 30,
8057 Zürich.
Tel 044 316 10 00.
www.eurotrek.ch

Swiss Hiking Association
Monbijoustr. 61, 3007 Bern.
Tel 031 370 10 20.
www.swisshiking.ch

Trekking Team
Casa Rossina, 6652 Tegna.
Tel 091 780 78 00.
www.trekking.ch

SKY SPORTS

Air Glaciers Helicopters
Sion Airport, 1951, Sion.
Tel 027 329 14 15.
www.air-glaciers.ch

Fly Time Paragliding
La Gare, 1934 Le Chable.
Tel 079 606 12 64.
www.fly-time.ch

Scenic Air Flights
Postfach 412,
3800 Interlaken.
Tel 033 821 00 11.
www.scenicair.ch

Swiss Balloon Association
Postfach 16,
4124 Schönenbuch, Basel.
Tel 061 481 32 22.
www.sbav.ch

WATER SPORTS

Aqua Park
Route de la Plage,
1897 Le Bouveret.
Tel 024 482 00 11.
www.aquaparc.ch

Swiss Adventures
Alpinzentrum, 3780 Gstaad.
Tel 084 816 11 61.
www.swissadventures.ch

Swiss Sailing Federation
Laubeggstrasse 70,
3000 Bern 22.
Tel 031 359 72 66.
www.swiss-sailing.ch

Swiss Windsurf Association
www.windsurf.ch

Swiss Windsurf Spot Guide
www.intermagnus.com/re
nato/windsurf/

Swissraft
Punt Arsa Promenade 19,
7013 Domat/Ems.
Tel 081 911 52 50.
www.swissraft.ch

CYCLING

Alpen Cross Mountain Biking
Gerbestrasse 8b,
8840 Einsiedeln.
Tel 078 818 48 58.
www.alpencross.ch

Bike Switzerland
22 Rue des Grottes,
1201 Geneva.
Tel 078 601 69 57.
www.bikeswitzerland.com

Veloland Schweiz
Spitalgasse 34, 3011 Bern.
Tel 031 318 01 28.
www.veloland.ch

ADVENTURE SPORTS

Alpin Center Zermatt
Tel 027 966 24 60.
www.alpincenter-
zermatt.ch

Caving and Canyoning
Casa Rosina, 6652 Tegna.
Tel 091 780 78 00.
www.trekking.ch

Garbely Adventure
In den Lussen,
3999 Oberwald.
Tel 027 973 25 75.
www.garbely-
adventure.ch

Outventure
Acheregg,
6362 Stansstad.
Tel 041 611 14 41.
www.outventure.ch

Sentier Suspendu
Place Centrale,
1936 Verbier.
Tel 027 775 33 63.
www.verbierbooking.ch

LEISURE SPORTS

Swiss Equestrian Association
Papiermühlestrasse 40H,
3000 Bern 22.
Tel 031 335 43 43.
www.fnch.ch

Swiss Franches-Montagnes Horse Association
Les Longs Prés,
1580 Avenches.
Tel 026 676 63 43.
www.fm-ch.ch

Swiss Golf Association
Place de la Croix-Blanche
19, 1066 Epalinges.
Tel 021 785 70 00.
www.asg.ch

Swiss Golf Network
Laupenstrasse 18a,
3008 Bern.
Tel 044 586 98 66.
www.swissgolfnetwork.ch

Swiss Tennis Federation
Solothurnstrasse 112,
2501 Biel.
Tel 032 344 07 07.
www.mytennis.ch

Skiing in Switzerland

Snowsports holidays were invented in Switzerland in the 19th century, and for that unmistakeable Swiss hotel or chalet experience, as well as unrivalled infrastructure both on and off piste, Switzerland remains the world's premier winter sports destination. Only here can you board a train right at the airport terminal (Zürich or Geneva), with connections to any of the country's major ski resorts. Nowhere else will you find so many car-free resorts, the most famous of these being Zermatt, Saas Fee, Wengen and Mürren. Switzerland has more 4,000-m (13,000-ft) peaks than any other alpine nation, the highest ski lifts and ski fields, and superb conditions.

Snowboarder in mid-jump with a stunning backdrop at Leysin

Young skiers riding a "magic carpet" ski lift at Wengen

SKIING

There are more than 250 skiing areas and some 2,400 cable cars and ski lifts, transporting more than 310 million passengers a year. "Magic carpet" conveyor-belt ski lifts transport beginners and children uphill. Zermatt and Saas Fee have underground "metro" trains, protected from weather and applauded by environmentalists, as they require no pylons.

Swiss resorts do not use chemicals in their snowmaking, and most have drastically reduced salt on the roads. Forests, and the animals that overwinter in them, are protected by fenced-off no-skiing zones. Free buses within resorts, some solar powered, are part of the strong pro-environmental policies.

Swiss ski passes are more expensive than elsewhere in Europe, though cheaper than in North America. Family discounts are the best in the world. Children under nine, for example, ski free in Zermatt and at all Lake Geneva region resorts.

SNOWBOARDING

The distinction between skiers and snowboarders is all but extinct now. For years the trend has been to shorter, fatter skis. Two such skis are about the same width as a snowboard. Skiers and boarders now share techniques: "carving" (making deep cuts in the piste), "freeride" (long, fast turns in deep snow) and "freestyle" (jumps or tricks).

No Swiss resorts ban snowboarders or restrict them to certain areas. Indeed, what used to be called "snowboard parks" are now renamed "terrain parks", where both skiers and boarders make jumps side by side.

WHEN TO GO

Swiss resorts with glaciers, like Zermatt and Saas Fee, are open summer and winter alike. High resorts like Verbier traditionally open at the start of November and close in May. But it is a fact of life that, for the past decade, early season skiing has lacked sufficient snowfall. The most expensive and crowded periods are Christmas, Easter and the entire high-season month of February. By contrast, most hotels and resorts offer tremendous bargains during the quiet month of January. March is the best month for a combination of reduced prices, most sunshine and deepest snowpack (*see pp30–31*).

CHOOSING A RESORT

Switzerland has skiing areas for all price ranges and abilities. **Zermatt**, **St Moritz**, **Davos**, **Gstaad** and **Verbier** are the most fashionable. High resorts with glaciers have the best guarantee of snow. In addition to Zermatt, Verbier and **Saas Fee**, these include the more family-oriented resorts of **Les Diablerets** and **Engelberg**.

Intermediates, who want to cruise long, well-groomed pistes, will find endless variety in resorts that have joined together on a single skipass. The **Portes du Soleil** straddling

The view from Blatten village looking towards Breithorn mountain

the Swiss-Franco border has 650 km (404 miles) of marked trails. Zermatt, joined with its Italian neighbour Cervinia, boasts 313 km (194 miles) of cross-border skiing.

For chalet charm and views, the small resorts of **Mürren**, **Wengen**, **Andermatt** and Saas Fee are unbeatable. For families, the pace and price of resorts like **Val d'Anniviers**, **Adelboden** and **Kandersteg** are particularly attractive.

ACCOMMODATION

One of the most memorable parts of a Swiss skiing holiday is staying in an authentic chalet or a grand old hotel. But there is also a wide choice of budget accommodation, including guesthouses. Self-catered apartments are a popular alternative; holiday costs can be cut considerably by buying groceries at chain super-markets like Migros. Another possibility is staying in a Swiss city and driving each day to a different resort *(see pp242–3)*.

OFF-PISTE SKIING

It is estimated that more than half of all skiers (tourists and locals) in Switzerland now ski

Off-piste skiing in pristine, powdery snow in Uri canton

off piste, defined as skiing off marked trails in natural snow which has not been packed down by machines.

There has been a consequent explosion in tours to the "back-country" by qualified mountain guides. Visitors should make sure their insurance covers such activities explicitly, including rescue by helicopter (common in Switzerland, even for minor accidents on piste).

AT THE TOP

Switzerland has 42 authorized landing zones where heli-copters may deposit skiers searching for the best quality

untracked snow. Mountain guides are always required, and groups are chosen according to ability level, which need not be expert.

Amazingly popular is the oldest way of getting to the top, sliding uphill on skis fixed with "skins" that prevent backward slippage. At high altitudes the Swiss have erected hundreds of "huts", really small hotels with food and wine served by a "guardian". These huts are spaced a day's tour apart. The most famous ski tour across the glaciers starts in Saas Fee and ends a week later in Chamonix (France).

DIRECTORY

PRACTICAL INFO

International Ski Federation
www.fis-ski.com

Meteo Swiss
www.meteoswiss.ch

Piste maps
www.alpineskimaps.com

Switzerland Tourism
www.myswitzerland.com

GUIDES, GEAR AND SCHOOLS

Air Glaciers Helicopters
Tel 033 856 05 60.

Mountain Air Sports
Tel 027 771 62 31.
www.mountainairverbier.com

Swiss Alpine Club
Tel 031 370 18 18.
www.sac-cas.ch

Swiss Mountain Guides
Tel 044 360 53 66.
www.4000plus.ch

Swiss Rent a Sport
Tel 081 410 08 18.
www.swissrent.com

Swiss Ski Schools
Tel 031 810 41 11.
www.snowsports.ch

Swiss Snowboard
www.swisssnowboard.ch

Terrain Parks
www.snowboardparks.co.uk

RESORTS

Adelboden
Tel 033 673 80 80.
www.adelboden.ch

Andermatt
Tel 041 888 71 00.
www.andermatt.ch

Davos
Tel 081 415 21 21.
www.davos.ch

Engelberg
Tel 041 639 77 77.
www.engelberg.ch

Gstaad
Tel 033 748 81 81.
www.gstaad.ch

Kandersteg
Tel 033 675 80 80.
www.kandersteg.ch

Les Diablerets
Tel 024 492 00 10.
www.diablerets.ch

Portes du Soleil
Tel 024 477 23 61.
www.portesdusoleil.com

Saas Fee
Tel 027 958 18 58.
www.saas-fee.ch

St Moritz
Tel 081 837 33 33.
www.stmoritz.ch

Valais Tourism
Tel 027 327 35 70.
www.valais.ch

Val d'Anniviers
Tel 0848 848 027.
www.sierre-anniviers.ch

Verbier
Tel 027 775 38 88.
www.verbier.ch

Wengen
Tel 033 856 85 85.
www.wengen.ch

Zermatt
Tel 027 966 81 00.
www.zermatt.ch

SPA RESORTS IN SWITZERLAND

With its pure alpine air and therapeutic hot springs, Switzerland has always been a favoured destination for those recovering from illness or seeking to improve their health or lifestyle. With the help of relaxing treatment courses using physiotherapy and natural spa resources, such as hot mineral springs and therapeutic

Guest at Clinique La Prairie

muds, countless people have regained their health and strength. Modern Swiss spas lead the world, not only in their standards of comfort and care, but with their pioneering treatments. Few other countries offer such a diverse choice of spa experiences, from traditional "cures" in thermal pools to the latest health and beauty treatments.

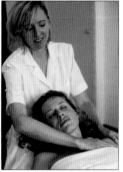

Therapeutic massage at Clinique La Prairie, near Montreux

THERMAL SPAS

Switzerland has an abundance of hot springs but just 20 thermal resorts. These spa towns are a pleasant mix of ancient traditions and 21st-century comforts, with public thermal baths, shops, gardens, sports amenities and a full calendar of cultural events. Spa "cures" are carried out in modern treatment centres following a medical consultation and include hydrotherapy, physiotherapy, mud treatments, massage and balneotherapy (therapeutic bathing).

In **Bad Ragaz**, mineral-rich water is piped down from a hot spring in a nearby gorge and used in the treatment of rheumatic, circulatory and neurological disorders. Aesthetic and cosmetic procedures are also offered in the town's medical clinics.

The strong sulphur waters in **Lenk** are good for treating respiratory disorders. The modern spa and health centre has a specialist inhalation

clinic with physiotherapy, lymph drainage and other lung-related treatments. Traditional spa rheumatism cures, dietary advice, slimming and beauty treatments are also available.

The village of **Leukerbad** is Europe's largest alpine spa, with 65 thermal springs, 22 thermal baths and a large hydrotherapy/balneotherapy treatment centre. The hot mineral-rich waters are used to treat rheumatic conditions, metabolic diseases and hormonal disorders, for rehabilitation after accidents, surgery or strokes and in sports medicine.

The sparkling carbonated springs of **St Moritz** are the highest in Switerland. The waters are used by doctors and therapists in the medical centre, combining traditional spa therapies with the latest medical advances.

The hot springs of **Yverdon-les-Bains** have eased rheumatic pain and respiratory conditions since Roman times. Today, spa treatments are carried out

in the public Centre Thermale – a large modern spa complex with indoor and outdoor thermal pools, fitness facilities, saunas, Turkish baths, solaria, mud baths and massages.

MEDICAL SPAS

Swiss medical spas are known for their rejuvenating treatments and clinical excellence. The exclusive **Clinique La Prairie** near Montreux specializes in rejuvenating treatments. A recent expansion has provided a dedicated spa floor with state-of-the-art amenities and new equipment in the medical centre, which carries out general as well as cosmetic surgery. Also in Montreux is **La Clinic**, a hospital with the luxury of a five star hotel, offering rejuvenating treatments, cosmetic surgery, dentistry and hair replacement. The sumptuous **Kempinski Grand Hotel des Bains** in St Moritz has a medical spa as well as a lavish wellness facility with treatments and access to the town's medical centre.

Taking the fresh alpine air and the hot thermal waters in the small village of Leukerbad, in the Valais

HOTEL SPAS

Many four and five star hotels offer outstanding spa facilities. The new ESPA spa has transformed Interlaken's **Victoria Jungfrau Grand Hotel & Spa** into a spa destination with state-of-the-art treatment rooms, thermal and relaxation areas and an extensive menu of fabulous treatments.

At **Le Mirador Kempinski Lake Geneva**, the spa adjoins the hotel and has a swim-through indoor/outdoor pool and an extensive spa menu that includes massage, hydrotherapy, wellness treatments and weight-loss programmes.

Grindewald's **Grand Regina-Alpin Well & Fit Hotel** offers spa treatments, massage and hairdressing. Facilities include pools and a thermal circuit with caves, baths, steam rooms, saunas and ice showers.

Vals' dramatic **Therme Vals** has thermal pools and a wellness centre with aromatherapy, kelp wraps, acupressure, manicures, pedicures and facials.

La Réserve's opulent spa on Lake Geneva provides indoor and outdoor pools, sauna, *haman* and 17 treatment rooms for massages, personalized treatments and facials.

ESPA spa at the Victoria Jungfrau Grand Hotel & Spa in Interlaken

The Tschuggen Bergoase at Arosa's **Tschuggen Grand Hotel** is built into a mountain over four levels and linked to the hotel by a glass bridge. Spring water flows throughout the spa and the spectacular open plan design encompasses thermal and relaxation areas, indoor and outdoor pools, treatment rooms and spa suites. A wide range of spa treatments are available.

At Lausanne's **Beau Rivage Palace Hotel**, the Spa Cinq Mondes offers Asian healing traditions and holistic health rituals. There are pools, tropical shower promenade and nine treatment rooms, some with Japanese flower baths.

The **Grand Hotel Bellevue** in Gstaad has a well-equipped spa with a thermal suite and spa menu that includes holistic rituals, Kneipp therapies, aromatherapy, body massages and wraps, spa baths and Shiseido treatments.

In Zermatt, **Hotel Mirabeau's** new Alpine Wellness Refuge uses natural products made from local mountain flowers, honey and herbs. Connected to the hotel by a tunnel, the spa has a warm indoor pool and a thermal circuit with scented hay mattress, Kneipp bath, mountain flowers steam bath, sauna with open sky shower and relaxation room with water beds.

DIRECTORY

SURVIVAL
GUIDE

PRACTICAL INFORMATION

A prime tourist destination, Switzerland attracts large numbers of visitors, both during the winter sports season and at other times of the year. As tourism is an important part of Switzerland's economy, the country has a highly developed tourist infrastructure and a positive attitude towards helping foreign visitors make the most of their stay.

Museums and other places of interest are well-maintained, with helpful

Tourist information sign

information in several languages, usually including English. English is also spoken at most tourist offices, as well as in almost all the larger hotels and major winter sports resorts.

Having one of the most efficiently run and convenient public transport systems in Europe, Switzerland is also a very easy country to travel around in, whether by road or rail, or at a more leisurely pace by boat on Switzerland's larger lakes.

WHEN TO GO

The best time of year to visit Switzerland depends on how you plan to spend your time here. The winter sports season runs from mid-December to late spring. The most crowded periods are the Christmas and Easter holiday weeks, and the entire "high season" month of February.

Summertime in Switzerland is pleasantly warm. The height of the summer season runs from the beginning of July to late August. Accommodation then tends to be harder to find, and visitor attractions are at their most crowded.

Spring and autumn are much quieter, and are excellent seasons for exploring the countryside. The mountains are particularly beautiful in spring, when wild flowers start to bloom, and in autumn, when leaves begin to turn. In the countryside, spring and autumn are also the time of year when you are most likely to witness folk festivals.

VISA AND CUSTOMS REGULATIONS

Citizens of the EU, the United States, Canada, Australia, New Zealand and South Africa need a valid passport to visit Switzerland and Liechtenstein but do not require a visa.

Information board in Parc Mon Repos, Geneva

However, individual visits are limited to three months, and total visits per year should not exceed six months. Visitors planning a longer stay (to work or study in Switzerland, for example) should contact the Swiss embassy in their own country. Switzerland is a member of the Schengen Agreement, which abolishes border controls on travel within member states.

Customs regulations are straightforward. Visitors from Europe may import 2 litres of wine and 1 litre of spirits, and 200 cigarettes or 50 cigars, or 250g of pipe tobacco. Visitors from other countries may import 400 cigarettes, 100 cigars and 500g of pipe tobacco. However, no visitors under the age of 17 may bring alcohol or tobacco into Switzerland.

Visitors may also bring in a variety of items for their own use while in Switzerland, such as camping and sports equipment, cameras and laptop computers, and gifts up to a value of 300 CHF.

OPENING HOURS

Most museums and visitor attractions are open six full days a week. Many close on Mondays and some on Tuesdays. Shops, post offices, banks and tourist offices are generally open from Monday to Friday, 8am–6:30pm. Shops also open on Saturdays, 8am–4pm, while post offices open until 11am or noon. However, shops in smaller towns and villages may close for lunch and those in smaller towns may be closed on Mondays. In many resorts, shops stay open all day on Sunday. Shops on station concourses have longer opening hours and are also open on Sundays.

The tourist information centre at the Bärengraben in Bern

◁ **Train on the Jungfrau railway and Jungfrau (13642 ft) in the Bernese Alps**

News kiosk with publications in German, French and Italian

Australia
Chemi des Fins 2,
1211 Geneva.
Tel 022 799 91 00.
Fax 022 799 9178.

Canada
Kirchenfeldstrasse 88,
3005 Bern.
Tel 031 357 32 00.
Fax 031 357 32 10.

Ireland
Kichenfeldstrasse 68, 3005 Bern.
Tel 031 352 14 42.
Fax 031 352 14 45.

New Zealand
Chemis des Fins 2,
1218 Grand-Saconnex.
Tel 022 929 03 50.
Fax 022 929 03 77.

South Africa
Alpenstrasse 29, 3006 Bern.
Tel 031 350 13 13.
Fax 031 351 39 44.

United Kingdom
Thunstrasse 50, 3005 Bern.
Tel 031 359 77 00.
Fax 031 359 77 01.

United States
Sulgeneck, Strasse 19, 3007 Bern.
Tel 031 357 70 11.

SWISS TOURIST OFFICES

United Kingdom
1st Floor, 30 Bedford Street,
London WC2E 9ED.
Tel 020 7420 4900; 00800 1002
0030 (toll-free in Europe).

United States
Swiss Center, 608 Fifth Avenue,
New York, NY 10020.
Tel (212) 757 59 44.

USEFUL WEBSITES

Tourism
www.MySwitzerland.com

Museums
www.museums.ch

Arts and Culture
www.prohelvetia.ch

LANGUAGES

German is the most widely spoken language in Switzerland, after which are French and Italian. German-speakers, followed by French-speakers, are most likely to speak English as well. Many organizations that have contact with foreign visitors speak English and most tourist offices have English-speaking staff.

Swiss German differs from the standard, or High, German of Germany and Austria. Swiss German (*Schwyzertütsch*), which has several regional dialects as well as its own syntax and vocabulary, is used in everyday speech and is hardly ever written. High German (*Hochdeutsch*) in Switzerland is primarily a written language, being used for public signs and notices and in the media but also in education and in formal situations such as public speaking.

Pillar with news and information

NEWSPAPERS

Switzerland's national press is dominated by French- and German-language titles. Among the leading dailies are the conservative *Neue Zürcher Zeitung*, the more liberal *Tages- Anzeiger* and the progressive *Le Temps*.

Swiss weeklies include *Die Weltwoche* and *Wochen-zeitung*. The daily *Corriere del Ticino* is widely read in Ticino.

British and American newspapers, such as *The Times, The Guardian, The International Herald Tribune* and *USA Today* are sold in large towns and cities and in most major resorts. *The Economist, Time* and *Newsweek* are also available.

TIME

Switzerland is one hour ahead of Greenwich Mean Time (GMT) in winter and two hours ahead of GMT in summer. The Swiss use the 24-hour clock. In German *halb* (half) refers to the half-hour before the hour; for example, *halb zwei* means 1:30, not 2:30.

ELECTRICITY

The current in Switzerland is 220v AC 50 cycles. Sockets are of the three-pin type, and they accept the two- or three-pin round-pronged plugs used elsewhere in continental Europe. Although many hotels provide adaptors on request, it can be more convenient to bring your own. For equipment designed for use in the USA, you will need a transformer.

Personal Security and Health

Logo of Zürich police

With efficient public services and one of the lowest crime rates in the industrialized world, Switzerland is generally a safe country for foreign visitors. The Swiss are helpful, polite and welcoming, so that travelling anywhere in their country is a pleasant experience. With a temperate climate, clean water and few natural hazards, Switzerland poses virtually no health risks to visitors. However, those who enjoy the more strenuous outdoor activities, particularly at high altitudes, should be aware of potential dangers.

Patrol car of Geneva police

PERSONAL SAFETY

Despite Switzerland's deserved reputation for safety, visitors should be vigilant, particularly when walking in unlit streets late at night, withdrawing cash at an ATM, travelling on public transport, or among large crowds of people in public places. Pickpockets in search of wallets and credit cards sometimes operate in the streets and squares of

large towns, as well as at airports, train stations and other transport hubs. Thieves may be on the look-out for opportunities to grab handbags and jewellery from unwary visitors. It is also wise to make use of hotel safes to store valuable items and never to leave valuables in cars, which should always be left locked. If you intend to stay in hostels, it is worth taking a padlock to secure a locker.

Municipal police patrol car

Generally, caution and common sense are the best defences. However, if you are the victim of theft, report it at once to the police. Obtaining a police report will enable you to make an insurance claim. Loss or theft of credit cards should also be reported as soon as possible to the issuing company (*see p298*).

Women travelling alone are unlikely to experience problems, but it is best to follow the same safety precautions you would usually and to keep away from lonely, unlit areas at night.

Policeman patrolling the streets on a bicycle

POLICE

The Swiss are scrupulously law-abiding and expect the same of foreign visitors. Simply crossing the street on a red pedestrian light may result in a police caution or a fine. More serious transgressions, such as the possession of drugs, may lead to imprisonment or deportation. At all times, you should carry your passport or ID, which the police will ask to see if they have reason to stop you.

Each of the country's 26 cantons has its own armed police force, as do individual towns and cities. Each canton also has its own laws, although the differences between them are minimal.

HEALTH

No vaccinations are required for visitors entering Switzerland, except for those who have visited a high-risk region in the two weeks preceding their arrival in the country.

Tap water is safe to drink everywhere in Switzerland, and the water gushing from fountains in towns and villages is also safe, unless otherwise indicated by the words *kein Trinkwasser, eau non potable or acqua non potabile*. It is, however, best not to drink from streams and springs, however pure they may appear to be.

At altitudes over about 3,000 m (10,000 ft), visitors should be aware of the risk of altitude sickness. Aspirin and bed rest may alleviate mild symptoms, which include nausea, headache and fatigue but which usually pass after 48 hours. If symptoms persist, the only effective remedy is to descend to a lower altitude.

Sunstroke is also more likely at high altitudes, where the air is thinner, or where snow or water reflect the sun's

Rescue helicopter in action in Crans-Montana

rays. To prevent sunstroke, drink plenty of water, wear a hat and sunglasses and use a sunblock with a high UV-protection factor. The best prevention, however, is to limit the amount of time you spend in the sun, especially in the first few days of your stay.

At any time of the year, the weather in the mountains can be very changeable, with cold wind, rain and sudden snow-storms posing the greatest danger. Skiers and hikers should wear several layers of warm clothing, a hat and waterproofs, and carry supplies of high-energy food and water. The best precaution of all is the decision to turn back when weather conditions threaten to deteriorate.

Entrance to a pharmacy in St Gallen

MEDICAL CARE

There is no national health service in Switzerland, so medical treatment of any kind must be paid for. Switzerland has a reciprocal agreement with all EU countries. Visitors must obtain a European Health Insurance Card (EHIC) – the form is available from post offices. However, taking out health insurance before your trip is still recommended. This is particularly important if you are planning a skiing, mountaineering or hiking holiday, or intend to practise any extreme sports. Insurance should also cover the cost of helicopter rescue. This is extremely expensive but is often the only means of rescue when someone has suffered serious injury in the mountains.

An auxiliary services vehicle

In case of illness or injury, lists of local doctors can be obtained from the more expensive hotels, the consulate of your own country *(see p295)* or from tourist information offices *(see p287)*. Almost every hospital *(Spital, hôpital, ospedale)* has a 24-hour accident and emergency department. However, before receiving hospital treatment, you are advised to contact your insurer or your country's embassy *(see p295)*.

PHARMACIES

All pharmacies *(Apotheke, pharmacie or farmacia)* are denoted by a sign in the form of a green cross. Pharmacies have helpful and knowledge-able staff who are able to give advice on minor health problems. Many pharmacies close on Saturday afternoon.

Duty pharmacies are open outside normal shopping hours, and their address is posted in the windows of pharmacies that are closed. In larger towns and cities, duty pharmacies stay open round the clock.

EMERGENCIES

If you are involved in, or witness, an emergency, immediately call the police by dialling 117, or the ambulance (144), fire brigade (118), road rescue (140) or helicopter rescue service (1414). If you are asked to sign a police document, do not do so unless you understand its content. Ask to have it translated. If you hold an insurance policy issued in your home country, you should immediately contact the insurer's central office, by ringing the number given on the policy document. Should you need legal assistance, your embassy can offer advice *(see p295)*.

DIRECTORY

EMERGENCIES

Police
Tel 117.

Fire Brigade
Tel 118.

Ambulance
Tel 144.

Duty Doctors and Dentists
Tel 111.

Road Rescue
Tel 140.

Helicopter Rescue
Tel 1414.

Note that almost all public telephones are card-operated. Road rescue and helicopter rescue numbers cost 0.40 CHF per call.

USEFUL NUMBERS

Weather Information
Tel 162.

Avalanche Information
Tel 187.

Clock
Tel 161.

Traffic
Tel 163.

Banking and Local Currency

Bureau de change logo

You may bring any amount of currency into Switzerland, but for any amount over 10,000 CHF the source must be declared. Travellers' cheques are the safest way to carry money abroad, but credit and debit cards, both of which can be used to withdraw local currency, are the most convenient. The unit of currency in Switzerland and in Liechtenstein is the Swiss franc (CHF).

PAYMENT

The preferred payment is the Swiss franc. However, euros are now widely accepted in shops, hotels and restaurants, though the rate of exchange is usually less advantageous than at a bank.

Ticket offices of SBB, the Swiss federal railway, *(see pp304–5)* accept payment in euros. Throughout Switzerland euros can often be used at airports as well as to pay motorway tolls. Some coin-operated telephones will accept euro coins *(see p300)*.

BANKS AND BUREAUX DE CHANGE

Most banks are open Monday to Friday from 9am to 5pm, although in smaller towns they may close from noon to 2pm. Currency can be exchanged over the counter at banks, or cash withdrawn with a credit

Basler Kantonalbank cash machine

or debit card at cash machines (ATMs). Even the banks in small towns have cash machines, and these can of course also be found at all airports and at major railway stations. Cash machines generally dispense both euros and Swiss francs.

The least favourable rates of exchange are usually those offered by hotels. Always check the rate, whether using a bureau de change, hotel, or bank, to get the best rate.

CREDIT CARDS

The use of credit cards is less widespread in Switzerland than in the United Kingdom and United States. Visitors should bear in mind that some shops, hotels and restaurants ask for payment to be made in cash. In general MasterCard and Visa have the widest use in Switzerland, with American Express and Diners Club less widely accepted.

TAX-FREE GOODS

Value-added tax (VAT) is levied at 7.6 per cent. Visitors to Switzerland can reclaim sales tax, or VAT, on individual purchases of 400 CHF or more made at a single store. Obtain a VAT refund form at the time of purchase and take the goods out of the country (unopened) within 30 days. The form should be

DIRECTORY

SWISS BANKS

Banque Cantonale de Genève
17 Quai de l'Ile,
1204 Geneva.
Tel 022 317 27 27.

Credit Suisse Group
Paradeplatz 8, 8001 Zürich
Tel 044 212 16 16.
www.credit-suisse.com

Raiffeisen Bank
Brandschenkestrasse 110d,
8002 Zürich.
Tel 0844 88 88 08.

UBS AG
Bahnhofstrasse 45, 8001 Zürich.
Tel 044 234 11 11.
www.ubs.com

Zürcher Kantonalbank
Bahnhofstrasse 9,
8001 Zürich.
Tel 044 293 93 93.

LOST/STOLEN CREDIT CARDS AND TRAVELLERS' CHEQUES

American Express
Tel +44 (0) 1273 69 69 33.

Diners Club
Tel 0870 190 00 11.

Mastercard
Tel 0800 96 47 67.

Thomas Cook/Travelex Worldwide Refund Service
Tel 0800 62 21 01.

Visa
Tel 0800 89 4732 (cards).

A branch of Credit Suisse, one of Switzerland's largest banks

presented to customs when you leave the country. To obtain your refund, either take the form to the refund counter or send it back to the store when you are home. For a fee, **Global Refund**, a Europe-wide refund service, will handle all the paperwork for you.

CURRENCY

The Swiss unit of currency is the Swiss franc, which is abbreviated as CHF and known as *Schweizer Franken* in German, *franc suisse* in French and *franco svizzero* in Italian. The franc is divided into 100 *centimes*, which are known as *Rappen* in German and as *centesimi* in Italian.

Because of the customs union that exists between Switzerland and the principality of Liechtenstein, the Swiss franc is also the official currency of Liechtenstein.

Banknotes
Swiss banknotes are issued in denominations of 10, 20, 50, 100, 200 and 1,000 francs. The different banknotes are distinguished by their size and colour. The smallest, both in terms of size and value, is the 10-franc note. The largest is the 1,000-franc note.

10 francs

20 francs

50 francs

100 francs

200 francs

1,000 francs

5 francs   2 francs   1 franc   50 centimes   20 centimes

10 centimes   5 centimes

Coins
Swiss coins are issued in denominations of 1, 2 and 5 francs, and of 5, 10, 20 and 50 centimes. All Swiss coins are silver-coloured, except the 5-centime coin, which is gold-coloured.

Communications and Media

Swiss post office logo

Like the country's other services, Switzerland's telephone, Internet and postal systems are efficient and reliable. Swisscom's modern public telephones have built-in electronic directories and also built-in facilities for sending e-mails and text messages. Switzerland's post office, known as Die Post in German, La Poste in French and La Posta in Italian, offers an equally modern and comprehensive mail service, as well as other useful services. Neighbouring Liechtenstein has its own separate telephone and postal systems.

USEFUL NUMBERS
- Country code for
  Switzerland: 41
  Liechtenstein: 423
- Useful country codes:
  Australia: 61
  Ireland: 353
  New Zealand: 64
  South Africa: 27
  UK: 44
  US & Canada: 1
- Directory enquiries for
  Switzerland and
  Liechtenstein: 111
  All other countries: 11 59

A Swisscom telephone box

INTERNATIONAL AND LOCAL TELEPHONE CALLS

Switzerland's principal telecommunications company is **Swisscom**. It has 6,700 public telephones, most of which are located outside post offices and in train stations. Every public telephone has a Teleguide. This provides access to an electronic directory and also enables users to send an e-mail, fax or text message. Instructions are given in four languages, including English.

Some public telephones are coin-operated. Those that are accept Swiss francs and euros. The easiest way of using a public telephone is with a pre-paid phonecard, known as a taxcard. Taxcards, in denominations of 5, 10, 20, 50 and 100 CHF, are sold at post offices and train stations as well as in news kiosks.

Calls within Switzerland are cheapest at weekends, and on weekdays between 7pm and 7am. Inland calls to 0800 numbers are free. Calls from hotels, which set their own phone tariffs, always cost more than from public telephones.

Swisscom alone has over 1,700 wireless LAN (local area network) hotspots, from which VOIP (voice over Internet protocol) telephone services like Skype, for example, can be used.

All Swiss telephone numbers now consist of ten digits. This means that you must always include the three-digit area code, even when dialling a local number.

MOBILE PHONES

There are three main mobile telephone providers in Switzerland: Swisscom (the largest), Sunrise and Orange.

Coverage varies across the country so some background research is a good idea if you're staying in the country for a while. Eastern Switzerland, for example, is not a good area to make calls for Orange customers, whereas the company claims it provides the fastest data connection.

Ready-to-use mobile phones with prepaid cards can be bought at department stores or electrical shops. Charges for Swiss mobile phone users are comparatively high, while roaming charges are some of the highest in Europe so be careful if you're travelling in neighbouring countries with a prepaid Swiss phone.

INTERNET

There are numerous **cafés**, special terminals and Wi-Fi hotspots throughout Switzerland. Many hotels offer free

An Internet booth in Lugano, southern Switzerland

Sign for a Post Office in a German-speaking region of Switzerland

Wi-Fi, as do restaurants and fastfood outlets. Train stations and Intercity trains have Wi-Fi (for a fee) in 1st class, while Swiss Post buses offer it for free. Note that Swiss telephone providers charge for a hotspot service.

POSTAL SERVICES

In large towns post offices are open from 8am to 6.30pm Monday to Friday, and from 8am to 11am or noon on Saturdays. In smaller towns, they close between noon and 2pm. In large cities, including Zürich, Geneva, Bern and Basel, post offices situated near railway stations have counters that remain open until 9–10pm. A small extra charge is made for using their services but be aware

that they don't handle the more complicated transactions, such as money transfers.

Many post offices also have fax machines as well as shops selling books, confectionery and writing and packaging materials.

STAMPS AND MAIL

Postage stamps are available at post offices, newsagents and hotel reception desks. They can also be purchased from machines, which are located within post offices and also beside some postboxes.

The Swiss postal system operates a two-tier delivery system. Inland letters sent by A-Post are delivered the next day. Those sent by B-Post, which is cheaper, reach their destinations in two to three days. For international letters there are two categories, Prioritaire and Économique. Prioritaire mail is delivered in two to four days within Europe and up to seven days everywhere else. Économique mail is delivered in four to eight days within Europe and up to 12 days elsewhere.

POSTE RESTANTE

A convenient way of receiving mail if you are travelling in Switzerland is by using Poste Restante. By this system mail is sent to any post office in the country that you designate, and is kept there until you come to collect it. Mail should be addressed with your name, the words Poste Restante, the letters CH (for "Switzerland") and the four-digit postcode of the relevant town. A full list of Swiss postcodes

A Die Post Postbox in Switzerland

is published in phone directories. The Post Restante fee for a short break of two weeks is approximately 8 CHF, if the account is set up online.

LIECHTENSTEIN

Liechtenstein has its own telephone company, **Telecom FL**, and its own postal service, **Liechtensteinische Post**. It also issues its own postage stamps, which are coveted by collectors. Swisscom and Telecom FL cards can be used in both countries. Calls from Switzerland to Liechtenstein are treated as international, and you should dial 00, then the country code (423). A call from Liechtenstein to Switzerland is treated as national.

DIRECTORY

TELEPHONES

Yellow Pages (business & services)
www.local.ch

INTERNET

Internetcafe Zurich
Urianastrasse 3, 8001 Zürich.
Tel 044 210 33 11.

Ispot Centre
Rue Pictet de Bock 3, 1205 Geneva.
Tel 548 06 36.

POSTAL SERVICES

Die Post/La Poste/La Posta
www.post.ch

Swisscom
www.swisscom.ch

LIECHTENSTEIN

Telecom Liechtenstein
www.telecom.li

Liechtensteinische Post
www.post.li

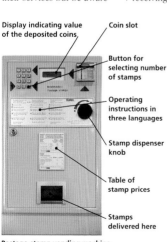

Display indicating value of the deposited coins

Coin slot

Button for selecting number of stamps

Operating instructions in three languages

Stamp dispenser knob

Table of stamp prices

Stamps delivered here

Postage-stamp vending machine

TRAVEL INFORMATION

L ying at the crossroads of major European routes, Switzerland has excellent transport connections. The country has air links with all major European cities, as well as frequent intercontinental flights.

An aircraft of the SWISS fleet

The country's internal transport system is also highly efficient, pleasant and easy to use, and a panoply of travel passes offer substantial discounts. Swiss trains

and passenger postal buses together cover almost every corner of the country, offering visitors some of the best views of Switzerland's dramatic mountain scenery. Well-maintained roads make driving in Switzerland a pleasure and allow motorists either to cover long distances quickly or to explore the country's remoter regions at a more leisurely pace.

Zürich **Flughafen** ✈

Sign indicating Zürich airport

BY AIR FROM THE UK

Several airlines operate frequent daily direct flights between the United Kingdom and Switzerland. The main carriers are **British Airways** and **SWISS**, the national airline. Several low-cost airlines, including **easyJet** and bmibaby, also operate flights between the United Kingdom and Switzerland.

SWISS flies daily direct from London City Airport to Geneva and from Heathrow to Geneva and Basel. Daily flights from Birmingham, Manchester and Heathrow to Zürich connect onward to Geneva and Basel.

Cheaper air fares can sometimes be obtained if you buy your plane ticket as part of a package from a tour operator. The London-based Swiss company **Switzerland Travel Centre**, which specializes in travel to and holidays in Switzerland, can advise on every type of requirement.

BY AIR FROM THE US

Flights between the United States and Switzerland are provided by **SWISS, American Airlines, United Airlines,** US Airways and **Delta**. Flights to Zürich and Geneva depart from New York, Boston, Atlanta, Miami, Philadelphia,

San Francisco, Washington D.C. and Los Angeles. The duration of flights is about seven or eight hours from the east coast of the United States, about 10 hours from the Midwest, and about 14 hours from the west coast.

SPECIAL-INTEREST PACKAGES

Tour operators both in the United Kingdom and in the United States offer many special-interest package holidays in Switzerland. Most of them revolve around skiing and other winter sports but there are a range of other options, including birdwatching and botanical tours led by specialists, and independent walking or cycling holidays, as well as rail tours and cultural explorations of the country.

SWISS AIRPORTS

Switzerland's three main international airports are Basel, Zürich and Geneva. Both of the latter conveniently house train stations within the air terminal complex.

Basel is served by EuroAirport. Split into Swiss and EU sectors, it is located on French territory and also serves Mulhouse (in France) and Freiburg (in Germany). In addition to internal flghts, EuroAirport provides links to several European cities.

Switzerland also has three smaller airports – Bern-Belp, Sion and Agno in Lugano – which provide a limited number of package and holiday flights, as well as internal connections. Most of the flights at Bern-Belp are to or from France, Germany and Italy, while Sion is ideally

Zürich's Kloten airport, one of the busiest in Switzerland

Zürich's international airport

placed for access to the largest ski resorts, as well as the thermal resorts.

FLY RAIL BAGGAGE

When flying to Switzerland via Zürich or Geneva from any airport in the world, you can make use of the convenient **Fly Rail Baggage Service**. From the check-in desk at your home airport, you can send your luggage direct to any one of 76 train stations in Switzerland, where you can collect it at your convenience. Some hotels will collect your luggage for you.

To use Fly Rail Baggage you must obtain a special luggage tag from SWISS or a Swiss tourist office. The service costs about 20 CHF per piece of luggage. It is not, however, available if you are flying with a low-cost airline or any US airline, and bulky items such as bicycles are not carried. As security concerns may also limit the availability of this service, you are advised to check with the airline or your travel agent.

STATION CHECK-IN

Passengers flying from Zürich or Geneva with certain scheduled airlines and charter flights can make use of the convenient station check-in service. This costs around 22 CHF per item of luggage and can make for a more leisurely journey to the airport without having to carry heavy bags. You can check in your luggage the day before at any one of 50 of the larger Swiss train stations. You will be given your boarding pass with your requested seat and your luggage is transported to the airport and loaded onto your flight. You can then forget about your luggage until you collect it from the carousel at your destination airport.

A list of 50 participating airlines can be found on the Swiss Federal Railways (SBB) website (www.sbb.ch).

DIRECTORY

American Airlines
Tel 1-800-433-7300 (US).
www.aa.com

British Airways
Tel 0844 493 0787 (UK); 1-800-247-9297 (US); 0848 845 845 (Switzerland). **www**.ba.com

Delta
www.delta.com

EasyJet
www.easyjet.com

Fly Rail Baggage
www.sbb.ch

SWISS
Tel 0845 601 0956 (UK); 1-877-359-7947 (US); 0848 700 700 (Switzerland). **www**.swiss.com

Switzerland Travel Centre
Tel 0207 420 4934 (UK).
www.stc.co.uk

United Airlines
www.united.com

TOUR OPERATORS

Alphorn Tours
Tel 877 257 4676 (US).
www.alphorntours.com

Great Rail Journeys
Tel 01904 521 936 (UK).
www.greatrail.com

Inn Travel
www.inntravel.co.uk

Naturetrek
Tel 01962 733 051 (UK).
www.naturetrek.co.uk

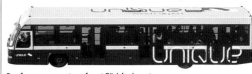
Bus for passenger transfer at Zürich airport

AIRPORT	INFORMATION	DISTANCE FROM CITY	JOURNEY TIME BY TAXI	JOURNEY TIME BY PUBLIC TRANSPORT
Basel	061 325 31 11	5 km (3 miles)	20 minutes	Bus: 15 minutes
Bern	031 960 21 11	9 km (6 miles)	30 minutes	Bus: 20 minutes
Geneva	022 717 71 11	5 km (3 miles)	20 minutes	Train: 6 minutes Bus: 20 minutes
Lugano	091 610 12 82	20 km (12 miles)	40 minutes	Bus: 10 minutes
Zürich	043 816 22 11	10 km (6 miles)	25 minutes	Train: 9 minutes

Travelling by Train

The comprehensive Swiss rail network provides an excellent means of transport. Trains are modern, clean and comfortable, and services are frequent and dependably punctual. Because the railway timetable is efficiently integrated with other forms of public transport, connections are very convenient. The train is also one of the best ways to see the country. Special excursions by train and boat enable visitors to enjoy exceptionally beautiful scenery on several routes through mountains and over passes, across lakes and along valleys.

An Intercity train

ARRIVING BY TRAIN

The most direct rail route from London to Switzerland is via the Channel Tunnel to Paris Gare du Nord. Transferring to Paris Gare de Lyon, three separate TGV

Bustling train station with blue information boards

(high-speed) train lines lead directly to Geneva, Lausanne, Basel and Bern. There are a number of TGV connections into Switzerland, although TGV trains do not travel at their maximum speeds within Switzerland, due to lack of suitable rails.

The quickest journey (from London to Geneva) takes at least eight hours and, although all these routes are scenic, passing through the French Alps, reaching Switzerland by train from the United Kingdom is not as cheap, quick and convenient as flying (see pp302–3).

Switzerland has good links with European high-speed-train networks, among which are Germany's ICE, France's TGV and Italy's Cisalpino. Comprehensive Swiss public transport timetables, including international connections, can be consulted on the website www.sbb.ch/timetable.

TRAINS

Switzerland's main train operator is Swiss Federal Railways, or SBB/CFF/FFS (Schweizerische Bundes-bahnen/Chemins de Fer Fédéraux/Ferrovie Federali Svizzere). SBB covers almost all the country, and over a dozen smaller operators run certain routes.

Most trains run from 6am to midnight, with hourly services operating between major towns. Smoking is forbidden on all trains at all times. Long-distance trains, including Intercity (IC), Eurocity (EC) and Interregio (IR) trains, have restaurant cars and trolleys serving drinks and snacks.

Trains also carry unaccom-panied luggage. You can send your luggage ahead from almost any station to another station or bus terminal. This is very useful if you are on the move, and want to spend the day unencumbered by baggage.

TRAVEL PASSES

A range of travel passes are available. Offering substantial discounts for rail travel, these passes can also be used on other modes of public

DIRECTORY

SBB Timetable
www.sbb.ch
Tel 0900 300 300.

Travel Passes
www.swisstravelsystem.ch
www.raileurope.com

SCENIC JOURNEYS

Glacier Express
Tel 027 927 77 77.
www.rhb.ch

Golden Pass Express
Tel 021 989 81 81.
www.goldenpass.ch

Bernina Express
Tel 081 288 6326.
www.rhb.ch

William Tell Express
Tel 041 367 67 67.
www.sbb.ch

transport, such as buses, trams, funiculars and boats.

The Swiss Pass allows unlimited rail travel on almost all train, bus and boat services, and on trams and buses in 37 towns. It allows reductions of up to 50 per cent on many railways, funiculars and cable cars. The Swiss Pass is available for periods of 4, 8, 15 or 22 consecutive days, or even a full month. It also gives free entry to 450 museums.

The Swiss Flexi Pass buys unlimited travel on any 3, 4, 5, 6 or 8 days within a month, and those travelling in groups of two to five receive a 15 per cent discount. Further discounts apply to those under 26. The Swiss Transfer Ticket covers one round trip from the Swiss border or any Swiss airport to anywhere in the country. The Swiss Card provides the same plus a 50 per cent discount on most other travel. The Family Card allows children up to the age of 16 to travel free when accompanied by an adult. Regional passes are also available.

To see the full range of travel passes, visit www.swisstravelsystem.ch. Most national travel passes can be purchased from travel agencies and Swiss tourist offices in your own country.

The concourse of Winterthur railway station

SCENIC JOURNEYS

Special trains take visitors on panoramic journeys through Switzerland's most spectacular scenery. Some trains have glass-roofed carriages that enable travellers to enjoy views in all directions.

Among the most popular of these rail journeys are the **Glacier Express**, from

Double-decker carriage of an SBB train

St Moritz or Davos over the Oberalp pass to Zermatt; the **Golden Pass Express**, from Montreux over the Brünig Pass to Luzern; the **Bernina Express**, from Davos, Chur or St Moritz over the Bernina Pass and down to Tirano, in Italy; and the **William Tell Express**, which starts with a cruise on Lake Lucerne, then cuts through the St Gotthard tunnel and descends to Lugano.

Tickets for these scenic journeys can be bought at any station. Most require reservation at least 24 hours in advance.

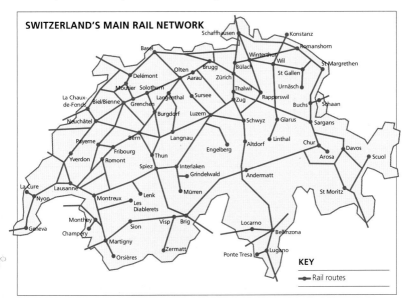

SWITZERLAND'S MAIN RAIL NETWORK

KEY

➤ Rail routes

Travelling by Car, Bus, Bicycle and Boat

Motorway links provide swift means of road transport the length and breadth of the country and well-maintained roads link Switzerland's major towns. Scenic routes also lead to high mountain passes and down Alpine valleys. Travelling through Switzerland by car is only one means of exploring the country. A fleet of passenger-carrying post buses traverse spectacular landscape to reach remote Alpine towns and villages. A slower but equally rewarding alternative is to travel by bicycle, using convenient bus and rail links. Switzerland can also be appreciated at a slower pace, by taking a cruise on any of its breathtakingly beautiful lakes.

Multistorey car park in Geneva

Road sign in western Switzerland

ARRIVING BY CAR

Fast car-carrying train services through the Channel Tunnel and good motorway routes eastwards across France make driving to Switzerland from the United Kingdom a viable alternative to flying. Frequent car ferries also cross the Channel from Dover to Calais and from Hull to Rotterdam or Zeebrugge. From Calais the quickest route is by motorway eastwards through France, entering Switzerland via the A40 to Geneva. From Zeebrugge or Rotterdam, there are fast motorways across Belgium, Luxembourg, France and Germany, from where the A5 leads to Basel. By either route, the journey from the Channel coast to the Swiss border is unlikely to take less than eight hours.

If you drive on French *autoroutes* remember that motorway tolls may add considerably to the cost of your journey.

RULES OF THE ROAD

In Switzerland, as in the rest of mainland Europe, driving is on the right. Overtaking on the right is prohibited and at junctions priority is given to drivers on the right, except when you are entering a roundabout. Unless road signs indicate otherwise, the speed limit is 120 km/h (75 mph) on motorways, 100 km/h (60 mph) on main highways, and 80 km/h (50 mph) on other roads. In built-up areas it is 50 km/h (30 mph) but can sometimes be as low as 30 km/h (20 mph). Speed cameras and radar are in widespread use.

The driver and passengers of a car must wear seat belts. Children under 12 years old must travel in the back seat, and those under seven must be strapped into a child seat. All vehicles must also carry a breakdown warning triangle. When entering a tunnel you are required to use dipped headlights. Any infringement of traffic regulations is likely to incur an on-the-spot fine, for which drivers should request a receipt.

The use of mobile phones while driving is considered to be a serious infringement, as is drink-driving. The blood-alcohol content limit is 0.05 per cent. Drivers should also carry their driving licence and the vehicle's registration document, which may be checked by the police.

DRIVING ON MOTORWAYS

To use Swiss motorways, which are indicated by green signs, drivers require a disk, or *vignette*. Costing 40 CHF, a *vignette* is valid until the end of January of the following year and can be purchased at border crossings, petrol stations, in post offices and at tourist offices. A *vignette* is also required for motorcycles and trailers. Driving on a motorway without a valid *vignette* incurs a fine.

DRIVING IN THE ALPS

Drivers are required by law to use snow tyres and/or chains on mountain roads when indicated by special

BP petrol station

warning signs. Road signs on routes leading into the Alps inform drivers of conditions ahead and whether passes are closed. The road tunnels beneath the Gotthard, San Bernardino and Great St Bernard passes are open year round, and some operate a toll system. The Lötschberg, Furka, Albula and Vereina tunnels have rail links, and cars are carried on trains.

Most of the country's high Alpine passes are generally open from June until October, although this is subject to weather conditions.

Drivers must always yield to post buses, which may swing wide on narrow curves.

CAR HIRE

The major international car-hire companies offer services in Switzerland, with offices in the main airports and in the town centres. Swiss Railways also offer a short-term Click and Drive car hire service. Cars are booked online and collected from any of the 1,300 SBB railway stations. Local firms usually offer cheaper rates, but for the cheapest deals it is best to pre-book in your own country. To hire a car in Switzerland, a driver must be over 20 years of age (in some cases 25) and must show a valid driving licence.

Sign to a motorway

A post bus on one of many Alpine routes inaccessible by rail

BUSES AND POST BUSES

Outside of the towns and cities, public transport can be provided by local bus companies or the yellow-coloured post buses. Most bus stations are located very near train stations, and bus and rail services are well coordinated, so that bus departures coincide with train arrivals and vice versa.

Alpine routes that are inaccessible by rail are also served by post buses (known as *postautos* or *postcars*), which are yellow and bear the Die Post, La Poste or La Posta logo. As well as carrying mail and passengers, post buses also carry unaccompanied luggage, which is convenient for hikers. Some of the routes taken by post buses lead over high passes and through stunningly beautiful mountain scenery.

Bus stop sign for the post bus

BICYCLES

Switzerland has a very cyclist-friendly infrastructure. **PubliBike** is a nationwide bike-sharing scheme. Bicycles (*velos*) can also be hired at some 100 train stations (follow signs indicating *Mietvelos, Location de Vélos* or *Bici da Noleggiare*), and need not be returned to the same station. Rental information is available from Swiss Federal Railways (*see p305*). For a fee, bicycles can be carried on post buses and on trains (unless otherwise indicated in the timetables). Reservations for cycles are mandatory on all InterCity tilting trains from March to October.

Recommended cycle routes are marked by red signs with a white bicycle symbol. Cycling maps are obtainable from local tourist offices. Several long-distance cycle routes traverse the country. The North–South Route runs for 360 km (225 miles) from Basel to Chiasso, in southern Ticino.

Post offices sell *vignettes* (6 CHF), which provides third-party liability insurance of 2 million CHF.

LAKE CRUISES

Taking a cruise on one of Switzerland's lakes is a relaxing way to explore. A fleet of paddle steamers ply Lake Lucerne and many other lakes, and there are scenic cruises of Lake Geneva, Bodensee and Lake Lugano. Most cruises run only from April to October.

All Swiss travel passes are valid for cruises on the lakes, except for Lake Maggiore. The **Swiss Pass** gives free travel on many cruises and journeys by public transport, as well as 50 per cent off most mountain railways.

Getting Around in Towns

Most Swiss towns, particularly the historic districts of larger cities, are compact, making them easy to explore on foot. Some major historic town centres are also pedestrianized, or barred to almost all motorized traffic. To reach outlying attractions, visitors will sometimes need to take buses, trams, suburban trains or in certain cases funiculars. These are all easy to use, especially as tickets and travel passes are valid for every mode of public transport. Taxis are also available, although they are expensive. Bicycles, which can be hired from many rail stations, are an alternative means of getting around. For unforgettable views of Switzerland's great lakeshore towns, visitors should take a boat cruise.

A conducted sightseeing tour of a town centre

TAXIS

Because the Swiss public transport system is so efficient, taking a taxi is rarely worth the extra expense. Although they vary from town to town, taxi fares are uniformly high, consisting of a flat rate and an additional charge for every kilometre (just over half a mile) travelled. These charges are higher at night and at weekends.

Taxis can be any colour and are identifiable by a "taxi" sign on the roof. They can be hired from ranks, which are almost always located in front of railway stations. They can also be booked by telephone.

BUSES AND TRAMS

The quickest and easiest way of getting around in towns is by hopping on a bus, trolley-bus or tram. These run at frequent intervals from about 5am until midnight. Night buses run only at weekends.

Inside buses and trams are maps showing the itinerary travelled, and the stops along the route. Each stop is announced by the driver, or by a recording.
To request a stop, press the button next to the door. The doors of buses open automatically. Tram doors are opened by passengers pressing a button.

S-BAHN & METRO

Zürich, Bern, Geneva and other cities are served by S-Bahn, or suburban, trains (known as RER in French). The hubs of these networks are the cities' main stations, from where you can travel not only to the suburbs but to neighbouring towns. Bicycles can be carried on almost all S-Bahn trains. The S-Bahn network map is displayed inside the carriages.

Some towns built on steep cliffs or clinging to hillsides, such as Lausanne and Fribourg, also have funicular railways. Lausanne's funicular trains run from the main train station, in two directions. One line leads up to the town centre, and the other leads down to Ouchy, the suburb on the shores of Lake Geneva. Lausanne is also the only Swiss town to have a metro.

TICKETS

Information on the various types of tickets available is displayed at bus and tram stops. In most towns, the public transport network is divided into zones, and the more zones you intend to traverse the more a ticket will cost. Also, tickets are valid for a limited period, ranging from an hour to a full day or more, and can be used on any mode of transport. In Zürich, for example, one ticket can be used on buses, trams, S-Bahn trains and boats.

In towns and cities there is an automatic ticket machine at every bus and tram stop. The machines accept coins (Swiss francs and sometimes euros) and special cards that are sold in all newsagent kiosks. When you board a bus or tram, you should validate your ticket by stamping it at a machine on board the vehicle. Ticket inspectors (some in uniform) regularly carry out checks. The penalty for travelling without a valid ticket is likely to be 40–60 CHF.

The Swiss Pass and Flexi Pass *(see p304)* are valid on all modes of public transport in 37 Swiss towns (listed on the ticket). Some towns issue special passes for visitors. The ZürichCard, for example, costs 20 CHF for 24 hours and 40 CHF for 72 hours. It also offers reduced rates

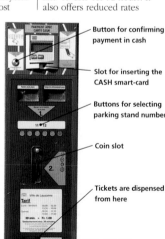

Button for confirming payment in cash

Slot for inserting the CASH smart-card

Buttons for selecting parking stand number

Coin slot

Tickets are dispensed from here

Coin- and card-operated parking-ticket machine

An SBB bus bound for Bülach, in the suburbs of Zürich

for guided tours, free entry to 37 museums and a free drink at some 20 restaurants.

PARKING

Using a car in city centres can be quite inconvenient. It is far easier to leave your car in an out-of-town car park (sign-posted P&R, for Park and Ride) and switch to a bus or tram to reach the town centre.

On-street parking and urban car parks are usually very expensive, especially in large towns and cities. Parking bays are colour-coded, or delineated with coloured lines. Those in a White Zone are usually pay-and-display. To use those in a Blue Zone you need a parking disc, which limits the parking time allowed. Discs are available from tourist offices, banks and other points. Bays in a Red Zone allow free parking for 15 hours, and the parking disc must be displayed. Illegal parking is likely to result in a fine. Most parking-ticket machines accept coins but do not accept cards other than CASH, a Swiss smart-card.

Sign for metered car parking

BICYCLES

Switzerland's zealous anti-pollution and anti-congestion ethic means that the use of bicycles is actively encouraged. Many towns have cycle lanes, filter lights at crossings and ubiquitous cycle racks. Bicycles can be hired at many main railway stations (see p307). Some towns offer free bicycle rental. To hire a bicycle under this scheme, all you need to do is show your passport and pay a deposit of 20–50 CHF, which is refunded when you return the bike. Details can be obtained from local tourist information offices or by visiting www.rentabike.ch or www.publibike.com.

SIGHTSEEING ON FOOT

Many of the oldest and best-preserved town centres have been partly or wholly pedestrianized, restoring their historic atmos-phere and making them very pleasant to explore on foot. Suggested itineraries are usually marked with a continuous line or a succession of painted footprints, and major historic buildings and other features of interest along the route have information panels.

The tourist offices in some towns organize guided tours, which are often led by English-speaking guides. Most tourist information offices also provide town maps and helpful information in English.

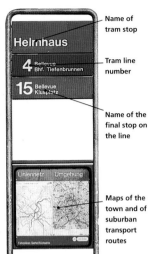

- Name of tram stop
- Tram line number
- Name of the final stop on the line
- Maps of the town and of suburban transport routes

Information board at a tram stop in Zürich

FERRIES

Ferry trips can offer quite a different perspective of Switzerland's lakeshore towns. Ferries operate from Zürich, Geneva, Lugano, Locarno, Thun, Luzern and other towns, whose beautiful lakeshore buildings may be seen to their best advantage when viewed from the water.

Most ferry companies run cruises only from early April to the end of October. Steamer services operate on Lake Geneva and Lake Lucerne. Longer cruises, on Lake Maggiore depart from Locarno or Ascona for Stresa in the Italian part of the lake.

Tickets can usually be bought either from the ticket windows at the boat landings or directly on the boat – the price is the same. The Swiss Boat Pass gives holders a 50 percent reduction on cruises on 14 lakes. The Swiss Pass (see p305) is valid for travel on all lakes except Lake Maggiore. Full details are available from tourist offices.

A tram on Zürich's network

Index

Acknowledgments

Dorling Kindersley and Hachette Livre Polska would like to thank the following people and institutions, whose contributions and assistance have made the preparation of this guide possible.

Publishing Manager
Kate Poole

Managing Editors
Helen Townsend, Jacky Jackson

Publisher
Douglas Amrine

Cartography
Uma Bhattacharya, Mohammad Hassan, Jasneet Kaur, Casper Morris

DTP
Vinod Harish, Vincent Kurien, Jason Little, Azeem Siddiqui

Revisions Team
Julie Bond, Louise Cleghorn, Kati Clinton, Caroline Elliker, Karen Fitzpatrick, Anna Freiberger, Priya Kukadia, Jude Ledger, Carly Madden, Kate Molan, Rada Radojicic, Catherine Richards, Conrad Van Dyk, Antoinette Verlan

Fact-Checker
Doug Sager

Picture Research
Rachel Barber, Rhiannon Furbear, Ellen Root

Proof Reader
Stewart Wild

Index
Helen Peters

Additional Contributors
Catherine Beattie, Doug Sager

Additional Photographers
Ian O'Leary

Special Assistance
Appenzellerland Tourismus; Artothek, Baud V. Maydell; Bellinzona Turismo; Biel/Bienne Seeland Tourismus; Burgerbibliothek, Bern; Corbis; Enteturistico Lago Maggiore; Furrer Jakob (photograph of beers, p266); Historisches Museum, Basel (Therese Wollmann); Kunsthaus, Zürich (Cécile Brunner); Kunstmuseum, Basel; Kunstmuseum, Bern (Regula Zbinden); Alicja Kusch (photograph of Bomi shop in Klif); André Locher (photographs of Yverdon-les-Bains and Mesocco); Lugano Turismo; Katarzyna and Wojciech Medrzak; Grzegorz Mościbrocki (World of Alcoholic Drinks); Mövenpick Wein, Zug (Brigitte auf der Maur); Musée d'Art et d'Histoire, Geneva (Isabelle Brun-Ilunga, Marc-Antoine Claivaz); Musée d'Art et d'Histoire, Neuchâtel (Marie-Josée Golles); Musée Romain, Avenches (Anne Hochuli-Gysel); Offentliche Kunstsammlung Basel, Kunstmuseum und Museum für Gegenwartskunst (Maria-Theresa Brunner); Schweiz Tourismus, Zürich (Fred Schreiber); Schweizerisches Landesmuseum (Angelica Condrau, Andrea Kunz); Swiss Embassy, Warsaw; Gerry Thönen (photograph of an orchard); Tourist Information Centre, Geneva (Frédéric Monnerat); Verkehrshaus, Luzern (Hans Syfrig, Martin Sigrist); Wistillerie Etter Soehne Ag, Zug (Eveline Etter); Zentralbiliothek, Zürich (Kristin Steiner).

Picture Credits

Key: a-above; b-below/bottom; c-centre; f-far; l-left; r-right; t-top.

Works of art have been reproduced with the permission of the following copyright holders: *Window in Fraumünster*, Marc Chagall ©ADAGP, Paris and DACS, London 2012 166ca; Poster (detail) Kirchner Museum Davos © Dr. Wolfgang & Ingeborg Henze-Ketterer, Wichtrach/Bern 191br; *Diego*, 1963–4, Alberto Giacometti ©ADAGP, Paris and DACS, London 2012 43c; *Sheep piece*, 1971–2 (LH627), Henry Moore, this image has been reproduced by kind permission of the Henry Moore Foundation 169t; *Fastnachtsbrunnen*, 1977, Jean Tinguely ©ADAGP Paris and DACS, London 2012 142tl; *Schwimmwasserplastik*, 1980, Jean Tinguely ©ADAGP, Paris and DACS, London 2012 143br. *Sheep piece*, 1971–2 (LH627), Henry Moore, this image has been reproduced by kind permission of the Henry Moore Foundation 169t.

4Corners Images: SIME/Fantuz Olimpio 11tl; SIME/Giovanni Simeone 288br; SIME/Johanna Huber 284cl; SIME/Siegfried Eigstler 60tl.
Alamy Images: Arco Images 10tc; Design Pics Inc./Natural Selection Dan Sherwood 284br; Eddie Gerald 290br; Marc Grimberg 263c; Andre Jenny 262cl; Jon Arnold Images/Gavin Hellier 10cl; Chris McLennan 286br; mediacolor's 10br; Mo Peerbacus 300br; Photo Mere Switzerland 296cla; StockShot/Karen Jones 288cl; StockShot/Mike Weyerhaeuser 288tr; tbkmedia.de 286tl.
Appenzellerland Tourismus: 188b.
Artothek: 54b.
Baud V. Maydell: 92.
Bellinzona Turismo: 220tl.
Berne Animal Park: RANDO 63cr.
Biel/Bienne Seeland Tourismus: P. Brisset 18tl.
Burgerbibliothek, Bern: 37b.
Clinique La Prairie: 290cl, 290tc.
Collectif d'enfants: *Le cinema*, ca. 1950, gouache et collage sur papier, 294 x 173.5cm © Collection de l'Art Brut, Lausanne/Photo: Claude Bornand, Lausanne 116bl.
Corbis: O. Alamany & E. Vicens 22d, 23crb, 177b; Paul Almasy 44–5; Roger Antrobus 2–3, 79t; Morton Beebe 84g, 107d; Bettmann 40clb, 40d, 42t, 42b, 43tr, 43bca, 43bl, 84t; Stefano Bianchetti 38bl; Jacques Bock/Sygma 104t; Barnabas Bosshart 60b, 64t, 174g; Christie's Images *Diego*, 1963–4, Alberto Giacometti ©ADAGP, Paris and DACS, London 2012 – 43ca: Corbis 41crb; Robert Eric/Sygma 105t; Farrell Grehan 8–9; Robert Harding World Imagery/H.P. Merten 292–293; Historical Picture Archive 40cla, 41c, 45c; Dave G. Houser 190b; Pat Jerrold/Papilio 23clb, 23bl; Wolfgang Kaehler 15t, 62t; Kelly-Mooney Photography 26tr; Listri Massimo 139t; Francis G.

Mayer 38br; Richard T. Nowitz 27tr, 158; Gianni Dagli Orti 39b; José F. Poblete 22–23c, 47br, 134; Annie Poole/Papilio 23tl; Christian Sarramon 83b; Leonard de Selva 41b; Ted Spiegel 36t; Ink Swim 41tl, 228c; Tim Thompson 23br; Vittoriano Rastelli 21t; Ruggero Vanni 27cl; Jean Bernard Vernier/ Sygma 43crb, 43br, 105b, 106cla, 107t; Scott T. Smith 22cl; Sandro Vanini 27br, 52b, 207b, 214tlb; Pierre Vauthey/Sygma 27cr, 31bl; Patrick Ward 27bl, 30t, 76–7; Werner Forman 141tl; Nik Wheeler 1; Adam Woolfitt 22t; Zefa/José Fuste Raga 284tc; Zefa/Uli Wiesmeier 289tr.
Enteturistico Lago Maggiore: T. Krueger 214tra.
Familie Grolimund: 300cl, 301tl.
Getty Images: LOOK/Bernard van Dierendonck 11cr, 285tl; Stephen Studd 235br.
Hemispheres Images: Patrick Frilet 11bc.
Hiltl AG: 260br.
Historisches Museum Basel: M. Babey 38ca.
Hotel Le Mirador Kempinski Genfer See: 243cr.
Oldrich Karasek: 5t, 68b, 79b.
Piotr Kiedrowski: 106t, 106crb, 107c.
Kunsthaus Zürich: 34, 41cra, 170cb, 170cla, 170bc, 171cb; *Dadaist work*, Hans Arp © DACS, London 2012 167tr; *Au-dessus de Paris*, 1968, Marc Chagall ©ADAGP, Paris and DACS, London 2012 170tr; *Entire City*, 1935–7, Max Ernst ©ADAGP, Paris and DACS, London 2012 171cra; *Bird in Space*, 1925, Constantin Brancusi ©ADAGP, Paris and DACS, London 2012 171tc; *Guitar on a Pedestal Table*, 1915, Pablo Picasso ©Succession Picasso/DACS 2012 171cr; *Big Torn Campbell's Soup Can (Vegetable Beef)*, 1962, Andy Warhol © Licensed by the Andy Warhol Foundation for the Visual Arts, Inc./ARS, NY and DACS, London 2012 171b.
Kunstmuseum Basel: 146t, 146clb, 146b, 147ca, 147cb, 147b; *Senecio*, 1922, Paul Klee ©DACS 2012 146tr; *Burning Giraffe*, 1936–7, Salvador Dalí © Kingdom of Spain – Gala-Salvador Dalí Foundation, DACS, London 2012 146br.
Kunstmuseum Bern: 56t, 56c; Peter Lauri 56b, 57cb; *Dans un Jardin Meridional*, 1914 Pierre Bonnard ©ADAGP, Paris and DACS, London 2012 57tc; *Ad Parnassum*, 1932, Paul Klee ©DACS 2012 57cra; *Drunken Doze*, 1902, Pablo Picasso ©Succession Picasso/DACS 2012 57br.
Landesmuseum Zürich: (2003) 35b, 36br, 37t, 37cr, 39t.
André Locher: 128t. **Lugano Turismo:** 210t.
Musée d'Art et d'Histoire, Neuchâtel: 40–41c.
Musée d'Art et d'Histoire, Geneva: MAH 102t; Jean Marc Yersin 102ca, 102cb, 103cra; Yves Siza 102b, 103b; Bettina Jacot-Descombes 103t; *Le Bain Turc*, 1907, Félix Edouard Vallotton 103cb.

Öffentliche Kunstsammlung, Basel: Martin Bühler 36cl, 38t.
Małgorzata Omilanowska: 4t, 26tl, 26cl, 26cr, 47tr, 47bl, 51b, 53tra, 58c, 58t, 58b, 59tl, 159b, 174b, 175t, 309tr, 309b.
Photolibrary: imagebroker.net/Meinrad Riedo 236bl; Mauritius Die Bildagentur Gmbh/Beuthan Beuthan 263tl.
Robert Harding Picture Library: Neil Emmerson 82cb.
photo SBB: 304cl, 304bl.
Schilthornbahn AG: 261br.
Schweizerishes Landesmuseum, Zürich: 4b, 162–3.
Schweiz Tourismus: 111t, 164t, 191t, 191blb; U. Ackermann 18b; D. Brawand 225b; R. Brioschi 172cr; L. Degonda 24t, 119cb; S. Eigstler 23cla; S. Engler 30b, 32b, 104b, 117b, 119bla, 172b; Ph. Giegel 228t; Höllgrotten Baar 209t; P. Maurer 18c, 28t, 232tlb; F. Pfenniger 25b; M. Schmid 17b, 25t, 119t, 225t; H. Schwab 17t, 23crb, 29br, 209b, 228b; C. Sonderegger 18b, 19t, 19b, 21b, 28ca, 28cb, 28bl, 28br, 29tl, 29tr, 29bl, 30c, 31t, 32t, 33t, 119ca, 119tr, 135b, 178, 179, 190t, 208b, 214b, 220b, 229b, 232tra, 232b; W. Storto 215b; Rausser 13t; K. Richter 20t.
Thun-Thunersee Tourismus: 74ca.
Verkerhaus Der Schweiz: 238–9 all.
Victoria-Jungfrau Grand Hotel & Spa: 291tr.
Widder Hotel: 242cl.
Ireneusz Winnicki: 262–3.
Paweł Wroński: 88c, 90b, 116b, 307b.
Zefa: J. Raga 108.
Zentral Bibliothek, Zürich: 36–7c, 38cb.
Andrzej Zygmuntowicz: 262–3.

JACKET Front – SUPERSTOCK: Prisma.
Back – DORLING KINDERSLEY: Katarzyna and Wojciech Medrzakowie tl, cla, clb.
Spine – SUPERSTOCK: Prisma t.

All other images © Dorling Kindersley
For futher information see www.dkimages.com

PHRASE BOOK

Phrase Book

German is the most widely spoken language in Switzerland, followed by French and Italian. Swiss German, which is used in everyday speech, differs from standard High German (see p295). Because it consists of several local dialects, each of which are almost impossible to transcribe, the phrases given below are in High German, with some of the most commonly used expressions in Swiss German marked by an asterisk.

In Emergency	German	French	Italian
Help!	Hilfe!	Au secours!	Aiuto!
Stop!	Halt!	Arrêtez!	Alt!
Call a doctor!	Holen Sie einen Artz	Appelez un médecin	Chiami un medico
Call an ambulance!	Holen Sie einen Krankenwagen	Appelez une ambulance	Chiami una ambulanza
Call the police!	Holen Sie die Polizei	Appelez la police	Chiami la polizia
Call the fire brigade!	Holen Sie die Feuerwehr	Appelez les pompiers	Chiami i pompieri
Where is a telephone?	Wo finde ich ein Telefon?	Ou y a-t-il un telephone?	Dov'è il telefono?
Where is the hospital?	Wo finde ich das Krankenhaus?	Ou est l'hôpital?	Dov'è l'ospedale?

Communication Essentials

	German	French	Italian
Yes	Ja	Oui	Si
No	Nein	Non	No
Please	Bitte	S'il vous plaît	Per favore
Thank you	Danke vielmals	Merci	Grazie
Excuse me	Entschuldigen Sie *Äxgüsi	Excusez-moi	Mi scusi
Hello	Grüss Gott *Grüezi	Salut!	Salve!/Ciao!
Goodbye	Auf Widersehen *Ufwiederluege	Au revoir	Arrivederci
Bye!	Tschüss!	Salut!	Ciao!
here	hier	ici	qui
there	dort	là	la
What?	Was?	Quel, quelle?	Quale?
Where?	Wo/Wohin?	Oé?	Dove?

Useful Phrases and Words

	German	French	Italian
Where is …?	Wo befindet sich…?	Oé est …?	Dov'è
Where are …?	Wo befinden sich…?	Oé sont …?	Dove sono?
Do you speak English?	Sprechen Sie Englisch?	Parlez-vous anglais?	Parla inglese?
I understand	Ich verstehe	Je comprends	Capisco
I don't understand	Ich verstehe nicht	Je ne comprends pas	Non capisco
I'm sorry	Es tut mir leid	Je suis désolé	Mi dispiace
big	gross	grand	grande
small	klein	petit	piccolo
open	auf/offen	overt	aperto
closed	zu/geschlossen	fermé	chiuso
left	links	à gauche	a sinistra
right	rechts	à droite	a destra
near	Es ist in der Nähe	près	vicino
far	weit	loin	lontano
up	auf/oben	en haut	su
down	ab/unten	en bas	giú
early	früh	de bonne heure	presto
late	spät	en retard	tardi
entrance	Eingang/Einfahrt	l'entrée	la entrata
exit	Ausgang/Ausfahrt	la sortie	l'uscita
toilet	WC/Toilette	les toilettes/les WCs	il gabinetto

Making a Telephone Call

	German	French	Italian
I'd like to place a long-distance call	Ich möchte ein Fernsgespräch machen	Je voudrais faire un interurbain.	Vorrei fare una interurbana.
I'd like to make a reverse charge call/call collect	Ich möchte ein Rückgespräch machen	Je voudrais faire une communication PCV	Vorrei fare una telefonata a carico del destinatorio
I'll try again later	Ich versuche es später noch einmal	Je rapellerai plus tard	Ritelefono pié tardi
Can I leave a message?	Kann ich etwas ausrichten?	Est ce que je peux laisser un message?	Posso lasciare un messaggio?

Staying in a Hotel

Do you have a vacant room?	Haben Sie ein Zimmer frei?	Est-ce que vous avez une chambre libre?	Avete camere libere?
double room	ein Doppelzimmer	une chambre à deux	una camera doppia
twin room	ein Doppelzimmer mit zwei Betten?	une chambre à deux lits	una camera con due letti
single room	ein Einzelzimmer	una chambre à une personne	una camera singola
with a bath/shower	mit Bad/Dusche	avec salle de bains/ douche	con bagno/doccia
How much is the room?	Wievel kostet das Zimmer?	Combien coûte la chambre?	Quanto costa la camera?
Where is the bathroom?	Wo ist das Bad?	Oé est la salle de bains?	Dov'è il bagno?
with breakfast	mit Frühstück	avec petit-déjeuner	con prima colazione
with half-board	mit Halbpension	en demi-pension	mezza pensione
dormitory	Schlafsaal	dortoir	il dormitorio
key	Schlüssel	la clef	la chiave
I have a reservation	Ich habe ein Zimmer reserviert	J'ai fait une réservation	Ho fatto una prenotazione

Sightseeing

bus	der Bus	l'autobus	el autobus
tram	die Strassenbahn	le tramway	el tram
train	der Zug	le train	il treno
bus station	der Busbahnhof	la gare routière	l'autostazione
train station	der Bahnhof	la gare	la stazione
information (office)	Information	les renseignements	l'informazioni
boat	Boot	le bateau	la barca
(steam) boat	(Dampfer) Schiff	le bateau (à vapeur)	il battello (a vapore)
boat trip	Schiffahrt	la navigation	la navigazione
parking	Parkplatz	la place de stationnement	il parcheggio
car park	Parkhaus	le parking	l'autosilo
(hire) bicycle	Fahrrad/Mietvelo	le vélo (de location)	la bicicletta (a noleggio)
airport	Flughafen	l'aéroport	l'aeroporto
bank	Bank	la banque	il banco
church	Kirche	l'église	la chiesa
cathedral	Dom	la cathédrale	il duomo/la cattedrale
main square	Hauptplatz	la place centrale	la piazza principale
post office	Postamt	le bureau de poste	la posta
tourist office	Verkehrsamt	l'office du tourisme	l'ente turistico

Time

morning	Vormittag	le matin	la mattina
afternoon	Nachmittag	l'apres-midi	il pomeriggio
evening	Abend	le soir	la sera
in the morning	morgens	le matin	di mattina
in the afternoon	nachmittags	l'après-midi	di pomeriggio
in the evening	abends	le soir	di sera
yesterday	gestern	hier	ieri
today	heute	aujourd'hui	oggi
tomorrow	morgen	demain	domani
Monday	Montag	lundi	lunedi
Tuesday	Dienstag	mardi	martedi
Wednesday	Mittwoch	mercredi	mercoledi
Thursday	Donnerstag	jeudi	giovedi
Friday	Freitag	vendredi	venerdi
Saturday	Samstag/Sonnabend	samedi	sabato
Sunday	Sonntag	dimanche	domenica

Shopping

How much does this cost?	Wieviel kostet das?	C'est combien, s'il vous plait?	Quant'e, per favore?
I would like...	Ich hätte gern...	Je voudrais...	Vorrei...
Do you have...?	Haben Sie...?	Est-ce que vous avez...	Avere...?
expensive	teuer	cher	caro
cheap	billig	pas cher/bon marché	a buon prezzo
bank	Bank	la banque	la banca
book shop	Buchladen	la librairie	la libreria
chemist/pharmacy	Apotheke	la pharmacie	la farmacia
hairdresser	Friseur/Frisör	le coiffeur	il parruchiere
market	Markt	le marché	il mercato
newsagent	Zeitungskiosk	le magasin de journeaux	l'edicola
travel agent	Reisebüro	l'agence de voyages	l'agenzia di viaggi

Eating Out

Have you got a table for...?	Haben sie einen Tisch für ...?	Avez-vous une table pour...?	Avete una tavola per ...?
The bill/check, please	Zahlen, bitte	L'addition, s'il vous plait	Il conto, per favore
I am a vegetarian	Ich bin Vegetarier	Je suis végétarien(ne)	Sono vegetariano(a)
waitress/waiter	Fräulein/Herr Ober	Madame/Mademoiselle/ Monsieur	cameriera/camariere
menu	die Spiesekarte	le menu/la carte	il mené
wine list	Weinkarte	la carte des vins	la lista dei vini
breakfast	Frühstück	le petit déjeuner	la prima colazione
lunch	Mittagessen	le déjeuner	il pranzo
dinner	Abendessen	le dîner	la cena

Menu Decoder: German

Ei	egg	Mineralwasser	mineral water
Eis	ice cream	Obst	fresh fruit
Fisch	fish	Pfeffer	pepper
Fleisch	meat	Pommes frites	chips
Garnelen	prawns	Reis	rice
gebacken	baked/fried	Rind	beef
gebraten	roast	Rostbraten	steak
gekocht	boiled	Rotwein	red wine
Gemüse	vegetables	Salz	salt
vom Grill	grilled	Schinken/Speck	ham
Hendle/Hahn/Huhn	chicken	Schlag	cream
Kaffee	coffee	Schokolade	chocolate
Kartoffell/Erdäpfel	potatoes	Schwein	pork
Käse	cheese	Tee	tea
Knödel	dumpling	Wasser	water
Lamm	lamb	Weisswein	white wine
Meeresfrüchte	seafood	Wurst	sausage (fresh)
Milch	milk	Zucker	sugar

Menu Decoder: French

l'agneau	lamb	grillé	grilled
l'ail	garlic	le homard	lobster
le bifteck/le steack	steak	le jambon	ham
le boeuf	beef	le lait	milk
le canard	duck	les légumes	vegetables
le chocolat	chocolate	l'oeuf	egg
le citron	lemon	le pain	bread
les crevettes	prawns	poché	poached
les crustacées	shellfish	le poivre	pepper
cuit au four	oven-baked	le poisson	fish
l'eau minérale	mineral water	les pommes de terre	potatoes
les escargots	snails	le porc	pork
le frites	chips	le potage	soup
le fromage	cheese	le poulet	chicken
le fruit frais	fresh fruit	le sucre	sugar
les fruits de mer	seafood	le thé	tea
le gâteau	cake	la viande	meat
la glace	ice/ice cream	le vin blanc/rouge	white/red wine

Menu Decoder: Italian

agnello	lamb	lesso	boiled
aglio	garlic	il manzo	beef
al forno	baked	le patate	potatoes
alla griglia	grilled	le patate fritte	chips
arrosto	roast	il pesce	fish
la bistecca	steak	il pollo	chicken
i carciofi	artichikes	il pomodoro	tomato
la carne	meat	il prosciutto cotto/crudo	cooked/cured ham
carne di miale	pork	il riso	rice
la cipolla	onion	la salsiccia	sausage
i contorni	vegetables	i spinaci	spinach
i fagioli	beans	il tè	tea
il fegato	liver	il tonno	tuna
il finocchio	fennel	l'uovo	egg
il formaggio	cheese	vino blanco	white wine
frutti di mare	seafood	vino rosso	red wine
il gelato	ice cream	gli zucchini	courgettes
il latte	milk	la zuppa	soup

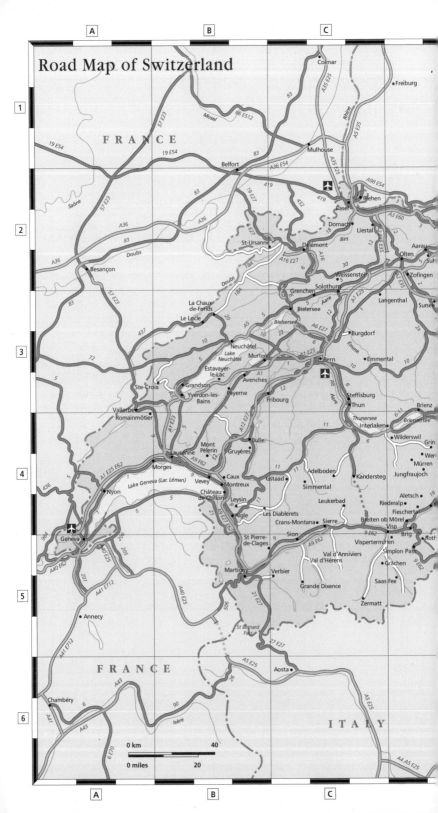

Road Map of Switzerland